AF791562

Advocates and Advocacy

ADVOCATES AND ADVOCACY

The Best of The Advocates' Journal 2005–2018

edited by

STEPHEN GRANT, LSM, ASM

THE ADVOCATES' SOCIETY

Advocates and Advocacy: The Best of *The Advocates' Journal* 2005–2018
© The Advocates' Society, 2018

All rights reserved. No part of this publication may be reproduced, stored in a retrieval system, or transmitted, in any form or by any means, without the prior written permission of the publisher or, in the case of photocopying or other reprographic copying, a licence from Access Copyright (Canadian Copyright Licensing Agency), 56 Wellesley St W, Suite 320, Toronto, ON, M5S 2S3.

Published in 2018 by

Irwin Law Inc
Suite 206, 14 Duncan Street
Toronto, ON M5H 3G8
www.irwinlaw.com

ISBN: 978-1-55221-480-0 e-book ISBN: 978-1-55221-481-7

Library and Archives Canada Cataloguing in Publication

Advocates and advocacy : the best of the Advocates' journal, 2005–2018 / edited by Stephen Grant, LSM, ASM.

Includes bibliographical references.
Issued in print and electronic formats.
ISBN 978-1-55221-480-0 (softcover).--ISBN 978-1-55221-481-7 (PDF)

1. Advocates' Society. 2. Actions and defenses—Canada. 3. Trial practice—Canada. I. Grant, Stephen M., editor II. Advocates' Society, issuing body

KE8370 A38 2018 347.71'0504 C2018-902135-7
C2018-902136-5

KF8863 A38 2018

Canada

Ontario
Ontario Media Development Corporation
Société de développement de l'industrie des médias de l'Ontario

Printed and bound by CPI Group (UK) Ltd, Croydon, CR0 4YY
1 2 3 4 5 22 21 20 19 18

Contents

President's Message *ix*

The Best of *The Advocates' Journal* 2005–2018 *xi*
From the Editor

Part One
ADVOCATES AS STORYTELLERS *1*

The power of context *3*
Benjamin Zarnett, LSM

The trial advocate as storyteller: The art and science of persuasion *11*
The Honourable Todd L. Archibald and J. Manuel Mendelzon

The charm of the narrator: The overlooked commonality between novelist and advocate *41*
Andrew Pyper

The only way to be paid well as an actor: Why I became a lawyer *47*
Yashoda Ranganathan

Did opposing counsel get your GOTE? *53*
Kate Southwell

PERSONAL REFLECTION | Advocacy at the crossroads *59*
Linda R. Rothstein, LSM

Part Two
WITNESSES 69

Why we can't trust witnesses 71
Paul Fruitman

If we can't trust witnesses, can we trust trials? 77
Matthew Milne-Smith

PERSONAL REFLECTION | Fostering connection, creating community 87
The Honourable Harriet Sachs

Part Three
EXPERTS, SCIENCE AND THE LIKE 93

Science in the courtroom: The mouse that roared 95
The Honourable W. Ian C. Binnie

Cross-examining the opposing expert 121
John McLeish

The independent expert witness: How did we get here? 137
Bryan Finlay, Q.C.

Asking ourselves the *Moneyball* question about expert evidence 149
Professor Adam Dodek, LSM

What irreproducible results mean for the law of scientific evidence 157
Jason M. Chin

PERSONAL REFLECTION | The advocate's calling 167
Guy J. Pratte

Part Four
TRIALS AND SETTLEMENTS 181

The unsettling truth about settling 183
The Honourable Joseph W. Quinn

The unsettling truth about settling: Part two 189
The Honourable Joseph W. Quinn

In support of open courts 205
Iris Fischer

PERSONAL REFLECTION | The advocate as loser 211
Jonathan Lisus

Part Five
APPELLATE ADVOCACY 221

Losing tip no. 16: 1066 and all that 223
The Honourable Marvin Catzman

Some appellate advocacy advice 229
The Honourable Marshall Rothstein

How to lose an appeal in the Court of Appeal: The next generation 235
The Honourable David M. Brown

PERSONAL REFLECTION | Beside the Supreme Court bench: A law clerk's reflections on advocacy 241
David Sandomierski

Part Six
STANDARD OF REVIEW 245

Tipping the balance in the Court of Appeal 247
The Honourable Kathryn N. Feldman

Advocacy in the Court of Appeal: One lawyer's perspective 257
Paul J. Pape

Standard of review: Ongoing chaos or a path to order? 267
Greg Temelini

PERSONAL REFLECTION | The heroic advocate 273
The Honourable Eleanore A. Cronk

Part Seven
ETHICS AND PROFESSIONALISM 283

The ethics of advocacy 285
Gavin MacKenzie

Professionalism: An old idea but a new ideal 291
The Honourable Joan L. Lax

Looking back and looking forward on learning in professionalism 301
The Honourable Stephen T. Goudge

PERSONAL REFLECTION | How I do it 313
Jasmine Akbarali

PERSONAL REFLECTION | Diversity and the future of advocacy 321
Iman Abokor and M. Greg Abogado

Part Eight
MEDIA RELATIONS 329

The care and feeding of reporters: A lawyer's guide 331
Tracey Tyler

When a journalist comes calling 341
Kirk Makin

Talk to reporters: It's your professional duty 347
Cristin Schmitz

What litigators and broadcast journalists have in common 351
Scott Arnold

PERSONAL REFLECTION | Why good judgment comes first 357
John Adair

Part Nine
HUMOUR 365

And the winner is ... 367
Marie Henein

PERSONAL REFLECTION | Why lawyers like baseball 371
Peter Hrastovec, LSM

President's message

"I consider this first meeting of the Society an historic occasion. In these times of unrest, when the rights and liberties of the people are slowly being infringed upon and taken away ... we need more than ever a strong, independent and courageous bar."

– Isadore Levinter, Q.C., May 17, 1965

WHILE THE NATURE of unrest changes over time, the fact of change and unrest is constant. Also constant is the unique role of advocates in defending the independence of the bar and the judiciary as enduring cornerstones of a free and democratic society. In fact, in our barrister's oath, we commit to improve access to justice, safeguard the rights and freedoms of all persons, and champion the rule of law.

The Advocates' Society proudly celebrates its 55th anniversary in 2018. From its roots in 1963 as a small group of senior litigators advancing their common interest in fostering a strong, courageous and independent bar, the Society has grown into a national network of more than 6,000 members. The Society's commitment to its original core values is unwavering – and pressing as ever. We are united by our dedication to access to justice and the administration of justice from coast to coast.

We are also officers of the court. Serving as the voice of our clients before decision-makers is a great privilege and a great responsibility. The Advocates' Society helps us fulfil our oaths and duties, collectively and individually, and inspires us to become the best advocates we can be.

Becoming a great advocate is a lifelong commitment. While each generation of advocates faces new challenges and demands, our history shows that we are stronger, better advocates when we support and learn from each other. To this end, the Society invests in the future of our profession by encouraging, mentoring and training young advocates. And, for all of our members, we tirelessly reinforce the essential commitment to professionalism and civility that is the hallmark of every truly great advocate.

There is no manual, rule book or recipe to make a great advocate. There is no mould or formula. In fact, our profession is notable for the remarkable array of personalities and styles from one great advocate to the next. This is what makes our vocation so special and rewarding. Just as we can learn from the considerable experience of advocates before and around us, we can still be true to ourselves and make it our own.

This collection of some of the finest articles featured in *The Advocates' Journal* memorializes a wide spectrum of skills, tips and techniques to help us refine our craft. It provides tools for tackling the endless challenges, demands and responsibilities we face, and reminds us that we are not alone in these – that we all need courage and resilience, introspection and inspiration. Without these, we as advocates cannot fulfill our duties to the courts, our clients and, of course, ourselves. This book celebrates advocacy because, whether we win or lose in our adversarial system, we should all be proud of our profession and our integral role in the justice system.

We hope these thoughtful reflections from advocates and judges of all ages and stages will reassure you, entertain you and inspire you.

Special thanks to Stephen Grant, who marks his 10th anniversary as editor of the *The Advocates' Journal*. Stephen has preserved and nurtured the finest traditions of the *Journal* established by previous editors Moishe Reiter, Q.C., and David Stockwood, Q.C. He has a gift for encouraging busy advocates and judges to pause from their daily demands to share their wisdom. We are all beneficiaries of these indelible, timeless gems ... these reminders that advocacy is a craft, and a privilege.

Sonia Bjorkquist
April 2018

Advocates and Advocacy:

THE BEST OF *THE ADVOCATES' JOURNAL* 2005-2018

FROM THE EDITOR

THE ADVOCATES' JOURNAL (formerly *The Advocates' Society Journal*) is a publication of analysis, critique and thought on our craft. Whether advocacy is an art, a science or both, in its purest form it is all about persuasion, powered by analytical skill and intuition. Usually, we are persuading a judge or a panel of judges, but as often as not these days, arbitrators and other tribunal adjudicators.

Persuasion may be simply trying to convince the other party, the other lawyer or your own client of the merits of a course of action. Paul Pape's charming and compelling theory is that if you can persuade your mother of the rightness of your cause, you have a winning argument. It might be no more complex than that.

It's been 13 years since The Advocates' Society published *Ethos, Pathos, and Logos: The Best of The Advocates' Society Journal 1982–2004*, recalling the classical lynchpins of rhetoric. The collection was co-edited by David E. Spiro and my predecessor, the late David Stockwood, Q.C., LSM, whose reins I assumed in the summer of 2008. It showcased the finest articles published in the *Journal* over a span of 22 years. *Advocates and Advocacy* picks up where *Ethos, Pathos, and Logos* left off, covering 2005 to 2018, now with contributors from across the country.

Have things changed? The digital age is undeniably pervasive, for better or worse. Advocacy continues unabated but has morphed into different forms and forums, especially with the rise of the regulatory society. Anecdotally, trials appear to be on the wane. This is not necessarily a bad thing as litigants find other means to resolve their conflict, but for the contraction, rather than expansion, of legal precedent. As arbitration, too, becomes prevalent, the decisions rendered, unless appealed, also don't find their way into the legal domain. Clearly, this is an unintended and troubling consequence of these developments.

Advocates now grapple with privacy, electronic communications, artificial intelligence and, in practice, the expansion of summary judgment. The delivery speed of legal information is nothing short of astonishing. Cases and commentary show up instantly on Facebook, Twitter, LinkedIn and other social media.

Trials and appeals can be conducted and argued by iPad, often paperless. And speaking of paper, written advocacy in motions and appeals is now more pronounced and important than oral advocacy. To the next generation of advocates, our older ways will seem archaic, but that's for then. As one sees in this volume, the clarity and cogency of our current writing on advocacy – print or electronic – remains solid.

I have collected here a selection of the best of the *Journal*, grouped into topics for ease of reference, from storytelling to humour with personal reflections in between.

With thanks to Irwin Law, our partner in this venture.

For me, being the editor of *The Advocates' Journal* remains a privilege.

Stephen Grant, LSM, ASM
April 2018

Part One

ADVOCATES AS STORYTELLERS

IN MANY WAYS, advocates are actors and storytellers, especially in front of a jury. They might write their scripts to begin, but the frailty of witnesses makes going off-script as much the rule as the exception. Like every story, each case, whether at trial or on appeal, has a moral. It generally portrays a party wearing a "white hat" and another wearing a "black hat," usually more nuanced than that distinction implies. The authors in this chapter – judge, advocates, former actors and novelist – reflect their different vantage points on lawyers and the "stories" we tell.

WINTER 2010

The power of context

BENJAMIN ZARNETT, LSM

MUCH HAS BEEN written, from many different perspectives, about good advocacy. Experienced advocates have described their own habits and practices, implicitly inviting emulation. Judges have pointed out what impresses them. Still others have detailed the misadventures of bad advocates, suggesting the possibility that one can reverse-engineer a good advocate by avoiding the pitfalls of an atrocious one.[1]

One comes away from reading about good advocacy struck by the variety of things one could or should do to achieve it. That impression is reinforced, at least for me, by years of working with and litigating against advocates who are superb yet who have different intellectual backgrounds, personalities and natural gifts, and who apply different skills. Yet despite the variety there is, for me, a certain mode of thinking, a core belief, that seems to be shared by those who excel in advocacy. To be a good advocate, one must believe in the power of context.

Context is the raw material of advocacy. It consists, to name only a few examples, of those facts that put bad facts in perspective; of the language in other parts of the contract that illuminates a contentious term's meaning; of the array of indicators of legislative meaning that helps to interpret the statutory provision in question; of those facts that

1 Some of the best writing on advocacy is collected in *Ethos, Pathos, and Logos: The Best of the Advocates' Society Journal, 1982–2004* (Toronto: Irwin Law, 2005).

distinguish the *ratio* of a previous decision from the case at hand. Advocates create and use context to argue, explain and persuade. Indeed, the use of context is one of the most powerful tools of advocacy. In important ways, it is the very essence of advocacy.

This is so, I think, for three essential reasons. First, for an advocate, context can drive the meaning of language. Second, context can provide the answer to our most basic advocacy questions, such as what do we say first and what do we say second. Third, context is the bridge between what the advocate's ultimate point is and what the advocate's audience, the judge, will take on board.

CONTEXT AND LANGUAGE

Most cases turn on language. What the contract means, what the legislature intended, what one party meant by what was said to another, what previous cases have decided and what they leave open – these questions all require an interpretation of the words used. Most lawyers can recite the words and suggest a meaning, but good advocates *argue* for a meaning, and do so by using context to drive the words to the meaning for which they contend. The good advocate's theory of language resembles one that was ascribed to the early legal realists:

> There was a time when words were thought to have a fixed, determined content, a meaning partaking of objective Platonic forms. In the absence of a belief in Platonic intelligible essences, however, *no interpretation or application of language can be logically required by the language itself. Words are created by people in history, and their definition inevitably varies with particular context and with the meaning brought to them by the judges who are asked to interpret them.*[2] [emphasis added]

If proof is needed that the meaning of any word can bend to the context, then consider the word "clear," a bedrock legal term so important that, for example, the rules of evidence about interpreting a contract change depending on whether the language is ambiguous (susceptible to more than one meaning) or "clear" (has only one meaning). But does

2 Elizabeth Mensch, "The History of Mainstream Legal Thought" in David Kairys, ed., *The Politics of Law: A Progressive Critique*, 3rd ed. (New York: Basic Books, 1998) 23.

the word "clear" have only one meaning? Let's examine the word in these two contexts:

a) "Now that you say it that way, *I see* your point precisely. It *is clear*. It *is obvious*."
b) "After they had been cleaned, I almost walked right into the sliding glass doors. I could *not see* them. They were *so clear*, they were *invisible*."

The meaning of the word "clear" isn't clear. It depends on the context – something the good advocate believes about all words and combinations of words. The recognition that the meaning of words can be driven by the context leads the advocate to introduce or stress all of the permissible context that will support a favourable interpretation.

The use of context by the skilful advocate extends not just to context that we might think of as bearing directly on meaning, but to context that does so indirectly because it speaks to the acceptability of the contended-for meaning. Consider the following two hypothetical contextual arguments on an appeal where the issue is whether an oral amendment to a written contract is enforceable in the face of a clause that the advocate says negates the validity of an amendment made that way:

- *Example A*: The trial judge found that after the written contract was made, the parties orally agreed to amend it. But the trial judge was technically wrong, because among the boilerplate terms in the contract was one that said the contract could only be amended in writing.
- *Example B:* The parties painstakingly defined, in writing, the terms of their business arrangement – with great precision and after legal advice. They included a clause excluding prior and contemporaneous oral contracts. Their intention was to define all their rights and obligations in writing.

They then included a clause that pointed to the future. Any amendment had to be in writing signed by the parties. In other words, if the contract was to be changed, a written document had to be signed; nothing less would do. Now what did the parties intend by that clause? Consistent with the rest of their dealings as shown by the contract, they did not want their rights to be left to the uncertainty of who said what to whom, to the faults and frailties of memories or to the admittedly imperfect system by which a trial judge must try to determine what had been orally agreed. They wanted the certainty of writing, and they did it by a perfectly even-handed clause that would operate to preclude assertions of oral amendments by *either* party. The trial judge was wrong to ignore these intentions and give effect to what one side said was an oral amendment.

Example A suggests, in a counterproductive way, that a favourable meaning should be given to something that is technical and boilerplate and that it should oust an oral agreement found to have been made. The second argument uses the context of the rest of the written agreement, and in effect acts out the parties' presumed negotiating intentions to rationalize the clause and to ease the acceptance of a meaning that will negate the oral amendment.

CONTEXT AND THE ORDER OF PRESENTATION

A primary determinant of the order in which good advocates say things, write things or even ask questions is that they do so as much as possible in an order that makes the best use of context. The belief that context will shape meaning is what leads good advocates to adopt "point first" advocacy, sometimes described as context (or a description of what the point is or where it is heading), before detail. Good advocates do this whenever they are communicating for the purpose of persuasion, be it in examination- in-chief, in pleadings, in oral argument or in written argument. They do so because it makes the arguments easier to follow by telling the listeners what they will be hearing and why they will be hearing it (or reading it) before the details are dumped upon them. This alone would be a sufficient reason. But they also do so because the context provided will influence the meaning, emphasis or significance of the detail that follows. Consider these two examples:

a) "This is an appeal by the Reverend Martin Luther King Jr. from an order forbidding a non-violent march to protest racial segregation and racially motivated violence in Birmingham, Alabama. Although the court will not hear an appeal from an order the appellant has not obeyed except in exceptional circumstances, the court should hear this appeal."[3]

3 See *Walker v. Birmingham*, 388 U.S. 307 (1967).

b) "This is an appeal by Mr. Smith from a series of child support orders with which he has not complied. The court will not hear an appeal from an order that the appellant has not obeyed except in exceptional circumstances. The court should not hear this appeal."

In the first example, the words "except in exceptional circumstances" practically jump off the page with significance; in the second they all but disappear. The difference results from the context first provided.

The recognition of the power of context also explains why good advocates know where to start a submission – for example, why some arguments should begin with the law and then move to the facts, whereas others should begin with the facts and move to the law. In some cases, the facts provide context for the law that the advocate wants interpreted, nuanced or viewed a certain way. In others, the law provides the context in which to appreciate and interpret the facts.

CONTEXT AND BRIDGE BUILDING

Compare the descriptions of advocates given by clients or other lawyers with the descriptions given by judges. To the former, advocates are aggressive, tenacious, forceful, plodding, boring, well-prepared and so on. But to judges they are either "helpful" or "not helpful." Good advocates present cases and argue in such a way that the judge thinks the advocate is there to help the judge reach the "right" result. That can only be done if the advocate is empathetic with his or her audience. Almost every judicial admonition about advocacy could be reduced to this: "When presenting your case, think about us." Beyond being civil and respectful, using context is the advocate's major way of being audience-friendly.

Good advocates are always thinking about how the argument works for the judge. They must free themselves from the baggage of detail that comes from having lived with a case for months or years and present the argument in a context in which the judge, who has little background in it, can easily receive it. This requires a careful ordering of the submission. It requires providing context before detail. And, most of all, it requires providing context that anticipates and renders unnecessary the always-looming judicial question "Why are you telling me this?" – a question that is the litmus test of whether an advocate is speaking with the judge, or someone else, in mind. Good advocates can, at any stage of argument, answer the "Why are you telling me this?" question – but their aim is to provide context in such a way and at such appropriate points that the question is answered before it is asked.

The good advocate also provides the context that will anticipate and address the judge's expected reaction to the consequence of a submission. Consider these two examples:

a) "My client has a valid default judgment, and it is irrelevant that the default was due to the sloppiness of the defendant's lawyer."
b) "Of course, your honour will be concerned that the effect of my submission to uphold the default judgment will be to deny the defendant her day in court against my client because of a default that is the result of her lawyer's neglect.

That concern in another case might be decisive. But here it is outweighed by the failure of the defendant, despite having a new lawyer, to show any defence worthy of a day in court with my client. If it is right for the defendant to blame her lawyer, the defendant can have her day in court with him."

The first argument provides no context and shows no empathy. It simply says to the judge, "You might not like the result, but suck it up." The second argument provides context – it "feels for" the judge's distaste for the result while gently talking the judge out of giving effect to that reluctance.

Good advocates also empathize with the judge by contextualizing the issues the judge must decide. They provide context by formulating the argument to identify the issues they are addressing and suggesting answers to the issues raised by the other party. They do not simply make points and leave it to the judge to do the heavy lifting – consider the point, try to relate it to what the opponent said, find the points of intersection, formulate the issues and then pick a side – all on the judge's own. Good advocates provide context by defining and suggesting answers to the issues.

Consider this hypothetical reply by the plaintiff's counsel:

> The defendants' argument can be encapsulated as raising two reasons why they should be excused from performing the contract. All of their submissions about the costs they incurred to resell the products made by my client are really an argument that the contract had become unprofitable for them to perform. And all of their submissions about the

> meetings they had with Mr. Jones of my client come down to a submission that they obtained an oral waiver of performance. My answer to the first issue is that continued profitability was not a term of the contract. They never bargained for or obtained any such guarantee from my client. My answer to the second issue is that what Mr. Jones said to the defendants does not meet the requirements of waiver either under the contract or under the Supreme Court's definition of waiver.

The importance of context to the way in which an argument will be received can be illustrated by returning to the example of the oral amendment given above. Some may think a submission should be right or wrong regardless of context. But how effective would the "had to be in writing" submission be if it were preceded by a lengthy and detailed attack on the correctness of the trial judge's findings of fact and credibility about what was orally agreed, coupled with a suggestion that the trial judge should have found an oral amendment consisting of different terms? That attack makes it sound like the parties really did think it was appropriate to address amendments orally and to litigate about what was said, and, by creating that context, deprives the "had to be in writing" submission of its contextual air of reality.

CONCLUSION

Shakespeare said, "There is nothing either good or bad, but thinking makes it so." A particular kind of thinking – a belief in the power of context – is an essential part of what makes up good advocacy. Arguments may not be either good or bad as much as they may be good in the right context and bad in the wrong context.

Others who know more about good advocacy than I may try to show that I am wrong. They may identify the arguments I have taken out of context and show what becomes of them if put in proper perspective. They may show that by setting things in the "right" order different conclusions may flow, gently pointing out that while they take no pleasure in cataloguing my errors, by doing so and providing corrections they will help the reader come to more correct views. They may even provide better bridges than I have toward getting the reader to understand what I have been trying to say.

And if they do, haven't I made my point?

The trial advocate as storyteller:
THE ART AND SCIENCE OF PERSUASION

THE HONOURABLE TODD L. ARCHIBALD AND J. MANUEL MENDELZON

Children, only animals live entirely in the Here and Now. Only nature knows neither memory nor history. But man – let me offer you a definition – is the story-telling animal. Wherever he goes he wants to leave behind not a chaotic wake, not an empty space, but the comforting marker-buoys and trail-signs of stories. He has to go on telling stories. He has to keep on making them up. As long as there's a story, it's all right. Even in his last moments, it's said, in the split second of a fatal fall – or when he's about to drown – he sees, passing rapidly before him, the story of his whole life.

~ Graham Swift, *Waterland*[1]

THE MOST PERSUASIVE litigator is a compelling storyteller. This oft-repeated maxim may seem trite, but many litigators consider this principle to be pertinent only to the preparation of a jury address and not to all stages of their litigation. In reality, a well-constructed and coherent case narrative will resonate with conviction from the beginning of the case to its successful conclusion. Many litigators fail to adopt a story- or theme-centred approach to litigation. They do not consider the strengths, weaknesses and structure of their case's

1 (London: William Heinemann, 1983) at 53.

narrative until it is too late. These lawyers all too often end up, as Stephen Leacock once wrote, "[riding] madly off in all directions."[2]

This article argues that the adoption of a story- or theme-centred approach to litigation will fundamentally change the way a case is prepared and presented. Story-centred litigation will assist in achieving the following important goals: conducting an effective examination for discovery, choosing what evidence to lead at trial, determining how to attack an opponent's case, engaging in effective settlement negotiations and, of course, presenting a persuasive argument to a judge or a jury. An acute awareness of the kind of story a particular case tells will provide a coherent framework for making effective and efficient litigation strategy decisions.

Similarly, applying narrative and storytelling techniques to oral advocacy will provide the key to successful courtroom presentations. The principles discussed in this article will assist litigators in creating simple, clear and credible stories, where strengths and weaknesses have been synthesized, characters have been well developed and strong themes have been drawn to the forefront through point-first advocacy.

A simple yet memorable example from the children's fairy tale "Goldilocks and the Three Bears" illustrates the power of using a story-centred model. Consider what the competing narratives would be if the Three Bears had sued Goldilocks for trespass. They might adduce the following evidence: "We were out hunting, and when we came home we couldn't believe it – our house was ransacked! It was destroyed. Everything was turned upside down, and all of our food was eaten." Goldilocks, on the other hand, might present a competing narrative: "Your Honour, I was desperate. I was lost. I was hungry. I was in the woods. I came upon this house and had to break in. I was dying of thirst and starving."[3]

Each story presents a familiar and relatable theme: in one, we see a family's peace and routine destroyed by a criminal intruder; in the other, we see a young victim seeking safety and assistance after enduring significant trauma. Both sides present narratives that contain strong elements of theme, plot and structure. Both stories have the capacity to resonate with a legal audience or decision maker who will try to help the

2 *Nonsense Novels* (Montreal: Publishers' Press, 1911) at 27.

3 Justice Todd L Archibald, "The Art of Persuasion: From the Boardroom to the Courtroom" (2007) 24:2 TM Cooley L Rev 169 [Archibald (1)].

parties achieve their goals. But neither story addresses the weaknesses in the other's perspective.

The Three Bears do not address the fact that the uninvited entry by Goldilocks was done out of a necessity to survive. On the other hand, the problem with Goldilocks's position is that there was no need for her to ransack the Three Bears' household. Breaking in and feeding herself makes sense given her situation, but to pillage the house does not. This is where her defence breaks down. This is where Goldilocks's narrative takes a bad turn and alienates its audience. Without addressing and mitigating the glaring weakness in her side of the case, Goldilocks will lose.

The better storyteller will assimilate and blend the strengths and weaknesses of its side into one homogeneous theme, so that the trier of fact is not left to choose between two stark and irreconcilable positions. As can be seen from this example, the science of persuasive advocacy is built on analysis and reflection. Every case must be evaluated from the beginning for its strengths and weaknesses. Then the case should be synthesized into a three-dimensional story with an overarching and compelling theme.

The question this article raises is: what are the elements of a persuasive story? In a nutshell, narrative theory tells us that a good story feels familiar to an audience. It has strong structure (i.e., a discernible beginning, middle and end), with characters that seem real and relatable. It also conforms to the norms and values of our society. This article will examine the development of narrative theory and its application to litigation, from the time of Aristotle's *Poetics* to modern Hollywood screenwriting theory.

We begin by identifying and classifying the building blocks of a good story: elements such as plot, theme, characters and archetypes. These are all elements that any litigator can use to build his or her case. Having identified the basic elements of a good story, the task is then to learn how to apply them. To that end, this article examines several examples that illustrate how the employment of narrative theory will affect the choices made by a litigator and the potential outcomes in a particular case. We must learn how to develop a narrative that most closely reflects a client's goals, and understand at the same time how audience biases should shape the way a case is presented.

Once the importance of narrative has been explored and a technique has been developed for approaching cases from the perspective of the storyteller, this article deals with the question of how to tell a good story. While drawing upon the rich literature available on the issue of persuasive advocacy, we will suggest ways in which a case narrative can be effectively conveyed to an audience, be it a judge, a jury, opposing counsel or an adverse party. We argue that the most persuasive oral presentation is one that is simple, clear and, most importantly, credible.

WHAT MAKES A COMPELLING AND PERSUASIVE STORY?

Narrative

Narrative is a characteristically human phenomenon that defines the way in which we understand our lives, the lives of others and the world around us. Roland Barthes describes narrative as follows:

> The narratives of the world are numberless. Narrative is first and foremost a prodigious variety of genres, themselves distributed amongst different substances ... Able to be carried by articulated language, spoken or written, fixed or moving images, gestures, and the ordered mixture of all these substances; narrative is present in myth, legend, fable, tale, novella, epic, history, tragedy, drama, comedy, mime, painting ... stained glass windows, cinema, comics, news item, conversation. Moreover under this almost infinite diversity of forms, narrative is present in every age, in every place, in every society ... All classes, all human groups, have their narratives ... Caring nothing for the division between good and bad literature, narrative is international, transhistorical, transcultural: it is simply there, like life itself.[4]

Another narrative theorist, David Herman, writes that the prototypical narrative can be characterized by the following aspects:

- The representation is situated in a specific discourse context or occasion for telling.
- This representation cues interpreters to draw inferences about a structured time-course of particularized events.
- These events are such that they introduce some sort of disruption or disequilibrium into a story-world involving human agents.

---

4 "Introduction to the Structural Analysis of Narratives," trans by S Health, in *Image Music Text* (New York: Hill & Wang, 1977) at 79.

- The representation also conveys the experience of living through this story-world, highlighting the pressure of events on consciousness affected by the various occurrences.[5]

Herman argues that narrative is centrally concerned with the sense of "what is it like" for something or someone to have a particular experience (what philosophers call *qualia*); that is, narrative is essentially about explaining the experience of being.[6] As the quote from Barthes demonstrates, narrative is an ubiquitous phenomenon that permeates our lives and defines how we understand our world. Narrative scholarship is equally prolific. Contemporary Western legal theorists and philosophers have extensively drawn on narrative theory to examine the adjudicative process, legal reasoning and jurisprudential thought.

Storytelling

The oldest and most familiar form of narrative is the story. Throughout history, humans have told stories to share information, to teach their children and to understand themselves and the surrounding world. In other words, narratives and stories are a basic human strategy for coming to terms with time, process and change. It is a strategy that contrasts with, but is in no way inferior to, scientific modes of explanation that describe the world through expressions of equations and various general laws of behaviour and cause and effect. Storytelling is not just a form of entertainment. It is a cognitive phenomenon that allows us, by ritually enacting human situations in an artistic or social realm, to come up with solutions for real-life problems.[7]

Aristotle was among the first Western philosophers to analyze the elements of a good story. In *Poetics,* he dissects the ancient Greek tragedy into six constituent elements: plot (*mythos*), character (*ethos*), thought (*dianoia*), diction (*lexis*), melody (*melos*) and spectacle (*opsis*). His observations of these elements survive today and are recognizable as the universal markers of a good story. For example, in describing character, Aristotle tells us that a protagonist should be as follows: good in the moral sense, and consistent in the sense that the protagonist's actions

---

5 *Basic Elements of Narrative* (Chichester: Wiley-Blackwell, 2009) at xvi.

6 *Ibid.*

7 Lisa Dethridge, *Writing Your Screenplay* (Crows Nest, AU: Allen & Unwin, 2003) at 23 [Dethridge].

should coincide with his or her age, gender and social class. Aristotle underscores the importance of consistency in character by explaining that even if a character's nature is to be inconsistent, he or she must remain consistently inconsistent to avoid audience confusion and misunderstanding.[8] This article underlines the importance of plot, character and diction (language). A case with a good theme (plot and language) built around a credible character will resonate with the trier of fact. It will have its own melody.

Screenwriting

Screenwriting is a type of storytelling that lends itself to the litigation context. Screenwriters, like litigators, have a limited amount of time to "hook" an audience. In this era of BlackBerrys and other forms of instant communication, the 21st-century audience's attention span is extremely short and accustomed to receiving information in sound bites. Thus, litigators must create an appropriate theme or headline for their case – a theme that can be instantly communicated to the trier of fact at the front end of a trial.

Unlike some novelists or historians, screenwriters have developed a science of telling stories that appeal to a broad range of audiences by using tried and true conventions and genres. The next section of this article examines storytelling and narrative theory through the lens of screenwriting. By adopting some of the pragmatic rules of screenwriting, litigators can develop a principled approach to constructing the narrative threads of their cases. A screenwriter will tell you that the measure of a good story is whether it can be easily retold. Being able to tell your story quickly and succinctly, while using easily recognizable conventions, is the key to getting a script on the producer's desk. Screenwriting theorist Lisa Dethridge described this phenomenon in her book *Writing Your Screenplay*:

> [I]n a pitch situation, when a writer is trying to "sell" an idea, the producer will be looking for a story with a "hook" that can be easily encapsulated and communicated in one line. Robert Altman's film *The Player* gives wonderful insights into the world of the commercial screenwriter. In the opening scene, a variety of writers pitch their stories to a producer. They each mention other movies as a way of describing their script. One

8 Aristotle, *Poetics*, trans by Malcolm Heath (London: Penguin, 1996).

> writer envisages her story as a vehicle for the actress Goldie Hawn: "It's like 'Goldie goes to Africa'. She's found by this tribe of small people and she becomes worshipped …" The producer interrupts her pitch asking, "Oh, so it's like *The God's Must be Crazy* only the coke bottle is a movie actress?" "Right," the writer agrees, "exactly. It's like *Out of Africa* meets *Pretty Woman.*"[9]

The pitch scene from *The Player* reveals how screenwriters use conventions such as stock stories and universal narratives to make their point powerfully and succinctly. Dethridge's advice is particularly well suited to a litigator approaching a case. Good stories are neither so obscure nor so complicated that they cannot be easily summarized or repeated. The central themes and dilemmas of any story should be clearly drawn for the audience to follow. The story must have a hook, and it must resonate on a variety of levels – mythic, cultural and psychological. Any deviation from this can cause audience confusion.[10]

The metaphor of the screenwriter "pitching" for the producer is especially apt for the litigator who has to quickly "sell" a client's story to a judge, a jury, an arbitrator, the public or even an opposing party during settlement negotiations. Modern screenwriting theory provides litigators with a simple, familiar and well-developed set of rules for narrative construction. These rules lend themselves to the task of developing a narrative for a civil case.

The four Ps

A good screenplay requires the development of four main structures known in screenwriting parlance as "the four Ps": protagonist, dramatic problem, plot, and premise.[11] Examining each of these Ps will assist a litigator in developing an effective approach to any new case.

The protagonist

A story's protagonist, or hero, is the focus of any narrative and is defined by five characteristics:

- The physical and psychological nature – the protagonist's inner and outer worlds.

9 Dethridge, *supra* note 7 at 24.

10 *Ibid* at 23–24.

11 *Ibid* at 47.

- The history of the protagonist up to the beginning of the story.
- The immediate dramatic problem.
- The character arc or journey.
- The premise or viewpoint of the writer.[12]

One of the most familiar human stories is the journey of a protagonist or hero, real or imagined, while struggling with a problem. The hero undertakes a journey. Along the way he or she encounters friends, foes and other obstacles. Author and screenwriter Christopher Vogler describes the hero's journey as an "ancient guide to storytelling" and characterizes the hero-story as follows:

> At heart, despite its infinite variety, the hero's story is always a journey. A hero leaves her comfortable, ordinary surroundings to venture into a challenging, unfamiliar world. It may be an outward journey to an actual place; a labyrinth, forest or cave, a stranger city or country, a new locale that becomes the arena for her conflict with antagonistic, challenging forces ... In any good story the hero grows and changes, making a journey from one way of being to the next: from despair to hope, weakness to strength, folly to wisdom, love to hate, and back again. It's these emotional journeys that hook an audience and make a story worth watching.[13]

In a compelling story, the members of the audience need to identify with the protagonist in order to relate to the problem he or she has faced and to allow them to stay committed to the story. Aristotle wrote that a complex process of identification must occur between the audience and the protagonist. The audience must become one with the protagonist, such that its members imagine themselves as the protagonist, identify with his or her problems, and experience a catharsis at the end of the protagonist's journey. To do this, a storyteller should develop a protagonist whose psychology is clear, that is, one whose needs, fears, goals and problems have been considered and developed by the storyteller.[14] To facilitate the creation of a well-developed protagonist, lawyers should always learn and understand the biography of their clients as an exercise in character development. To convey a likable and credible protagonist,

12 *Ibid.*

13 Christopher Vogler, *The Writer's Journey: Mythic Structure for Writers* (Studio City, CA: Michael Wiese Productions, 2007) at 13 [Vogler].

14 *Supra* note 7 at 48.

lawyers must present the client as a person either with whom the audience can empathize or in whom its members can see themselves.

A perfect example of this process is depicted by Sara Ramshaw in "'He's My Man!': Lyrics of Innocence and Betrayal in *The People v. Billie Holiday*,"[15] which examines the reasons for the famed jazz singer Billie Holiday's 1949 acquittal on five narcotics possession charges. Ramshaw examines how Holiday was able to beat her charges by relying on her "unlucky in life" public persona as the premise underlying her defence. Ramshaw notes the attention paid throughout Holiday's trial to the race and class distinctions and gender components of her narrative of innocence and betrayal by the men in her life. Ramshaw argues that this public persona was well known and accepted as valid by her audience of jurors. It became an effective legal narrative in her defence.[16]

Billie Holiday had created a name for herself in the United States through her music. Her public persona evolved into that of a woman "unlucky in life" due to the fact that almost all her songs contained lyrics that drew on the romantic conventions of unrequited love, loneliness and frustration. This persona took on some authenticity because of the ultra-racist view in the United States at the time that many black women were "unsophisticated" people who were condemned to poor relationships with men.[17] It was in this context that a successful defence was poignantly mounted for Holiday against the charges of narcotics possession in 1949 by criminal defence attorney Jake Ehrlich.[18]

The narrative suggested, with almost no evidence, that Holiday, as always, was the victim of her abusive boyfriend/manager, John Levy, who had framed her. The defence used Holiday's well-known and ongoing struggle with men as the central dramatic problem in her journey, emphasized betrayal as the premise of her story and played to stereotypes of black women by presenting Holiday as an uneducated, unsophisticated victim. While issues of race and gender should normally be ignored in a modern courtroom, Ramshaw shows how they were brought into the foreground in Holiday's trial:

15 (2004) 16 Can J Women & L 86.

16 *Ibid* at 87–88.

17 *Ibid* at 89–90.

18 *Ibid* at 97–99.

> To begin, Holiday entered the courtroom looking uncharacteristically "unkempt in a beige suit." Her eyes were puffy from crying and one eye was bruised and swollen. She told a reporter in the courtroom that Levy had hit her ... Ehrlich used Billie's obvious emotional and physical pain to his advantage, "let[ting] her pour it out while the indictment was being read and the first twelve jury candidates took their places." Holiday's visible anguish and drab appearance enabled the jury to more readily accept her "unlucky in life" persona.[19]

Ehrlich stuck closely to his premise in defending Holiday by questioning her extensively on (selectively chosen) episodes of her humble childhood, her past drug use and her relationship with Levy. Holiday was portrayed as a victim at all times. Ehrlich even pressed Holiday to account for her $200,000 annual income (a "bad fact" that may have worked against her portrayal as a poor and unfortunate victim), which Holiday explained was controlled by Levy and was a source of contention between them: "I keep asking him to give me some money and he keep beating me limp."[20] Ramshaw notes that this questioning, although irrelevant to the issue of the narcotics possession, directed attention towards Holiday's "unlucky in life" persona, which resonated with the jury.[21] In the end, Ramshaw demonstrates that "jurors came to despise the absent, abusive Levy, a man who, they were told, stole all of Holiday's money and refused to marry her."[22] The jury quickly returned with a unanimous verdict of not guilty.[23]

Ramshaw's article underscores how a strong narrative can fill gaps, attenuate weaknesses and solve contradictions in evidence to tie together a compelling defence in what was described as an "ironclad" case for the prosecution.[24] Ramshaw concludes that "the heightened authenticity that her ... public persona lent to her trial narrative of innocence and betrayal gave Holiday's testimony the quality of truthfulness needed to get a jury to overlook the evidence (or lack thereof) in front of them."[25] The Billie Holiday example also demonstrates how important outside

19 *Ibid* at 101.
20 *Ibid* at 102–103.
21 *Ibid* at 104.
22 *Ibid.*
23 *Ibid.*
24 *Ibid* at 105.
25 *Ibid.*

influences, such as popular culture, form part of the narrative of a lawyer's case.

Faced with Holiday's celebrity and well-known public persona, Ehrlich harnessed it and used it to his advantage to connect with his audience. It could easily have gone the other way. If her salary, luxurious lifestyle and long history of substance abuse had become the centrepiece of the trial, it is unlikely that the blue-collar jury would have empathized with the defence position.

Archetypes

In addition to focusing on the protagonist, a litigator must also wrap his or her mind around the other characters in the narrative. In determining how the other players in a litigator's story relate to the protagonist and the narrative as a whole, a litigator should look for archetypes, or stock characters, whose presence an audience will implicitly understand and accept. Archetypes are characters in stories and narratives that symbolize recurring patterns of universal human behaviour. Archetypal characters play supporting roles in a hero's story, roles that everyone can relate to and understand. Some typical archetypes are the mentors, or hero's guides, who assist and provide wisdom to the hero for his or her journey; the enemies or gatekeepers that stand in the way of the hero, and the family and friends who stand with the hero and journey with him or her.[26]

Archetypes serve to express patterns of behaviour collected from the rich wealth of human history. They are ideals derived from past collective experiences, which many Jungian psychologists believe are present in the individual unconscious.[27] Archetypes are useful in developing the case because they provide a context that will resonate with an audience. They help confirm the legitimacy and credibility of the story. The audience will better relate to the story because it has a familiar ring and reverberates with the audience's common sense and life experiences.

---

26 Vogler, *supra* note 13. See also Northrop Frye, *Anatomy of Criticism: Four Essays* (Princeton: Princeton University Press, 1957); Joseph Campbell, *The Hero with a Thousand Faces* (Princeton: Princeton University Press, 1968).

27 See David Herman, Manfred Jahn & Marie-Laure Ryan, *Routledge Encyclopedia of Narrative Theory* (New York: Routledge, 2005) at 26–27 [Herman]. See also Carl G Jung, "Approaching the Unconscious," in Carl G Jung, ed, *Man and His Symbols* (London: Dell, 1968).

Stereotypes

On the other hand, litigators must be careful to avoid stereotypes, which are conventional, formulaic and oversimplified representations of individuals or groups. The use of these types of characters in constructing a legal narrative will ring hollow with a modern audience and may even cause offence. Litigators who employ stereotyping to convey a message about the nature of a particular character in a legal narrative or to predict how a jury will react to a particular person will likely fail because they underestimate the ability of today's audience to understand and relate to complex, nuanced characters. Juries and judges may well feel that they are being "played to" or manipulated when presented with stereotypes. Archetypes, on the other hand, can be multifaceted and complex, despite their universal nature, because they symbolize various aspects of our own humanity – which is never simple. Archetypes ring true, whereas stereotypes fall flat.

The second step in developing a protagonist is to chart his or her journey. Most Western storytelling, whether ancient or modern, dramatic, religious or otherwise, employs a simple linear narrative in which three acts represent the beginning, middle and end of a protagonist's story. The protagonist journeys forward on this line, or "arc," while encountering a series of problems. The protagonist's journey sets the stage for the introduction of the second "P": the dramatic problem.

The dramatic problem

A good story presents an organized series of problems or obstacles for the protagonist to solve in his or her journey towards self-actualization.[28] The resolution of the dramatic problem is a crucial step towards catharsis. The problem must be resolved in a way that satisfies the audience. An effective resolution of the dramatic problem is a key consideration for the litigator. If the litigator has created a compelling narrative for his or her case, the resolution to the dramatic problem will be obvious: members of the audience will gravitate towards the solution that most closely relates to their identification with the actions of an empathetic protagonist. In litigation, the solution to the dramatic problem in a client's story lies in the outcome. This will often manifest itself in a jury or a judge wanting to "do the right thing" in terms of delivering an appropriate verdict. If the "right thing" is

---

28 Dethridge, *supra* note 7 at 48.

unclear, or if there seem to be many possible "right" endings to the story, then the narrative will have been incoherent and muddled.

The plot

In *Poetics*, Aristotle posited that a "whole" drama is one that has a beginning (*protasis*), middle (*epitasis*) and end (*catastrophe*). This classical three-act structure prevailed until the Roman period, when Horace introduced the five-act drama.[29] In the 19th century, German playwright and critic Gustav Freytag created a simple diagram to illustrate the plot line of the five-act story.[30] Known as "Freytag's Triangle," this diagram charts the progress of the classical dramatic arc.

Freytag identified the first stage of a dramatic plot as the "exposition." In this stage, the protagonist is introduced, and the initial or normal state of affairs of a particular story-world is established. At the end of the exposition, the inciting incident is revealed; this fuels the further development of the plot. Following the exposition comes the "rising action" where the protagonist of the story attempts to realize his or her goals in the face of the central inciting incident as well as from any secondary complications and obstacles. The protagonist's journey through the rising action will eventually lead to the turning point, or "climax." This stage is where the protagonist's fortunes turn, for better or for worse, and leads to the falling action, where, in a tragedy, the declining fortune of the protagonist is portrayed.[31] As an example, in a personal injury trial, the exposition and rising action would depict the plaintiff's life before the accident and the events leading to the accident itself (the turning point, or climax). The falling action would depict the nature of the injuries and the difficult road towards rehabilitation.

Lastly, and most importantly for litigators, comes the dénouement.

The name for this final stage in Freytag's Triangle comes from French and means the untying, or literally "un-knotting." In this stage, conflicts are resolved. A sense of catharsis, satisfaction or release of tension is created for the audience.[32] In a story constructed by a litigator, the

29 Barret Harper Clark, *European Theories of the Drama from Aristotle to the Present Day* (New York: Crown, 1947).

30 Herman, *supra* note 27 at 189. See also Gustav Freytag, *Die Technik des Dramas* (Stuttgart: Reclam, 1983).

31 Herman, *ibid.*

32 *Ibid.*

closing address is part of the dénouement. It is the protagonist's opportunity to have the knots untied and the conflicts resolved. When the litigator's audience, usually a judge or a jury, reach the dénouement, they begin to play an active role in the story and will want to assist the protagonist in reaching the natural resolution of his or her story arc through providing a proper verdict, which resolves the conflict in the case. In the personal injury example, a finding of liability against the defendant and an appropriate award of damages would reflect the resolution of the conflict in favour of the plaintiff.

The premise

The last and, in many ways, most important screenwriting "P" is the premise. This "P" is described by Lisa Dethridge as "the writer's secret weapon."[33] The premise, or theme, of the story will be the element that ties the other three Ps together; the moral or philosophical elements that underpin the story and drive it forward. The premise is the most important story element for litigators. A strong case premise will allow the lawyer to relate to his or her audience through commonly held values. A strong premise for the case narrative should be readily identifiable and should be announced up front – for example, the search for truth, or justice, or reconciliation or appropriate compensation for injuries. A litigator with a well-developed case premise (like a screenwriter pitching to a producer) should be able to simply and succinctly answer the questions "What is this case about?" and "Why should my client succeed?"

A useful example of premise at work in case theory can be found in Janice Schuetz and Lin S. Lilley's book *The O.J. Simpson Trials: Rhetoric, Media, and the Law*.[34] In the chapter on final summations, Schuetz and Lilley examine and contrast the central themes, or premises, in the closing arguments presented by both sides in O.J. Simpson's infamous criminal and civil trials. In the civil trial, the authors note that the defence attorneys failed to present a complete or compelling storyline. Instead they presented a disorganized series of attacks on the plaintiffs' evidence. They divided their focus on police misconduct, the alleged immoral behaviour of Nicole Brown Simpson, the plaintiffs' greed and the existence of unknown assailants who may have committed the

33 *Supra* note 7 at 50.

34 (Carbondale: Southern Illinois University Press, 1999).

murders in question. These disparate themes never coalesced into a unified story. Instead of presenting a persuasive counterpoint to the plaintiffs' tragic loss, the defence simply maligned the victims and impugned their motives.[35]

In contrast, the defence attorneys in the criminal trial were able to construct a cohesive narrative with an overarching theme of police racism. They successfully characterized O.J. Simpson as a victim of an unfair and racist police system, as opposed to a homicidal domestic abuser. The defence suggested that because the lead detective, Mark Fuhrman, was a racist, it was likely that he and other police had framed Simpson because he was a famous black man. This simple and understandable theory resonated powerfully both with the jury and with many segments of the public.[36]

In the civil case, the successful plaintiffs' attorneys constructed their case theory around the theme of domestic violence as a driving force that led to Simpson's jealousy, rage killing and cover-up. The suffering of the victims as well as the impact on their families were also underlined.[37] These examples from the O.J. Simpson trials illustrate how important theme or premise is to the development of a successful and cohesive case narrative.

Another example of the power of "the fourth P" is found in the article "Eve Was Right to Eat the 'Apple': The Importance of Narrative in the Art of Lawyering," by Professor Sally Frank.[38] In that article, Frank uses the biblical story of Eve to illustrate how narrative theme can shape a client's case and reveals how premise can be used not only to present a successful case but also to achieve a particular client goal.

Frank imagines that Eve has just walked into the office of a criminal defence lawyer. She seeks vindication after over 5,000 years of vilification for committing the crime of eating the forbidden fruit from the Tree of Knowledge in the Garden of Eden. Frank uses examples from hypothetical closing addresses to reflect the various legal defences that could be mounted for Eve with varying degrees of success. Some of the

---

35 *Ibid* at 109.

36 *Ibid* at 108.

37 *Ibid* at 112.

38 (1996) 8 Yale JL & Feminism 79.

approaches fail to justify her conduct. Others attempt to exonerate her actions with reasonable success.[39]

Frank writes that one of the important features of a coherent legal narrative is that it can create a link between the exceptional and the ordinary. Narrative obtains meaning by explaining a deviation from the ordinary in an understandable and realistic manner. Frank suggests that the stories lawyers tell are often specifically intended to explain and justify a deviation from the normal in order to obtain a successful result.[40] This is clearly the goal of the storytelling criminal defence lawyer, who must explain the client's alleged deviant conduct in a rational way that will make the audience relate to that client and accept his or her conduct as excusable or not blameworthy in the circumstances.

In the sentencing process, while the analysis undertaken is often portrayed as a balancing of enumerated mitigating and aggravating factors, the reality is that this process involves a judicial choice between the competing narratives of the offender who is deserving of justice, but also a second chance, versus the offender who is inherently evil and deserving only of punishment. We now turn from the structure of a strong legal narrative to the role that the audience plays in developing a good story.

Know the audience

A good story necessarily interacts with and understands its audience. Frank's article raises the important issue of being tuned in to the audience's makeup:

> The reader interprets the story based on that reader's own culture and the resources of his or her imagination. The reader then assimilates the narrative into the drama of his or her own life. The subjectivity of the reader is developed both by his or her position in society and his or her personal history. Accordingly, when people encounter a narrative, they view it from their own perspective, which is shaped by their culture, their identity, and various aspects of their individual lives. Within a given audience, therefore, there are multiple perspectives and multiple realities from which to interpret a text.[41]

39 *Ibid.*
40 *Ibid* at 82.
41 *Ibid* at 83.

Frank cautions that lawyers must take all of these factors into account when listening to the viewpoints of their clients and witnesses, and when reconstructing the narrative of their clients to present to a judge or jury.

Schuetz and Lilley describe the legal narrative as a "transactional process in which audiences participate in the creation of the meaning of stories."[42] These narratives take on persuasive character because legal audiences experience them with "a stock of stories" in their minds. That background of stories is used to decide whether a particular narrative rings true when compared with the stories the audiences know and understand.[43]

This "stock" is built from an audience's social knowledge and life experience. In their analysis of the O.J. Simpson trials, Schuetz and Lilley describe the use of parallel imagery as a way to connect with the juries by using the legal audience's social knowledge. Through the connection with the audience's sense of what they value, their common sense and life's experiences, the lawyer begins to persuade the triers of fact of the rightness of his or her position. In the criminal trial, the prosecution used the image of a burning fuse, which traversed the long history of Simpson's domestic violence. This burning fuse inevitably led to his explosively homicidal behaviour. Schuetz and Lilley identify a clear misconnect in the prosecution's fuse imagery, in that some jurors had experienced domestic violence in their own lives and did not believe that it created an inevitable path to murder.[44]

Jury demographics

In addition to the topics of theme and premise, Shuetz and Lilley explain that the differences between the verdicts in the O.J. Simpson criminal and civil trials may also be rooted in the demographics of the respective juries. They argue that the more ethnically diverse jurors of the criminal trial in Los Angeles may have been more open to accepting the police racism theory than were the predominately white jurors in the Santa Monica civil trial.[45] Thus, the importance of knowing the backgrounds and potential

---

42 *Supra* note 34 at 104.

43 *Supra* note 34. See also Nancy Pennington & Reid Hastie, "The Story Model for Juror Decision Making" in Reid Hastie, ed, *Inside the Juror: The Psychology of Juror Decision-Making* (Cambridge: Cambridge University Press, 1993) at 192 [Hastie].

44 *Supra* note 34 at 118.

45 *Ibid* at 120.

biases of the triers of fact is spotlighted.[46] We appreciate that, within the framework of the rules of civil procedure in our provinces, the ability to learn about a prospective juror's background is limited. Nonetheless we should glean as much as we can from the information provided about jurors, such as occupation, residency and background.

The litigator's background

Another important audience consideration is the credibility of the narrator (the lawyer). Schuetz and Lilley adopt a definition of credibility as referring to "the judgments made by a perceiver concerning the believability of a communicator."[47] While much attention has been paid to the importance of the credibility of witnesses in a lawyer's case, an awareness of the importance of the credibility of the legal narrator is also crucial for creating a connection with an audience and promoting the validity of a particular narrative.

Unlike the lead, but treacherous, voice in some fascinating works of fiction, the litigator wants to avoid the appearance of being the "unreliable narrator" at all costs. The litigator's credibility in any particular case depends on many factors, including his or her level of preparation, the language employed to convey the key themes, his or her perceived integrity, his or her level of courtroom experience and even the nature of his or her employment. For example, a litigator representing the Crown may be viewed differently by a judge or jury than a litigator who is a partner at a large law firm, or a sole practitioner or even one who is working pro bono. The recognition that those elements may affect how the litigator is viewed by a jury or judge during the construction of a case narrative will avoid potential pitfalls with a legal audience. We will discuss these elements in greater detail under the section "How to Tell a Good Story," on page 30.

Popular culture

Another subjective type of audience bias, one that may be particularly problematic when dealing with a jury, is the way in which litigators are represented in popular culture and the effect of those representations

46 See, for example, Hubert S Field, "Juror Background Characteristics and Attitudes toward Rape: Correlates of Jurors' Decisions in Rape Trials" (1978) 2:2 Law and Human Behaviour 73.

47 *Supra* note 34 at 110.

on the credibility of the lawyer. Professor Steven Penney's article on the influence of Hollywood film on Canadian mass tort litigation examines *Erin Brockovitch* and *A Civil Action* and how they shape the public's view of law and lawyers.[48] Penney argues that the depiction of law, lawyers and legal institutions in film has the potential to deeply impact public attitudes about legal issues in the sense that they exist as a form of "popular jurisprudence."[49] Penney demonstrates that both of the above-mentioned films used traditional narrative techniques to create compelling stories that led audiences to specific moral conclusions about the legal profession and justice system. Litigators need to be aware that their audiences, legal and non-legal alike, come to a case with these deeply ingrained popular cultural notions of law, lawyers and justice. Most of these cultural notions are not positive and need to be dispelled. An example is a serious personal injury jury trial, in which the perception of avarice may envelop the jury's innate reaction to the plaintiff and his lawyer. That bias needs to be tackled head-on in an opening address and dispelled before it takes root and poisons the outcome of the trial.

The jurist's background

Lastly, the innate perspective of the jurist must also be considered. Judges come to a case with their own varied backgrounds, experiences and opinions.[50] To ignore this and expect that the personality and the background of a judge will play no role in the construction of the legal narrative is to forget the vital importance of connecting with your audience. The old adage of "know your judge" and his or her background still applies, and now it is easier than ever to learn about your judge's history and to access his or her prior decisions in the age of the Internet.

---

48 "Mass Torts, Mass Culture: Canadian Mass Tort Law and Hollywood Narrative Film" (2004) 30 Queen's LJ 205.

49 *Ibid* at 206–208.

50 For a study on how the background and ideology of judges affect decisions in Canadian Federal Court immigration matters, see Jon B Gould, Colleen Sheppard & Johannes Wheeldon, "A Refugee from Justice? Disparate Treatment in the Federal Court of Canada" (2010) 32:4 Law & Pol'y 454. See also Candace C White, "Gender Differences on the Supreme Court" in FL Morton, ed, *Law, Politics and the Judicial Process in Canada*, 3rd ed (Calgary: University of Calgary Press, 2002) at 85.

HOW TO TELL A GOOD STORY

What is the best way to present a successful narrative in court? Many of the principles of screenwriting reviewed above apply equally to the art of legal storytelling, with some modifications. Whether the legal narrative is presented orally or in writing, to a court or to another interested party, these principles will assist litigators in telling compellingly persuasive stories. In examining what makes a good legal story, we return for a moment to the analogy of the screenwriter pitching an idea to a producer. Like the screenwriter, the litigator has a limited amount of time to make the pitch. The litigator's audience, like a Hollywood producer, is busy, sometimes distracted and often expert in the subject matter. The story must be focused, resonate with the audience (on both rational and emotional levels) and use conventions that make it easily understood. We know this already from having examined Aristotle's schema and "the four Ps" of screenwriting. The following three principles will also help litigators translate a strong legal narrative into a successful legal argument: simplicity, clarity and credibility.

The simplicity principle

Often, the civil litigator's task is to turn a warehouse full of boxes of documents and thick volumes of examination transcripts into a simple, understandable story. To tell a successful story, a litigator should create a good sketch of the proposed progression of the case. Whether the case concerns a complex commercial transaction or a personal injury, the litigator should break the legal narrative down into its constituent parts by using Aristotle's beginning, middle and end, or Freytag's Triangle, as a guide to mapping out the narrative's milestones, turning points and climaxes. In doing so, the litigator will ensure that each section of the case has its own discrete elements and its own beginning and end.

Once the story is broken down into sections and the path that the story will take is identified, the litigator needs to consider the biography of the protagonist (the client) and identify the important supporting characters. Audiences find it difficult to relate to more than one protagonist at a time,[51] so the legal narrative should more closely resemble the journey of the classical hero than the sprawling character study of a Victorian novel.

---

51 Dethridge, *supra* note 7 at 61.

Not every character or witness in a case needs to be included to move the story forward. Litigators should not be afraid to "edit out" characters who do not either aid or challenge the protagonist or move the case ahead. The same goes for the level of detail necessary in evidence. Just because evidence exists that may be relevant to a cause of action does not mean that it is of sufficient probative value or so important that it needs to be highlighted in the narrative. Counsel should edit out unimportant detail to lead only the evidence that moves the narrative's action forward.

Evidence that is just distracting noise should be deleted. The story should be kept as simple and straightforward as possible so that it can be easily digested by the trier of fact. The road map should be clear from beginning to end; the road should not have any unexpected bumps or detours. The presentation must at all times be focused, coherent and clearly understandable.

Lisa Dethridge provides a screenwriting *mantra* for this purpose that is equally useful to a litigator.[52] In deciding which details are important, litigators should constantly ask themselves "So what? Who cares?" In so doing, they will be challenged to step back from the story and see the big picture, to understand what the story is *really* about and ultimately to adduce only truly important evidence, not just filler. Practically speaking, this principle encourages litigators to make effective use of admissions and concessions, agreed statements of fact and skilful amendments to pleadings, which will assist them in focusing on the important details at trial.[53]

Weaknesses and omissions

Notwithstanding the above, the principle of editing out minor unnecessary details does not mean that a litigator should gloss over or omit evidence that contradicts the client's position or otherwise hurts the case. Those omissions will invariably damage the story and the storyteller's credibility and alienate the audience. An interesting example of how editing can backfire is found in the legendary television series *Seinfeld*. In a 1997 episode entitled "The Yadda Yadda,"[54] Jerry and George are

52 *Ibid* at 35.

53 See Justice Todd L Archibald, "11 Negative Advocacy Tips – How to Lose Without Really Trying" (Paper presented to the Law Society of Upper Canada, Toronto, 11 January 2011) [unpublished].

54 *Seinfeld*, 1997, DVD (Beverly Hills, CA: Columbia/Tristar Video, 2007).

both dating women who gloss over apparently unimportant details in their stories by replacing them with the phrase "yadda yadda yadda." Jerry appreciates his girlfriend's concision and simplicity, and remarks that her approach to storytelling is "like dating *USA Today*." George, on the other hand, is suspicious that his girlfriend is misusing the "yadda yadda" to leave out crucial and negative parts of her life story. In the end, George's suspicions are shown to be correct. Audiences, especially legal ones, are savvy and know when details are being left out disingenuously and will come to doubt and mistrust the "yadda yaddaing" lawyer. Similarly, litigators must resist the temptation to edit out the weaknesses of their case to avoid leaving gaping holes that foster the audience's mistrust. Weaknesses are important details in any case and must be dealt with head on; otherwise, audiences (or worse, opposing counsel) will sniff them out. Opposing counsel will seize on them if a litigator does not highlight them first and attenuate them or explain them away. The case's warts and weaknesses will not be so significant if they are exposed early in the case, especially in the opening address.

From a purely practical perspective, addressing a case's weaknesses allows a litigator to take ownership of the case's "bad facts," put them in context, explain them away or make them work in the overall story of the case. Most importantly, it prevents the litigator's opponent from weaving weaknesses into the narrative of his or her own case.[55] The perfect example of this theory at work comes from the world of advertising and the very successful and memorable campaign for Buckley's cough syrup that announced "It tastes awful but it works great."[56] The slogan acknowledged the weakness of the product but turned it into an advantage.

The persuasive burden

The Honourable Justice John Laskin of the Court of Appeal for Ontario, while quoting from the venerable judge and legal scholar Richard Posner, instructs litigators to persuade with simplicity by "reducing the persuasive burden" on a decision maker.[57] The key to reducing the persuasive

55 Justice John I Laskin, "What Persuades (or, What's Going on Inside the Judge's Mind)" (2004) 23:1 Advocates' Soc J 4 [Laskin (1)]. See also Justice Todd L Archibald, "Tips for an Effective Closing Address in a Judge Alone Trial" [2002] Annual Review of Civil Litigation 255 [Archibald (2)].

56 Laskin (1), *ibid* at 5.

57 *Ibid* at 6–7.

burden is to shorten the distance a court or judge must travel to agree with the position. This can be done by presenting a reasonable solution to a dispute or by presenting the court with a narrow ground to decide in your favour. Justice Laskin articulated the principle as follows:

> As Cardozo reminds us in his famous lectures on "The Nature of the Judicial Process," each of us has our own philosophy of life, and try as we may to see things objectively we can never see them with any eyes but our own. Many unseen forces guide our thoughts and actions – our likes and dislikes, our moods, instincts, emotions, habits, and convictions. All these forces make judges resist radical change to their beliefs. Judges look for consistency between their existing beliefs and any new information presented to them. The less they have to travel to agree with you and the smoother the journey to get there, the more likely you are to persuade them.[58]

Note the use of the metaphor of a journey to describe the persuasive process. If the litigator has constructed a simple, well-structured narrative with a credible protagonist and a tenable story arc that takes into account the biases of its audience, then the distance a court must travel to reach that litigator's conclusion will likely be perceived as shorter and the ride much smoother.[59]

Brevity

Lastly, simplicity also demands brevity. Litigators should in most cases limit their submissions to the three most important points. In today's increasingly busy courts, where judges and juries have limited time and are accustomed to sound bites, litigators have at most only a few minutes to hook their audience and get their message across. Condensing a narrative into three strong points is no easy task and takes great effort

---

58 *Ibid* at 7.

59 Social science research has shown much the same to be true with juries who often decide cases based on a model of story-centred decision making, arguing that juries decide cases based on a process of selecting the best-fit narrative. See Benjamin L Berger, "The Rule in Hodge's Case: Rumours of its Death are Greatly Exaggerated" (2005) 84 Can Bar Rev 47; D Schum & A Martin, "Formal and Empirical Research on Cascaded Inference in Jurisprudence" in Hastie, *supra* note 43 at 136; W Bennett & M Feldman, *Reconstructing Reality in the Courtroom: Justice and Judgment in American Culture* (New Brunswick, NJ: Rutgers University Press, 1981); J Holstein, "Jurors' Interpretations and Jury Decision Making" (1985) 9 Law and Human Behaviour 83.

and reflection. Remember the comments attributed to Samuel Langhorne Clemens (a.k.a. Mark Twain): "I did not have time to write a short letter, so I wrote a long one instead."[60] If you deluge a trier of fact with a downpour of points, your main message may be diluted by the impact of many lesser points or lost in a forest of extraneous arguments. At a minimum, your road map will become complicated and unappealing. The trier of fact will not want to join you on the journey.

The clarity principle

It may seem obvious that a good legal narrative or argument needs to be clear. There are, however, some features of legal argument and narrative that will help a legal audience to interpret and understand your position.

First, a strong legal narrative cannot resemble a mystery novel. The conclusion must be presented at the beginning. A litigator needs to position his or her case premise in the opening address and to provide the audience with a clear road map of the hero's journey. This approach allows the audience to process the details and trust that the narrative is going somewhere. Judges, like many movie audiences, are not passive listeners; rather, they are always looking to make sense of what they are hearing.[61] The members of the audience will readily absorb details and new information when they know why it is significant and why it matters as soon as they hear it. Justice Laskin calls this approach "cognitive clarity" and suggests that it is especially important in oral argument before judges, who will always be asking themselves "Why are you telling me this?"[62] That question will be answered if the litigator adopts the cognitive clarity approach and considers the screenwriter's "So what? Who cares?" mantra in crafting submissions.

Point-first advocacy

Put another way, the most effective way to present any argument is to employ point-first advocacy. The premise of any submission should be stated immediately. Many counsel do not take this approach;[63] instead,

60 The origin of this phrase, often attributed to Mark Twain, may be Pascal's *Lettres Provinciales* (XVI) (4 December 1656).

61 Laskin (1), *supra* note 55 at 5.

62 *Ibid* at 6.

63 Justice John I Laskin, "Forget the Windup and Make the Pitch" (1999) 18:2 Advocates' Soc J 3 [Laskin (2)].

they are convinced their audience first needs to understand how the argument will develop and that their point will not be understood until the audience is familiar with a long set of facts.[64] These concerns have some validity, but putting the point first allows the members of the audience to orient themselves and prepares them to receive the detail, context and other information necessary to support the point. Point-first advocacy makes all submissions clearer and provides a crucial road map for the trier of fact.

Secondly, putting the premise up front not only allows an audience to understand the details of the narrative that will follow, but also serves to make the point more memorable. Cognitive psychologists have shown that where storytellers position their premise in the piece will affect how well the audience retains the information. This phenomenon is known as the "serial position effect," a term coined by psychologist Hermann Ebbinghaus.[65] Using the concepts of "primacy" and "recency," the serial position effect demonstrates that people are most likely to absorb and retain the first and last items in a list.[66] This theory underscores the importance of a litigator's opening and closing comments, and suggests that the premise of the legal narrative should be presented at the beginning and repeated at the end. The classic advocacy adage on this point rings with poignancy: Tell your audience what you intend to prove; prove it; then remind them at the closing that you fulfilled the promises made in your opening address.[67]

The power of emotion

Charles Evans Hughes, former Chief Justice of the United States, once said: "Ninety percent of any decision is emotional. The rational part of us supplies the reasons for supporting our predilections."[68] A strong story with emotional appeal will also serve a litigator in constructing a

---

64 *Ibid.*

65 Hermann Ebbinghaus, *Memory: A Contribution to Experimental Psychology*, trans by Henry Alford Ruger & Clara E Bussenius (New York: Dover, 1964).

66 Laskin (1), *supra* note 55 at 6; Archibald (2), *supra* note 55 at 259. See also Harry Mills, *Artful Persuasion* (New York: AMA, 2000) at 137–138.

67 Archibald (2), *supra* note 55 at 261.

68 William O Douglas, *The Court Years, 1939–1975* (New York: Random House, 1980) at 8 and 33.

clear story. Aristotle identified *pathos*, or emotion, as one of the three elements of rhetorical persuasion.[69]

Consider this brief example from a plaintiff's opening address in a fatal personal-injury trial:

> Ladies and gentlemen, think about that stormy night last November with the last leaves blowing around. There was a hot fire glowing inside the home of the plaintiffs, Gene and Martha. They were in their home having tea at 10 p.m. as they have done for 40 years. They loved their tea and they loved their quiet time together. It was a chance for this elderly couple to replay the events of the day or even just to be in the emotional and intellectual embrace of each other. Then Martha turns to her husband and says "I think it's time, dear, for you to go to the store and get some cream, you know I love cream in my tea." Her dutiful husband says "Don't worry, I'll be back in two minutes. I'll go in the car to the corner store and get the cream." But he never again comes home because, ladies and gentlemen, a drunk driver, the defendant in the courtroom, kills him.[70]

This example sets the stage for a compelling narrative, appeals to an audience's emotions and creates a strong theme that spotlights the drunk driver's actions as a stark incursion into, and direct contrast to, the peaceful and loving existence of Gene and Martha. Counsel tend to undervalue the power of emotion in their presentations. That is not to suggest that lawyers should ever intentionally play to the trier of fact's emotions – that kind of craven appeal will be seen for its meretricious value. The point is that counsel should be alive to the positive and negative visceral elements in a case.

Justice Laskin instructs litigators to "activate the judges' senses" and "paint word pictures that judges can see" by being concrete in their descriptions, avoiding generalities and eliminating abstract legal concepts whenever possible. To do this, litigators should show instead of tell:

> Do not say "she felt sad" when you can say "she had tears streaming down her face." Do not say "Carter tried to mitigate his losses but could not find other employment" when you can say "Carter applied for eight other jobs but did not get a single interview." One effective way of "showing" is to read

---

69 Aristotle, *On Rhetoric: A Theory of Civil Discourse*, trans by GA Kennedy (New York: Oxford University Press, 1991).

70 Archibald (1), *supra* note 3 at 174.

a compelling excerpt of a witness's testimony so that the court can see and hear the evidence in the witness's own words.[71]

In addition, forceful language is more persuasive. In "Forget the Windup and Make the Pitch," Justice Laskin makes many helpful suggestions to assist in simplifying and strengthening language, such as avoiding the use of false intensifiers, avoiding the overuse of the word "not," avoiding needless words and eliminating the "dreaded couplets" (i.e., null and void, cease and desist, due and payable, free and clear, force and effect).[72]

Most importantly, we urge lawyers to "romance the verb" and use the active voice to create more forceful submissions. The passive voice exposes a reluctance to admit that something is happening and can create the appearance that something is being concealed. For example, the passive sentence "An order was rendered by the court requiring that the defendant be paid $600,000 in damages by the plaintiff" would in the active voice be "The court ordered the plaintiff to pay the defendant $600,000 in damages." The active phrase is stronger and easier to understand. A familiar example of the passive voice being used to distance a subject from an object and conceal a particular fact is the use of the phrase "mistakes were made." The phrase, uttered to avoid responsibility for misdeeds, is so often heard in Washington that American political consultant William Schneider claims that its use has created a new tense, which he refers to as "the past-exonerative tense."[73]

The credibility principle

We have already seen that the credibility of a narrator is an important factor when an audience is evaluating the validity or truth of a story. An unreliable narrator may provide a dramatic twist – perfect for the ending of a Hollywood thriller like *The Sixth Sense* or *The Usual Suspects* – but the dissonance caused by such a surprise in a legal narrative will cause a litigator to lose a case. In any story, the narrator is the audience's guide through the journey of the protagonist. That journey should not

71 Laskin (1), *supra* note 55 at 14.

72 Laskin (2), *supra* note 63 at 10.

73 John M Broder, "Familiar Fallback for Officials: Mistakes Were Made" *New York Times* (14 March 2007), online: New York Times <www.nytimes.com/2007/03/14/washington/14mistakes.html>.

have any unexpected stops. The landscape should be illuminated in its entirety in the opening address.

Here we consider three qualities of narrators that contribute to their credibility: preparation, conviction and honesty.

Preparation

A good guide should have extensive knowledge of the path to be followed and the landmarks to be viewed along the way. What this means for a legal narrator is that he or she must always be well-prepared. It is difficult to overemphasize the importance of preparation in oral advocacy. A litigator who knows the record of a case inside out will not only be helpful to a busy decision maker, who may not be as acquainted with the case, but will also instil trust in the audience.[74]

Conviction

Hand in hand with preparation comes conviction. Persuasive and prepared litigators believe in the narrative they are advancing. American president Lyndon Johnson once said: "What convinces is conviction. You simply have to believe in the argument you are advancing. If you don't, you are as good as dead. The other person will sense that something isn't there."[75] The bottom line is that litigators who do not know their record inside out will not be able to deal effectively with whatever unexpected curve comes their way and will not be persuasive. Their tentativeness and/or unfocused performance will undermine the strength of their presentation.

Honesty

The audience will more easily accept the truth of a narrator's story if the narrator is perceived to be honest. Like the hero or protagonist, the narrator must be human and relatable to be considered credible. Justice Laskin argues that nothing instils more trust in a legal narrator than a lawyer who can own up to his or her case's weaknesses.[76] A litigator who clearly acknowledges the weaknesses of a case is more credible because

74 Laskin (1), *supra* note 55 at 4.

75 Robert A Caro, *The Years of Lyndon Johnson: Master of the Senate* (New York: Alfred A Knopf, 2002) at 887.

76 Laskin (1), *supra* note 55 at 4.

he or she seems more human and reasonable, and a legal audience can relate to a story in which no one or nothing is perfect.

Too perfect a story can also create mistrust in the narrator and damage credibility. Like George and his "yadda yaddaing" girlfriend, the legal audience will quickly suspect that information is being hidden if the weaknesses in a case, whether obvious or subtle, are not addressed. In addition, narrators who appear reasonable and acknowledge the weaknesses in their case will be given deference by the triers of fact when they object to the admissibility of evidence or to the inappropriateness of opposing counsel's submissions or questions. If a narrator appears reasonable, that atmosphere will carry over to the times in the trial when he or she is unwilling to concede a point. Narrators who are perceived to be fair through previous concessions will also be perceived to be fair when they object.

Christopher Vogler gives similar advice to writers when constructing a story's protagonist. Vogler argues that while heroes must possess admirable and noble qualities, they must also have character flaws, which make them human, relatable and ultimately more likable and trusted.[77] Audiences recognize themselves in the small (or large) flaws of a protagonist: "Weaknesses, imperfections, quirks, and vices immediately make a hero or any character more real and appealing."[78] The plaintiff or defendant must appear human and be empathetic.

CONCLUSION

Compelling advocacy is virtually all science and little art. It is built on the inspired diligence of counsel who understand the case from every perspective. With sufficient preparation and intellectual perspiration, a case can resonate with clarity and conviction. Screenwriting and narrative theory give litigators the tools necessary to adopt a story-centred approach and to conduct litigation in an effective and persuasive manner. By applying the principles introduced in this article, such as "the four Ps" and the "so what, who cares?" mantra, lawyers will learn to make focused litigation decisions aimed at constructing more persuasive case narratives. Strong, classic stories with recognizable trajectories,

77 *Supra* note 13.

78 *Ibid.*

clear beginnings, middles and ends, and relatable characters with flaws will go a long way towards persuading a decision maker that a particular outcome is just.

Similarly, the application of literary narrative theory to a litigator's advocacy and presentation style will increase the persuasiveness of oral argument. The focus on credibility, clarity and simplicity, as well as an awareness of the audience's innate subjectivities, will inevitably result in stronger arguments that will reduce the "persuasive distance" that a decision maker must travel to reach an outcome favourable to a client.

The main theme of this article has been to underline the importance of preparation. The distillation of the good and bad facts into a cohesive and persuasive narrative overlaid with a powerful premise require hard work and discipline. But it can be done. A quotation attributed to legendary trial lawyer Louis Nizer is apt here: "Preparation is the be-all of good trial work. Everything else – felicity of expression, improvisational brilliance – is a satellite around the sun. Thorough preparation is that sun."[79]

79 Louis Nizer, *Newsweek* (11 December 1973).

The charm of the narrator:

THE OVERLOOKED COMMONALITY BETWEEN NOVELIST AND ADVOCATE

ANDREW PYPER

THE NOVELIST'S LIFE is blessed in innumerable ways, but among its few plagues is the taxi driver/waiting room/barstool/cocktail party questioner, the know-it-all who, upon learning one writes fiction for a living, confesses to having always planned on a side career of literary fame ("If only I had the *time!*") and then, conspiratorially, asks about "the hook." Because that's what a prize-winning bestseller requires above all, right? A sprinkling of fairy dust that grabs the reader right off the top, a trick of the trade that compels the turning of pages into the night. A grimy mechanism that makes us *care*.

Generally, this mechanism – this hook – is assumed to be a structural bit of business: opening with a dead body, a blast of high-voltage action, the introduction of a Big Mystery. Later, these come-hithers will pay off in more trickery. A twist, a nifty tying together of loose ends, a Shocking Revelation.

In the name of changing the subject I always say they're right, though in fact they're not. Because what's most important for building a compelling narrative isn't plot, but a main character who convincingly feels and experiences and endures the trials of plot. And what's most important to creating a character is voice. This is as true of the courtroom as it is of the novel.

Whether the words are delivered by a fictional narrator or a flesh-and-blood lawyer (or his or her client), voice tells the story. And the voice that wins – where winning is understood as seizing our attention, the "hook" of sympathy – isn't necessarily the loudest nor the smartest nor even the one in command of the most favourable facts or interpretations of the law, but the one with the most charm.

What do I mean by "charm"? It is, sadly, a term of narrowed range in contemporary usage. For most, charm today means only one thing: George Clooney. A grinner, a joker, a well-tailored rake. Yet the *Oxford English Dictionary* reminds us of the word's broader definition: "The power or quality of delighting or fascinating others." It's the fascinating part that is too often overlooked. Note too that there is no mention of us having to *like* or *approve* of the charmer, merely that we pay attention, that we are involved in his or her story. And it is the winning of attention and involvement that is the threshold challenge of advocate and fiction writer alike.

Seen in this light, lawyers and novelists do the same thing, though at regrettably different hourly rates.

* * *

In my research among the legal community (where "research" largely consists of having drinks with litigator friends), charm is often dismissed as superfluous, an at best minor factor in decision making that stands far behind the facts and fine legal argument.

Certainly judgments are written in a way that makes it seem this is so. And yet, given that the facts and the properly applicable law are in question at the outset of every trial, the more foundational point remains how a judge or jury decide *which* facts. *Which* argument.

To an underestimated degree, the answer lies in how the reader (or the trial judge) determines her sympathies, in the way the story charms us to see things one way over another. Storytelling isn't part of advocacy, it *is* advocacy. And it is the human need for narrative that judges and readers have in common. The issue isn't necessarily "Who do you believe?" as it is, more fundamentally, "Whose story will you follow?" It is in this sense that the legal implications of charm overlap with the literary. Who gets to be narrator of the story? Who is the protagonist? Antagonist? How a reader/judge answers these questions will, more often than not, decide the case.

I must clarify that charm, in the context we are discussing it here, is not the same thing as likability or moral purity. Indeed, being "in the right" is certainly of assistance to the courtroom advocate, and having a "role model" as a narrator may be soothing to readers of a certain temperament. But some of the most charming literary figures – and successful advocates, not to mention their clients – are anything but squeaky clean. A good thing, too, given that clients, as with the people we meet in fiction as well as in our everyday lives, are guilty of something.

Consider Holden Caulfield of *The Catcher in the Rye*, one of the most charming narrators in literature. We sympathize with Holden, follow him, ultimately judge in his favour. And yet he is, at the same time, a sour, self-pitying, spoiled brat. How does he pull this off? Charm. His search for authenticity and loathing of all that's "fake" might have otherwise struck readers as self-congratulating, even delusional. Yet his humour and vulnerability convince us that he is right. As an advocate for his own character, he couldn't be more effective.

By way of example, take the novel's opening sentence:

> If you really want to hear about it, the first thing you'll probably want to know is where I was born, and what my lousy childhood was like, and how my parents were occupied and all before they had me, and all that David Copperfield kind of crap, but I don't feel like going into it, if you want to know the truth.

It's that "crap" that does it. Funny, dismissive, air-clearing. Just a couple dozen words into the novel and a figure as great as Dickens has been pushed off the stage. It sets a tone, a point of view, establishes a voice. Though he would likely have hated law school, I suspect Holden would have made a pretty good lawyer.

And then there's the greatest triumph of charm over the authority of the law in all of literature: Milton's Satan from *Paradise Lost*. Imagine you had to represent Satan as your client! The defiler of Man, the serpent in the garden, the father of all temptation. Most advocates would beg for a plea bargain, take anything on offer, and move on. And yet Milton (despite his declared intentions to "justify the ways of God to men") manages to subtly have Satan win the role of protagonist over Adam, over Eve, over God Himself. How is this done? The charm of sympathy.

> All hope excluded thus, behold instead
> Of us outcast, exiled, his new delight,
> Mankind created, and for him this world.

> So farewell hope, and with hope farewell fear,
> Farewell remorse: all good to me is lost;
> Evil be thou my good.

This is Satan declaring his allegiance to darkness, to evil. Yet even in these lines there is something that draws us to the character, a tremendous sadness and solitude and loss. His grumpy, authoritarian father has cast him out and favoured mankind over him, going so far as to create an entire world for Adam and Eve, the fawned-over newlyweds. It denies Satan hope, and with it the range of feelings that were once his. The humanity in these responses causes us to sympathize, to cheer him on, even as we acknowledge his literally biblical moral corruption.

* * *

If advocates and novelists share the job of casting director, both trying to get their client or main character the role of protagonist, how is this best achieved? And aren't some people "simply bad"? Don't the facts sometimes unavoidably determine the outcome no matter how charming the representation?

People are complex, as are well-realized fictional characters. Complexity is a large part of what makes a protagonist charming, an attribute that trumps even goodness. Take Edward Ashburnham from Ford Madox Ford's *The Good Soldier*. While he is not the novel's narrator (that job is unreliably performed by the metaphorically – and probably actually – impotent John Dowell), Ashburnham is the winning enigma who stands, somehow at once emptily and honourably and tragically, at the heart of the book.

Is Ashburnham a classic protagonist? Decidedly not. Yet he is charming. We try to see things the way he sees them, to feel his pain, to be on his side. And he achieves these sympathies by way of fascinating complexity.

At their first meeting, Dowell describes Edward as "So well set up, with such honest blue eyes ..." Yet later, those eyes aren't so simple a matter. "I had forgotten about the eyes," Dowell observes. "When you looked at them carefully you saw that they were perfectly honest, perfectly straightforward, perfectly, perfectly stupid. But the brick pink of his complexion, running perfectly level to the brick pink of his inner eyelids, gave them a curious, sinister expression ..."

The same eyes – the same character – at once honest, stupid, good and sinister. We are, most of us, at least potentially all of those things ourselves. By drawing the contradictions within Edward Ashburnham, Ford creates an unexpected protagonist out of an adulterer who, based only on the facts, seems to ruin two or three lives. Is Ford showing his capacities as advocate in this, or as novelist? The distinction is unnecessary to draw.

* * *

Recently, over drinks (again), an accomplished litigator friend summarized the task of a trial judge as "Making the law fit what feels right." It was a frank observation that sounded not only apt, but echoed my own practical insights into what the novelist does. Both my lawyer friend and I are specialists in our fields, holders of unique knowledge, the rules of procedure and precedent. And yet, at bottom, our task remains fundamentally human, intuitive.

We are both storytellers. There are rules and moral judgments and history and facts and an elusive "truth" shaping the narratives we nudge and coach and craft into existence, but more than this our success or failure will turn on "what feels right." Viewed in this context, the common law is the recorded history of readerly sympathy, which is another way of saying the history of judicial intuition. Judges are readers, just as readers are judges. And lawyers and novelists ignore the demands of narrative, of charm, at their peril.

Unsurprisingly, this is an insight more accepted in literary than in legal circles. We pretend, as lawyers and judges and clients, that we are always secondary to the law, that we "serve under" it, "honour" it, "obey" it, as though the narrative of the facts could only be one thing, and the law an indifferent machine that generates ever-predictable outcomes. This is a necessary fiction, but a fiction nonetheless.

And as for fiction, the novelist deals with the same material as the lawyer: a set of facts. It is the arrangement and priority of those facts that make a story. But every story requires a storyteller: the voice who, through the fascinations of charm, commands our attention and inspires our sympathy in order to turn a mere character into a protagonist.

The only way to be paid well as an actor:

WHY I BECAME A LAWYER

YASHODA RANGANATHAN[1]

PEOPLE OFTEN ASK me why I decided to leave my career as a professional actor and become a lawyer. I am always surprised at this question. I believe that, aside from the obvious financial considerations, acting and advocacy are similar crafts.

At the core of both crafts is the mastery of persuasion.

The advocate must persuade you of the merits of her case; the actor must first persuade you that he is a depressed Prince of Denmark and then persuade you of the merits of his case. In short, the actor's job is harder, if not better compensated.

SPEAK TRUTH

Some people accuse advocates and actors of deception. This is a misconception. Truth is all that an advocate or actor can offer. The truth is what persuades.

An actor must believe the truth of his role. Similarly, an advocate must find and believe the truth of her position. If necessary, an advocate must assume a role in order to speak from a place of truth. Effective advocacy requires this.

1 The views expressed in this article are those of the author and do not necessarily reflect those of the Ministry of the Attorney General or the Government of Ontario.

SPEAK SLOWLY

Here, the Shakespearean actor is akin to the commercial litigator explaining asset-backed commercial paper or the IP litigator describing the differences in the molecular structure of pharmaceutical products. They cannot speak slowly enough.

For the actor speaking Shakespeare, the pauses allow the language to land within the comprehension of the listener. There is a similar need, when explaining complex scientific or commercial concepts, for time, space and breath to exist between concepts. The pauses allow listeners to chew on and swallow each idea. Once they have digested an idea, listeners can be led to the next one. Here the analogy to Shakespeare is particularly apt. Shakespeare's speeches are arguments: they begin either with a problem or a thesis statement; both sides of the argument are weighed, and listeners are led to a logical conclusion.

If listeners are taken along from one logical concept to the next, they will reach the logical conclusion on their own.

Nothing will be more persuasive to listeners than a conclusion they have reached on their own.

BE PREPARED

It is expected that actors will be at rehearsal on time, warmed up, ready to go and well prepared. Preparation involves knowledge of the play (its history and roots), knowledge of the playwright (the genre or style), knowledge of the character (his or her history and background) and knowledge of the subject matter of the play.

Well before opening night, the actor must become an expert on the play and her part in it.

It goes without saying that an advocate must also be an expert on her case by the time she stands up in court.

BE OFF BOOK

An actor cannot truly play a scene until he is off book – until he knows his lines. A good actor will be off book by the second or third time he has rehearsed a particular scene. Even at a staged reading – an early reading of a play in which the actors sit, with their scripts on lighted music stands in front of them – a good actor will only occasionally glance at his text.

Before an actor even knows his lines precisely, he will have some idea of what he is trying to achieve in the scene. In other words, he will know his objective. He will then "play the scene" – try various approaches to achieve his objective – until he hits an approach that meshes with the director's vision for the play. This requires the actor to know, even before he knows his lines, what it is he has come to say. If the advocate is reading her lines, how can the audience trust her? They will feel that she doesn't know what she has come to say.

A good advocate is off book.

BE PRESENT

Someone who is not present cannot persuade. Why? If the speaker is not present, the listener cannot sense the speaker's humanity. If the listener cannot sense the speaker's humanity, the speaker cannot appeal to the listener's sense of fairness, justice and truth.

What is presence? One of my acting coaches summed it up: "It's not that easy, but it's that simple." Presence is the most natural state of being; yet for most people it is the most foreign state of being.

- *Breathe.* Observe yourself breathing.
- *Listen.* Observe yourself listening.
- *See.* Observe yourself seeing.
- *Feel* the sensation of your feet planted on the earth.

It's not that easy, but it's that simple.

In acting school, we were given a simple exercise to understand the power of presence. We were in a large proscenium theatre, and we were each asked to walk on stage right, stop at centre stage and walk off stage left.

I watched my colleagues do this simple exercise. They were not "acting." There were no lines. There was no action. Nevertheless, some of their walk-ons were truly interesting to watch. What made them so interesting? Presence. These people were fully engaged in walking on stage right, fully engaged in standing at centre stage and fully engaged in walking off stage left. I could sense their humanity.

PLAY THE SCENE ON STAGE, NOT OFF

In my third year of theatre school, I played Thomasina in Tom Stoppard's play *Arcadia*. At the beginning of the play Thomasina, an English noble and a math genius, is 13 years old. It was a challenging role. I was excited to have it and I was well prepared, but I didn't trust my preparation or training. I would go over every scene in my head a dozen times before each entrance. The director saw me doing so one day and gave me some simple but important advice: "Play the scene on stage, not off."

If the goal is to be present on stage, your preparation should help you to be present. Ruminating over what you will do once you are on stage or hunching over your notes will not help you to be present.

In the minutes before you get up to speak, remember to breathe, listen, take space in the room and trust in your training and your preparation.

REACT, DON'T ACT

An actor must play the scene. This means he must be responsive to his environment, that is, to his fellow actors and to the other moving parts on stage.

Imagine a scene in which an actor is to come on stage, say a line and juggle the apples he finds in a bowl on stage. In the prior scene, however, another actor has mistakenly removed the bowl from the stage. A good actor will omit the juggling or mime it comically if it is appropriate in the context of the scene. A bad actor, unable to do anything other than what was rehearsed, will bring the production to a standstill until the apples are returned to the stage.

Similarly, a good advocate who is peppered with unexpected questions from the bench will not carry on blindly with her prepared speech, but will respond to the question.

The positive side effect of reacting to what is going on around you is that it immediately makes you present. If you have ever coached a moot, you will have noticed that students are much more engaging when they are answering questions than when they are delivering their prepared speeches.

Listening, breathing, thinking, speaking – all of which are required when responding to questions – make you present and allow the listener to sense your humanity.

BE A PASSIONATE STORYTELLER, BUT TELL A SIMPLE STORY

The most significant commonality between great actors and great advocates is that they are great storytellers. However, the greatest advocates and actors keep the story simple. "Suit the action to the word, the word to the action ..." Hamlet's admonition to the actor applies equally to advocates. Discretion must be the advocates' tutor. When passion is not genuine – when it is pushed – it will be distracting and will turn off the listener.

The last thing an advocate wants is to have "so strutted and bellowed" that her listener thinks, as Hamlet did, that "some of nature's journeymen had made men and not made them well, they imitated humanity so abominably."

At the same time, the advocate should not be too tame. Passion that genuinely arises from the advocate's belief in her position will engage and persuade in the same way that passion arising from the actor's genuine pursuit of his objective will convince the audience of the real stakes involved for the character.

While their goals may differ, the traits and skills that make actors and advocates excel at their craft are the same.

Did opposing counsel get your GOTE?

KATE SOUTHWELL

IN THE COURSE of your legal practice, have you ever asked yourself: *What on earth was that guy thinking? Why did opposing counsel just say that? What does my client really want to get out of this?*

GOTE can help.

Not a truth serum or a crystal ball, GOTE is an acting theory that, when used effectively, can help you to make better choices, more fully understand others, and approach the world in a constructive and goal-oriented way.

Yes, I said an acting theory – acting, as in theatre. Bear with me.

WHAT IS GOTE, AND WHY SHOULD YOU CARE?

GOTE is a technique developed by Robert Cohen, the author of *Acting One*, which is one of the seminal acting textbooks for beginners. The GOTE technique is often one of the first things taught to young actors. It can build a foundation for almost any acting technique and, really, for almost any personal interaction.

GOTE is an acronym for **G**oal, **O**bstacle, **T**actic and **E**xpectation. The basic theory holds that every interaction between people, whether in real life or fictional, is driven by these four elements.

It is rare that people engage in communication for no purpose at all. Instead, people almost always have a reason for interacting with one another. Even inane small talk can serve a goal, such as reducing awkward silences or building rapport.

Most people intuitively use the four elements of GOTE in everyday interactions, but becoming consciously aware of them in both yourself and the person you're interacting with can help you communicate more effectively. For example, imagine that you bump into a senior partner in the hallway and briefly chat about the stunning success of the Toronto Blue Jays. You might assume that you're merely chatting for no particular reason. However, in fact, both you and the senior partner are using complex tactics to achieve something from the other person. GOTE can help you to comprehend this interaction more fully, to achieve your goals and to understand what other people are attempting to achieve by communicating with you.

Goal: Everyone wants something

The first and arguably most important element of GOTE is Goal. In short, every time you interact with someone, both you and that person are trying to achieve a goal.

Take the above example in which you chat with a senior partner about the Blue Jays. Your goal may be for the partner to remember your name. It may be to get the partner to offer you one of the firm's playoff tickets. It may be simply to make a favourable impression. Similarly, the partner's goal may be to gain a reputation among junior associates for being approachable. Or it may be just to soften you up so that you're more likely to agree to pull an all-nighter on the next closing.

But wait, you might say. *Aren't we over-thinking this?* Maybe you were just chatting with the partner because it would be rude to walk by without saying anything. Well, that is a goal in itself. In that case, your goal was for the senior partner to think you are polite.

Everyone always has a goal, no matter how seemingly insignificant. By becoming aware of the goals motivating you and others, you can more effectively understand and control your communications strategy.

When trying to determine what your goal is, it's helpful to think in terms of the simple phrase: *I want* ______________. Goals should be concrete, short and simple.

Throughout the course of a conversation, or even throughout the course of a relationship, you may have several smaller goals that build toward a larger one. For instance, as an overall goal you may want to develop a relationship with a particular client so you become her first choice when retaining counsel. Smaller interim goals may be that you want the client to trust you, that you want to inspire confidence and that you want the client to think of you as a friend.

By being aware of your goal, you can ensure that all your interactions with the client are building toward – not hindering – your ultimate objective. Similarly, being aware of the client's goal can help you achieve your own goal because you're more likely to negotiate successfully if you know what the other person wants. For example, maybe the client's goal is to find a go-to lawyer that she trusts. By knowing that your goals are aligned, you can work to achieve a positive resolution for both of you.

Obstacle: What is standing in your way?

The second element of GOTE is Obstacle. This element asks, quite simply: *What is standing in the way of achieving your goal?*

In the example of chatting with a senior partner about the Blue Jays, the obstacle may be that you know he is in a hurry. It may be that you know nothing about baseball. It may even be that you're a Yankees fan.

By identifying the challenges you must overcome to achieve your goal, you can best strategize effective ways to address them. Similarly, identifying what the other person perceives to be an obstacle may give you a strategic advantage in the conversation.

For instance, you and opposing counsel may both have the goal of finalizing a settlement quickly. However, she may keep presenting various, seemingly insignificant reasons why it can't be done. Rather than just getting frustrated, if you're able to identify what she perceives to be the real obstacle (maybe she is unable to draft the settlement documents this weekend because she has plans to go to the cottage) you can more effectively achieve your goal, perhaps by offering to draft the settlement documents yourself.

Tactic: How are you going to get there?

Once you know what your goal is and what the obstacles are, the next step is figuring out how you're going to get what you want. This element is called Tactic. Goals are achieved and obstacles are overcome by using tactics.

Let's go back to the example of chatting with the senior partner about the Blue Jays. If your goal is to make a favourable impression, a poor choice of tactic would be to annoy him or bore him. For instance, if you perceive that he is getting annoyed because you keep praising the Yankees, then perhaps it's time to switch tactics. A more successful choice would be to engage him, surprise him or humour him. You might do that by asking him about his favourite player.

Similarly, if the senior partner's goal is to seem approachable, it would not serve him well to use the tactic of intimidating you. Instead of demanding that you recite the ERA of all Blue Jays starting pitchers, he would do better to start with more basic topics or to ask how avidly you follow the team.

Tactics are typically expressed as a single active verb, such as I charm, I intimidate, I entice or I threaten. Tactics don't have to be literal, and the most effective tactic may be something more extreme, such as I shove, I seduce, I shake or I hug. These figurative images can help you to tailor the manner in which you approach your communications. For instance, when your goal is to comfort a distraught client, you may use the tactic of "I comfort" or "I hug" to frame the conversation. (To be clear, I am not advocating that you physically hug or shove anyone, much less a client or senior partner. These are merely images that can help you strike the right tone and manner.)

By tailoring your tactics to the other person's reactions, you can make sure you're effectively working toward your goal. Tactics can, and should, change multiple times throughout the course of an interaction. If one tactic isn't effective, try another. Perhaps "I hug" is no longer appropriate once the client has calmed down. Or maybe if "I comfort" isn't working, what the client really needs is "I take control" or "I shake."

Similarly, by being aware of the other person's tactics, you may be less easily manipulated into doing something that you don't want to do. Opposing counsel may be trying to charm you in order to convince you to agree to more favourable settlement terms. Similarly, your client may be trying to intimidate you in order to obtain a reduction in fees. By becoming aware of the other person's tactics, you can more easily work with, or against, her to achieve your goals.

Expectation: What did you think was going to happen?

The final element of GOTE is Expectation. By analyzing your expectations and considering the expectations of the other person, you can more effectively tailor your tactics, overcome your obstacles and achieve your goal.

Returning to the well-worn example of the baseball-loving senior partner, perhaps you expect that he is going to be too busy to want to speak with you. You might then begin the conversation with, "I know that you're terribly busy, but I hope you've had time to catch some of the ball games." If you know that the senior partner expects you to be intimidated by him, you may make a more favourable impression by displaying confidence and self-assurance.

Similarly, when dealing with opposing counsel, perhaps you expect that she will try to intimidate or bully you. Being aware of this expectation may allow you to focus your approach and decide on effective tactics before the conversation even begins. Similarly, if you know that opposing counsel expects you to be stubborn on a particular point of contention, you may choose to steer the conversation around that point until agreement is reached on other issues.

Just as tactics may shift throughout a conversation, expectations may shift as well. After chatting with the senior partner for a few minutes, it may become clear that your expectations were incorrect and that he is not in any hurry at all. Alternatively, opposing counsel may be unexpectedly friendly rather than bullying. By listening to the other person and remaining engaged in the conversation, your expectations can and will shift fluidly.

Being aware of expectations, both your own and the other person's, can help you make a strategic decision whether to meet, exceed or defy them.

HOW CAN YOU USE GOTE IN YOUR PRACTICE?

GOTE is a flexible tool that can be used in various ways to enhance interactions both big and small.

Before calling opposing counsel to make a settlement offer, I often take the time to write out my goal, obstacle, tactics and expectations. This routine helps me to focus my thoughts and brainstorm effective approaches to the negotiation.

GOTE can also be helpful when analyzing a conversation after the fact. When you find yourself wondering *why on earth did he say that?*, it is helpful to consider what the other person was hoping to achieve – consciously or unconsciously. Trying to understand people's goals, perceived obstacles, tactics and expectations can help you to determine why they said a specific thing or approached the conversation in a certain manner.

Finally, GOTE can also be used in the moment to communicate more effectively. For instance, a client may repeatedly tell you what her goals are. However, if the client's tactics, expectations and stated obstacles are inconsistent with her stated goals, then you may want to consider whether she has another goal – one about which she may not even be consciously aware. I recently used GOTE to negotiate a settlement in a protracted and acrimonious litigation by helping the client to realize that, while her stated goal was to drag the plaintiff to trial and cause him pain, what she actually wanted most was to save her co-defendant from the expense and stress of litigation.

GOTE is an acting theory, and most successful lawyers are probably already intuitively applying it. However, becoming more familiar with its elements and using them as a framework for planning and analyzing conversations may help you to communicate more effectively with others, become a better negotiator and, ultimately, achieve your goals. (Although it may not help the Blue Jays win the pennant.)

Advocacy at the crossroads

LINDA R. ROTHSTEIN, LSM

PERHAPS EVERY GENERATION of Canadian advocates has wondered whether and how great advocacy will survive the ascendancy of a new generation of advocates. Or maybe it's the oft-described collective narcissism of my generation, the baby boomers, that makes us convinced we are always at some sort of crossroads. But I think that whether you choose advocacy in the courtroom or in the boardroom, the challenges will be daunting. And I worry that those of us who practise civil litigation have already lost our way – that we must respond to the dramatic ways in which law and advocacy have changed in the last 20 years if advocacy is to continue to be the fuel of a fair and robust justice system.

CHANGING TIMES

My generation of advocates has moved through a period of unparalleled and rapid social and technological change. Our laws, our legal culture and society's basic notions of fairness and equity are dramatically different from what they were when I was in law school almost 30 years ago.

Consider the sweeping changes in the law. I know you still read contracts and torts cases that are decades, maybe even centuries, old: *Hadley v. Baxendale*, *Donohue v. Stephenson*, to name just two. You may not yet appreciate how much our laws have changed since you were born, but they have. Even if one ignores the impact of the *Canadian Charter of Rights and Freedoms*, changes in family law, human rights law, professional regulation and environmental law (to name a few about which I know something) have brought about statutory regimes that bear little resemblance to the ones we pored over in my law school classroom. Back then, family law was still a reflection of male supremacy in the family unit. Professional self-regulation didn't really have a name. Human rights law was mostly a gleam in the eye of law reform commissions and the Canadian Civil Liberties Association. And environmental laws were, well, not very environmental.

Change in the law has not just been the work of legislatures but of judges, too. Indeed, the fundamental approach of judges to the interpretation of legislation and legal documents has also changed significantly. Today, there is little reliance on "blackletter" interpretations of the law. In contrast, when I started practising it was considered foolish for a young lawyer to make arguments based on the "policy" of the legislation. I remember well the icy glare from the aging and humourless judge who challenged me to show him where the word "policy" could be found in the 60-page statute that governed the case. When I thought I had cleverly sidestepped the question by referring to the "statutory scheme," he asked me if I had another life as a legislator of which he wasn't aware. It is impossible today to imagine a case that turns on the interpretation of legislation in which the leading arguments are not premised on public policy, the scheme of the Act and on a purposive, as opposed to a strict constructionist, interpretation.

CHANGING LEGAL CULTURE

The culture of the legal profession has also changed over the course of my career – more than ever I dared hope. When I began practising, the legal profession was patriarchal in both look and feel: 38 per cent of the students in my law school class were women, and only 1 per cent were visible minorities. When we entered working life through the door of the legal profession, it felt pretty much like an elite male club on a good day, a male locker room on a bad one.

There were few women judges – no matriarchs anywhere in sight. The Honourable Bertha Wilson was the only woman on the Court of Appeal for Ontario at the time. This was before she was appointed to the Supreme Court of Canada (in 1982), and I don't remember a lot of favourable reviews of her talents. To the contrary, I remember her judgments being ridiculed by my law professors and male colleagues, and her career as a legal researcher at a highly regarded Toronto law firm, which preceded her appointment to the bench, being treated as a kind of "soft qualification" for judicial office.

Men were everywhere. They were the clients, the partners, the politicians, the opposing lawyers and, of course, the judges. It's not that legal culture is barrier-free or all-inclusive now. Clearly it isn't; but significant changes in the law, statutory and judge-made, have been paralleled by significant changes in legal culture. Laws change culture, and culture changes laws – like some sort of postmodern *pas de deux* in which it is not clear which of the two partners is doing most of the heavy lifting.

CHANGING TECHNOLOGY

The pace of technological change makes the legal and social changes I've described seem lacklustre. When I started practising, the photocopier was the only technology that assisted our advocacy. Factums were literally cut with scissors and pasted with glue brushes in the last, fatal hours before they had to be filed in court. Then they were hand-delivered by articling students to opposing counsel and to the courthouse. The fax machine, which wasn't ubiquitous until the late 1980s, was initially traumatizing – not because its operation was hard to master, but because of its ability to dramatically accelerate the pace of a case.

Imagine this: when I was a young advocate, there was almost never a document – a letter, memo, or anything on paper – passed between my law firm and another, or between a client and a lawyer *after* regular business hours, that is, after 6 p.m., Monday to Friday. Nothing at all was transmitted over the weekend.

E-mail, Blackberry and the Internet had little impact on what we did or on the nature of advocacy only a dozen years ago. In the early '90s, I had to call a university professor of computer science as an expert witness to teach a tribunal what the Internet was. Its use was still restricted to university campuses and the odd governmental research agency. Few people outside those circles had heard of it; even fewer predicted it would develop a broader audience. Today, driven by information technology, the pace of litigation and of every kind of legal work means "keeping up" is increasingly a 24/7 commitment. Many of our clients assume that we don't have a life outside the office. Some clients consider it part of our professional obligation to put our families, loved ones and other interests aside to deal with their ever-increasing list of urgent and time-sensitive issues.

It's not just about the speed of our responses. It's also about the volume of written material that our clients create and collect. The pressure is now on to create paperless files and conduct paperless trials. Lawyers now brag to each other about their cases by comparing the number of documents – how many hundreds of thousands? – in their databases.

A year or so ago, the *Law Times* reported that a paperless trial against four software executives "broke new ground in Ontario." But, if you read the fine print, you will learn that the substantial $11 million judgment nevertheless required 295 days of trial that spanned more than three years, with 2,893 exhibits and a total of 70,000 pages – all of which were filed and viewed in an electronic format. One of the counsel on the case remarked that "it's scary to think how long the trial might have [taken] if we *hadn't* used an electronic courtroom." I'll have more to say about the perils of documentary overload soon. But for now, just consider that statement: a 295-day trial could have taken longer? How is that possible?

Then there's the problem that the law isn't just rapidly changing, it's ballooning. The unwieldy labyrinth of legislation and regulation that comprises Canadian law increasingly forces specialization and sub-specialization by lawyers. Of course, if we look to the United States, it appears as if that nation is drowning in regulatory minutiae. A few years ago, a prominent secretary of a large federal department described new health and safety regulations this way:

> There are more words in these regulations than there are words in the Bible. They are a lot less inspired to read and a lot harder to understand.

The historic healthcare bill that was passed by the U.S. Senate in 2009 is a 2,943-page bureaucratic monstrosity. In ten years, will Canadian legislation be similarly obese? I hope not.

Law students and young lawyers have to contend with the reality that the common law is an unwieldy and ever-growing web of decision-making. Until ten years ago, if a case wasn't reported by an official reporting service, such as the *Alberta Reports*, *Ontario Reports*, D.L.R.s or *Canadian Criminal Cases*, it was of no significance to anyone other than the parties to the litigation who had either won or lost. In today's litigation, it's not uncommon to be deluged with hundreds of authorities, many of them quite useless, more the product of a key word search or Quicklaw or CanLII than any thoughtful sifting and analysis.

The dramatic changes don't end there. In both the United States and Canada, "blawgs" compete for our attention. These are not written by disgruntled litigants. A high-profile U.S. legal publication notes that a handful of U.S. judges maintain a regular blawg and that a vast and growing number of U.S. law professors and law students find the time to post daily. The article concludes that "the real bones and guts and sinew of the [U.S.] national conversation is happening online and not in print." The debate on these blawgs covers a wide range of fascinating and legally important topics: free speech on college campuses, Yale's decision to admit a Taliban student, the military commissions at Guantanamo Bay. There is even a sentencing blawg, increasingly cited in U.S. judicial opinions, which tracks the fallout from the U.S. Supreme Court's sentencing guidelines. I ask again: ten years from now, will cutting-edge legal analysis be posted in daily blogs that only those advocates nearing retirement feel free to ignore?

CHANGING ADVOCACY

Changing times; changing law and legal culture; changing technology and communications also means changing advocacy. First of all, it is less often found in courtrooms. Although the settlement rate for civil litigation hasn't changed much in the last 15 years, almost every litigator has noticed that trials appear to be less frequent. In the United States and Canada there is constant and sweaty hand-wringing by aging advocates over "the vanishing civil trial." Clients may well be better off without trials. No one can agree on how to assess whether having fewer trials benefits litigants, but what we know for sure is that without trials there is no proven way to train young lawyers in the art and science of advocacy. At the same time, advocacy has been dispersed to a huge range of no-gown-required venues – administrative tribunals, domestic and statutory, too numerous to count, each with its own legal culture, advocacy style and rules. Some of these are almost as formal and traditional as a courtroom, whereas others are remarkably informal and procedure-free.

If one includes the many forms of alternative dispute resolution – fact-finding, mediation, mediation/arbitration, arbitration – the kinds of advocacy one must master appear to be endless. Judges today are less authoritarian and exert less control on advocates than did the stern, sharp-tongued judges of the past. In tribunal settings, where laypersons often preside, advocates are mostly free to take as long as they like to get to the point and to make as many of them as they wish to make.

The increased significance of written advocacy cannot be overstated. Until the late 1980s, the *Rules of Civil Procedure* described the two components of a factum as comprising the facts and the law "without argument," as if written advocacy separated from argument was either achievable or beneficial. As a young lawyer, I had the good fortune of junioring for one of Ontario's great advocates, Ian Scott, who eventually left the practice of law and became the Attorney General of Ontario. I remember being stunned by the audacity of his written advocacy: he gleefully crossed out the words "the law," which headed the second section of the factum and replaced them with the single word "argument." I think he was trying to goad the Court of Appeal judges into reprimanding him for his nose-thumbing so that he could demonstrate the sophistry of suggesting that the "law" could ever be stripped bare of argument. Legal writing then was often wordy, clumsy and impregnable.

And that was the good stuff. Lawyers weren't supposed to speak or write in language that was understandable to non-lawyers. Remember that Lord Denning, Master of the Rolls, was heralded not so much because his judgments were groundbreaking or progressive (although they sometimes were) but because he wrote in understandable, compelling prose. He told a story. We can all aspire to the style that was used to describe the reasons of a well-known American judge: "clear, compact and complete, carrying no immaterial discussions and losing no weight through grammatical leaks or rhetorical cracks."

Today, if you are not a good writer, you are not a good advocate. Period. Leave to appeal applications are almost always in writing. Time limits for oral argument are the norm in the Supreme Court of Canada and the Ontario Court of Appeal. After long civil trials, many judges have come to expect pithy, authoritative, persuasive written submissions. Often one has only 48 hours to produce a written submission. If you can't "win" the case on paper, it's unlikely you can do so in oral submissions.

Even more, legal proceedings are often more public and more publicized than they once were. I think this is a good thing. As I remember the 1980s and early '90s, very few cases other than local murder trials found their way into the newspaper. There were no televised legal proceedings in the Supreme Court of Canada, or anywhere else; no cable TV shows reporting every titillating detail of the latest celebrity shoplifting, divorce or white-collar crime. Thus advocates didn't fret about whether to speak to a reporter; they didn't take media training or review press releases for their clients.

Good advocacy is also, thankfully, much less parochial than it was when I was beginning my career. Today, in every substantive area of law, good advocates look outside Alberta and Ontario, outside Canada – to the Commonwealth, to the United States and elsewhere – to find the answers, the strategies and the common law that can offer lessons and analysis. Our courts are more curious and less inclined to dismiss another nation's jurisprudence. Similarly, the scholarship and research of scientists and social scientists has more influence on individual cases and on legislative provisions. Yes, sometimes the science is weak and unreliable, but good advocacy will normally reveal these hazards.

In essence, legal scholarship, advocacy and decision-making have all taken a giant step forward in terms of quantity, comprehensiveness and complexity. This demands more of advocates: it's much harder, I believe, to be good. You must be a good writer. You must be comfortable with technology. You must be media-savvy. You must not be intimidated by ever-changing laws and mountains of evidence. Fewer cases go to trial, and those that do are longer and more complex. Few legal or factual questions are simple anymore, no answer is straightforward or briefly stated. We are at a crossroads. We can shrink under the burden of information overload and spiralling complexity, or we can consciously and consistently recommit ourselves to the defining principles of great advocacy. What are those principles?

FIRST, WE MUST NOT ABANDON JUDGMENT IN FAVOUR OF EXHAUSTIVENESS

The temptation to include everything in the opinion letter, the memorandum, the factum, the examination of a witness or the trial has never been greater and easier to accomplish. Our computers allow us to produce volume with dizzying speed. But in advocacy, more is rarely more; it is just overwhelming and unaffordable.

In civil litigation, we will have to become better at sifting the relevant from the irrelevant, the important from the unimportant, the persuasive from the unpersuasive. It requires choices, lots of them, based on a finely tuned assessment of the strengths and weaknesses of one's case. The emphasis on *judgment* means that litigators must not default to the "no stone unturned" approach to advocacy and equate that with good advocacy. This is especially true in our new era of "proportionality," a theoretical cost-benefit analysis in large measure.

One of my partners says that all lawyers fall into one of two categories: complicators or simplifiers. Twenty-five years ago, almost all the great advocates were simplifiers. Today, an alarmingly higher percentage of the bar are complicators. Beware of this trend. Unnecessary complexity is unaffordable. It leads to litigation by exhaustion. It puts the courts and legal services beyond the economic reach of most of the population. This is also an access to justice issue.

It takes *judgment* to isolate the main points from the morass of other tangential ones, but that's what we are being hired to do. Conscientious advocates worry that if they simplify, they risk missing a key piece of evidence. I disagree, but it takes a commitment to exercising good judgment to make one's factual investigations proportionate to the significance and value of the case.

SECOND, WE MUST CONSCIOUSLY VALUE REASON OVER RHETORIC

We live in an age when rhetoric is widely celebrated, even rhetoric of the ungrammatical sort. In November last year, Rex Murphy, the CBC commentator who also writes for *The Globe and Mail*, described Sarah Palin as one of the "two great speakers in America today." I shudder. President Barack Obama was the other one. Which is why I emphasize this point: the advocacy of lawyers must not devolve to political language, which in George Orwell's famous words is "designed to make lies sound truthful and murder respectable, and to give an appearance of solidity to pure wind."

I admit I have rarely turned away from a rhetorical flourish that I thought could persuade a client, an opposing lawyer, a judge or an adjudicator. So perhaps I should be the last one to talk. But it is vital to great advocacy and to the survival of great advocacy that we consciously choose reason over rhetoric and clarity over obfuscation. In his great novel *Bleak House*, Charles Dickens took the symbolism of fog to characterize the way lawyers argue cases and judges rule on them:

> Fog everywhere, fog up the river, fog down the river, fog in diverse streets ... Never can there come a fog too thick as some score of members of the High Court of Chancery are mostly engaged in one of ten thousand stages of endless cause, tripping one another up slippery precedents, groping knee deep in technicalities and making a pretence of equity...

Choosing reason over rhetoric means that we must:

- avoid overstatement – expressing conclusions in superlatives,
- support conclusions with facts and logic,
- support facts with evidence, and
- finally – and this is often the most difficult – state the opposing case fairly.

In short, our advocacy must not degenerate into "spin." Spin isn't credible, and credibility is all we advocates have.

THIRD, WE MUST FIND THE COURAGE TO BE ADVOCATES

We rarely choose our clients. More often, they choose us or happen upon us. Sometimes they are longstanding clients of the firm where we work, and "who chose who" has little to do with it. We will not always like our clients or their causes. It takes great courage to defend unpopular causes or clients. Those of you who choose criminal law will learn courage early on, or you will be driven to look for another specialty. But even if you don't choose criminal law, you will need courage to stand up for your clients. Most have imperfections, sometimes gaping ones. The husband who is ungenerous with child support to his children. The employer – a power-hungry perfectionist – who expects the impossible of her employees. The business titan who wants to crush his former partner.

There's another often overlooked side to this coin: the courage to stand up to a client is also a prerequisite of good advocacy. I've mentioned this in passing. It takes not just mental discipline but quiet courage to pick the best arguments and abandon the weak or frivolous ones. Clients will rarely support you in doing it. In fact, a long-suffering client will often cling to arguments that do not address the legal reality or are *ad hominem*, overstated or illogical. Some lawyers include these points in their briefs, their cross-examinations and their arguments simply to appease the client. It's the path of least resistance, but it is not good advocacy. In the end, it's not very sound client management, either.

FOURTH, GOOD ADVOCACY REQUIRES EMPATHY

Few lawyers talk about empathy,[1] but I have met very few great advocates without it. The best lawyers I know are good listeners – not always, and certainly not when they are in full flight – but always when they need to be. They are good at connecting with a client, eliciting information that he or she is reluctant to share. They are good at providing the client with some comfort even when no legal alchemy can set the matter entirely right. These same great advocates are also in tune with the other side's issues, concerns and thinking. And they are able to put themselves in the judge's, arbitrator's or mediator's chair and see the world from that perspective.

CONCLUSION

Technique is essential to great advocacy. Mastery of technique is as necessary for great advocates as it is for sports heroes or celebrated artists. But as you learn the art of cross-examination and opening statements, as you develop the skills to think on your feet and to communicate in a concise and compelling way, I urge you to remember this: your success as an advocate will be influenced more by your judgment and reason, more by your courage and your empathy, than it will be by your technique. The future of advocacy and the justice system depends on these qualities. Make them define you.

1 I credit my friend Ben Zarnett, past president of The Advocates' Society, with this insight.

Part Two

WITNESSES

IN 1957, HUMOURIST Art Linkletter (from Moose Jaw, Saskatchewan, no less) published a book, later made into a TV series, called *Kids Say the Darndest Things*. This expression could equally apply to witnesses, although using a much stronger adjective.

At a trial years later, I kept objecting to a lawyer leading her client. Finally, the trial judge said, "Ms. X, the evidence must come from your client, not you." "I know, Your Honour," she protested. "But she's *telling* it wrong." Amusing as that is, I'm sure we've all had that experience. There's a critical point or two, for which we extensively prepare the witness, and he or she gets it dead wrong. And there's precious little we can do about it. Of course, as backdrop, there's the fine line in our work between preparing and "wood-shedding" a witness. Here, our two well-regarded practitioners dissect the problem of the fallibility of witnesses and offer some thoughts.

Summer 2017

Why we can't trust witnesses

PAUL FRUITMAN

THE MOST FASCINATING witnesses are those I call "credible fabricators." They confidently recount their recollections, although it is clear that those recollections do not match the documentary record. In another time, we simply called these witnesses "liars," even sociopaths. However, with the benefit of recent research into human psychology, it is just as likely that these witnesses are telling the truth – as they observed and remember it.

It turns out the human mind has serious deficiencies. We do not think clearly, and we have questionable observational skills and poorer memories. Yet we think our memories and powers of observation range from great to fantastic.[1]

This reality has profound implications for our common law, which is grounded in and depends heavily on witness testimony. We require facts be proven through witnesses, and witness credibility weighs heavily in

1 Expounding on the failings of the human mind has become its own cottage industry over the past decade. Some notable examples include Rolf Dobelli, *The Art of Thinking Clearly* (New York: HarperCollins, 2013); Richard H Thaler, *Misbehaving: The Making of Behavioral Economics* (New York: Norton, 2015); Daniel Kahneman, *Thinking Fast and Slow* (New York: Farrar, Straus and Giroux, 2011); and Christopher Chabris and Daniel Simons, *The Invisible Gorilla* (New York: Crown Publishing Group, 2010).

judges' reasons. Our system trusts that witnesses who testify credibly and confidently are telling the truth. It appears that trust is misplaced.

However, this realization coincides with an explosion of hard data – email, social media and cellphone cameras – that more accurately capture every moment of our lives. The future development of the common law will likely depend more on data than witness testimony, as technology improves and we face growing evidence of our limited cognitive abilities.

WE HAVE BAD MEMORIES, INCLUDING OF THINGS WE "REMEMBER" WELL

Scholars have been challenging the accuracy of witness memory for nearly a century.[2] They have shown our memories to be amalgams of things that actually happened and details we invent to make those events conform to our views of the world and ourselves. Until recently, however, it was believed that we could comfortably rely on so-called "flashbulb memories," those that leave an indelible imprint on our minds such that we "remember them like they were yesterday."[3] It turns out that even our most vivid memories are not especially accurate despite our subjective belief in them.[4] Studies of memories of the 9/11 attacks and Michael Jackson's death, among other events, show that "flashbulb" memories decline over time just as other memories do.[5]

2 See e.g. Hügo Mustenberg, *On the Witness Stand: Essays on Psychology and Crime* (New York: Doubleday, Page, 1908).

3 Roger Brown and James Kulik, "Flashbulb Memories" (1977) 5 Cognition 73.

4 Dr Julia Shaw, *The Memory Illusion: Remembering, Forgetting and the Science of False Memory* (New York: Random House, 2016) at 159–186 [Shaw].

5 The 9/11 study examined participants' memories, one week, six weeks and 32 weeks after the attacks, and compared them with memories of everyday events at the same time intervals. The study posed similar questions – such as "where were you?" and "who else was there?" – about each memory. The participants assessed their memories of 9/11 as being better than their memories of everyday events at each interval, but both sets of memories in fact declined equally over time: Jennifer M Talarico and David C Rubin, "Confidence, Not Consistency, Characterizes Flashbulb Memories" (2003) 14 Psychological Science 455. The Michael Jackson study tested participants' memories of his death shortly after it occurred and again 18 months later. Those who felt a stronger emotional attachment to Jackson expressed greater confidence in their memories of his death at the second interval than did those who

In addition, we are susceptible to creating flashbulb memories of events that never really happened to us. It is apparently easy to implant false memories through suggestion and the use of photographs.[6]

Why do we place so much trust in these inaccurate (and perhaps untrue) flashbulb memories? One theory is that the emotional nature of flashbulb memories breeds false confidence in them. What we fail to appreciate is that the brainpower used to capture these memories so vividly comes at the expense of processing their peripheral details.[7] We clearly remember seeing the twin towers fall but might misremember where we were when we heard of the attacks.

This tendency to misremember provides an explanation for witnesses who appear credible but whose testimony does not fit with the documentary record. I have had this experience with witnesses on several occasions. My instinct was to think these witnesses were lying, and some of them likely were. However, some probably believed what they were saying – which explains their apparent credibility – even though their memories had failed them.

As Hollywood producer Robert Evans (*The Godfather, Chinatown*) said, "There are three sides to every story: your side, my side, and the truth. And no one is lying. Memories shared serve each differently."[8]

---

were not fans, but the memories of the attached group were no more enduring: Martin V Day and Michael Ross, "Predicting Confidence in Flashbulb Memories" (2014) 22 Memory 232.

6 Shaw, *supra* note 4 at 170–182; Kimberly A Wade et al, "A Picture Is Worth a Thousand Lies: Using False Photographs to Create False Childhood Memories" (2002) 9 Psychonomic Bulletin & Review 597.

7 Maria Konnikova, "You Have No Idea What Happened" *The New Yorker* (February 4, 2015); online: <newyorker.com/science/maria-konnikova/idea-happened-memory-recollection>.

8 The quote comes from the 2002 documentary about Evans, *The Kid Stays in the Picture*. A decade earlier, the glam rock-funk band Extreme used the title *Three Sides to Every Story* for its third record, the follow-up to the *Extreme II: Pornograffitti*, which contained the smash hit ballad "More Than Words." *Three Sides to Every Story* was a "concept record" that grouped its songs into three "sides": "Yours," "Mine" and "the Truth." However, the album and cassette versions still used two-sided records and tapes. Despite their prescience, and technical proficiency (and pretentiousness), the rockers in Extreme could not figure out how to make a three-sided piece of vinyl.

WE MISS WHAT IS RIGHT IN FRONT OF US

Not only do we have suspect memories of events we witness, our initial observations of these events are also questionable. A great example is "Gorillas in our midst," perhaps the most famous study in modern psychology. The study asked participants to watch a short video of people passing around a basketball and to count the number of passes. In the middle of the video, a woman in a gorilla suit walks from the right of the screen, pounds on her chest and walks off. Amazingly, 50 percent of participants failed to notice the gorilla.[9]

A 2000 study of changing scenes in videos and in real life produced similar results. The video scenes featured changes to actors and dinner plate colours in a restaurant scene. The real life scene involved a pedestrian asking for directions, interrupted by two people walking by carrying a door. During the interruption, the actor playing the pedestrian changed into a different person. An average of 83 percent of participants across the experiments predicted they would notice the changes. Only 11 percent did.[10]

The authors of the original gorilla study, Christopher Chabris and Daniel Simons, argue that our recognition failures are due to the limited processing power of the human brain and our consequent tendency to view life through a series of mental models.

> When we focus on a specific task, we tend to miss things that do not fit in within those models, such as a gorilla walking through a game of basketball. We fail to recognize our limitations because we wrongly assume that unusual or distinctive objects will attract our attention. It is the reason drivers say they did not see the pedestrian they hit until just before the body bounced off the windshield.[11]

---

9 Not surprisingly, many of the participants who missed the gorilla refused to believe that it was there. In a separate study, 90 percent of participants said they would expect to see the gorilla, although the 50 percent rate of actually seeing it has remained constant through various subsequent iterations of the gorilla experiment: Christopher Chabris and Daniel Simons, *The Invisible Gorilla* (New York: Crown Publishing Group, 2010) at 5–8, 31 and 249 (fn 11).

10 Daniel T Levin et al, "Change Blindness Blindness: The Metacognitive Error of Overestimating Change-detection Ability" (2000) 7 Visual Cognition 397.

11 Chabris and Simons, *supra* note 9 at 7, 15 and 24–30.

I can think of several occasions where witnesses have been baffled at failing to have noticed a key fact, be it a fateful clause in a document or a dangerous spot on an X-ray. Such facts seemed obvious after the fact, but, being unexpected, they were missed as they happened.

WE ARE OVERCONFIDENT AND EASILY SWAYED BY THE CONFIDENCE OF OTHERS

One reason witnesses fail to see the limitations of their memories and observational skills is an inflated sense of self. It is a well-documented human trait. Everyone thinks he or she is above average, at pretty much everything,[12] which of course is statistically impossible. In addition, we are more likely to believe individuals who express confidence in themselves, irrespective of their level of ability. Juries[13] and study groups alike[14] have demonstrated this susceptibility to assurance. Humans mistake confidence for competence in an individual, until we have enough exposure to the person to assess his or her ability fully.

All things being equal, the more confident a witness is in his or her memory, the more likely the trier of fact is to believe that witness. However, the research on flashbulb memories shows that the confident witness is no more likely than the hesitant one to be telling the truth.

12 This is known as the Dunning-Kruger Effect. In 1999, Justin Kruger and David Dunning of Cornell University subjected participants to tests of humour, grammar and logical reasoning. In general, participants overestimated their abilities, and those in the bottom quartile assessed themselves in the upper half. Interestingly, the more those in the bottom quartile improved their skills, the more realistic their self-assessments became. See Justin Kruger and David Dunning, "Unskilled and Unaware of It: How Difficulties in Recognizing One's Own Incompetence Leads to Inflated Self-Assessments" (1999) 77 Journal of Personality and Social Psychology 1121.

13 Gary L Wells et al, "The Confidence of Eyewitnesses in the Identification from Lineups" (2002) 11 Current Directions in Psychological Science 151.

14 Cameron Anderson and Gavin J. Kilduff, "Why Do Dominant Personalities Attain Influence in Face-to-Face Groups? The Competence-Signaling Effects of Trait Dominance" (2009) 96 Journal of Personality and Social Psychology 491.

OBJECTIVE DATA CAN COMPENSATE FOR HUMAN FRAILTIES

Among the modern advocates' chief complaint is being "drowned in data." We claim the ubiquity of email, for example, has made the discovery process overwhelming. However, such data can compensate for our poor memories and observational skills. Data are objective and do not miss gorillas or misremember.

The most obvious example of data's superiority over witness testimony is the use of DNA evidence to exonerate the wrongly convicted. Eyewitness testimony engages all the pitfalls listed above. Crimes involve unexpected events that do not engage our typical mental models. Because of their traumatic nature, crimes also tend to generate flashbulb memories, which are inaccurate but imbue the witness with confidence owing to their vividness. Not coincidentally, false witness identifications account for fully 70 percent of wrongful convictions overturned as a result of DNA testing.[15]

In the same way, contemporaneous documents more accurately reflect what really happened than does the testimony of witnesses. Video and audio records are better still. Even when witnesses are certain of their testimony, there is a good chance they are misremembering their observations. There is also a good chance those observations were themselves inaccurate. My recollections of the anecdotes shared in this article are, I now realize, just as uncertain. The more we can rely on objective data, the more likely we are to do justice to the dispute.

15 Innocence Project; online: <innocenceproject.org>.

If we can't trust witnesses, can we trust trials?

MATTHEW MILNE-SMITH

TRIALS ARE OVERRATED.

Heresy, I know – particularly so when appearing in *The Advocates' Journal*. But hear me out.

A growing body of scientific research indicates that human beings are not very good lie detectors. Drawing on this research, Paul Fruitman persuasively argued in the Summer 2017 issue of this *Journal* that "[o]ur system trusts that witnesses who testify credibly and confidently are telling the truth. It appears that trust is misplaced."

Nor is this problem limited to intentionally untruthful witnesses. Even well-intentioned witnesses who take seriously their oath or affirmation to tell the truth fall prey to reconstructing the past to fit their desired narrative. Every counsel can certainly recall the client or witness who forcefully and credibly insists on a particular version of events, only to be contradicted by contemporaneous documents or physical evidence.

It is difficult to overstate the significance of this problem for our adversarial system of justice, founded as it is on parties leading oral evidence from witnesses, and triers of fact making assessments of credibility based on that evidence. If cases can turn on credibility assessments, and human beings' ability to assess credibility is poor, what does that say about the quality of justice? Unless triers of fact have an innate or acquired ability to assess credibility that far exceeds that of the population at large, the implications are troubling.

There is, of course, an alternative means of adjudicating civil disputes on their merits: summary judgment. Traditionally, the bench and bar have been extremely reluctant to decide cases by way of summary judgment, wary of denying litigants their proverbial day in court. Summary judgment was perceived as a less desirable form of justice reserved for cases so obvious that a proper trial was unnecessary. Trials were necessary for anything but the easiest cases. However, if trials are in fact overrated as a means of determining the truth and providing justice, our veneration of them may be misplaced.

As a trial lawyer, I do not want to see trials become even less frequent than they already are. Trials are to litigators what the stage is to actors. All the grinding work of preparation is directed to being ready for trial, or at least to the superior bargaining position that comes from being ready for trial. For most of us, trial advocacy is no small part of why we chose to become litigators. Moreover, the difficulty of training young lawyers in trial advocacy has become almost trite. It grows more difficult by the day.

With all that said, trials are dreadful for clients. They are expensive, lengthy and risky. It can take years to get to trial. Our civil justice system is perpetually short of judges, courtrooms or both. The capacity of the civil system to try cases in a timely manner is likely to be strained even further by the demands of the criminal justice system in light of the Supreme Court of Canada's decision in *R. v. Jordan*.

A LONG-STANDING RELUCTANCE TO EMBRACE SUMMARY JUDGMENT

The historical rules and jurisprudence surrounding summary judgment reflected the veneration of trials as a means of resolving civil disputes. Before 1985, summary judgment was available to plaintiffs only on enumerated claims for a debt or liquidated demand. A defendant could never seek summary judgment, no matter how spurious the case.

The 1985 amendments to the *Rules of Civil Procedure* implemented a modest expansion of summary judgment. Rule 20 permitted defendants as well as plaintiffs to seek summary judgment, but only where the motions judge was satisfied that there is no "genuine issue" for trial with respect to a claim or defence.

The key words were "genuine issue" for trial. Summary judgment was not conceived as a true alternative to trial. Rather, reflecting the traditional skepticism of summary judgment, it was a measure available only where a trial would essentially be a waste of time. There are not many cases where there is *no* genuine issue for trial. Even in cases that turn on the interpretation of a contract, which one might expect would lend themselves to summary adjudication, it is relatively easy to generate a genuine issue for trial given the evolution of the law to recognize that contracts must always be interpreted in light of their surrounding circumstances.

The jurisprudence on summary judgment reflected the skeptical approach embodied in the Rules. While Justice Henry's suggestion in *Pizza Pizza Ltd. v. Gillespie* that the motions judge was to take "a hard look at the merits" gave hope to proponents of summary judgment,[1] those hopes were relatively short-lived. Eight years later, in *Aguonie et al. v. Galion Solid Waste Material Inc.*, the Court of Appeal held that, on a motion for summary judgment, "the court will never assess credibility, weigh the evidence, or find the facts." Rather, the court's role was limited to "assessing the threshold issue of whether a genuine issue exists as to material facts requiring a trial."[2]

RECENT REFORMS ENCOURAGING SUMMARY JUDGMENT

In 2007, former Associate Chief Justice Coulter Osborne released his report on making the civil justice system in Ontario more accessible and affordable. One section of his report was dedicated to summary judgment and made a series of recommendations that were ultimately incorporated into the 2010 amendments to the *Rules of Civil Procedure*. Chief among these amendments were ones specifically empowering a judge hearing a motion for summary judgment to (1) weigh the evidence; (2) evaluate the credibility of a deponent; and (3) draw any reasonable inference from the evidence.[3] Critically, however, the motions judge was not to exercise those powers where it was "in the interests of justice for such powers to be exercised only at a trial."

While the initial jurisprudence under the new Rule 20 adopted a more liberal approach to summary judgment, the Court of Appeal quickly

1 (1990), 75 O.R. (2d) 225 at 237 (Gen. Div.).

2 (1998), 38 O.R. (3d) 161 at 173 (C.A.).

3 *Rules of Civil Procedure*, Rule 20.04(2.1).

reversed that trend with its decision in *Combined Air Mechanical Services Inc. v. Flesch* ("*Combined Air*")."[4] The court's interpretation of whether it was "in the interests of justice" to require a trial was extremely broad and traditional. Echoing the Supreme Court of Canada's paeans to the trial process in standard of review cases such as *Housen v. Nikolaisen*,[5] the court noted that the trial judge "is a trier of fact who participates in the dynamic of a trial, sees witnesses testify, follows the trial narrative, asks questions when in doubt as to the substance of the evidence, monitors the cut and thrust of the adversaries, and hears the evidence in the words of the witnesses."[6]

The Court of Appeal was just as deferential to the role of trial counsel. The court noted that

> the order in which witnesses are called, the manner in which they are examined and cross-examined, and how the introduction of documents is interspersed with and explained by the oral evidence, is of significance. This "trial narrative" may have an impact on the outcome.[7]

The poetry of the trial process was juxtaposed with the prose of summary judgment:

> The deponents swear to affidavits typically drafted by counsel and do not speak in their own words. Although they are cross-examined and transcripts of these examinations are before the court, the motion judge is not present to observe the witnesses during their testimony. Rather, the motion judge is working from transcripts. The record does not take the form of a trial narrative. The parties do not review the entire record with the motion judge.[8]

Taking these factors into account, the court concluded that summary judgment was available beyond the traditional categories only where "the full appreciation of the evidence and issues that is required to make dispositive findings can be achieved by way of summary judgment."[9]

4 2011 ONCA 764.
5 2002 SCC 33.
6 *Combined Air, supra* note 4 at para 47.
7 *Ibid* at para 48.
8 *Ibid* at para 49.
9 *Ibid* at para 50.

THE SUPREME COURT REINVIGORATES SUMMARY JUDGMENT

The Court of Appeal for Ontario's decision was short-lived. On appeal, the Supreme Court of Canada overturned the "full appreciation test" as being too restrictive and recognized that summary judgment could be "a proportionate, more expeditious and less expensive means to achieve a just result than going to trial."[10]

While the result was welcome, the decision still represented only a limited and conditional embrace of summary judgment that emphasized its expediency and cost-efficiency, not its accuracy. The Supreme Court framed its decision by adopting the *Advocates' Society*'s submission that, given the cost of trial, "the trial process denies ordinary people the opportunity to have adjudication."[11]

Notably, the Supreme Court continued to presume a "tension between accessibility and the truth-seeking function."[12] The more expansive (and expensive) procedures associated with a trial were presumed to be superior at serving courts' truth-seeking function.

The Supreme Court's judgment in *Combined Air* was a welcome corrective to the Court of Appeal's veneration of the trial process. Welcome as it was, the Supreme Court's decision still did not accept summary judgment as a co-equal method of adjudicating cases alongside trials. Rather, summary judgment was effectively acknowledged as merely being "good enough" in light of the goals of proportionality and efficiency.

NOT JUST "GOOD ENOUGH"

My suggestion is that, in many civil cases, summary judgment is not just "good enough"; it is "as good as," or "better than," for at least three reasons.

First, as Paul Fruitman's article pointed out, human beings (which, last I checked, included judges) are not nearly as good as we think we are at assessing credibility. By placing so much weight on assessments of credibility, trials are prone to turn not on which side's witnesses are

10 *Hryniak v Mauldin*, 2014 SCC 7 at para 4.

11 *Ibid* at para 24.

12 *Ibid* at para 29.

in fact truthful, but on which are successful in projecting truthfulness. These two are often not the same thing.

Second, particularly in commercial cases, the contemporaneous documentary record should usually be far more important than witnesses' recollections (or, more cynically, their *post hoc* rationalizations). This is most obviously true in contract cases, where the witnesses for each side miraculously just happen to recall that the factual matrix was most consistent with their preferred interpretation of the contract. These *post hoc* rationalizations are far less probative than what the relevant parties actually said and did in the contemporaneous documents.

Third, the role of counsel in drafting affidavits is a feature, not a bug. It is hard to reconcile the Court of Appeal for Ontario's distaste for this aspect of summary judgment with its praise for counsel's role in crafting a "trial narrative." The fact is, the skill of counsel will play a role whichever method of adjudication is chosen. If anything, however, the ability of skilful counsel to win a losing case is somewhat mitigated in summary judgment, where the focus is properly on the documents rather than on the witnesses.

AN EXTREME EXAMPLE OF A CASE FOR SUMMARY JUDGMENT

The expanded approach to summary judgment that I propose is not limited to straightforward cases involving a handful of documents. It could and should be used in even complex commercial cases. For example, one of the more prominent trials in recent years was the so-called "allocation dispute" arising out of the insolvency of Nortel. Debtor groups from Canada, the United States and EMEA (Europe, the Middle East and Asia) were fighting over the allocation of approximately $7 billion in proceeds from the sale of Nortel's worldwide assets.[13]

Nortel was a unique trial. It was tried in a joint session of the Superior Court of Justice, Commercial List in Toronto and the US Bankruptcy Court for the District of Delaware. Justice Newbould presided in Toronto, and Judge Gross in Delaware. As a result of the joint nature of the proceedings, the parties engaged in American-style depositions, conducting more than 125 depositions of fact and expert witnesses located

13 The author acted as Canadian counsel to the EMEA Debtors.

around the world over a span of several months. This was followed by a 21-day trial and then three days of argument. The parties submitted evidence-in-chief at trial principally by way of affidavits, with brief oral examinations-in-chief followed by full cross-examinations.

At the end of all of this litigating, most witnesses proved to be of little assistance. Much of the evidence at trial consisted, to the obvious and understandable frustration of the trial judges, of witnesses' self-serving interpretations of contracts entered into years or even decades earlier. Even less helpful were cross-examinations that consisted largely of lawyers arguing with witnesses concerning their interpretations of the documents.

Typical of Justice Newbould's frustration with witnesses giving evidence about their interpretations of the relevant agreements was the following description of the parties' position on the Master R&D Agreement (MRDA), the interpretation of which was central to the dispute:

> There was a great deal of evidence led by the U.S. and EMEA interests as to the subjective views of the witnesses, mostly tax personnel, regarding the rights of the parties under the CSA or MRDA or what the witnesses understood the language to mean, or in one case as to the witness's understanding of what others understood the documents to mean. Apart from the latter being inadmissible hearsay, all of this evidence was not admissible as it amounted to subjective views as to the meaning of an agreement. Nor was it admissible under the factual matrix rule permitting objective surrounding circumstances at the time of the execution of the agreement to be considered, and I do not consider it. For example, what Mr. Henderson thought about the rights under the CSA license, that he copied from an earlier version of the CSA, or what others thought the MRDA meant or what they thought the intent of it was is not to be taken into account. See *Sattva, supra,* at para. 59.[14]

Throughout the trial and again in his Reasons, Justice Newbould repeatedly referred to the parties' subjective views of the evidence as being inadmissible or irrelevant.[15] Ultimately, Justice Newbould's conclusion was that he did "not consider the surrounding circumstance or factual matrix evidence to provide much clear assistance in construing

14 *Re Nortel Networks Corporation*, 2015 ONSC 2987 at para 119.

15 *Ibid* at paras 120–121.

the meaning of the terms in the MRDA."[16] Even expert evidence was occasionally criticized as being an "inadmissible subjective view as to how the MRDA license should be interpreted."[17]

Where Justice Newbould did give effect to the evidence of witnesses, it was usually on relatively uncontroversial subjects, such as the fact that the MRDA was driven by tax concerns,[18] that Nortel assigned all worldwide patents to one corporate entity as a matter of best practices[19] or that the majority of Nortel's bonds were issued without guarantees.[20] In addressing the important issue of whether a substantive consolidation of worldwide assets would be permissible, Justice Newbould emphasized that the relevant evidence was "clear beyond peradventure," and "clear and uncontested".[21]

In the result, Justice Newbould and Judge Gross agreed on a *pro rata* allocation that was not even advocated by any of the three main debtor groups; rather, it was advanced as a primary argument only by counsel representing Nortel's UK pensioners. No witness gave testimony indicating that a *pro rata* allocation was required by the agreements between the parties; rather, the evidence led in support of this outcome was simply that nothing precluded a *pro rata* allocation, and it was a just solution in the circumstances.

Given this result, it raises the question of whether the extensive trial and pre-trial procedures in Nortel were even necessary. The deposition transcripts were barely referred to at trial or in the judgments. Even the trial evidence was typically relied on only where it was uncontroversial or uncontradicted. Far more important were the documents themselves, and the judges' overall assessment of what was fair in all the circumstances in light of the relatively undisputed underlying facts. Summary judgment would likely have achieved the same result.

I believe the same is true in many commercial cases. The evidence of the witnesses is rarely probative of anything unless supported by

16 *Ibid* at para 157.
17 *Ibid* at para 166.
18 *Ibid* at paras 174, 176.
19 *Ibid* at para 196.
20 *Ibid* at para 230.
21 *Ibid* at paras 222, 223. While Justice Newbould did not order a substantive consolidation or conclude that it was necessary to effect the resolution of the case, he did find that, if his order did amount to a substantive consolidation, it was permissible.

the contemporaneous documents. Commercial cases are not like, for example, personal injury cases where only the disputed evidence of eyewitnesses can determine what actually happened, and who did what. In commercial cases, the documents are the most important thing, and the documents are presented just as well by summary judgment as they are by traditional trial. Indeed, one might argue they are better presented by summary judgment, without the distracting spectacle of witnesses putting their gloss on the documents.

A PROCESS ALREADY BEGUN

The move toward summary judgment–style procedures has in fact already begun in various forums. On the Commercial List, it is now routine for evidence-in-chief to be given principally by way of evidence-in-chief.[22] Parties never waste time proving documents through witnesses; a document brief is routinely agreed on in advance of trial.

Arbitration is another forum where summary judgment–style procedures have become routine. Parties routinely submit evidence by way of affidavits, with minimal cross-examinations in court. Rare is the commercial litigator who has not tried any number of cases in this manner.

Finally, the leave-to-proceed test for securities misrepresentation cases under Part XXIII.1 of the *Securities Act* is, in essence, a summary judgment test. While it of course is just a test for whether a case can actually proceed to a trial, if the defendant prevails, it is the final adjudication on the merit of a claim on behalf of, typically, thousands of class members.

22 *Nortel Networks Corporation (Re)*, 2015 ONSC 2987; *The Catalyst Capital Group Inc v Moyse*, 2016 ONSC 5271; *Husky Injection Molding Systems Ltd v Schad*, 2016 ONSC 2297.

Fostering connection, creating community

THE HONOURABLE HARRIET SACHS

THANK YOU FOR this great honour. I am overwhelmed, and when I am overwhelmed my usual response is to retreat into a book, not give a speech. I love to read, but if I get to choose, my books come with happy endings. I have learned that life does not always deliver happy endings; however, if you're lucky, it can deliver wonderful moments. For me, this is one of those moments, not only because of the honour I have received but because I get to share it with all of you and, most particularly, my eldest daughter, Emma, who is being called to the bar today.

I look at you and I see myself, sitting in what was then the O'Keefe Centre, waiting to be called up to the stage. I remember that my feet hurt and that the collar of my court shirt felt way too tight. I don't remember feeling triumphant, but I do remember feeling unsure and scared – unsure about my choice of profession, and scared because, having made that choice, I could not see how I would ever find my way in a profession that had not yet made a place for women.

When I started law school my class of 300 was divided into sections of 60. My section had three women. I had never had a woman law professor, and when I articled at a medium-sized downtown law firm there was one woman associate. When I got called to the bar, there were a handful of women on the trial benches; there had never been a woman appointed to the Court of Appeal of any province, and there had never been a woman on the Supreme Court of Canada.

I had tried my hand in the courts during the summer and semester that I spent in a legal clinic during law school. By any standards, it had not gone well. My first court appearance, on behalf of a regular attendee in what was then referred to as "drunk court," came to an abrupt end when, just after I'd nervously given the judge my name, a voice boomed from the back of the courtroom asking the judge to have *me* arrested. It was my client's wife, another drunk-court regular. She pointed at me and yelled to a packed courtroom that I was having an affair with her husband. For the record, it wasn't true. On my second appearance – also in drunk court, fortunately in front of another judge – I fared no better. This time I pled my client guilty and gave what I thought was an effective presentation about how he had changed and should therefore receive a light sentence. The judge listened and then turned to my client, saying, "It's bad enough that you would try and deceive this court with this tale of reformation, but what's worse is that you actually got this nice young girl to believe you."

I have to confess that when I first thought about this speech, my plan was to talk about how I now realize that not having a ready slot to fit into forced me to find my own path in the law – in retrospect, a gift. That is, until I read Frank Bruni's article in the Sunday *New York Times* a few weeks ago. It was a column about the struggle that this year's commencement speakers are having giving the usual messages about the triumphs awaiting the graduating class when, in so many ways, the realities facing that class seem so grim. He went on to summarize what he called the leitmotif of this year's commencement speeches. As he put it,

> Speaker after speaker recalls nail-biting national conditions at their own graduations – or simply miserable personal stories from their youth – as a way of assuring their audience that life's ordeals are plentiful, survivable and, as the trajectories of the speakers themselves demonstrate, preludes to great accomplishment. Message: it's tough now, but you could be on a dais in a tasseled cap receiving an honorary degree and dispensing some assertive optimism of your own in 30 years.[1]

I read that column and my heart sank. If he hadn't summarized my speech, he'd at least lampooned its subtext, and I hadn't even written it

1 Frank Bruni, "Buck Up, Graduates!" *New York Times* (30 May 2009) <www.nytimes.com/2009/05/31/weekinreview/31bruni.html>.

yet. If I couldn't talk about triumphing over adversity and the opportunities it presents, what could I talk about? Then I thought about what the law had offered me over the past 30 years. I realized there was something I wanted to share with you, because it is how I survived – and, believe me, survival, not triumph, was my aim.

After I was called to the bar, I set up a firm with three other women. For the rest of my professional life as a lawyer, I continued to work with women and, more importantly, with people I cared about and who cared about me. My workplace offered me a place to connect – and when I use the word "connect," I mean more than just keeping in touch or making contacts. We were women facing an array of challenges, and we reasoned and laughed our way together toward solutions. What we did for each other gave us the strength and the will to interact in the same way with our clients and our communities.

In the over 30 years I have been in the law, I have seen real changes. The profession has become much more diverse. Women, particularly, are now a huge presence. They go to law schools in the same numbers as men. They get hired by the firms that did not want me, in the same numbers as men. This is a good thing. What has been disturbing, however, has been to watch how, within five to seven years, so many of them are gone – often leaving the profession for good.

* * *

The realities that have caused women to flee the workplaces that my generation had fought to get them access to have also affected the men in those workplaces. To make this point Joshua Perry, a law professor at Vanderbilt University, composed a fictionalized letter based on conversations he had had with practising lawyers he knew – some were his former classmates, but most were his former students. It began as follows:

> Dear Professor Perry,
>
> I am writing to seek your advice regarding my life. I graduated from law school two years ago, passed the bar exam and I have been in the practice of law for about 18 months. I am earning a good salary – enough to make my monthly school loan payments, drive the standard-issue BMW, make the mortgage on my new house, and drink $3 cups of coffee. Financially speaking, things are pretty good. I think I'm earning about twice what my father earned when he retired. I'll turn 29 next month.

> But I'm writing today because I am restless. I feel disconnected and empty. I do not enjoy my practice, much less feel fulfilled by it. In fact, I dread the thought of going into work every day. And I don't know what to do ...[2]

For his former students, Professor Perry's response is to return to them a copy of the personal statement they wrote when they applied to law school.

In the past three decades, life in the law has come to be dominated by the billable hour. The more hours you bill, the more you earn. If you do not bill up to expectation, there is no place for you. The problem, as Professor Marina Angel so succinctly put it when she spoke to the New York Women's Bar Association a few years ago, is that "two thousand billable hours a year are incompatible with human life."[3]

Billable hours have become the measure of participation and contribution. Yes, that measure offers the advantage of objectivity. But, in a fundamental way, it misses the point. Participation – human participation in a collective enterprise – cannot be reduced to a number. If you do that, you destroy what makes working together and living together worthwhile – a sense of connectedness, the recognition that we can depend on each other for our mutual survival and well-being. When we feel connected, we learn to trust each other. We learn to rely on each other to solve the problems that we all face. We learn to believe and act in a way that reinforces the development of reciprocal relationships, relationships that recognize that mutual self-interest is also our own self-interest.

I have a friend. I call him my inspiration. His name is Ric Young. He is not a lawyer, but he is one of the leading thinkers about how to effect social change in this country – change directed at creating healthier communities and, from that, a better world. I cannot do justice to his message, but I have heard him quote Marcus Aurelius, the Roman emperor and philosopher, who 2,000 years ago put it this way: "Always remember this doctrine: Reasoning beings were created for one another's sake."[4] I have also heard him talk about the research that shows that, ultimately, the

---

2 Joshua Perry, "Thinking Like a Professional" (2008) 58 Journal of Legal Education 159 at 161.

3 Marina Angel, "What It's (Really) Like to Practice Law in New York as a Woman," conference presentation, New York, April 21, 2005.

4 Marcus Aurelius, *Meditations*, iv, 3.

quality of people's lives depends not upon whether they earn hundreds of thousands of dollars, but on the quality of the bonds between them.

If the tap that fed the billable-hour culture has not been turned off, it has at least been reduced to a trickle. In a sense, the music has stopped. That silence may feel scary, but it is also your opportunity to demand something better for yourself, for the people you work with and for your community. Because here is another connection. Alienation breeds alienation. People who feel alienated in the place where they spend most of their waking hours become alienated from each other and from their social and political institutions. Robert Putnam, a professor of public policy at Harvard, observed that "this disengagement poses a critical threat to our personal health, local communities and national well-being."[5]

Who is better equipped than you to rebuild our workplaces and our profession so that they foster, rather than destroy connection? You are among the best and the brightest of your generation – a generation that has started to speak out about the need for change. You have spent four years studying an enterprise that is fundamentally about the ordering of human relationships. You have been trained to understand that decision-making requires listening, hearing both sides, thinking and reflecting. You have been taught the importance of process: if the process is not fair, the result is compromised. You have been taught to examine and test the principles that guide our relationships with each other and to adjust those principles to meet new, unanticipated situations.

You know that there are no easy answers, but that if we take the time to reason our way together, we can create environments that foster human dignity, environments that are based on the concepts that lawyers have helped develop – values such as freedom of speech, freedom of association and equality. So my message to you is use what you have learned and know. Don't compromise on connection. Start with yourself. Integrate who you are with who you become as a lawyer. Take that into the world in which you work. If that workplace does not seem to exist, work with others to make the one that you're in change, or create a new one of your own. Care about yourself and the others around you. For, truly, we are in it together. Without each other, we will not survive.

5 As cited in Eric Young, keynote address, Canadian Public Relations National Conference, June 16, 2005.

I am going to end this speech with a benediction of sorts. In doing so, I realize that I no longer care what the *New York Times* would think about what I say. It is a slightly modified quote from Paul Goodman, a philosopher, teacher and artist who, in his time, was compared to Rousseau. He believed in a Utopian society, which he described as follows:

> Where the community is planned as a whole, with an organic integration of work, living and play ... Where it is the policy to give an adequate voice to the unusual and unpopular opinion ... Where people are not afraid to make friends ... Where ... sexuality is taken for granted ...[6]

To which I would add, "where happiness means people to love, a community to work for and a world at peace." That is my wish for you and for us.

6 Paul Goodman, *Growing Up Absurd: Problems of Youth in the Organized Society* (New York: Random House, 1960) at 229–230.

Part Three

EXPERTS, SCIENCE AND THE LIKE

TO SAY DNA evidence has been a game-changer, especially for the wrongly accused, is to understate the case. Yet, all purported scientific methods and methodologies aren't necessarily the last word in evidence, as we saw in the Goudge Inquiry into Pediatric Forensic Pathology in Ontario. And experts, now required to hew to a statutory duty to the court of fairness and objectivity, still stray into advocacy from time to time. Our distinguished retired jurist, three practitioners and a law school dean weigh in on this aspect of advocacy. Who, I ask, doesn't enjoy debunking expertise where it proves to be flawed and misleading? No advocate worth his or her salt that I know.

September 2008

Science in the courtroom: THE MOUSE THAT ROARED

THE HONOURABLE W. IAN C. BINNIE*

> [I]f matters arise in our laws which concern other sciences and faculties, we commonly call for the aid of that science or faculty which it concerns, which is an honourable and commendable thing. For thereby it appears that we do not despise all other sciences but our own, but we approve of them and encourage them ... [1]

WE LIVE IN an age dominated by science and technology. The question I want to address is whether the courts are doing a proper job of resolving disputes in which an appreciation of such technical matters is necessary. The litigation of scientific and technological issues – symbolized perhaps by the mouse in the courtroom, whether it be the Harvard Mouse[2] or the Stuart Little mouse, a rodent with human brain cells[3] or, even worse, the mysterious Schroedinger's cat, which can be

* The Honourable Mr. Justice W. Ian C. Binnie is a member of the *Supreme Court of Canada*. This article is based on the Viscount Bennett Memorial Lecture delivered at the Law School, University of New Brunswick, on October 5, 2006. Justice Binnie expresses his thanks to his law clerks, Emilie Taman and Maia Tsurumi, for their indefatigable research into these issues.

1 *Buckley v. Rice Thomas* (1554), 1 Pl. Com. 118, 75 E.R. 182 at 184, Saunders J. [*Buckley*].

2 *Harvard College v. Canada (Commissioner of Patents)*, [2002] 4 S.C.R. 45.

3 The *London Times* reported on 2 September 2006 that scientists at Stanford University in California are introducing human brain cells into mice. Stuart Little, you will recall, is the mouse that can talk and had human parents, but was still a mouse and

shown by physicists to be simultaneously alive and dead[4] – is a prospect that leaves much of the legal community justifiably shaking in its Luddite boots. But however daunting, the task of making courts more science friendly is important to sustaining the legitimacy of courts as dispute resolution institutions.

Science disputes are hitting the courts at an increasing velocity. In cases involving tort, environmental, intellectual property and criminal law, the admission and use of expert scientific or technical testimony is often crucial to the outcome. These cases frequently raise policy concerns that collide. For example, there have been very interesting disputes dealing with customized bacteria used to fight oil spills and other pollution, where scientists have designed a bacterium that has no counterpart in nature. But of course, once the pollution is eaten up, the bacteria keep on reproducing. If a court does not understand exactly what was modified and what the consequences of unleashing such organisms into the environment are, how can it determine legal questions related to liability and remedies? From a scientific standpoint, one of the solutions to the problem of natural reproduction is to build into the organisms a so-called "suicide gene," so that at a certain point the bacteria simply die. That sounds like a good idea, but then Monsanto came along with a genetically modified soybean containing a suicide gene and critics said, "This is contrary to the *Competition Act* because you're forcing the farmer to go back to Monsanto every year to buy seed."[5]

Recently, a group of scientists visited the Supreme Court of Canada. They told us that nanotechnology[6] will create the next big wave of

---

the *Times*'s headline read: "A human brain trapped inside a mouse's body – Not a good idea." A Stanford law professor responsible for overseeing the legal and ethical aspects of the Stuart Little experiment was quoted as saying, "Frankly, if we made a mouse that had a fully human brain, I would be concerned." When you have fully human children suing their parents in the United States for wrongfully bringing them into the world, I suspect Stuart Little might have a winner of a lawsuit.

4 Schroedinger's cat is a creature that inhabits the wonderland of quantum physics. You and I may think that a physical object has one state. The book is either open or it is closed. You may be surprised to hear that quantum physicists do not agree and can prove by the principle of "super position" that a physical object can be both – at least at the molecular level.

5 See *Monsanto Canada Inc. v. Schmeiser*, [2004] 1 S.C.R. 902.

6 A nanometre is a billionth of a metre. A sheet of paper is about 100,000 nanometres thick. Using various new techniques, in particular something called a

litigation. Harnessing so-called quantum nanotechnology, governments will be able to make devices to listen to private communications, however cleverly encrypted, and the legitimate parties to the communication will not be able to tell whether their communication has been intercepted or not. Other nanoscientists are working on a customized molecule to dust the site of brain surgery. It seems the dust will prevent scar tissue from forming and thus allow the tissue to knit. But what if the dust has disastrous unexpected side-effects? There are also applications of nanotechnology to deliver medicines to the right place in the body. But what is the legal liability if the delivery fails or runs amok and the patient is injured or dies? It is important that parties injured by such scientific initiatives, as well as those defending against the claims, have confidence in a court's ability to understand and evaluate the expert evidence.

LAWYERS AND SCIENTISTS SEEM TO INHABIT DIFFERENT UNIVERSES

Superficially, and misleadingly, the cultures of the lawyer and the scientist *seem* to have much in common.[7] We all try to act on "evidence" and use comparable indicia of expertise and testing in the search for reliability. Conclusions are drawn from the accumulated evidence through logic, deduction and induction. Yet, in truth, we largely inhabit mutually skeptical solitudes, and where these solitudes rub together the result is often not pleasurable for either discipline, especially for the judge. For instance, the idea of "evidence" seems to mean something quite different to scientists than to judges. In science, "evidence" is not equivalent to "proof."[8] For the most part, theories cannot truly be "proved" in the sense that they become indisputable. Almost all scientific conclusions are considered provisional.[9] Theories can be supported by more or less

scanning tunnelling microscope, scientists can construct new forms of matter at an atomic level.

7 See generally Alan D. Gold, *Expert Evidence in Criminal Law: The Scientific Approach* (Toronto: Irwin Law, 2003).

8 *Federal Judicial Center Reference Manual on Scientific Evidence*, 2nd ed., 2000 at 80, online: The Federal Judicial Center <http://www.fjc.gov/public/home.nsf/pages/610> [*Reference Manual on Scientific Evidence*].

9 Justice Thomas Cromwell & Ronald-Frans Melchers, "Testing the Validity of Scientific Evidence" (National Judicial Institute Conference, *Managing Science in the*

evidence and may eventually come to be accepted as the dominant or most likely explanation of observed phenomena. The phrase "consistent with" to a scientist merely means that something cannot be excluded as an explanation. It does not connote any particular weight, association or commonality. However, to judges, lawyers and the public this phrase is often interpreted to mean that there is a "match."[10]

The average judge is likely to have little background in science generally, much less particular expertise in the field to which the dispute relates. Even worse, whereas the lawyers have had months and perhaps years of preparation, the judge hits a dispute cold and is expected to get "up to speed" within a few of days on matters which the expert witnesses have spent a professional lifetime attempting to understand. The predicament of the judge was well summarized by Justice Frank Muldoon, a larger-than-life figure who sat for years as one of the leading judges in the Federal Court, Trial Division. The topic was a patent dispute involving the dryer-added clothes fabric conditioner called Bounce. Unilever had claimed that the coating (animal fat and sugar extract) on the substrate of Procter & Gamble's dryer sheet violated a Unilever patent. Legions of experts were called by both sides to argue about how this animal-fat mixture distributed itself on clothing during the dryer cycle. Millions of dollars hung in the balance. After a lengthy trial in which there were periodic outbursts from Muldoon J. complaining that all this talk of surfactants, contact angles and surface tension was incomprehensible, he eventually exploded in his final reasons for judgment as follows:

> A judge unschooled in the arcane subject is at difficulty to know which of the disparate, solemnly-mouthed and hotly contended scientific verities is, or are, plausible. Is the eminent scientist expert with the shifty eyes and poor demeanour the one whose "scientific verities" are not credible? Cross-examination is said to be the great engine for getting at the truth, but when the unschooled judge cannot perceive the truth, if he or she ever hears it, among all the chemical and other scientific baffle-gab, is it not a solemn exercise in silliness?[11]

As counsel for Unilever, I took little comfort in this *cri de coeur* (although Unilever won the case), but the fact of the matter is that judges

Courtroom, Toronto, 23 November 2005) [unpublished].

10 Gold, *supra* note 7 at 200.

11 *Unilever PLC v. Procter & Gamble Inc.* (1993), 47 C.P.R. (3d) 479 at 488.

and jurors may have no means of assessing credibility except through the usual clues applicable to witnesses generally. Even body language and physical appearance, as Muldoon J. observed, may well be misleading when it comes to expert witnesses.[12] In the absence of anything better, the court may be overly impressed with credentials and reputation and too little focused on the validity and content of the scientific testimony itself, which may have been presented in a disjointed and confusing manner.

In one criminal case, the Manitoba Court of Appeal criticized the way in which a scientific point was argued for just this reason:

> It can be seen that Crown counsel was inviting the jury to determine a question of science on the basis of their impression of the demeanour of the witnesses.[13]

Yet the same flaw appears frequently in judge-alone cases. In *Lubrizol Corp. v. Imperial Oil Ltd.*,[14] a patent case involving heavy-molecular-weight dispersants in motor oils, the evaluation of the expert witnesses by the trial judge, Mr. Justice "Bud" Cullen, a former minister of national revenue, includes the following:

> Each witness, especially the expert witnesses, received very careful scrutiny by myself with attention paid not only to their answers, but also to their demeanour, out-of-line advocacy, evasiveness.[15] My note on that day reads: "Dr. Klaus would be a better witness if he showed more confidence in counsel who are experienced and competent."[16]
>
> After hearing Billmeyer's evidence in reply, I had written as one of my comments: "Impressive, straightforward, very convinced that he's right in his observations and conclusions."[17]

What is the scientific community to think about the administration of justice if experts are to be judged like travelling salesmen on the basis

12 See also Sanja K. Ivkovic & Valerie P. Hans, "Jurors' Evaluations of Expert Testimony: Judging the Messenger and the Message" (2003) 28 Law & Soc. Inquiry 441.

13 *R. v. Medvedew* (1978), 43 C.C.C. (2d) 434 at 440 (Man. C.A.).

14 (1991), 33 C.P.R. (3d) 1. Although I was not involved in the trial, I disclose that I was one of the lawyers who appeared for Imperial Oil on the appeal(s).

15 *Ibid.* at 37, Cullen J.

16 *Ibid.* at 41.

17 *Ibid.* at 42.

of their ability to project confidence and conviction? One hesitates even to ask. Here are a few representative complaints from some experts who felt "burned" by their trial experience:

1. "There is no opportunity to explain evidence or interpretation oneself, no assurance that counsel will explain it clearly or in a sophisticated fashion, and no opportunity to correct errors or crudities which creep in."
2. "There is no guarantee that counsel will even understand the arguments the expert has made, and consequently no guarantee that questions which may be posed by the judges will be correctly or clearly answered."
3. "The expert witness is almost entirely at the mercy of counsel on both sides. The expert must depend on counsel to present his or her views fairly and forcefully ... [Scientists] do not get an opportunity to defend themselves against misquotation or selective quotation by opposing counsel."[18]

A common thread woven through these complaints is the impression (perhaps false) among some scientific experts that the legal system suffers from amateurishness when it deals with scientific matters. Our courts are said not to be scientific enough in their approach to scientific evidence. Legal academics, too, sometimes offer observations surprising enough to make scientists rub their eyes, as in the case of Stéphane Beaulac and Pierre-André Côté, professors of law at the Université de Montréal, who recently wrote with a somewhat shaky grip on the law of gravity:

> Consider a flight from Montreal to London. The pilot must plan such a flight based on a conception of the earth that is round, otherwise the aircraft would end up in outer space.[19]

From a scientist's point of view, a disturbing feature of litigation is the adversarial process itself, under which judges and lawyers assume that the truth is best arrived at by contending parties stating their own (one-sided) point of view simply, forcefully and with the least amount of

18 J. Morgan Kousser, "Are Expert Witnesses Whores? Reflections on Objectivity in Scholarship and Expert Witnessing" (1984) 6:1 *The Public Historian* 5.

19 See S. Beaulac & P.A. Côté, "Driedger's 'Modern Principle' at the Supreme Court of Canada: Interpretation, Justification, Legitimization" (2006) 40 R.J.T. 131 at 168.

nuance possible. Rather than acting as an independent scientific investigator, the judge sits and listens to both adversaries and is supposed to distill from all the conflicting (and perhaps overstated) evidence the "true facts," to which he or she then applies the law. This is the jurist's equivalent of Adam Smith's "invisible hand" in *The Wealth of Nations.*[20] If every litigant furiously pursues his or her own self-interest in the courtroom, then, at the end of the day, the truth will emerge. Many scientists think that this approach is naive and is hardly likely to get to the truth in a matter involving serious learning and sophistication.

Another problem is that, as scientists see it, courts rush in where experts fear to tread. How can a court possibly resolve a product liability case involving the alleged adverse effects of using oral contraceptives,[21] for example, when the experts themselves are divided over the increased risk of strokes? In a class action in the United Kingdom brought by a group of women against Schering Health Care and others,[22] six studies on this relationship were put before the court.[23] Three of these studies, all published in the British medical journal *The Lancet*, said that there was an approximate doubling of the risk to a woman who was taking the third generation of this pill.[24] There were also three industry-sponsored reports which said that there was no increase in the risk. The studies, written largely in algebra, landed before the unfortunate Mr. Justice Mackay. He accepted as persuasive the industry reports, dismissed the action and was then virtually universally condemned in the medical literature. An editorial in *The Lancet* stated that "trying science in a court of law is doomed to failure."[25] It went on to say, "Despite millions of pounds spent, and numerous intelligent minds locked in combat, the judge failed utterly to get to the heart of the matter."

---

20 Adam Smith, *An Inquiry Into the Nature and Causes of the Wealth of Nations* (London, 1776).

21 See, for example, *Buchan v. Ortho Pharmaceutical (Canada) Ltd.* (1986), 54 O.R. (2d) 92 (C.A.), aff'g (1984), 46 O.R. (2d) 113 (H.C.J.).

22 *XYZ & Others v. Schering Health Care Ltd., Organon Laboratories Ltd., John Wyeth & Brother Ltd.*, [2002] EWHC 1420 (Q.B.).

23 See Editorial, "Epidemiology on Trial" (2002) 360 *The Lancet* 421; News, "Third Generation Pill Not More Risky" (2002) 269 *The Pharmaceutical Journal* 149.

24 Haroon Ashraf, "UK High Court Dismisses Risk of VTE in 'Pill' Test Case" (2002) 360 *The Lancet* 391.

25 Editorial, *supra* note 23.

There is a further problem. The judge may not have the luxury of waiting until scientists in the relevant field have reached a consensus. The court is a dispute resolution forum, not a free-wheeling scientific inquiry, and the judge must reach a timely decision based on the information available. Even if science has not figured it out yet, the law cannot wait. This problem was in the forefront of the late Justice Sam Grange's mind when he was faced with reaching conclusions in his commission of inquiry into deaths at the Hospital for Sick Children in Toronto. He wrote:

> I cannot await the research. I am charged to find the cause of death of thirty-six children. Obviously toxicologic information is important. I must accept the best information available at least if it is not seriously challenged in the present state of science. I may eventually be proven wrong because the toxicologic evidence upon which I in part based my conclusion may be proved wrong or inadequate [but] that is how I interpret obedience to my mandate.[26]

IT IS EASIER FOR LAWYERS TO ATTACK THE TESTIFIER THAN THE TESTIMONY

Even if they are knowledgeable about the specific scientific issues in a case, lawyers, being practical people, are sensitive to the dangers of overloading the finders of fact, whether judges or jurors, with too much jargon and complexity, scientific or otherwise. The skilful cross-examiner may have soaked up the elements of the science at issue in a particular case, but will often find it easier and more effective to discredit the expert witness than to demolish the scientific basis on which the witness's testimony rests.

A good example is the cross-examination of a scientific expert conducted by one of Canada's great criminal lawyers, G. Arthur Martin, in the celebrated Stephen Truscott murder case when it was "retried" before the Supreme Court of Canada in 1966.[27] The accused was a teenager; the victim was a girl named Lynn Harper, who was of about the same age and was last seen alive

26 Ontario, *Report of the Royal Commission of Inquiry into Certain Deaths at the Hospital for Sick Children and Related Matters* (Toronto: Ministry of the Attorney General, 1984) at 29–30.

27 *R. v. Truscott*, [1967] S.C.R. 309.

in Truscott's presence. One of the strongest arguments for the defence was that Truscott could not have murdered Lynn Harper in the narrow window of opportunity contemplated by the prosecution. The evidence was that Lynn had eaten her supper at a quarter to six the evening she was killed. Steven Truscott had a strong alibi from 8 p.m. onwards. The Crown therefore had to establish that Lynn was murdered within two hours of her last meal, and for that purpose called a pathologist to testify that the precise time of death could be established from the state of digestion of the contents of her stomach. Arthur Martin's task was to undermine the testimony of the pathologist. He did so by using a dry sense of humour rather than by debating the correctness of the pathologist's science. Here is an extract from the trial transcript:

Q. Now, you have written extensively, Dr. Simpson, in the field of forensic medicine.

A. Yes.

Q. Now, I have read a good many of your books and one of the books you have written is entitled *Forensic Medicine* and, as my learned friend Mr. Scott says, it has gone through five editions now?

A. Yes.

Q. And in the last edition, indeed, you say this edition has been combed to insure it is abreast of the times. I notice at page 7 of the book – of course, I quite realize here you are dealing with a post-mortem event – you say under the heading of "Cooling": "This is the only real guide to the lapse of time during the first eighteen hours after death, and its *early* measurement is often vital to the establishment of an approximate time of death."

A. Yes, sir.

Q. Do you, anywhere in this book, suggest that the stomach contents and the state to which digestion has proceeded following the last meal is a reliable guide to the time of death?

A. No sir: I think that that is, as may be evident to you, a short book for the student.

Q. It would not have made it much bigger to put in a sentence indicating that stomach contents were also a reliable guide?

A. No sir: I appreciate that, but it is not intended to be a comprehensive work, of course.

Q. It should contain the things upon which there is greater consensus –

A. I think you may expect the next edition, sir, to contain some reference.

Q. You are going to change the next edition?
A. I think it is how one improves one's textbooks, by experience.
Q. When did you decide to change the next edition?
A. Each time I am writing I am learning and each case I have helps me to improve the next edition.
Q. I will throw this away and buy the next edition ...[28]

The striking feature of the cross-examination is that it essentially ignored the merits of what the pathologist was trying to say. Counsel declined to take the witness (and the court) into the underlying science. The trier of fact was no doubt struck by the inconsistency between what the pathologist had written in his book and what he was now ready to swear to, but would have been none the wiser as to which version was correct. Arthur Martin's possible distrust of a non-expert court to appreciate the underlying science may have been wise, although in the end the conviction of his client was affirmed.[29]

DOES THE TRIAL PROCESS WORK EFFECTIVELY WHERE SCIENCE IS INVOLVED?

In some cases, it is clear that the scientific issues have not been properly understood. Take as an example the 7,000 lawsuits pending against Merck in respect of its drug Vioxx. In the first of those lawsuits to go to trial, Merck was found liable by a jury to pay US$253 million to a single claimant. Merck said that the deceased did not at all fit the Vioxx risk profile because he had taken Vioxx for only a few weeks before his fatal heart attack, whereas Merck's scientific evidence suggested a danger threshold

28 Reproduced in Arthur Maloney, "Expert Evidence" in *Special Lectures of the Law Society of Upper Canada, Defending a Criminal Case* (Toronto: Richard De Boo, 1969).

29 Interestingly, in the August 2006 inquiry into the case, referred to the Court of Appeal for Ontario by the federal Justice Minister, experts were called who said that it was simply impossible to judge, by the state of digestion, the time from ingestion to death: Tracy Tyler, "Noted pathologist slams 'ludicrous' methodology" *The Toronto Star* (8 July 2006) A15. [*Editor's note*: The Court of Appeal ultimately admitted this evidence as fresh expert evidence, and concluded that it demonstrated that there was no scientific justification for the opinion given by the Crown's pathology expert at the original trial as to time of death. Largely on the basis of this evidence, the Court of Appeal held that the verdict of guilt could no longer stand, and entered an acquittal: *Truscott (Re)*, 2007 ONCA 575].

of about 18 months.[30] Merck brought experts to court in an effort to show that there was no reputable scientific basis to the plaintiff's claim. Not only was Merck's evidence not accepted, but the following was reported from a post-trial press conference held by the jurors:

> "Whenever Merck was up there it was like 'wah wah wah,'" juror John Ostrom told reporters. "We didn't know what the heck they were talking about."[31]

Whether or not Merck's case was valid, such an outcome is wholly unsatisfactory. In some measure this may be the fault of the trial process, which, some critics argue, includes the following weaknesses:

- the non-sequential presentation of evidence, which can be confusing (for example, skipping from issue to issue or back and forth between fact witnesses and expert opinion witnesses);
- evidence selected and arranged by parties in a way that may be self-serving but that is potentially misleading unless effectively countered;[32]
- counsel who may not have sufficient background and familiarity with a particular scientific area to cross-examine the opposing party's experts effectively;[33]
- "professional" hired-gun, incompetent or ideological witnesses who may deflect the debate from the real issues;

30 Ann Woolner, "A thin case against Vioxx" *Ottawa Citizen* (27 August 2005) B7.

31 *Ibid.*

32 In *R. v. F.(D.S.)* (1999), 23 C.R. (5th) 37 (Ont. C.A.), the court declined to set aside the conviction because, in part, at trial it was open to the defence to challenge the expert's general statements about the empirical or scientific support for her opinions and it failed to do so. In *R. v. Blanchard*, [1996] N.J. No. 319 at para. 6 (Nfld. C.A.) (QL), the court dismissed an appeal, stating that "in light of [the expert's] education, experience, research and extensive history in analysis of animals, which includes 160 appearances before courts in Ontario, the Maritimes and Newfoundland, it is difficult to see how the trial judge could do otherwise than admit the evidence in the absence of testimony on a *voir dire* supporting the contention of the defence that no such field of expertise exists."

33 In *R. v. D.D.*, [2000] 2 S.C.R. 275 at 300, the court stated that "expert evidence is highly resistant to effective cross-examination by counsel who are not experts in that field. In cases where there is no competing expert evidence, this will have the effect of depriving the jury of an effective framework within which to evaluate the merit of the evidence."

- cross-examination that can undermine trustworthy sources for reasons other than scientific validity, yet fail to discredit opposing testimony of less merit that is delivered with greater presentational skill; and
- some evidence that may be important from a *scientific* perspective may be excluded because of admissibility rulings, while other weak or controversial evidence may be admitted, depending on how the judge exercises the gatekeeper role.

The result of these weaknesses? Wah wah wah.

A REVISED APPROACH TO THE ADMISSION OF SCIENCE AND TECHNOLOGY EVIDENCE

Historically, the common law courts judged science by seeking to ascertain the prevailing consensus (if any) in the scientific community.[34] This came under criticism as the velocity of scientific advances accelerated. The courts were frequently faced with "novel science,"[35] where there was no opportunity for consensus to form about its validity or invalidity.

The consensus approach was rejected in the United States in 1993 in the *Daubert* case, where the U.S. Supreme Court held that *legal* admissibility should henceforth be based on *scientific* validity, not scientific *consensus*, writing: "In a case involving scientific evidence, *evidentiary reliability* will be based upon *scientific validity*."[36] The real issue is not what the experts say, how qualified they are to say it or whether a consensus has formed in the relevant scientific community, but whether the experts have established in their evidence a scientific basis for their testimony. The judge should take a more active gatekeeper role,

34 Under the consensus approach, the scientific principle on which the evidence is based must be "sufficiently established to have gained general acceptance in the particular field in which it belongs": *Frye v. United States*, 293 F. 1013 at 1014 (D.C. Cir. 1923) [*Frye*].

35 By "novel science" is meant "science at the frontiers of knowledge" where "theories are vulnerable," versus "textbook science," which is known with "great confidence"; see David Goodstein, "How Science Works" in *Reference Manual on Scientific Evidence*, *supra* note 8 at 79. The line between novelty and general acceptance is fuzzy – referred to in *Frye*, *ibid.* as the "twilight zone between the experimental and the demonstrable."

36 *Daubert v. Merrell Dow Pharmaceuticals*, 509 U.S. 579 at n. 9 (1993) (emphasis in original) [*Daubert*].

perhaps reflecting a lingering mistrust of juries who, under the *Daubert* approach, would never get to hear the evidence if the judge slammed shut the metaphorical gate.

The present position is this: scientific opinion, to be admissible before the jury (or the judge sitting alone), must be:

- necessary (that is, not within the usual understanding of non-experts);
- valid (the science measures what it is supposed to measure); and
- reliable (the result is reproducible).

The presumption is that to be scientific, a statement must be testable, that is, susceptible to evidence that could potentially show it to be false (if it is indeed false).[37] As a result, post-*Daubert*, the courts have found it harder to evaluate the validity of the science than pre-*Daubert*, when all they had to determine was whether a consensus did or did not exist.[38] The *Daubert* approach requires a level of scientific sophistication on the part of the judge that the earlier consensus approach did not.[39]

The *Daubert* test has gained acceptance in Canada, particularly when screening novel science, which is subjected to "special scrutiny to determine whether it meets a basic threshold of reliability."[40] In *R. v. J.-L.J.*,[41]

---

37 See Susan Haack, "Trial and Error: The Supreme Court's Philosophy of Science" (2005) 95: S1 *American Journal of Public Health* S66, reproduced in (2006) 41 *The International Society of Barristers Quarterly* 376 at 378.

38 At least one commentator says that *Daubert* "has produced a minefield clogged with '*Daubert* hearings' that are more lengthy, technical, and diffuse than anything that preceded them." See David Crump, "The Trouble with *Daubert-Kumho*: Reconsidering the Supreme Court's Philosophy of Science" (2003) 68 Mo. L. Rev. 1.

39 An expertise modestly disclaimed by some U.S. lower-court judges, including the lower-court judges in *Daubert* itself, when the case was returned to the courts in California. Kozinski J. observed: "Our responsibility, then, unless we badly misread the Supreme Court's opinion, is to resolve disputes among respected, well-credentialed scientists about matters squarely within their expertise, in areas where there is no scientific consensus as to what is and what is not 'good science,' and occasionally to reject such expert testimony because it was not 'derived by the scientific method.' Mindful of our position in the hierarchy of the federal judiciary, we take a deep breath and proceed with this heady task." See U.S. Court of Appeals for the Ninth Circuit following remand of *Daubert* by the Supreme Court: *Daubert v. Merrell Dow Pharmaceuticals*, 43 F.3d 1311 at 1316 (9th Cir. 1995).

40 *R. v. Mohan*, [1994] 2 S.C.R. 9 at 25.

41 [2000] 2 S.C.R. 600.

a prosecution for sexual abuse of children, the defence called an expert to testify that the accused had no disposition toward pedophilia. The Supreme Court of Canada explicitly accepted the four *Daubert* factors as "ones that could be helpful in evaluating the soundness of novel science." These are:

- whether the theory or technique can be and has been tested ("Scientific methodology today is based on generating hypotheses and testing them to see if they can be falsified; indeed, this methodology is what distinguishes science from other fields of human inquiry.");
- whether the theory or technique has been subjected to peer review and publication ("[S]ubmission to the scrutiny of the scientific community is a component of 'good science', in part because it increases the likelihood that substantive flaws in methodology will be detected.");
- the known or potential rate of error or the existence of standards; and
- whether the theory or technique has been generally accepted ("A 'reliability assessment does not require, although it does permit, explicit identification of a relevant scientific community and an express determination of a particular degree of acceptance within that community'" ... "Widespread acceptance can be an important factor in ruling particular evidence admissible, and 'a known technique which has been able to attract only minimal support within the community' ... may properly be viewed with skepticism."[42]).

Chief Justice Rehnquist, dissenting in *Daubert*, expressed skepticism about the new test. He thought it unlikely that the quality of a scientific proposition could ever be properly evaluated by a court that lacks the necessary background knowledge and expertise. In later cases, the U.S. Supreme Court has somewhat refined its approach.[43]

TESTING FOR "JUNK SCIENCE"

The courts have responded with varying degrees of enthusiasm to this new role, as have the experts, some of whom obviously believe that giving

42 *Ibid.* at para. 33.

43 *General Electric Co. v. Joiner*, 522 U.S. 136 (1997); *Kumho Tire Co. v. Carmichael*, 526 U.S. 137 (1999).

the judges too much disclosure about the methodology risks confusion. In *J.-L.J.* itself, for example, the accused was exposed to various suggestive photographs while his penis was attached to an instrument called a penile plethysmograph. His penile response was measured. Lack of any measurable response was equated with repugnance to sex with small boys. The legal question was whether this sort of test could be remotely helpful to the court in determining the guilt or innocence of the accused. The expert declined to share his data with the trial court. Here is the somewhat offensive explanation he provided:

> Listen, Your Honour, we have to understand that if we start – normally we do not submit the psychological tests in detail or the curves because at that point if we start calculating everything in centimetres or millimetres, we will be here all morning. Let's just say that this curve, properly analysed, demonstrates the following results, that there are no, according to how those curves are normally evaluated, there are no signs of deviant behaviour in him.[44]

Elsewhere, the expert explained why he had not produced for the court the data on which he based his opinion:

> Okay. But it is not normally produced because otherwise, it would be too complicated to produce all the details, there would be battles over the little details.[45]

The Quebec Court of Appeal had ordered a new trial on the basis that the trial judge ought to have admitted the evidence and left its weight to be assessed by the jury. The Supreme Court reversed the Court of Appeal decision and upheld the trial judge's ruling that the evidence was simply inadmissible because it had not been shown to be either relevant or reliable.[46]

---

44 *R. v. J.-L.J.*, *supra* note 41 at para. 57.

45 *Ibid.* As pointed out in *General Electric Co. v. Joiner*, *supra* note 43 at 146, "[C]onclusions and methodology are not entirely distinct from one another ... [N]othing in ... *Daubert* ... requires the ... court to admit opinion evidence which is connected to existing data only by the *ipse dixit* of the expert. A court may conclude that there is simply too great an analytical gap between the data and the opinion."

46 The top four problems identified by U.S. Federal judges: experts abandoning objectivity; excessive expense; questionable validity or reliability; and conflict among experts that defies reasoned assessment. See Carol Krafka et al., "Judge and Attorney Experiences, Practices and Concerns Regarding Expert Testimony in Federal Civil Trials" (2002) 8 Psychol. Pub. Pol'y & L. 309.

Penile plethysmography is a technique that is said to have some utility in measuring the success of treatment of known pedophiles, but has no track record in diagnosing pedophilia in the case of an individual who categorically denies any such orientation. In other words, the expert had overstepped the boundary of his admitted expertise.

In other cases, both the experts and the judge have taken each other seriously, as in the recent rerun of the 1925 Scopes "monkey trial" in Pennsylvania.[47] The parents of some school children challenged their local school board's directive to include "intelligent design" in the curriculum of a high school biology class as an alternative to Darwin's theory of evolution. The school board was overruled by the court on the basis that the theory of intelligent design "is grounded in theology not science" and has no place in a biology class. Intelligent design was found to be lacking in testability.

Honourable mention might also be made of the bizarre U.S. case of *Iowa v. Harrington*,[48] where the trial court was asked to admit novel scientific evidence of alleged brain fingerprinting. According to *The Globe and Mail*:

> For two decades, Terry Harrington protested his innocence from his Iowa prison cell, insisting that he had not shot and killed a retired police officer when he was 17 years old. Then he decided to try brain fingerprinting. It's a computerized mind-reading technique developed by Jerry Farwell, an American researcher and entrepreneur who says he can tell if the details of a crime scene are stored in a suspect's brain. If Mr. Harrington were innocent, the test would show that his brain did not recognize details about the murder, details the killer would know. "The brain never lies," Dr. Farwell says.
>
> In February 2003, a judge in Iowa accepted the results of the brain-fingerprinting test, the new testimony from a key prosecution witness and the suppressed police reports. The Iowa Supreme Court overturned his conviction, and ordered a new trial. By then, he had been in prison for 25 years. He was released on bail. In October, 2003, the charges were officially dropped. Mr. Harrington is suing the police.[49]

---

47 *Kitzmiller v. Dover Area School District*, 400 F.Supp.2d 707 (M.D. Pa. 2005).

48 *Iowa v. Harrington*, 659 N.W. 2d 509 (Iowa Sup. Ct. 2003).

49 Anne McIlroy, "Not guilty: 'The brain never lies'" *The Globe and Mail* (5 November 2005) F6.

The idea of brain fingerprinting has some intuitive attraction as a technique to record an involuntary response – much as a lie detector is supposed to do – but there is considerable doubt as to whether, at this stage of its development, the technique achieves what it is claimed to do and whether its results are reproducible.

DIFFICULTIES WITH THE GATEKEEPER FUNCTION

It must be admitted that many courts are continuing to have serious difficulties in digesting and evaluating scientific evidence, even rather crude scientific evidence. This is for both institutional and procedural reasons.[50] Institutionally, judges hesitate to exclude such evidence in a jury case for fear of usurping the fact-finding function of the jury. Procedurally, in a judge-alone case, there is always a temptation to let the evidence in, fully understood or not, and for the judge to leave it to the end of the trial to determine what weight, if any, it is to be given. Either way, the result can be an enormous waste of time and money and, in some cases, a miscarriage of justice.

In 2005, for example, the media were full of reports of another wrongful conviction based on the identification of an accused as a murderer by the novel science of barefoot morphology.[51] Mr. Dimitre Dimitrov, a Bulgarian immigrant living in Ottawa, had been convicted four years earlier of murdering his landlord, who was also Bulgarian, by beating him to death with a blunt instrument. There was some evidence of mutual hostility, but there was nothing to tie Dimitrov to the murder

---

50 See, for example, Sidney N. Lederman, "Judges as Gatekeepers: The Admissibility of Scientific Evidence Based on Novel Theories" in Joost Blom & Hélène Dumont, eds. *Science, Truth and Justice – Canadian Institute for the Administration of Justice* (Montréal: Les Éditions Thémis, 2000) 217. Justice Lederman suggests that Canadian courts should adopt American-style "*Daubert* hearings" that would require experts to file comprehensive reports and that would permit discovery of the experts. The application of the *Mohan* criteria already requires a *voir dire*, which can become quite lengthy in some cases. Ideally, a *Mohan* hearing should be done before the trial is underway, to give a judge more time to rule on the admissibility of the preferred testimony. This would also assist counsel, who would know in advance whether their expert will be allowed to testify. Pre-trial discoveries or hearings would require advance disclosure by counsel, including disclosure of the methodology on which the expert anchors his or her conclusions.

51 *R. v. Dimitrov* (2003), 68 O.R. (3d) 641 (C.A.) [*Dimitrov*].

except, according to the prosecution, a pair of boots that were covered with bloodstains which the Crown alleged belonged to the victim. There were no eyewitnesses. The onus was on the prosecution to connect the boots to the accused. RCMP Sergeant Robert Kennedy testified that the impressions people's feet leave on the insoles of footwear are quite distinct and that by applying techniques of barefoot morphology he could say that Dimitrov was "likely" the usual wearer of the boots.[52]

Sgt. Kennedy is an expert in footprint identification. He could opine whether a running shoe imprint in the mud beside a body was consistent with the type of running shoe worn on the day in question by an accused. But here there was none of that; there was only a bloodstained boot. However, Sgt. Kennedy had also developed a sideline expertise trying to identify suspects by the imprint left by feet *inside* shoes or boots, specifically the pattern left by the weight-bearing portions of the bare foot on the insole.[53] The main proponent of barefoot morphology in Canada and the United Sates is Sgt. Kennedy himself.

---

52 "Barefoot morphology" theory is a "novel science" that forms part of an explosion of identification techniques. In *People v. Davis*, 304 Ill.App.3d 427 (1999), a man was convicted of first-degree murder where the only evidence connecting him to the scene of the crime was a set of lip prints on a roll of duct tape found nearby. A forensic specialist testified that the same procedures used in the comparison of fingerprints could apply to "lip prints," which, he said, are just as individualized as fingerprints. The man was convicted. His appeal was dismissed, notwithstanding the fact that the trial judge failed to even hold a "gatekeeper" hearing as required by Illinois law. The Illinois Court of Appeal concluded at 437–438 that "the method they employed to identify the lip print was the same as the well-accepted method of fingerprint identification which is accepted as a means of identification by the forensic science community ... Consequently we find that the method employed to identify lip prints, a side-by-side comparison, is reliable." The court appeared to be satisfied by the fact that the expert who performed the analysis was "unaware of any dissent in the field regarding the methodology used to make a positive identification lip print." Convincing? Similarly, in another case, a man was convicted on the basis of "ear print" identification, although the conviction was overturned on appeal: *State v. Kunze*, 112 Wash. App. 1023 (2002).

53 In Canada, evidence of "barefoot morphology" was accepted in *R. v. Légère* (1994), 156 N.B.R. (2d) 321 (C.A.), but rejected in *R. v. Sood*, [1997] O.J. No. 5417 (Gen. Div.). Sgt. Kennedy has also testified in some American cases: *State (South Carolina) v. Jones*, 541 S.E.2d 813 at 818–819 (S.C. 2001) and *State (North Carolina) v. Berry*, 546 S.E.2d 145 (N.C. 2001).

The Ontario Court of Appeal concluded in 2003 that Sgt. Kennedy should have been stopped at "the gateway" by the trial judge.[54] His evidence of "barefoot morphology" failed to meet any of the criteria set out in *Daubert* and *R. v. J.-L.J.*: there was no serious test of Sgt. Kennedy's hypothesis, and as such there was no opportunity for peer review and no error rate could be established. The court therefore set aside Dimitrov's original conviction on the basis that the trial judge had not performed a proper gatekeeper role. At the retrial in 2006, Dimitrov was readily acquitted.

WHAT IS TO BE DONE?

There are many kinds of science, and courts may therefore have to develop different approaches to gatekeeping, depending on the type of science or technology at issue.[55] Some areas of claimed expertise are more easily validated and reproduced than others. DNA evidence methodologies, for example, lend themselves more easily to testing, critique and the generation of error rates than do theories in the "softer" sciences, such as psychology. Nonetheless, there are a number of ways to try to help non-scientists evaluate science to the extent necessary to resolve a particular dispute. Among them are judicial education, judicial recruitment and modification of the adversarial system.

JUDICIAL EDUCATION

Much greater effort on both the general and particularized education of judges and lawyers is overdue. (This may not help jurors, but it is the judge who acts as the gatekeeper.) The National Judicial Institute has

54 *Dimitrov, supra* note 51. In setting aside Dimitrov's original conviction, the court said the trial judge had not performed a proper gatekeeper role (at paras. 55–56): "In our view, the slight probative value of Sergeant Kennedy's evidence was outweighed by its prejudicial effect. The risk that the jury might be over-awed by Sergeant Kennedy's expertise was a real one in this case. The evidence occupied a day and was augmented by diagrams, a lengthy discussion of the study of barefoot analysis and technical language about anatomy and laboratory procedures … In light of the significant issues as to reliability of the evidence, its lack of logical relevance and the risk of distortion in the fact-finding process, the trial judge erred in principle in admitting Sergeant Kennedy's evidence."

55 Michelle M. Mello & Troyen A. Brennan, "Demystifying the Law/Science Disconnect" (2001) 26 J. Health Pol. 429.

taken the lead to bring groups of Canadian judges together to explore scientific concepts and subjects that may give rise to litigation. On a more specialized level, the Einstein Institute for Science, Health & the Courts (EINSHAC), a Washington-based non-governmental organization, has held many seminars for judges in genetics and biotechnology.[56] By attending these seminars, judges gain some familiarity with the jargon and methodology in a setting less stressful than that of a trial. Of course, judges would be better off still if their education had started at a younger age, but scientific legal education has traditionally been a matter largely neglected in our law schools. Recently, this shows signs of improvement.[57] At Dalhousie, there is now a course on law and technology that covers genetic modifications in plant and animal materials for food and agriculture, developments in telecommunications, privacy concerns, access to information, ethics in technology and so on. The Université de Montréal has a course dealing specifically with "*la preuve scientifique au soutien des recours civiles et pénaux.*" These courses try to teach law students how to manage scientific proof. Other universities are also beginning to get their students into this area.[58]

JUDICIAL RECRUITMENT

Traditionally, little effort has been made in Canada to recruit judges with a scientific or engineering background. This is true even of the

56 Some critics are concerned that a little knowledge is a dangerous thing. Professor Susan Haack is "a little worried about the danger of giving judges the false impression that they *are* qualified to make subtle scientific determinations, when it is hardly realistic to expect that a few hours in a science seminar will transform judges into scientists competent to make subtle and sophisticated scientific judgments – any more than a few hours in a legal seminar could transform scientists into judges competent to make subtle and sophisticated legal determinations": *supra* note 37 at 388.

57 Surveyed 21 July 2006.

58 For example, McGill University offers a course on medical liability, the University of Ottawa has a course on forensic science, Osgoode Hall has a medical/legal seminar that covers expert scientific witness testimony and basic medical information, UBC has a quantitative methods in law course, l'Université de Sherbrooke has a course on molecular biology and the law and the University of Windsor has a law and medicine class.

Federal Court, where most intellectual property litigation takes place.[59] This lacuna should be addressed. In the *Lubrizol v. Imperial Oil* litigation mentioned earlier, the German Patent Court, which seems to be composed entirely of expert scientists, had invalidated Lubrizol's Meinhardt patent, on which its case in Canada depended, as "obvious" in light of the prior science. The trial judge in our Federal Court disagreed. In an era in which intellectual property is global, it is unfortunate to have inconsistent pronouncements of this sort. Where our judges differ from foreign courts on matters of science and technology, it is important that commercial litigants are satisfied that the courts in both jurisdictions, despite their differences, have understood and properly weighed the conflicting scientific perspectives.

MODIFICATION OF THE ADVERSARIAL SYSTEM

Assuming that the judge does take his or her role as the evidential gatekeeper seriously, whether presiding with a jury or alone, the present trial system still has too many systemic problems that get in the way of the court truly understanding the underlying science and technology.[60]

In the first place, our present system contemplates that a case must be resolved on the evidence heard in the courtroom. Yet the courtroom, with all its formalities and evidentiary rules, is a poor schoolhouse, and

59 This seems to also be the case in the United States, where a judge put it this way: "Judges, trial and appellate, generally are not recruited from within the ranks of behavioral research scientists. They tend to have little formal, post-secondary, science education ... except as provided in continuing judicial education programs. They tend to have no particular training in statistical analysis as it relates to scientific research. In short, they tend to be scientifically ignorant, which means they are not acquainted with, let alone conversant with, scientific practice or language." See Gold, *supra* note 7 at 19, citing Alan G. Gless, "Some Post-*Daubert* Trial Tribulations of a Simple Country Judge: Behavioural Science in Trial Courts" (1995) 13 Behav. Sci. & L. 261 at 262–263.

60 In Alberta, the *Rules of Court Project* is concerned with such procedural matters as efficiency and the cost of expert evidence, but some of the proposed reforms may have a secondary benefit of tempering some of the excesses of the adversary system by providing for court-appointed experts, referees or advisers. See Tania M. Bubela, "Expert Evidence: The Ethical Responsibility of the Legal Profession" (2004) 41 Alta. L. Rev. 853.

duelling experts may make bad teachers.[61] Courts are, however, the masters of their own procedure and have the flexibility to modify to their own advantage the framework within which experts testify. Why, for example, in a case that requires a judge to grapple with serious scientific evidence, can the parties not arrange for an out-of-court seminar on the basic science specific to the dispute? This was done for a panel of judges in the House of Lords in *Kirin-Amgen Inc. v. Hoechst Marion Roussel Ltd.*,[62] a patent case, in which it was explained at paragraph 135 of the decision:

> [T]he work which Professor Yudkin did by means of carefully prepared seminars enabled all those involved to concentrate on the issues of law in the appeal without having to spend a good deal of extra time in the course of the hearing on learning about the technology. This had the result of shortening the length of time that it was necessary to devote to the hearing by several days. It was at Lord Hoffman's suggestion in the course of a preliminary hearing that this was done as there was no dispute about the technology. I suggest that it is a course which might usefully be adopted in the future in cases of this kind, where the technology is complex and undisputed and the parties are willing to consent to it.

As previously stated, the case of *Lubrizol v. Imperial Oil* involved patent claims to certain heavy-molecular-weight dispersants in automotive

61 "Developments in the Law: Confronting the New Challenge of Scientific Evidence" (1994) 108 Harv. L. Rev. 1481 at 1586. See also Paul Michell & Renue Mandhane, "The Uncertain Duty of the Expert Witness" (2005) 42 Alta. L. Rev. 635 on the possibility of court-imposed codes of conduct for experts. In Australia and some other common law jurisdictions, there is a move towards emphasizing the duty of an expert to provide the court with complete, objective and non-partisan information; to this end, some courts have developed guidelines and codes of conduct that must be signed by the expert. In the United States, the American Medical Association and the American Psychological Association have professional responsibilities and ethics explicitly incorporated in their respective codes of conduct for members involved in litigation. See also United Kingdom, *Civil Procedure Rules*, r. 35.7; Australia, *Uniform Civil Procedure Rules 2005* (N.S.W.) Sch. 7, r. 31.23 and r. 31.30; Australia, *Uniform Civil Procedure Rules 1999* (Qld) r. 426; and New Zealand, High Court Rules (N.Z.), r. 330A. See generally Bubela, *ibid.* at para. 28; and Peter Wardle & Danny Cappe, "Reforming Ontario's Expert Evidence Rules" (paper presented to Into the Future: The Agenda for Civil Justice Reform, April 2006), online: Canadian Forum on Civil Justice <http://www.cfcj-fcjc.org/IntoTheFuture-VersLeFutur/advocatesPapers.htm>.

62 [2005] 1 All E.R. 667.

lubricating oils. This required such esoteric exercises as comparing *number*-average molecular weights with *weight*-average molecular weights of certain components. The scientific concepts and definitions were not contested, only their application. It would have been desirable, I think, to have locked the judges alone in a room, with a couple of experts appointed and paid for by the parties, to go over the common ground informally. In that setting, the judges could have engaged themselves in an open discussion and asked questions that no doubt they would have hesitated to ask in court, where judges are expected to sit Madame Tussaud–like, listening passively to what they are being told, often without knowing where the common ground ends and the controversy begins.

Prior to a trial, better use could also be made of case management.[63] A judge who is assigned early in a "science" case to deal with all interlocutory issues may acquire a decent understanding over time of the underlying science. This may also provide an early springboard to discuss issues about the presentation of technical evidence at trial. At present, in many Canadian jurisdictions, interlocutory matters in the same case may be assigned to different judges according to the vagaries of the judicial calendar, and the trial judge may have no prior exposure to the issues until the case opens. Judging from the reaction of Muldoon J. in the Bounce case, that initial *dévoilement* can be an appalling experience for everyone concerned.

Once the hearing begins, consideration might be given to a court-appointed expert nominated by the parties to sit with the judge or jurors to respond to their questions within the relevant field of expertise. In some cases, it may be appropriate for the court to take the initiative in appointing its own scientific *amicus curiae* to provide assistance in evaluating the scientific evidence, even without the consent of the parties.[64] This is the tradition in some European legal systems and is the practice

63 For example, a case management judge could impose trial segmentation to separate causation, liability and damages phases. This might help address problems caused by technological inexperience of the decision makers. It would also limit the number of issues that a judge or jury must consider in a single phase of the trial. The downside is that it may also result in a measure of duplication and repetition.

64 See, for example, Federal Rule 706 in the United States, and Order 34 of the Australian Federal Court Rules, *Statutory Rules 1979 No. 140* made under the *Federal Court of Australia Act 1976*, which provides:

"2. Appointments

in British admiralty courts[65] (which have a civil law genesis) as well as our own Federal Court sitting in admiralty.[66] Care must be taken, of course, to ensure that the litigants are not ambushed by the advice given by the assessors and that the principles of natural justice are observed.[67] In England, there is a rule of practice permitting the Court of Appeal to appoint its own scientific adviser in a patent appeal.[68]

As to the expert evidence presented by the parties, the rules of procedure should be modified to require experts to exchange reports and meet face-to-face for an unmediated discussion before trial. Evidence of the results of scientific experiments done specifically for the trial should be excluded unless witnessed by the other side. The court should be

---

(1) If a question for an expert witness arises in a proceeding, the Court may, at any stage of the proceeding:

(a) appoint an expert as court expert to inquire into and report upon the question;
(b) authorize the court expert to inquire into and report upon any facts relevant to the inquiry and report on the question;
(c) direct the court expert to make a further or supplemental report or inquiry and report; and
(d) give such instructions as the court thinks fit relating to any inquiry or report of the court expert. ...

(3) Instructions pursuant to paragraph (1)(d) may include provision concerning any experiment or test for the purposes of any inquiry or report of a court expert."

65 See, for example, *The "British Resource"* (1942), 73 Li. L. Rep. 143 (H.L.) at 144–145: "One could understand the difficulty of a layman appreciating that on a dark night ships could be seen at a distance sufficiently great to enable [the collision] to be avoided. Therefore it was particularly a matter for expert opinion, and in this case our nautical assessors had advised that the ships should have seen each other."

66 *Federal Court of Canada Rules*, S.O.R./98-106, Rule 56, "Role of Assessor."

67 See *Porto Seguro Companhia De Seguros Gerais v. Belcan S.A.*, [1997] 3 S.C.R. 1278, McLachlin J. at para. 40: "I conclude that the old admiralty rule appointing assessors to assist the judge in making findings of fault to the exclusion of expert evidence should be revised. First, assessors should be permitted to assist judges in understanding technical evidence. Second, assessors may go further and advise the judge on matters of fact in dispute between the parties, but only on condition of disclosure and a right of response sufficient to comply with the requirements of natural justice."

68 See *Supreme Court Act 1981* (U.K.), ss. 54 and 76, and *CPR Civil Procedure Rules*, r. 35.15. See also *Halliburton Energy Services Inc. v. Smith International (North Sea) Ltd.*, [2006] EWCA Civ. 1599 (Eng. C.A.), citing in part *Porto Seguro, ibid.* at paras. 18–20.

able to order opposing experts to produce a joint report that defines key terms as well as the points of agreement and disagreement. Moreover, the court should be able to require opposing experts to testify on the same panel and be subject to questioning in each other's presence, with the right to question each other in the presence of the trier of fact. The procedure whereby opposing experts testify together on the same panel is regularly used in continental legal systems as well as by administrative agencies in Canada, such as the National Energy Board, and is employed with success in the Federal Court of Australia (where it is known as the "Australian hot pot").[69] Experts testifying in the presence of one another are likely to be more measured and complete in their pronouncements, knowing that an exaggeration or errors will be pounced upon instantly by a learned colleague, rather than being argued about days later, perhaps by unlearned opposing counsel.

Finally, the parties to these complex cases have a legitimate expectation that the reasons for judgment (where the case is tried without a jury) will make it clear the judge has heard and understood the technical aspects of the case. Although in Canada jurors cannot be asked about their deliberations (therefore no "wah wah wah"), a case heard by a judge alone should result in a decision that traces the judge's pathway through the scientific evidence to the result. In this way, the trial judge establishes a better record for review by the appeal court and provides assurance to the parties as well as the broader public that the issues have been properly addressed. Appeal courts should be prepared to consider the rejection of boilerplate reasons from a trial judge that fail to come to grips with the scientific debate underlying the issues being litigated.[70]

CONCLUSION

Despite the conciliatory (if somewhat superior) tone adopted by the English judge over 450 years ago ("we do not despise all other sciences but our own, but we approve of them and encourage them"[71]), it must be said

69 See Rule 3 of Order 34A of the Australian Federal Court Rules.

70 This approach is consistent with what the Supreme Court has set out in *R. v. Sheppard*, [2002] 1 S.C.R. 869, and *R. v. Braich*, [2002] 1 S.C.R. 903, for determining the adequacy of reasons for appellate review. The principle is that the reasons must be sufficient for an appellate court to determine the correctness of the trial decision.

71 *Buckley, supra* note 1.

that judicial progress in matching reality to these fine words has been slow. Our courts may approve and encourage other sciences, but the real question is whether or not we adequately understand the science; and if not, are we doing enough to make our courts more "science friendly"? Procedures designed to deal with garden-variety legal disputes have often been found inadequate, if not actually counter-productive, with respect to cases involving science and technology. The legitimacy of a court's judgment in such cases is tied to the rigour of its fact-finding and to the ability of the judge or juror to evaluate the expertise involved. Reforms have been implemented, but more needs to be done if we are to be ready when Schroedinger's cat arrives on the courthouse steps.

Cross-examining the opposing expert

JOHN McLEISH

IN ALMOST EVERY cross-examination of an opposing expert, there are points to be scored. Cross-examining an opposing expert is an opportunity to tell your client's story, gain admissions from the opposing expert, emphasize the strengths in your client's case and expose weaknesses in your opponent's case. It is a rare situation where an opposing expert cannot be used to achieve some of these objectives. In preparing your cross-examination, you will need to define your goals clearly and know what it is that you want to achieve with the cross-examination.

THE AMMUNITION YOU REQUIRE

The following are the key documents that you can have available to you to provide ammunition to accomplish your goals as cross-examiner:

1. The expert's resumé.
2. The report.
3. Reports and statements of other experts in the case.
4. The foundation documents the expert reviewed.
5. The foundation documents that were not sent to the expert and that he or she did not review.
6. Articles and texts authored by the expert.
7. Authoritative literature in the field.

8. Prior transcripts of the expert in other cases.

This ammunition is material that can be generated in every case with the appropriate amount of work.

THE "DO'S" OF CROSS-EXAMINATION

The general rules of cross-examination apply to the cross-examination of an opposing expert witness. Some of the "do's" of cross-examination are as follows:

1. Cross-examine softly.
2. Start and close strongly.
3. Ask leading questions.
4. Ask short questions.
5. Use simple words.
6. Use headlines.
7. Ask for facts, not evaluations or opinions.
8. Get one fact straight at a time.

Cross-examine softly

You may know the opposing expert by reputation and think he or she is a biased, side-that-hires-the-expert "hack." However, the jury certainly does not know this and the judge likely will not. If on cross-examination you treat this witness on the basis of the way you feel, you will be the loser. Remember, you are trying to sell one version of the facts, while your opponent is attempting to sell another version. Who is the jury going to buy from – the person who tries to sell in a loud, boisterous, overly aggressive fashion, or the person who tries to sell quietly? If you cross-examine softly, a number of things happen: you build credibility and trustworthiness with the jury, the witness thinks that the cross-examiner is not so bad after all and becomes more co-operative, and the cross-examiner's opponent does not get edgy and tense and interrupt you constantly.

Start and close strongly

The first engagement with a witness can be the most important one. There are going to be times when you will start with a constructive cross-examination, that is, a cross-examination to obtain helpful admissions, contribute to the theory of your case or corroborate the favourable testimony of other witnesses. At other times you will want to unnerve the witness at the beginning of the cross-examination. No matter what initial approach you take, you want the initial points to be those on which you are confident of success.

The situations in which you may want to start with a constructive cross-examination are those in which the witness possesses evidence helpful to your case. You will want to obtain helpful admissions from the witness before you think about attempting to unnerve the witness and at the same time aggravate him or her.

It is difficult to end most cross-examinations on a dramatic note. You do not, however, want to let the cross-examination dissipate and lose all the gains you made during the cross-examination. Accordingly, if you have just made a strong point and have only several minor points left to cover in your notes, it is likely better to forget about the minor points and sit down.

Ask leading questions

The way to follow this rule is to remember that cross-examination is not designed to obtain information. On the contrary – cross-examination is not for the witness, but for you. It is your opportunity to present your side of the case, punctuated by the witness's reluctant agreement that what you say is true. If you break this rule by asking for information, two important things happen: you lose a measure of control with the witness, and you send a message to the jury that the witness is reliable. Ask for information if you must, but understand the potential cost. A leading question is a question that can be answered "yes" or "no." However, the unconscious mind cannot hear or respond to negatives. If someone says, "Do not think of pink elephants," the first thing one thinks about is pink elephants. If one of the goals of your cross-examination is to create an impression of agreement, bearing in mind that the unconscious mind cannot recognize or deal with negatives, you should try to get "yes" answers and not "no" answers. This is difficult to do when you are attacking the foundation of the expert's report and asking questions about information he or she did not have when preparing the report. Many of these questions start with "Did you know..."

Just as there is a crutch for asking non-leading questions in chief, there is a crutch to asking leading questions such that the answer will be "yes" rather than "no." Try to avoid these types of questions if you can, but if you must, use introductions to the sentence such as "Isn't it true ..." and tag endings such as "...isn't that correct?"

Sometimes, however, following the leading-question rule can hamper a cross-examination. If you want to show that a witness is a braggart or is giving carefully rehearsed testimony, remember that leading questions do not let you expose the witness.

Ask short questions

First, short questions are easy to understand. Second, aside from their content, long questions invite long answers. For example, in the cross-examination of a defence orthopaedic surgeon, say:

Q. You are an orthopaedic surgeon?
Q. You no longer have operating room privileges at the Victoria General?
Q. Or any other hospital?
Q. You have not had operating privileges at any hospital for five years?
Q. You now do only medical/legal consulting?
Q. Almost exclusively for insurance companies and lawyers representing defendants?

Instead of:

Q. Doctor Simms, I put it to you that you are an orthopaedic surgeon, who no longer has operating privileges at the Victoria General Hospital or any other hospital, and you haven't had such privileges for five years and that now most of your time is doing defence assessments for insurance companies and defence lawyers?

Again, there is a time to break this rule. One situation in which the question might be somewhat lengthy occurs when you are coming to the end of a section of cross-examination. An effective way to finish an area of cross-examination is to sum up the important parts of the expert's evidence without really caring what the answer is. You will see several examples of this approach in this article.

Use simple words

Law school seems to ruin the way most of us speak. This may be because we read cases that are over 100 years old and adapt to the language in the cases. Or it may be that when we graduate from law school, we think we have to speak in the way we think that lawyers should speak. Whatever the reason, it is a mistake. If at the start of an examination for discovery your first question is "Would you state your name for the record please" instead of "What is your name," and follow this with your second question, "And where do you at present reside?" rather than "Where do you live?" or "What is your address?" you have some work to do. Plain language goes hand in hand with short questions that help orient the jury and control the witness. Some examples of words to avoid and of words to use in their place appear in the following list.

Avoid	*Use*
prior to	before
aforementioned	previously mentioned
by reason of	because
cease	stop
in lieu of	instead
on or before	on
said	the
commence	begin, start
endeavour	try
during the course of	during
proceed	go, go ahead
obtain	get
utilize	use

Use headlines

Using topic sentences as verbal headlines to introduce new subjects is a valuable technique. For example, in cross-examining an orthopaedic surgeon, you can state the following: "Now I am going to ask you about the physical examination you conducted." The topic sentence is not a question. It requires no response; it simply announces a subject. It is permissible because it gives meaning to the questions that follow. Use a new headline every time you change subjects. One of the advantages of headlines is that you can frame them to suit the case and the mood of the examination. For example, another way of announcing questions about the physical examination is as follows: "As part of the medical assessment you performed for the defence, you conducted a physical examination. I am now going to ask you some questions about that examination."

Headlines orient the judge and jury and help everyone follow your questions. They also tend to keep witnesses from being nonresponsive and from changing the subject.

Get one fact at a time

You are not permitted to ask multiple or double-barrelled questions on either examination-in-chief or cross-examination. Take, for example, the question "On February 22, 2008, you conducted a defence medical assessment, which lasted 60 minutes, and as part of that assessment you conducted a physical examination, which lasted approximately five minutes?" If you break the question down into its components, your cross-examination becomes simple and powerful.

Q. You conducted a defence medical assessment?
A. *Yes.*
Q. On February 22, 2008?
A. *Yes.*
Q. That is more than a year ago?
A. *Yes.*
Q. The total examination took approximately 60 minutes?
A. *Yes.*
Q. Much of that 60 minutes was used to get biographical information from Mrs. Appelby, such as her birth date and whether she was married and had children?
A. *Yes.*
Q. More time was taken up getting information regarding her activity level?
A. *Yes.*
Q. Your assessment included a physical examination?
A. *Yes.*
Q. The physical examination took approximately five minutes?
A. *No. It took longer than that.*
Q. No more than ten minutes?
A. *That is probably closer.*

Occasionally there is a time to break the simple-question-one-fact-at-a-time rule, and that is when you want to summarize a series of helpful answers:

Q. Doctor, so that we are clear, your opinion is based on a physical examination that took place three years after the collision, more than a year ago and lasted no more than ten minutes?
A. *That's right.*

THE "DON'TS" OF CROSS-EXAMINATION

There are certain types of cross-examination we want to avoid. Some of the "don'ts" of conducting a cross-examination appear below.

Avoid introductions and tag endings[1]
Cross-examination is better paced, and the witness is better controlled, if the following words and phrases are avoided:

- *Introductions*
  - » Let me ask you this question ...
  - » Isn't is a fact that ...
  - » It is true, is it not ...
  - » In fact ...
  - » Didn't you testify that ...
  - » Am I correct in assuming that ...
  - » Would you tell the judge and jury ...
  - » Would you tell us, please ...
  - » I put it to you ...
  - » I suggest ...
- *Tag Endings*
  - » ... isn't that true?
  - » ... isn't that correct?
  - » ... right?

These introductions and tag endings might seem to make leading questions stronger, perhaps even more leading. But in fact, the reverse is true. Extra words like these just make questions longer. They blunt the force of the question and provide the witness with more time to think, which makes it easier for him or her to squirm out from underneath the

1 This is taken from J.W. McElhaney, *McElhaney's Litigation* (Chicago: American Bar Association, 1995) at 117.

question. Do not respond to a witness by answering "Okay." You may only mean that you have heard and understood the response, but the jury may think you accept that what the witness said is true. There are two situations in which to break the rule against introductions and endings. First, you can use an occasional introductory phrase for emphasis: "Dr. Cameron, this is an important question ... " Second, you can use a tag ending to prod the witness into an answer if he or she does not respond promptly. However, be sparing.

Do not wing it

Do not "wing it" with pointless cross-examination. If you receive a good answer, hold it, never go back to it and do not disturb it in any way.

Do not be offensive

Do not prejudice the judge or jury against your client by demonstrating a quick temper, demonstrating an offensive personality or using seemingly unfair tactics.

Do not be sarcastic

Do not ridicule or be sarcastic with a witness, or treat every witness as a perjurer, unless there are facts to substantiate that the witness is dishonest.

Do not misrepresent

Do not misrepresent the facts or use false insinuations or innuendos.

Do not argue

Do not argue with a witness. It is usually a sign that the cross-examiner is receiving damaging answers and knows that he or she is receiving damaging answers.

Do not become angry

Do not become angry, except when, as a tactical and strategic matter, righteous indignation is appropriate. Anger, real or assumed, kindles anger. A cross-examiner accomplishes much more with a difficult witness through a tone of friendliness rather than with a threatening, reproachful voice. Although I never saw him perform, I understand that when former Chief Justice of Ontario Charles Dubin was cross-examining, he treated each witness as a fair, honest person. If the person appeared badly, however, Dubin would demolish him or her – but he would do it with the air of a surgeon performing a disagreeable amputation, and as if he were profoundly sorry for the necessity. If you can be nice, gentle and dignified, the jurors will never bear any resentment towards you. You will go a long way towards establishing credibility, trustworthiness and sincerity, all of which are so crucial in winning a lawsuit.

Do not ask "Why?"

Do not ask the question "Why?" unless you do not care what the answer is.

Do not ask one question too many[2]

Edward Bennett Williams, the great American trial counsel who began his career on the staff of a Washington streetcar company because the company had many accidents and he wanted to get into court, learned this lesson early and well. A streetcar had hit and killed an old man. The old man was a well-known alcoholic who had spent almost his entire life sitting on the curb drinking cheap wine. At the time he was struck, the old man was staggering and drunk and was at least partially at fault. The defence had a witness who was half a block away but who did not see exactly what happened.

The witness did, however, see the streetcar hit the old man and did see the old man drop to the street. He then observed a middle- aged alcoholic, who was the son of the victim and who had also been sitting on the curb drinking cheap wine, proceed to the place where his father was lying after he had been struck. The independent witness saw the middle-aged alcoholic lean over the body, do something and then walk away. The witness thought the middle-aged alcoholic must have taken a whisky bottle from the victim. That is the answer Edward Bennett Williams, who was cross-examining the son, wanted. That was the point of the cross-examination.

Q. You were sitting on the curb before the accident?
A. *Yes.*
Q. Fifteen feet from where your father was hit?
A. *Yes.*

2 This anecdote is from J. Porter, *Cross-Examination Techniques* (Toronto: Law Society of Upper Canada, 1989) at 12, quoting I. Younger, *Advocacy Symposium* (Toronto: Canadian Bar Association, 1982) at 242.

Q. What happened when you saw your father hit?
A. *I went right to his body.*
Q. Were you the first person to get to his body?
A. *Yes.*
Q. And did you have a couple of seconds alone with his body?
A. *Yes.*
Q. You just listen to me and answer "yes" or "no."
A. *Yes, sir.*
Q. You bent over your father's body, didn't you?
A. *Yes.*
Q. And you did something, didn't you?
A. *Yes.*
Q. And then you stood up and walked away?
A. *Yes.*

At this point, Williams had enough. He should have stopped. But he expected too much from the cross-examination. He thought he could get more from it than he should have, so he continued:

Q. Isn't it a fact that when you bent over your father's body, what you did was take the whisky bottle out of his pocket?
A. *No, Sir.*

Williams did not know the answer and should have sat down at this point. Perhaps opposing counsel would not have rectified the answer in re-examination. If opposing counsel had not interviewed the son that carefully, he or she might not have known the answer. Even Edward Bennett Williams, the great cross-examiner, did not stop:

Q. All right, Mr. Witness, you tell the ladies and gentlemen of the jury just what you did when you leaned over the body.
A. *Well, Mr. Williams, he may have been a drunken old bum to you, but he was my father, and what I did, when I leaned over his body, was kiss him goodbye.*

Ask no question to which you do not know the answer

Cross-examination is not the time to be curious. It is not the time to learn information you do not already know. Accordingly, most of the time a cross-examiner should never ask a question to which he or she does not know the answer. There are, however, several reasons why this rule should not be considered absolute. First, the question may be far more important than the answer, and you may not really care what the answer is. For example, a defence neurologist may be taking an extreme position that notwithstanding the plaintiff suffers periodic dizzy spells, he can still go back to work as a pipe fitter, even though it involves working at great heights on small platforms. You may want to ask as your last question, for rhetorical effect, something like the one that follows. Although the question breaks many of the rules of cross-examination, it is a nice way to end the cross-examination of a witness whose evidence defies common sense and who is obviously being an advocate for the defence.

> Q. Doctor, you want these members of the jury to believe that notwithstanding the fact that Adam Scott suffers from periodic dizzy spells, and notwithstanding the fact that he works at great heights on platforms, and notwithstanding the fact that if he has a dizzy spell while working on one of these platforms he could fall and kill himself, he should still go back to work as a pipe fitter? Is that what you want this jury to believe?

A second situation in which you may ask a question without knowing the answer is if you feel that the odds favour your getting the answer you want and you are prepared to take the chance. Before doing so, however, you must weigh the potential gain from the answer you want against the potential harm of getting the wrong answer, and then decide whether to ask the question.

Do not nitpick

Do not harp on minor inconsistencies, as the jurors will understand that people can make errors.

CONTROLLING THE WITNESS

Every cross-examiner frequently encounters witnesses who are evasive or argumentative or who answer a question other than the one you are asking. Controlling a witness is one of the most difficult aspects of cross-examination – especially controlling an expert witness who has been advised by the lawyer who hired him or her not to answer "yes" or "no" and who is skilful enough to make speeches without sounding like an advocate for the side who hired him or her. For example, in the cross-examination of a defence neurologist:

Q. Dr. Cameron, did the plaintiff (in actual fact, you would not say plaintiff, but use the plaintiff's name) tell you he suffered from headaches?

A. *Yes, the plaintiff did tell me this, but in my view, the headaches were not serious, could easily be controlled by medication and would probably disappear in about three months.*

When a witness is trying to explain an answer, some lawyers will try to cut off the witness by saying "Thank you" or "You have answered my question" or "Just answer the question" or "Your Honour, would you instruct the witness to give only responsive answers?" In the last scenario, the chances are almost 100 per cent that the judge will allow the witness to answer.

Trying to cut off the witness draws a lot of attention to the answer you do not like, especially if you succeed in cutting it off. On re-examination your opponent will say, "Mr. McLeish did not let you answer this question, so let me. Why is it that you think the plaintiff's headaches will disappear in three months' time?" Would you rather hear an answer on cross-examination, when you can deal with it, or on re-examination, when there is nothing you can do?

Remember that in most cases the jury is rooting for the witness, not the lawyer. The jury is looking for a reason to dislike or mistrust the lawyer. Even though you may do a technically perfect cross-examination that follows all of the rules, you can alienate the jury by reinforcing the lawyer stereotype. The short, leading questions and the refusal to let the witness explain anything can seem terribly unfair. A lawyer has to convince the jury that he is a decent person and that he is scrupulously fair. One of the ways you help convince the jury of this is by handling witnesses with great courtesy. Jurors think lawyers are conceited people. You have to deflect that. You cannot do so by rudely trying to cut off a witness's answer.

Controlling a witness is one of the most difficult aspects of cross-examination

There are several ways of handling an answer that is not responsive to the question to gain at least some measure of control of the witness. Here are some of them.[3]

Restate the question

Simply repeat the question.

3 Some of the methods that follow are taken from J.W. McElhaney, *supra* note 1 at 128–132.

Is that a "yes"?

"Excuse me, doctor, does that mean the plaintiff did tell you he suffered from headaches?"

Appear puzzled

Appear puzzled and ask the question again: "Dr. Cameron, I thought the question was clear. Did the plaintiff tell you he suffered from headaches?"

Tell the witness you are repeating the question

"Dr. Cameron, I'll ask the question again [or, 'My question was ...']: Did the plaintiff tell you he suffered from headaches?"

The subject is ...

"Dr. Cameron, the subject is the plaintiff's headaches. My question is, did the plaintiff tell you he suffered from headaches?"

We will get to that

Q. Dr. Cameron, you want to talk about the seriousness of the headaches and how they could be controlled and how long they would last, don't you?

A. *Yes.*

Q. We're going to get to that in a few minutes. But before we do that, you need to answer my question.

A. *What's your question?*

Q. Did the plaintiff tell you he suffered from headaches?

A. *Yes.*

Have the reporter read it back

Q. Madam Reporter, would you please read the last question back to the witness?

A. *Did the plaintiff tell you he suffered from headaches?*

Q. Thank you. Dr. Cameron, please answer the question.

It's up to the jury

"Dr. Cameron, it is going to be up to the jury as to whether the headaches were serious or could be controlled by medication or would disappear. I will ask the question again."

Are you through?

After a long narrative by a witness, you may consider asking, "Are you through?" or "Now, will you answer my question?" Often, the witness will ask what the question was.

Let the witness ramble

Let the witness ramble, and then ask the witness if he or she remembers the question.

Hold up your hand

It is surprising how often a witness will stop an answer if you simply hold up your hand in a fashion indicating that you want the witness to stop answering.

The save-time approach

"Dr. Cameron, I will ask the question again. I want you to listen carefully to the question and simply answer what I am asking. If you do that, we will get through this a lot quicker, you will get to go home sooner and the jury will get to go home sooner."

The rules say ...

"Dr. Cameron, under the rules that govern the conduct of civil proceedings, I am entitled to ask questions and you are obligated to give answers which are responsive to those questions. Do you understand that, and will you please try to be responsive to the questions asked?"

Ask the judge for help

"Your Honour, the witness is not being responsive to the questions asked. He is engaging in speech-making and is wasting a lot of the court's time. I ask that you direct him to confine his answers solely to the questions asked."

If the witness insists on speech-making, you can ask the trial judge for help. This is, however, a desperate approach. It shows the jury that you have lost control of the witness. Also, often opposing counsel will get up and say the witness is entitled to give a complete answer to the questions asked and that that is all he or she is doing. There are a few judges who will make a witness answer the question being asked, but they are scarce. Most will simply say that the witness can answer as he or she deems fit. In other words, many judges will say the witness can give long answers that are non-responsive to the question.

Make an agreement with the witness at the outset

At the outset of the cross-examination, one approach is to try to reach an agreement with the expert you are cross-examining, as follows. You are going to ask a series of questions, which in your view can be answered "yes" or "no." You would like to reach an agreement with the expert that the question be answered either "yes" or "no," or alternatively, if the expert cannot answer "yes" or "no," then he or she is to tell you that the question cannot be answered "yes" or "no" and you will rephrase the question so that it can be answered "yes" or "no." An example of this technique is as follows:

Q. Dr. Cameron, my name is John McLeish and I represent the plaintiff, Mrs. Jones, in this case. Dr. Cameron, I noticed during your examination-in-chief how you tried to co-operate with the defendant's lawyer in answering questions, and I wonder if I might have the same co-operation?
A. *I will try.*
Q. Dr. Cameron, as the lawyer for Mrs. Jones and as an officer of this court, it is my job to ask you some questions about your testimony. You understand that, don't you?
A. *Yes.*
Q. I am going to try to ask you questions that will call for a "yes" or "no" answer.
A. *What if I cannot answer "yes" or "no?"*
Q. Well, doctor, as I was saying, I am going to try to ask you questions that will call for a "yes" or "no" answer. If you can answer them "yes" or "no," would you be willing to do that?
A. *Yes.*
Q. But if I should ask you a question that you cannot answer "yes" or "no," then please tell me that you cannot answer the question and I will try to rephrase it so that you can, or I will go onto another question. Is that fair?
A. *Yes, I guess so.*
Q. So, then, Dr. Cameron, the answers you will give will either be "yes" or "no" or "I'm sorry, Mr. McLeish, but I cannot answer that question." Can we agree on that?

A. *Yes.*

Q. Thank you, Dr. Cameron. As I understand it, a spinal tap is one of the diagnostic techniques commonly used by doctors to help determine the nature of possible brain injury. Is that correct?

A. *Yes.*

Q. Nevertheless, doctor, you did not perform a spinal tap on Mrs. Jones, the plaintiff in this case, did you?

A. *I did not need to.*

Q. Dr. Cameron, do you remember our agreement?

A. *Yes.*

Q. And you agreed that you would answer either "yes" or "no" or "I'm sorry, Mr. McLeish, but I cannot answer that question "yes" or "no." Is that correct?

A. *Yes.*

Q. Thank you, Dr. Cameron. So tell us, please, whether or not you performed a spinal tap on the plaintiff in this case.

A. *No. I did not.*

No one can think that the agreement you have reached with the witness is unfair, because you are indicating that if the questions cannot be answered "yes" or "no," the witness will tell you so. The agreement stops the expert from going into full oratorical flight – because once the expert goes into flight, starts giving a speech and gets away from the ten pages of the medical text that you understand, you are in trouble.

A potential issue with this approach is that defence counsel can stand up and object to the type of agreement you are trying to make with the witness, and indicate that Dr. Cameron is entitled to answer each question the way he sees fit.

CONCLUSION

With planning, lots of hard work and specific objectives in mind, you should be able to at least neutralize most opposing experts. Sometimes you will be able to have them provide favourable evidence that supports your theory. On rare occasions, you might even be able to totally undermine the opposing expert's opinion. A good cross-examination of an opposing expert can have a significant impact on the outcome of a case.

The independent expert witness: HOW DID WE GET HERE?

BRYAN FINLAY, Q.C.*

IN A PAIR of decisions released within weeks of each other, the Supreme Court has effectively hollowed out the requirement that an expert witness be independent.[1] On the one hand, the Court has found it permissible for an expert witness to be a founding member and a current officer of a party to the litigation, that party seeking as consistent with its goals, the relief claimed in the litigation.[2] On the other hand, the Court has held, at the same time and in the name of independence, that the trial judge may well draw the line against the proposed expert who has a financial interest in the litigation, who is an advocate for a party or who has a close familial connection with one of the parties.[3] This result is incomprehensible: the expert whose professional rationale includes the achievement of a particular result in the litigation may give opinion evidence, so long as he or she has no direct financial interest in the result or does not "appear" to be an advocate.

How did we get here? I believe the answer is that, although the Supreme Court pays homage to the importance of the independence of

* The author wishes to acknowledge the assistance of James White (Fox Scholar) and Kayla Theeuwen in the preparation of this note, including many fine conversations. He claims sole responsibility, however, for any errors or omissions.

1 *White Burgess Langille Inman v. Abbott and Haliburton Co.*, 2015 SCC 23 [*Abbott SCC*]; *Mouvement laïque québécois v. Saguenay (City)*, 2015 SCC 16 [*Saguenay SCC*].

2 *Saguenay SCC, supra* note 1 at paras. 106–107.

3 *Abbott SCC, supra* note 1 at para. 49.

the expert, the effect of its decisions in *Saguenay* and *Abbott* is to marginalize it.[4]

SAGUENAY

Though *Saguenay* was, at its core, a freedom of conscience and religion claim under the Quebec *Charter of Human Rights and Freedoms*, the Supreme Court's rehabilitation of an expert is what I wish to focus on.

In deciding whether there was a discriminatory interference with the applicant's freedom of conscience and religion under the Quebec Charter, the Human Rights Tribunal considered expert evidence on the religious significance and nature of a prayer that was recited at the beginning of municipal council meetings in Saguenay, Quebec. The Tribunal qualified the expert, Daniel Baril, notwithstanding the fact that he was a co-founder and member of the Mouvement laïque québécois (MLQ), the moving party in the litigation and, at the time of the tribunal hearing, was the MLQ's vice-president.[5] The Quebec Court of Appeal reversed this finding, holding instead that the relationship between Mr. Baril and the MLQ rendered his evidence inadmissible on the basis of a lack of objectivity and impartiality. Reasonably, the three-judge panel considered the expert's independence and impartiality (or lack thereof) from the perspective of both the opposing party and the "well-informed person." The Court held that the expert must have a requisite amount of impartiality so that the opposing party does not doubt that the expert witness's opinion is objective.[6] The Court stated that:

> [a] *well-informed person, aware of the duty of impartiality that must animate any expert called to appear before a court, would easily agree that the [expert witness] lacked the necessary perspective to act in this case.* The association, of which he was Vice-President at the time of the proceedings, has a financial interest in the outcome of this case. He himself is the propagandist of a well-established ideology and does not hesitate to personally

4 While it is observed that some sources draw a clear distinction between the concepts of "independence" and "bias," this article is conscious of both when referring to either term. For sources drawing a clear distinction, see Glenn R. Anderson, *Expert Evidence* (3d ed 2014) at ch 16 [*Anderson*]; Paul Michell & Renu Mandhane, "The Uncertain Duty of the Expert Witness" (2005) 42 Alta. L.R. 635 at para. 7.

5 *Simoneau c. Tremblay*, 2011 QCTDP 1 at paras. 177–178.

6 *Simoneau c. Tremblay*, 2013 QCCA 936 at para. 48.

> institute an action against a city for its actions that he considered to be contrary to his values.[7]

Gascon J., for the Supreme Court, reversed the Court of Appeal's decision and deferred to the Tribunal.[8] In rehabilitating Mr. Baril, he held that "more than a simple appearance of bias is necessary" for expert testimony to be inadmissible, and that an admissibility assessment does *not* contemplate "whether a reasonable person would consider that the expert is not independent."[9] Instead, the assessment must be fact-driven and will consider whether the "expert's lack of independence renders him or her incapable of giving an impartial opinion in the specific circumstances of the case."[10] By this holding, it is now acknowledged that the expert may lack independence and the test is whether the tainted witness, in the opinion of the court, is incapable of giving an impartial opinion. Remarkably, nowhere are considerations for the administration of justice examined: the need for independence of an expert as an essential ingredient to insure that the integrity of the litigation and trial process is not diminished. Regardless of what any court finds, how is the integrity of the litigation advanced where the judge accepts the opinion of a tainted (non-independent) expert witness?

ABBOTT

Saguenay set the stage for *Abbott*. There, a unanimous Supreme Court effectively restricted the exclusion of expert evidence for lack of independence to only the most extreme cases of actual bias and, as the Court did in *Saguenay*, dismissed the appearance of bias as irrelevant to admissibility.

In *Abbott*, the respondent shareholders brought a professional negligence action against the appellants, the former auditors of their company, after retaining a different accounting firm, the Kentville office of Grant Thornton LLP (GT), to audit their company. The action was commenced after GT revealed alleged problems with the auditors' work. The auditors brought a motion for summary judgment and, in response, the

7 *Ibid.* at para. 51 [emphasis added].

8 Abella J. concurred, in part, with the decision, but did not comment on any of the expert evidence issues.

9 *Saguenay SCC, supra* note 1 at para. 106.

10 *Ibid.*

shareholders retained Susan MacMillan as an expert witness. Ms. MacMillan was a forensic accounting partner at the Halifax office of GT.

The auditors applied to strike out Ms. MacMillan's affidavit on the ground that she was not an impartial expert. One of the central arguments regarding Ms. MacMillan's lack of impartiality was that, if her expert opinion was not accepted, then as a partner of her firm she might be personally liable. In the auditors' view, this gave her a personal financial interest in the outcome of the litigation and ought to render her evidence inadmissible.

At the Nova Scotia Supreme Court, Pickup J. held that in order to be admissible, an expert's evidence "must be, and be seen to be, independent and impartial." Given the relationship between the two GT offices, Pickup J. concluded that Ms. MacMillan's evidence could not be "seen to be" independent and impartial, and therefore refused to admit it.[11]

A majority of the Nova Scotia Court of Appeal concluded that the motions judge erred in excluding Ms. MacMillan's affidavit evidence, and that the test he adopted was wrong in law.[12] In dissent, MacDonald CJNS held that the motions judge had applied the relevant legal principles and properly excluded Ms. MacMillan's evidence.[13]

The Supreme Court dismissed the appeal and, building on *R. v. Mohan*[14] and *R. v. Abbey*,[15] reiterated the well-known framework used to assess the admissibility of expert opinion evidence: the two-step admissibility test. At the first step, the party calling the expert must meet the threshold requirements for admissibility, which are the four *Mohan* factors (relevance, necessity, absence of an exclusionary rule, and a properly qualified expert). At the second step, the judge then exercises his or

11 *Abbott and Haliburton Co. v White Burgess Langille Inman*, 2012 NSSC 210 at para. 99 [*Abbott First Instance*]. Pickup J. relied on three authorities in coming to this conclusion: *Lunenberg Industrial Foundry & Engineering Ltd. v. Commercial Union Assurance Co. of Canada*, 2005 NSSC 62 at para. 32; *Tingley v. Wellington Insurance Co.*, 2008 NSSC 317 at para. 16; *Ocean v Economical Mutual Insurance Co.*, 2010 NSSC 315 at para. 22. None of these cases held that an appearance of bias renders expert evidence inadmissible.

12 *Abbott and Haliburton Co. v White Burgess Langille Inman*, 2013 NSCA 66 at paras. 59–60 [*Abbott CA*].

13 *Ibid.* at paras. 43–47.

14 *R. v. Mohan*, [1994] 2 S.C.R. 9 [*Mohan*].

15 *R. v. Abbey*, 2009 ONCA 624 [*Abbey*].

her role as gatekeeper by "[balancing] the potential risks and benefits of admitting the evidence."[16]

A test within the test

The Court discussed how an expert's duty to provide independent assistance to a court or tribunal by giving objective and unbiased opinion evidence fits into the two-step analysis. The Court acknowledged the expert's duty to the court as an additional threshold requirement and situated that issue within the "qualified expert" element of *Mohan*.[17]

Absent a challenge to the expert's independence and impartiality, "the expert's attestation or testimony recognizing and accepting the duty will generally be sufficient to establish that this threshold is met."[18] Once the expert attests on oath to this effect, the burden shifts to the party opposing the admission of the evidence to show that there is a realistic concern that the expert is unable or unwilling to comply with that duty.[19] If the opponent is successful in demonstrating this concern, the burden shifts back to the party calling the evidence, who must establish, on a balance of probabilities, this aspect of the admissibility threshold.[20]

The Court emphasized that only in "very clear cases" where the proposed expert is unable to provide fair, objective and non-partisan evidence, should the evidence be excluded at the first, threshold step of the analysis.[21] The Court contrasted some examples: an expert's "mere" interest or relationship to the litigation – including an employment relationship – will not qualify as a "clear" case in which his or her evidence should be excluded.[22] However, a "direct financial interest" in the outcome of the litigation may qualify.[23] The Court stated that "[c]onsistent with the structure of the analysis developed following *Mohan* ... the

16 *Abbott SCC*, *supra* note 1 at paras. 23–24.

17 *Ibid.* at para. 53. The Court briefly explains that the independence and impartiality of an expert (separate from the expert's duty) has been addressed at various points of the *Mohan* admissibility test: see para. 52 for the Court's explanation and examples.

18 *Ibid.* at para. 47.

19 *Ibid.* at para. 48.

20 *Ibid.*

21 *Ibid.* at para. 49.

22 *Ibid.*

23 *Ibid.* The Court also indicated that a "very close familial relationship with one of the parties" or situations in which the expert's liability depends on his or her opinion will similarly be of concern: para. 49.

judge must still take concerns about the expert's independence and impartiality into account in weighing the evidence at the gatekeeping stage."[24] While it is not clear, it would appear that this statement refers to the second step of the analysis (weighing the probative values against the prejudicial effect). If so, then the Court provides no guidance as to the criterion to be applied at this second step. Might it allow for a more rigorous application of the independence test? In light of the holdings in *Saguenay* and *Abbott*, I do not see how it could.

INDEPENDENCE AND THE APPEARANCE OF INDEPENDENCE

The contemporary origin of the principles of independence and the appearance of independence is the English case *National Justice Compania Naviera SA v. Prudential Assurance Co. Ltd.* (the "*Ikarian Reefer*").[25] That case articulates the numerous duties to which expert witnesses are subject, the most relevant of which in this discussion are:

1. *Expert evidence presented to the Court should and should be seen to be* the independent product of the expert uninfluenced as to form or content by the exigencies of litigation.
2. An expert witness should provide independent assistance to the Court by way of objective unbiased opinion in relation to matters within his expertise.[26]

These passages have been unqualifiedly endorsed by the courts in Canada.[27]

---

24 *Ibid.* at para. 54.

25 *National Justice Compania Naviera SA v. Prudential Assurance Co. Ltd.*, [1993] 2 Lloyd's Rep. 68, aff'd on appeal [1995] 1 Lloyd's Rep. 455 (C.A.) at 496 [*Ikarian Reefer*].

26 *Ikarian Reefer*, *supra* note 25 at 565. The first duty listed was derived from *Whitehouse v. Jordan*, [1981] 1 All E.R. 267 at 276 (H.L.), where Lord Wilberforce held that "[I]t is necessary that expert evidence presented to the court should be, and should be seen to be, the independent product of the expert, uninfluenced as to form or content by the exigencies of litigation. To the extent that it is not, the evidence is likely to be not only incorrect but self-defeating." [Emphasis added.]

27 See, e.g., *Perricone v. Baldassarra*, [1994] O.J. No. 2199 at para. 21 (Ont. Gen. Div.); *Fellowes, McNeil v. Kansa General International Insurance Co.* (1998), 40 O.R. (3d) 456 at paras. 7–10 [*Fellowes*]; *Prairie Well Servicing Ltd. v. Tundra Oil and Gas Ltd.*,

While it is interesting that courts have repeatedly endorsed the *Ikarian Reefer*, its principles did not feature in the *Mohan* test for admissibility.[28] This state of affairs obfuscated the way in which independence, in both fact and appearance, came to be treated at the admissibility stage. An examination of the case law from the 1990s to date demonstrates that, rather than robustly analyzing what the *Ikarian Reefer* might be taken to mean in this regard, Canadian courts have tended to shoehorn its principles into one of the *Mohan* criteria on a case-by-case basis.[29]

Perhaps it was this lack of clarity that led the Supreme Court in *Saguenay* and *Abbott* to limit the domain of actual and apparent independence with respect to admissibility. What is now left of the principles stated in the *Ikarian Reefer*?

"Independence"

As recognized in *Abbott*, there are numerous cases in which it was determined that a lack of independence alone might suffice as a reason to exclude expert evidence. The examples identified include where the expert acts as an advocate;[30] where the expert represents the client in a related matter;[31] where there is a familial relationship between expert and client;[32] and in circumstances where the expert is the plaintiff.[33] Importantly, while declining to espouse a clear statement of principle with respect to an independence requirement, these cases did not consider it to be a total anomaly as a ground for inadmissibility, despite the absence of independence as one of the *Mohan* factors.

R. v. Docherty[34] suggested that impartiality is a prerequisite for admissibility: "the rules permitting the introduction of opinion testimony are

---

2000 MBQB 52; *Kirby Lowbed Services Ltd. v. Bank of Nova Scotia*, 2003 BCSC 617 at para. 38; *R. v. Inco Ltd.* (2006), 80 O.R. (3d) 594 [*Inco*]; *United City Properties Ltd. v. Tong*, 2010 BCSC 111 [*United City*]; *R. v. Docherty*, 2010 ONSC 3628 at paras. 1, 11–12 [*Docherty*]; *Sagl v. Cosburn, Griffiths & Brandham Insurance Brokers Ltd.*, 2009 ONCA 388 at para. 85, leave to appeal refused [2009] SCCA No 303.

28 *Mohan*, *supra* note 14.

29 *Abbott SCC*, *supra* note 1 at paras. 52–53.

30 *Fellowes*, *supra* note 27.

31 *Ibid.*; *CC&L Dedicated Enterprise Fund (Trustee of) v. Fisherman* (2000), 49 O.R. (3d) 187.

32 *Docherty*, *supra* note 27.

33 *Ocean v. Economical Mutual Insurance Co.*, 2010 NSSC 315.

34 *Docherty*, *supra* note 27.

clearly predicated on impartiality."[35] It is evident from *United City Properties Ltd. v. Tong*[36] that Romilly J. shared a similar view. He concluded that "an approach which allows any expert evidence to be adduced and considers bias only as a factor affecting the weight of the evidence is not supported by the rationale underlying the exception for expert evidence" and that an expert's degree of bias should be considered as part of *Mohan*'s relevancy criterion.[37]

Further, *R. v. Inco Ltd.*[38] went so far as to consider a *perceived* lack of independence as a factor to consider when assessing the admissibility of expert evidence on the basis that the expert is *actually* biased.[39] Hennessy J. held that, where there is a perceived lack of independence, the judge should conduct a *voir dire* to test whether the opinion is actually impartial; after this examination, the judge will be in a "much better" position to assess whether the witness should be rejected.[40] These decisions indicate that independence requires holistic consideration at the admissibility stage, and one should not approach the issue as exceptional.[41]

Despite recent suggestions that independence might well be a viable ground for inadmissibility, the Supreme Court's limitation of the issue to "clear" cases, being those where the expert is incapable or unable to fulfill his or her duty,[42] effectively marginalizes this consideration. Now, so long as the expert acknowledges that he or she is able and willing to comply with the duty to present fair, objective and non-partisan evidence to the court, it is very likely, absent some very damaging evidence to the contrary, that the expert's evidence will be admitted (assuming that the four *Mohan* factors are satisfied). The earlier cases are likely to be confined to their facts. This result is reinforced by *Saguenay*, which provides an example of what, in my view, is one of the clearest of cases in which an expert's evidence should not be admitted; and yet, the Supreme Court's current position on expert independence allows for its

35 *Ibid.* at para. 11.

36 *United City, supra* note 27.

37 *Ibid.* at para. 65.

38 *Inco, supra* note 27.

39 *Ibid.* at para. 45.

40 *Ibid.* at para. 49.

41 Indeed, Anderson identifies a range of cases in which independence was found to disqualify the expert: *Anderson, supra* note 4 at 16.3.

42 *Abbott SCC, supra* note 1 at para. 50.

admission. Further, leading by *Saguenay*'s example and following the *de facto* limitation of the independence requirement, it is equally unlikely, again in the absence of some very damaging evidence to the contrary, that partial expert evidence will be excluded at the gatekeeper stage.

Therefore, the first principle in the *Ikarian Reefer*, "expert evidence presented to the Court should be ... the independent product of the expert uninfluenced ... by the exigencies of litigation," has largely been rendered meaningless.

"The appearance of bias"

This second principle has been well and truly lost through the ambiguous interaction between the *Ikarian Reefer* and *Mohan*. Although it has regularly been mentioned in relation to an expert's duties of independence, the case law has seldom analyzed what an appearance of bias means in terms of the admissibility of evidence. The closest a Canadian court has come to finding the appearance of bias to be a bar to admissibility was in *R. v. Docherty*,[43] where Wein J. considered both bias and the appearance of bias to be reasons not to admit the expert evidence before the court. Accepting that "little precedent exists for legal rejection of expert opinion evidence on the basis of bias or the apprehension of bias,"[44] Justice Wein concluded:

> [I]t cannot therefore be said that there was a necessity to rely on an expert whose objectivity would clearly be in question and whose evidence could only cause concern to the court that the public perception of the administration of justice would be impaired if any weight was given to it.[45]

Unfortunately, this case is an anomaly. And *Saguenay* and *Abbott* have now slammed shut the door on this idea, holding that the appearance of bias is insufficient to establish inadmissibility.[46] It is important to observe that the decisions in *Saguenay* and *Abbott* are entirely consistent with the case law in this respect. Judicial attempts to exclude evidence on this ground drew on cases that did not establish the appearance of

---

43 *Docherty*, *supra* note 27.

44 *Ibid.* at para. 12.

45 *Ibid.* at para. 21.

46 *Abbott SCC*, *supra* note 1 at paras. 50, 57; *Saguenay*, *supra* note 1 at para. 106.

bias as a stand-alone bar to admissibility,[47] causing appellate courts little trouble in rejecting the argument.[48]

That said, it is unfortunate that the appearance of bias is now completely foreclosed from consideration. There was the opportunity in these two cases for the Court to examine this issue from a wide policy perspective including the public interest. Too many judges have cited the appearance of bias for it to have been completely abandoned. Three judges of the Quebec Court of Appeal in *Saguenay* and two of the four lower court judges in *Abbott* relied on it. As earlier stated, for the losing party – and the public at large – the judicial endorsement of a witness who appears biased will be difficult to understand.

WAS THERE AN ALTERNATIVE?

In my view, the *Ikarian Reefer* could have been read as *requiring* an expert not only to be independent, but also to appear to be independent. The situation with respect to independence itself could easily have taken the form suggested by pre-*Abbott* cases, in that courts look at the facts in the round and determine whether there is a real issue as to the expert's independence (what is sometimes referred to as "actual bias" or a "clear case" of a lack of independence). Residual doubts regarding an expert whose evidence was admitted could then have gone to weight. Further, the appearance of independence could have been afforded similar treatment: courts would look to the extent to which the public's perception of the justice system might be affected if the expert's evidence is admitted and determine whether it ought to be admitted. Again, concerns not strong enough to exclude the evidence could go to weight. Although one must acknowledge the weight of opposing views, much of it cited in *Abbott*,[49] there are cases that do identify the rationale behind independence and its appearances.

In addition to *Docherty*, there is, in this context, clear authority addressing the need to maintain the integrity of the justice system. For example, in *MacDonald v. Sun Life Assurance Co. of Canada*,[50] Spiegel J. explained that anything that detracts from the all-important objective

47 *Abbott First Instance*, *supra* note 11.

48 *Abbott CA*, *supra* note 12.

49 *Abbott SCC*, *supra* note 1 at paras. 41–44, 47.

50 *MacDonald v. Sun Life Assurance Co. of Canada*, [2006] O.J. No 4977, 2006 CarswellOnt (WL Can.) [*MacDonald*].

of an expert witness' evidence being and appearing to be independent "diminishes the integrity of the litigation and trial process and should be met with appropriate sanctions designed to send a clear message that such conduct will not be tolerated."[51]

In *Frazer v. Haukioja*,[52] Moore J. similarly emphasized the importance of expert evidence appearing to be independent so as to protect the administration of justice:

> At trial, the expert must be and appear to be independent of the party or counsel who retained the services of the expert and must demonstrate objectivity and impartiality in the analyses and opinions that she or he is allowed to give. Because the opinions stated by an expert are predicated upon expertise that the court does not possess, the court must be confident in relying upon the expert to provide a thorough, balanced and technically sound analysis. Independence and impartiality; the court expects nothing more and it will accept nothing less.
>
> The court endeavors to adjudicate each matter coming before it fairly and free from bias. To the extent that the court must receive and rely upon the expert opinions of others and to the extent that those opinions are tainted, the administration of justice is imperiled.[53]

As stated, what is regrettably missing in both *Saguenay* and *Abbott* is any consideration by the Court for the administration of justice, including the public's view of the fairness of the trial process and the integrity of the litigation. In ignoring such consideration, we only feed cynicism about the administration of justice. As the Honourable Ian Binnie has said when discussing expert witnesses, "the courts ignore public shock at their peril."[54]

WHERE DO WE GO FROM HERE?

While the Court in *Saguenay* can say that independence is important and in *Abbott* maintain that independence goes to admissibility, the

51 *Ibid.* at paras. 102–103.

52 *Frazer v. Haukioja*, [2008] O.J. No. 3277 (Sup. Ct.), 2008 CarswellOnt (WL Can.) [*Frazer*].

53 *Ibid.* at paras. 139–140.

54 The Honourable Ian Binnie, *The Changing Role of the Expert Witness* (2010) 49 S.C.L.R. (2d) at 191.

question to be asked after these two cases is "what meaning is left to the word independence?" I suggest very little. In practice in the future, absent some truly egregious circumstance (which is difficult to imagine after *Saguenay*), I doubt that counsel will rely on issues of independence as a means by which to oppose the admission of expert evidence other than in some supporting role. This, I believe, is most dangerous. In jettisoning the importance of "independence," we have turned our back on a long tradition of what we have acknowledged to be an essential ingredient of opinion evidence.[55]

55 See e.g. the Honourable Coulter A. Osborne, Q.C., *Civil Justice Reform Project* (November 2007), available online: <www.attorneygeneral.jus.gov.on.ca/english/about/pubs/cjrp>; The Advocates' Society, "Position Paper on Communications with Testifying Experts" June 2014, online: <www.advocates.ca/assets/files/pdf/news/The%20Advocates%20Society%20-%20Position%20Paper%20on%20Communications%20with%20Testifying%20Experts.pdf>; The Advocates' Society, "Principles Governing Communications with Testifying Experts" June 2014, online: <www.advocates.ca/assets/files/pdf/news/The%20Advocates%20Society%20-%20Principles%20Governing%20Communications%20with%20Testifying%20Experts.pdf>.

Asking ourselves the Moneyball question about expert evidence

PROFESSOR ADAM DODEK, LSM*

BRAD PITT IN THE COURTROOM

LAWYERS LOVE BASEBALL. This shouldn't be a surprise. Baseball is a game that is full of tradition and rules, and it's very slow. Whoops! I meant "slow to change." Baseball has also become more protracted and more expensive over time. Just like litigation. In the movie *Moneyball*, Brad Pitt stars as Oakland Athletics general manager Billy Beane, a contrarian who takes on baseball's conventional wisdom and wins.[1] The movie – based on the best-selling book by Michael Lewis[2] – is about how the low-budget Oakland A's were able to compete with big-budget, free-spending teams such as the New York Yankees and the Boston Red Sox by challenging long-held sacred cows of baseball and instead employing an analytical, evidence-based approach. *Moneyball* changed how baseball players are evaluated and spawned the whole analytics industry in sports. It has also become a popular business school case study that is applied to many different subject areas.[3] We can also apply *Moneyball* to the use of expert witnesses

* This article is based on the J. Donald Mawhinney Lectureship in Professional Ethics delivered by Prof. Dodek at the University of British Columbia in 2016.

1 *Moneyball* (Sony, 2011). See IMDB, "*Moneyball*," online: imdb. com/title/tt1210166.

2 Michael Lewis, *Moneyball: The Art of Winning an Unfair Game* (New York: Norton, 2003).

3 See eg Frances X Frei, Dennis Campbell and Eliot Sherman, Harvard Business Review, Case Study: Moneyball (A): What Are You Paying For? (August 2005)

in Canada. One baseball writer said that the core message of *Moneyball* is an intellectual one, a philosophical challenge: "If we weren't already doing it this way, is this how we would do it?"[4] Canadian legal consultant Jordan Furlong picked up on this observation immediately and wrote an article that every managing partner, law school dean, law society bencher and senior manager should read. It was called "Ask Yourself the Moneyball Question."[5] Furlong asserted that every law practice should be asking itself the Moneyball question. He was right. And so should every law school, every law society and every government department. We should also be asking the Moneyball question about the administration of justice and our court system. My point here is that if we ask ourselves the Moneyball question about expert testimony, there is no way we would construct the current system that we have. Here is why.

THE SPECIAL NATURE OF THE EXPERT WITNESS

The expert witness is a special type of witness. The expert is the only type of witness who is permitted as a matter of course to offer an opinion. Not only are experts allowed to offer their opinion, their opinion is the *raison d'être* for their testimony. Expert witnesses are permitted to offer their opinion for two reasons: first, because they have a special type of expertise or knowledge that is beyond the grasp of the trier of fact – whether that trier of fact is a judge or a jury; and second, because they have a duty to assist the court. That duty to assist the court has existed for decades under the common law and was codified in the English case known by the colourful title of the ship involved –*The Ikarian Reefer*.[6] In

---

Harvard Business Review, online: hbr. org/product/Moneyball--A---What-Are-Y/an/606025-PDF-ENG. See also "Moneyball for Government," online: moneyballforgov.com/app/uploads/2014/10/Case-Studies.pdf.

4 Mike Cormack, "Moneyball Movie: Q&A with Rob Neyer" Sportsnet.ca (September 5, 2011), online: sportsnet.ca/baseball/mlb/moneyball-neyer.

5 Jordan Furlong, "Ask Yourself the Moneyball Question" *Attorney at Work* (September 19, 2011), online: attorneyatwork.com/themoneyball-question.

6 *National Justice Compania Naviera SA v Prudential Assurance Co.*, [1993] 2 Lloyd's Rep 68, rev'd [1995] 1 Lloyd's Rep 455; cited with approval in *White Burgess Langille Inman v Abbott and Haliburton Co*, 2015 SCC 23 at para 27.

2015, the Supreme Court explicitly adopted and emphasized certain of the *Ikarian Reefer* duties in *White Burgess Langille Inman v. Abbott and Haliburton Co.*[7] These are:

1. Expert evidence presented to the Court should be, and should be seen to be, *the independent product of the expert uninfluenced as to form or content by the exigencies of litigation* ....
2. An expert witness should provide independent assistance to the Court by way of *objective unbiased opinion* in relation to matters within his [or her] expertise .... An expert witness in the High Court should never assume the role of an advocate.[8]

To recap: We demand that experts be independent of the parties and that they provide their objective unbiased opinion. Experts cannot have their testimony influenced by the exigencies of litigation, nor can they assume the role of advocate. These are the goals or the purposes of expert evidence.

Let us now ask ourselves the Moneyball question, slightly rephrased: How would we go about attempting to achieve these objectives if we weren't doing things the way we are currently doing them? If we are being honest, we would acknowledge that there is no way that we would set up the system we currently have where the parties (a) recruit the prospective expert witness; (b) instruct them; (c) prepare them; and (d) remunerate them. These factors create an insurmountable conflict of interest between the expert's duty to his or her "client" and duty to the court.

Collectively, these elements stack the deck against having an expert who is independent, objective and impartial. The last thing counsel want is an expert who has these qualities. Counsel will retain only an expert who will support their client's cause. And rightly so. Consequently, litigation privilege has buried communications and reports from many experts who turned out to be independent, objective and impartial – unless their independent, objective and impartial opinion aligned with the client's position. In which case, those expert reports are okay.

7 *White Burgess Langille Inman v Abbott and Haliburton Co*, 2015 SCC 23.
8 *Ibid* at para 27 (emphasis and editing by Supreme Court of Canada).

Regime change or just rule change?

Defenders of the status quo – including the Supreme Court of Canada – point to rules of court that require experts to acknowledge their duties.[9] For example, Ontario's Form 53 requires experts to acknowledge their duty, *inter alia*, to provide opinion evidence "that is fair, objective and non-partisan," and to acknowledge that their duties prevail over any obligation they may owe to a party on whose behalf they are engaged. Such rules and acknowledgements are necessary, but they are not sufficient. In fact, they are deficient in several ways. First, at least with Ontario's Form 53, the acknowledgement need not be signed until after the expert completes his or her report. It must be included with the expert's report. This is too late in the process. An acknowledgement of the expert's duties should be required when the expert is retained. Second, there is nothing that requires lawyers to explain these duties to the expert. There is thus a risk that Form 53 becomes just another standard form among the many we are required to sign in our day-to-day lives. This leads to the third and final problem with such forms: They are not self-executing – their mere existence does not necessarily change behaviour.

More than 20 years ago, Gavin MacKenzie wrote a law review article entitled "The Valentine's Card in the Operating Room: Codes of Ethics and the Failing Ideals of the Legal Profession."[10] MacKenzie took the title of his work from a statement that an American law professor had made to the effect that the American Bar Association's canons of legal ethics were about as much use to a lawyer in a courtroom as a Valentine's card would be to a heart surgeon in the operating room.[11] Granted this analogy is extreme. However, the point is that codes of conduct have limited effect on the conduct that they purport to regulate.

The scourge of adversarial bias

No code of conduct is likely to be able to address the biggest problem with expert evidence: adversarial bias. As my former colleague (now) Mr. Justice David Paciocco has written, "Without question, the most pernicious and common form of partiality related to expert witnesses is 'adversarial

9 See eg Ontario, Rules of Civil Procedure, RRO 1990, Reg 194, r 53.03(2.1)(7).

10 Gavin MacKenzie, "The Valentine's Card in the Operating Room: Codes of Ethics and the Failing Ideals of the Legal Profession" (1994) 34 Alb LRev 859.

11 *Ibid* quoting MH Freedman, *Lawyers' Ethics in an Adversary System* (New York: Bobbs-Merrill, 1975), vii.

bias,' an umbrella term that catches all of the pressures that are inherent in a litigation model where the parties select and call the expert witnesses."[12]

Adversarial bias includes *association bias*, "the natural bias to do something serviceable for those who employ you and adequately remunerate you ... the litany of conscious and unconscious pressures on experts to work in the interests of those they are associated with in litigation."[13] It also includes *confirmation bias*, "the unconscious tendency of those who desire a particular outcome to search for things that support that outcome and to ignore or reinterpret contradictory information."[14]

We are all too familiar with both these problems from the Inquiry into Forensic Pediatric Pathology in Ontario (the Goudge Inquiry). Dr. Charles Smith – the head pediatric forensic pathologist at the Hospital for Sick Children in Toronto – was implicated in more than a dozen questionable cases, some of which resulted in wrongful convictions. Smith was doubly biased: He displayed association bias by thinking it was his duty to help the Crown convict, and confirmation bias through the culture of "think dirty" when a child died without explanation.

The problem of adversarial bias was identified by judges more than 170 years ago, although they didn't call it that. More recently, it has been confirmed by scientific studies. In an 1843 case, Lord Campbell commented:

> I do not mean to throw any reflection on [the expert witness]. I dare say he is a very respectable gentleman, and did not mean to give any evidence that was untrue; but really this confirms the opinion that I have entertained that hardly any weight is to be given to the evidence of what are called scientific witnesses; they come with a bias on their minds to support the cause in which they are embarked ...[15]

Lord Campbell suggested that if the expert had been a witness in a different case and was asked his opinion, he would have provided a "totally different account of it." This suggestion is cynical and perhaps unduly harsh, but it reflects a widely held perception of the expert witness.

And then there is Sir George Jessel. Many will be familiar with Sir George, Master of the Rolls, from his seminal statement on solicitor-client

---

12 David M Paciocco, "Unplugging Jukebox Testimony in an Adversarial System: Strategies for Changing the Tune on Partial Experts" (2009) 34 Queen's LJ 565 at para 12.

13 *Ibid* at para 16.

14 *Ibid* at para 17.

15 *Ibid* at 715.

privilege in *Anderson v. Bank of British Columbia* (1876).[16] We continue to treat his words in that case as the gospel. However, forsaken as heresy is his caution against expert evidence three years earlier in *Lord Abinger v. Ashton* (1873).[17] Sir George was more polite than Lord Campbell. The Master of the Rolls stated that it was natural for an expert, however honest he may be, to be biased in favour of the person employing him. He complained that the courts "constantly see persons, instead of considering themselves witnesses, rather consider themselves as the paid agents of the person who employs them."[18] These warnings have been largely ignored for two centuries.

The pathology of the common law

Adversarial bias is a pathological problem of the common law. Virtually every report over the past two decades dealing with civil justice reform in every common-law jurisdiction mentions the problem of expert witnesses and adversarial bias. A study of American lawyers and judges conducted by the American Judicial Center found that American lawyers and judges believed that adversarial bias was "the single most important problem with expert evidence" in US courts.[19]

Adversarial bias is so much of a phenomenon that it has attracted the attention of social scientists. Studies done in the United States found strong evidence of allegiance, even where the "pull" of allegiance was relatively weak: minimal interaction with retaining lawyers (15 minutes), and minimal remuneration. Controlled studies have shown "strong evidence" of what researchers term "an allegiance effect" among some forensic experts.[20]

We are left with a very problematic paradox. Trials are exercises based on evidence. However, when it comes to how we run trials and how we

---

16 *Anderson v Bank of British Columbia* (1876), 2 Ch D 644 (CA).

17 *Lord Abinger v Ashton*, (1873) LR 17 Eq 358.

18 *Ibid* at 374.

19 Carol Krafka et al, "Judge and Attorney Experiences, Practices, and Concerns Regarding Expert Testimony in Federal Civil Trials Psychology," (2002) 8:3 Psychology, Public Policy, and Law 309 reprinted by Federal Judicial Center, online: fjc.gov/public/pdf.nsf/lookup/judattex.pdf/$file/judattex.pdf.

20 See Daniel C Murrie et al, "Are Forensic Experts Biased by the Side That Retained Them?" (2013) 24 Psychological Science 1889.

administer justice in this country, we ignore the very strong evidence of bias.

So what should we do?

SOLUTIONS

If we want experts who are independent, objective and unbiased, we should tether them to an institution that is independent, objective and unbiased rather than to counsel who are dependent, non-objective and biased in favour of their clients (as they are required to be). We should rely more on court-appointed experts. Rules in most jurisdictions allow this but they are used infrequently – no doubt because of cultural resistance both from judges and from lawyers.

If we want experts who are independent, objective and unbiased, we should provide training for experts in being independent, objective and unbiased. Simply passing a rule and making experts sign an acknowledgement form will not magically make them independent, objective and unbiased. We should provide for certification and accreditation of experts, as the UK does with the Academy of Experts and the Expert Witness Institute.

What about the issue of payment?

If we were being really principled, we might say that experts should be paid like jurors. Maybe they should not be paid at all – like experts (including some law professors) who appear before parliamentary committees. After all, there is only one other witness who is paid for giving testimony – the confidential informant – and we don't think very highly of that witness's reliability.

Alternatively, the court could set a tariff for expert fees as it does for other court-annexed matters.

The public policy rationale that allows some expert witnesses to earn extremely lucrative income under the auspices of a publicly funded judicial system is not apparent to me.

CONCLUSION

If we asked ourselves how best to do things, we would come up with a variety of options. But it is highly unlikely that we would come up with the current system for experts. Change is hard, but the greatest hurdle is our willingness to confront our own biases about the legal system. If we start to do that, we will have taken the first step into the batter's box and we will be ready for the pitch.

What irreproducible results mean for the law of scientific evidence

JASON M. CHIN

IN 2015, BRIAN NOSEK and several collaborators reported the results of perhaps the most important scientific study of the year – it was a study they performed by copying the work of others. That is not as contradictory as it sounds, or at least it should not be.

While the conventional wisdom is that most scientific findings have been vetted and reproduced many times before they reach scientific consensus, the reality is that such rigour is exceedingly rare. Nosek sought to remedy this situation, wrangling up a group of 270 other researchers (collectively the Open Science Collaboration, or OSC) and attempting to redo 100 psychology experiments already published in leading peer-reviewed journals.[1] The question: Would these re-creations find the same results as the initial studies?

Prior to the OSC's endeavour, the conventional wisdom was that, yes, published science contains some false positives, but they are a small minority and quickly identified through a robust self-correction process. The OSC's results suggest that this conventional wisdom is wrong – only 36 percent of the studies in the sample were reproducible. This finding surprised even the alarmists, who long suggested the number was closer to 50 percent.[2] The OSC's results also garnered widespread

1 Open Science Collaboration, "Estimating the Reproducibility of Psychological Science" (2015) 349 Science 943.

2 John PA Ioannidis, "Why Most Published Findings Are False" 2:8 PLoS Med e124.

media coverage, drawing attention to a problem that had been brewing for years.[3]

And while the OSC's study was in the context of psychological science, the picture is no rosier in other disciplines. For example, a large-scale replication attempt focused on cancer treatments was able to confirm the results of the original study just 11 percent of the time.[4] And, in December 2015, it was reported that a significant portion of research in clinical genetics (i.e., the type of research that provides for screening of genetic diseases) was unreliable.[5] Especially relevant to law, recent findings have put large swaths of the field of bite-mark forensics in doubt.[6]

Indeed, the legal community should heed the warnings flowing from the OSC's startling finding. Legal decisions often turn on scientific evidence. For example, courts use science to determine questions as varied as whether marijuana is addictive[7] and whether DNA links a suspect to a crime scene.[8] The problem may be even more immediate in law – whereas science self-corrects (although, as we shall see, it takes longer than most expected), litigants rarely get more than one kick at the can.

Issues with scientific evidence rose to prominence in Canada with concerns over the practice of pediatric forensic pathology and the subsequent report prepared by a commission of inquiry led by Justice Stephen

---

3 Ed Yong, "How Reliable Are Psychology Studies?" *The Atlantic* (27 August 2015), online: <theatlantic.com/science/archive/2015/08/psychology-studies-reliability-reproducability-nosek/402466>; Joel Echenbach, "Many Scientific Studies Can't Be Replicated: That's a Problem," *The Washington Post* (27 August 2015), online: <washingtonpost.com/news/speaking-of-science/wp/2015/08/27/trouble-in-science-massive-effort-to-reproduce-100-experimental-results-succeeds-only-36-times>; Benedict Carey, "Many Psychology Findings Not as Strong as Claimed, Study Says," *The New York Times* (27 August 2015), online: <nytimes.com/2015/08/28/science/many-social-science-findings-not-as-strong-as-claimed-study-says.html>.

4 C Glenn Begley & Lee M Ellis, "Drug Development: Raise Standards for Preclinical Cancer Research" (2012) 483 Nature 531.

5 Ed Yong, "Clinical Genetics Has a Big Problem That's Affecting People's Lives," *The Atlantic* (16 December 2015), online: <theatlantic.com/science/archive/2015/12/why-human-genetics-research-is-full-of-costly-mistakes/420693>.

6 Erik Eckholm, "Lives in Balance, Texas Leads Scrutiny of Bite-Mark Forensics" *The New York Times* (12 December 2015), online: <nytimes.com/2015/12/13/us/lives-in-balance-texas-leads-scrutiny-of-bite-mark-forensics.html>.

7 *R v Smith*, 2015 SCC 34, [2015] 2 SCR 602.

8 *R v B(SA)*, 2003 SCC 60, [2003] 2 SCR 678.

Goudge.[9] The report described serious flaws in the practice of forensic pathology, including with the skill and objectivity of expert witnesses.

The OSC reported a more pervasive problem, going beyond the practice of experts in a field to the basic science that girds their opinions. In other words, the safeguards built into the very *process* of scientific inquiry have long been inadequate to weed out erroneous findings. That process is changing (for the better) and legal actors must be aware of these changes.

In what follows, I first provide a brief review of the legal standard for the admission of scientific evidence. Then, I review several reasons why science has proven unreliable. These reasons inform the steps legal actors can take to effectively screen out unreliable science. In short, they should demand science's best rather that what has been generally accepted. I conclude with some tangible recommendations for the justice system.

THE ADMISSION OF SCIENTIFIC EVIDENCE

The admission of scientific expert evidence in Canada,[10] US federal courts, and most US state courts is governed by the landmark US Supreme Court decision *Daubert v. Merrell Dow.*[11] *Daubert* provides four questions trial judges should consider when determining whether proffered scientific evidence is admissible: (1) Is it generally accepted? (2) Has it been peer reviewed and published? (3) Has it been tested? (4) What is the error rate of the finding or method? In Canada, this inquiry accompanies the general test for the admission of expert evidence found in *R v. Mohan.*[12]

Daubert has attracted a great deal of scrutiny from both academics and practitioners.[13] The test's critics focus on the enhanced gatekeeper role played by judges under its framework. They argue that trial judges, who frequently do not come from a scientific background, do not possess

9 Ontario, *Inquiry into Pediatric Forensic Pathology in Ontario: Report* (Toronto: Ontario Ministry of the Attorney General, 2008) (Commissioner Stephen T Goudge); online: <attorneygeneral.jus.gov.on.ca/inquiries/goudge/index.html> [Goudge].

10 *R v J(LJ)*, 2000 SCC 51 at para 33, [2000] 2 SCR 600 [*JLJ*].

11 509 US 579–595 (1993).

12 [1994] 2 SCR 9, 1994 CarswellOnt 1155; *JLJ*, *supra* note 10 at paras 25–62.

13 See e.g. Ken J Chesebro, "Taking Daubert's 'Focus' Seriously: The Methodology/ Conclusion Distinction" (1994) 15 Cardozo L Rev 1745.

the scientific fluency to apply *Daubert*. Indeed, some empirical research shows that judges fail to spot key flaws in scientific studies presented to them.[14]

In Canada, there appears to be more agreement that an enhanced gatekeeper role under *Daubert* is desirable. Indeed, this is one of the primary themes arising from the Goudge Report.[15] And, in a 2015 Ontario Court of Appeal decision, Chief Justice George Strathy cited that report in enunciating Ontario's strong position regarding judicial gatekeeping: "[T]here has been growing recognition of the responsibility of the trial judge to exercise a more robust gatekeeper role in the admission of expert evidence."[16]

To understand fully what science's reproducibility problem means for courts, more background is required. The following section reviews the sources of the problem, which all flow from a flawed incentive system.

SOURCES OF THE FAILURE TO REPLICATE

Science's incentive structure values publishability over truth.[17] When one contemplates a research project, the goal line is almost inevitably publication. It is the metric by which scientists are measured. Indeed, publishing has been described as "the very heart of modern academic science – at levels ranging from the epistemic certification of scientific thought to the more personal labyrinths of job security, quality of life and self-esteem."[18]

The problem is that the qualities that make findings publishable are not the same ones that make them true. In fact, the competition to publish often encourages shortcuts and questionable practices that further bias the body of published research. This disconnect between

14 Margaret Bull Kovera & Bradley D McAuliff, "The Effects of Peer Review and Evidence Quality on Judge Evaluations of Psychological Science" (2000) 85 J Applied Psychology 574.

15 Goudge, *supra* note 9.

16 *Meady v Greyhound Canada Transportation Corp*, 2015 ONCA 6 at para 37, 2015 CarswellOnt 46.

17 Brian A Nosek, Jeffrey R Spies & Matt Motyl, "Scientific Utopia: II. Restructuring Incentives and Practices to Promote Truth over Publishability" (2012) 7:6 Perspectives on Psychological Science 615 [Utopia].

18 Michael J Mahoney "Open Exchange and Epistemic Process" (1985) 40 Am Psychologist 29.

publishability and truth manifests in several ways: (1) research is rarely independently replicated; (2) studies failing to find a statistically significant effect (i.e., negative results) are almost never published; and (3) researchers sometimes misbehave. These issues are reviewed below.

Journals value novelty, not replication

Replication is commonly referred to as the *sine non qua* of science,[19] and for good reason. Direct replication by an independent party substantially increases the confidence in a result.[20] In particular, direct replication helps confirm that the finding was not a statistical artifact and reduces the possibility that the experimenter deliberately or subconsciously affected the result.

Despite unanimous acceptance of the importance of replication, leading journals rarely publish direct replications of previous research. The reason for this is simply that journals value novelty over truth. In other words, they prefer to publish findings that are exciting, novel and counterintuitive, rather than replications of previous work.[21]

Both anecdotal accounts and empirical studies demonstrate the preference for novelty over replication. For example, surveys of editors find most agree that replications are a waste of valuable journal space.[22] Further, a 2012 study found that only 1.07 percent of psychological studies were replicated.[23]

Journals value positive results rather than negative ones

Similar to the problem with publishing replications, researchers also struggle to find an outlet for studies that find a negative result (i.e., that a treatment had no discernible effect). As a result, the publicly available body of evidence is positively biased, giving the impression that a

19 David C Funder et al, "Improving the Dependability of Research in Personality and Social Psychology: Recommendations for Review and Educational Practice" (2014) 18 Personality and Social Psychology Rev 3 at 8.

20 Harold Pashler & Christine R Harris, "Is the Replicability Crisis Overblown? Three Arguments Examined" (2012) 7 Perspectives on Psychological Science 531 at 534.

21 Utopia, *supra* note 17 at 617.

22 James W Neuliep & Rick Crandall, "Editorial Bias against Replication Research" (1990) 5 J Social Behavior and Personality 85.

23 Matthew C Makel, Jonathan A Plucker & Boyd Hegarty, "Replications in Psychological Research: How Often Do They Really Occur?" (2012) 7 Perspectives on Psychological Science 537.

finding is robust, when in fact there are many unpublished studies that show no effect. This bias against negative results is empirically verifiable: A 2012 study estimated that 90 percent of published results across all scientific fields are positive results.[24]

Questionable research practices

The incentive to publish creates a conflict between the personal interests of the scientist and the goal of knowledge accumulation (i.e., accuracy).[25] When personal motivations supersede accuracy, researchers may engage in questionable research practices (QRPs). QRPs are techniques used by researchers to strategically (but artificially) inflate the persuasiveness of their findings. These practices do not rise to the level of academic fraud, but undoubtedly they bias the state of knowledge in a field.[26]

More than 60 percent of researchers responding to an anonymous survey admitted to using one particular QRP – selectively reporting the measurements that confirmed the study's hypothesis and refraining from reporting those that did not.[27] Although this practice may seem relatively benign, it skews error rates by increasing the chance that researchers will find a statistically significant result.

Although use of QRPs represents misbehaviour by scientists, journals share some of the blame. In particular, they have failed to scrutinize adequately the findings they publish. *Nature*, a leading scientific journal, expressly admitted its culpability in the replicability crisis:

> The problems arise in laboratories, but journals such as this one compound them when they fail to exert sufficient scrutiny over the results they publish and when they do not publish enough information for other researchers to assess results properly.[28]

---

24 Daniele Fanielli, "Negative Results Are Disappearing from Most Disciplines and Countries" (2012) 90 Scientometrics at 891.

25 Utopia, *supra* note 17 at 616.

26 Joseph P Simmons, Leif D Nelson & Uri Simonsohn, "False Positive Psychology: Undisclosed Flexibility in Data Collection and Analysis Allows Presenting Anything as Significant" (2011) 22 Psychological Science 1359.

27 Leslie K John, George Loewenstein & Drazen Prelec, "Measuring the Prevalence of Questionable Research Practices with Incentives for Truth Telling" (2012) 23:5 Psychological Science 524 at 525.

28 Editorial "Announcement: Reducing Our Irreproducibility" (2013) 496 Nature 398; see also Eric Eich "Business Not as Usual" (2014) 25 Psychological Science 3.

THE MYTH OF SELF-CORRECTION

Science's claim to fame has long been that it self-corrects – erroneous findings are quickly and efficiently scrutinized and, if necessary, weeded out by other scientists. As Nosek described the problem:

> If a claim is wrong, eventually new evidence will accumulate to show that it is wrong and scientific understanding of the phenomenon will change. This is part of the promise of science – following the evidence where it leads, even if it is counter to present beliefs. ... We do believe that self-correction occurs. Our problem is with the word "eventually." *The myth of self-correction* is recognition that once published, there is no systemic ethic of confirming or disconfirming the validity of an effect. False effects can remain for decades, slowly fading or continuing to inspire and influence new research. ... Further, even when it becomes known that an effect is false, retraction of the original result is very rare.[29]

Fortunately, and thanks to scientists who have spent the past decade examining the problem, solutions are falling into place. Armed with these lessons, the law of scientific evidence can develop to ensure reproducible science takes centre stage in legal disputes.

WHAT CAN THE LEGAL SYSTEM DO ABOUT IT?

Daubert provides a useful framework for courts to evaluate science. But the *indicia* of good science *Daubert* directs judges to consider (i.e., peer review, testing and error rates) have themselves failed to track best practices. For example, the OSC's results suggest that the fact that a study was peer reviewed carries little weight. It is not the mere act of peer review that matters, but how thorough that process was. I will now review the *Daubert* factors and note how legal actors can employ them in the context of the OSC's findings, to ensure that bad science does not have an impact on legal decisions.

Peer review and publication

The OSC's results suggest that peer review and publication, in and of itself, is a poor *indicium* of scientific reliability because only a minority of such studies prove replicable. In fact, a poorly carried out peer review

29 Utopia, *supra* note 17 at 619.

process may do no more than increase the superficial believability of a study without providing any guarantees of reliability. Recall that some journals have expressly admitted culpability, stating that they failed to scrutinize sufficiently the results they published or did not publish enough information for others to scrutinize them. By placing weight on peer review for its own sake, *Daubert* may also distract judges from unpublished work containing valuable data.

Several initiatives can help to ensure that *Daubert*'s peer review component is effectively used. For instance, the Goudge Report recommended judicial training programs, which appear effective in several US jurisdictions.[30] These programs, as well as guides prepared for use by courts, could draw attention to the levels of scrutiny provided by various journals. (Nosek's organization, for example, awards badges to publications that adopt more open practices, such as by making their data publicly accessible and thus open to scrutiny.[31])

Informed lawyers would do well to cross-examine experts not only on whether the findings they rely on have been peer reviewed and published, but also on *how* that process was carried out. Are the authors' data available to the public? Are the instruments they used to make measurements available and accessible? Compelling proprietary reasons may exist for non-disclosure, but that is often not the case.

Even when expert evidence passes the threshold for admissibility, a battle continues over which expert's evidence will be accorded greater weight. In such cases, one relevant factor should be the quality of peer review the scientific evidence has endured. Peer review is not always rigorous and, all else being equal, scientific evidence that has withstood a higher level of scrutiny should receive the greater weight.

Ontario courts have been especially vigilant to the importance of properly performed peer review and publication. For instance, in *R. v. Truscott*,[32] a five-justice panel of the Ontario Court of Appeal was extremely critical of the Crown's expert witness whose opinion rested on little more than anecdotal experience. Instead, the court endorsed an approach centred

---

30 GT Harrell Jr et al, "Deployment of Science and Technology Trained Judges: Settling on a Plan" (Washington DC: Advanced Science and Technology Adjudication Center, 2009).

31 Online: <osf.io/tvyxz/wiki/home>.

32 2007 ONCA 575, 2007 CarswellOnt 5305.

on a "*critical analysis* of peer-reviewed literature."[33] Ontario advocates may wish to refer to *Truscott* in arguing that recent insights into the reliability of science demonstrate that the bar for critical analysis of peer-reviewed evidence is high.

In addition, expert witnesses in Ontario are now required to sign an acknowledgement of their duties. As part of this process, scientific experts could be asked to acknowledge that they attempted to canvass fully the relevant subject area and sought unpublished research that either confirms or casts doubt on the science at issue. Experts would need to contact scientists known to be active in a field and request their unpublished data. A major contributor to the replicability crisis is that high-quality research with negative findings, although available through informal channels, is seldom published. Likewise, court-appointed experts in cases involving complicated scientific issues may be directed to undertake a similar endeavour.[34]

Testing and error rates

Scientists use a variety of tactics to artificially inflate the persuasiveness of their results. Although these testing practices were once generally accepted, there is now no doubt that they have introduced bias into several bodies of scientific findings. Fortunately, it is relatively easy for courts and lawyers to be on the lookout for QRPs.

Scientific journals increasingly require researchers to adopt open methods. For example, some require researchers to "pre-register" their studies (or at least make note of those who do so). Pre-registration means that the researcher used one of several existing web-based databases to pre-record the experiment's parameters and helps to ensure that the researcher did not engage in QRPs. For example, because researchers must publicly pre-record the measurements they are going to make, pre-registration catches the QRP of failing to report them.

Absent a compelling reason, most modern scientific research should be pre-registered. Well-informed litigators would also be wise to inquire about pre-registration during cross-examination, when appropriate. And, once again, even if the scientific evidence is admitted, the presence or absence of pre-registration should inform the evidence's weight.

---

33 *Ibid* at para 169 [emphasis added].

34 Goudge, *supra* note 9 at 506.

Large-scale replication attempts, like the OSC's, are exceedingly rare. While it is unsettling that so many of the studies in its sample proved irreproducible, 36 percent were directly replicated by researchers acting independently of those who first made the finding. This type of direct replication, when it does occur, allows scientists to hone in on an accurate estimate of the error rate associated with a finding or technique. There are few situations, if any, in which non-replicated research should be admitted to influence the ultimate decision on the merits. Adjudicators should therefore adopt a skeptical attitude toward unreplicated evidence, questioning whether the extant evidence has been sufficiently tested and represents an accurate representation of the error rate of the finding or technique.

CONCLUSION

The meta-scientific insights described herein have not gone unnoticed. Nosek's own organization has received millions of dollars of support and now provides a host of tools for pre-registration of studies and support throughout the life of a scientific experiment.[35] Journals have also taken note and are enhancing their review processes. The legal community should take heed of these changes.

Although the situation sounds dire, science is still the best way to accumulate knowledge about the world. There are, however, more – and less – accurate ways of accomplishing this goal. We now know more about the dangers of the less accurate ways, and we have improved guidance on the more accurate ways. By attending to the methods that foster reproducibility, courts can better ensure that legal disputes are adjudicated accurately.

35 Online: <osf.io>.

PERSONAL REFLECTION | SUMMER 2013

The advocate's calling

GUY J. PRATTE

IT IS A singular honour for me to assume the Milvain Chair in Advocacy for 2013, particularly as I look at the list of previous incumbents, from John J. Robinette through to Sheila Block and Linda Rothstein, along with many others.

Only a great jurist and mentor like Chief Justice Milvain could have inspired the creation of this remarkable advocacy program in 1979 – one of the first, if not the first, of its kind in Canada. As the advocate's craft has a history of more than 2,000 years, going back to at least Roman times and Cicero, it should go without saying that I have no ambition today of revealing some secret recipe that will ensure you win all your cases.

And, just in case I were tempted to deceive myself – and you – into thinking that my experience as an advocate could be a source of unique wisdom, I keep in a well-lit corner of my mind, etched in bold letters, Abraham Lincoln's reminder in the notes he prepared in 1850 for a lecture on the practice of law: "I am not an accomplished lawyer. I find quite as much material for a lecture on those points where I have failed, as in those where I have been moderately successful."[1]

In fact, I will not discuss advocacy skills as such: that is the proper subject of the course many of you are taking. Nor have I come here

1 S. Sheppard, ed., *The History of Legal Education in the United States: Commentaries and Primary Sources* (Pasadena: Salem Press, 1999) at 489 [Sheppard].

to regale you with a tale of uninterrupted successes and heartwarming stories, glossing over the extraordinary demands of the profession and the valleys of despondency that most of us experience as we struggle to make advocates of ourselves. Instead, I want to ponder some ostensibly unrelated questions:

- What is the advocate's *raison d'être*?
- What are the advocate's basic duties?
- What essential quality does the aspiring advocate need?
- What are some of the key challenges facing the advocate?
- Is the advocate still relevant in the 21st century?

I have been asking myself these questions lately, as one is wont to do after more than a quarter of a century toiling at the same occupation. While I realize that my own reflections on these matters will not be particularly original, perhaps the fact that I should share them with you *now*, at the dawn of your careers in the practice of law, from the perspective of someone upon whom dusk is fast descending, could be intriguing, perhaps even helpful.

As I broach these questions, I am sure that what I have to say will sound somewhat old-fashioned, recalling values that appear out of place in a world suffused with commercial imperatives. Still, I should like to persuade you of the fact that, although one cannot live in the past, one should nevertheless sift through its sediments to extract the few gems it may have left behind as enduring lessons to us all.

For if you are going to choose the law as your profession, and advocacy as your calling, you may as well know *now* what will – in all likelihood – be required of you, and most important, why it should rightly be. And that is what I shall try to persuade you of, as candidly as I can.

That is my challenge, and it will put my modest advocacy skills to the test ...

THE ADVOCATE'S CALLING

The advocate's raison d'être

To begin with, we should start by reminding ourselves that we are *all* advocates, from our earliest days. The child making a scene upon being denied his second scoop of ice cream is making an argument; the candidate at a job interview is trying to charm and persuade the would-be employer that the company's future would be brighter if she were part of it; and anyone who has ever visited an emergency room with a sick family member knows how important advocacy is to obtaining timely attention.

Many of you are this week learning specialized, technical advocacy skills – tools that have been developed over centuries – since well before Cicero's time – to be fitted to their special purpose in a civilized society, namely, the peaceful resolution of disputes in public courts of law.

For we know that human beings cannot live without some set of rules to govern their myriad relationships with each other and with the state.

The complexity of these rules and the consequences of being found to have violated them – to one's reputation, one's liberty or one's economic situation – are such that a separate profession evolved to lend its voice and know-how to assist those grappling with those rules. Its *raison d'être* is to ensure that anyone's case does not founder simply because a litigant possesses neither the requisite legal knowledge nor the necessary persuasive skills. So, when you are retained by clients, you really hold the fate of their rights on the tip of your tongue, as a surgeon holds a patient's life in his hands. And that is no exaggeration, as I hope to demonstrate toward the end of these remarks.

I am sure that you had many other career paths open to you. But know that if you should choose to become an advocate, you will by that choice be representing that your skills are such that you can put forth your client's case as well as it can be put. You are telling your clients that *you* are better than *they* in ensuring that justice be done to *their* cause. You assume the duty to represent your clients in the way that *they* cannot.

This heavy responsibility requires that you develop your skills – as many of you are doing – so as to be equal to the tacit yet no less unequivocal representation you are making just by calling yourself an "advocate."

The advocate's duty: The cab-rank rule

There is another duty that you accept by assuming the title of advocate – one quaintly expressed by the so-called "cab-rank rule." That rule, which is most entrenched at the British bar, is described as follows by Lord David Pannick, one of England's foremost barristers:

> This "cab-rank rule" requires a barrister to accept any brief to appear before a court in which he professes to practice, to accept any instructions and to act for any person on whose behalf he is briefed or instructed

> irrespective of the party on whose behalf he is being briefed … the nature of the case and any belief or opinion which he may have formed as to the character, reputation, cause, conduct, guilt or innocence of that person.[2]

While it is true that, in Canada, this rule is not honoured as strictly as it may be in England, it nonetheless captures a core value of the best tradition of the bar, namely, that the duty of the advocate is to assist his or her client with the case and, once instructed to proceed with it, to refrain from judging the client or the cause: that is the job of the judges.

As David Pannick further writes:

> [N]o matter how hopeless the cause, however unmeritorious the client, notwithstanding the antipathy of the judge, irrespective of the risks to his own reputation, and despite the other pressing concerns which may be praying on the mind of the lawyer, what counsel must do is to follow and defend the great tradition of advocacy: to make mountains out of molehills, to find a point of law where none had previously been known to exist, to ensure that his client does not lose the case without everything possible (and, on occasion, some things impossible) being said on his behalf.[3]

This is something that many people – including some lawyers – have difficulty understanding.

I have had the privilege of representing some high-profile people who were not universally popular. In one instance, I got a flurry of hate e-mails and even highly critical personal voicemails from people strongly disapproving of my acting for a particular individual. One message said: "You are a disgrace to the profession! You should be ashamed of yourself." And that was from my mother!

Often those critical of the cab-rank rule see it as a thinly disguised form of intellectual prostitution – that the advocate will argue any case, regardless of merit, that he or she is paid for. Indeed, that charge was levied at me once, in virtually those terms. I concede that it may seem so to members of the public (and even to some members of the legal profession) who do not see a duty in the rule, but rather a pretext for commercial opportunism. But the rule does not exist to create a market for lawyers. Its true justification is that no one should be denied access

2 *Advocates* (Oxford: Oxford University Press, 1992) at 135–136.

3 *Ibid.* at 5.

to competent counsel because of negative public sentiment toward the client's cause, or, indeed, as a result of lawyers choosing to represent only clients that are likely to be successful. In other words, it is designed to promote access to justice, a core value of our legal system.

This should be understood at the very outset of one's career at the bar: one is simply not free to refuse a brief merely because it may be controversial or difficult. Abiding by the dictates of that rule is not always easy, and will require on occasion of the advocate that he or she summon the quality that is the *sine qua non* of any advocate worthy of the name: I speak of the quality of courage.

The advocate's courage

When I was a teenager, there was a sports program on television entitled *The Wide World of Sports.* As you watched the intro to the program of great athletic feats, pathetic failures and horrific accidents, of athletes alternately overcome with joy or overwrought with pain, the announcer would gravely intone: "The thrill of victory and the agony of defeat!"

No slogan better captures the life you can expect at the bar, as an advocate. While it is a life replete with thrilling experiences, these experiences come at the cost of some agony. This calling requires not only determination, but actual courage.

It may seem odd to think that the most important quality of the advocate is courage. We are not talking here about a calling like the military, which may ask of you to put your life at risk. But advocacy demands courage nonetheless if you are to be the very best you can be:

- The courage to fight self-doubt and confront daily the knowledge that you could have done better for your client.
- The courage to deal with sleepless nights and ever-present stress, worrying about how to present a cogent argument, to anticipate your opponent's points as well as the bench's questions, so that you are not caught unaware, momentarily frozen, staring blankly at the judge.
- The courage to have your public performances assessed by judges and colleagues alike – particularly if they are friends – whom you will undoubtedly hear murmur "Well, he wasn't very good today," in the same voice that speaks to you when you realize that, indeed, you were not that very good that day.

- The courage to pick yourself up and believe that the pain will abate eventually.
- The courage to stand up to the occasional ornery judge and to persist in making the case on behalf of your client with civility, yet firmness.
- The courage to resist the pressure of partners who may be over-concerned that your firm's reputation will suffer in the eyes of the public if you accept a controversial case.
- The courage to tell a less-than-honest but profitable client that your duty on its behalf ends where the court would be misled by any representation you might be asked to make.
- The courage to take a principled position in a case, notwithstanding the controversy it might provoke or the jeopardy to your career it might entail.

Few if any of us will ever have to muster the kind of courage Cicero summoned when, as a young advocate, he famously challenged the Roman aristocracy and led the prosecution of a case of extortion against the brutal and corrupt Verres, the former governor of Sicily.

But all of us will be confronted, almost daily, with situations that, albeit more mundane, call upon us to act courageously if we claim to deserve the title of advocate.

Some challenges of the profession

The public perception of dishonesty

Lawyers have been criticized for their alleged lack of honesty and have had their true motives questioned, at least as far back as Dickens's 19th century. Indeed, there is virtually no novel Dickens wrote that does not contain some criticism of lawyers – most notably *Bleak House*, where the famous case of *Jarndyce v. Jarndyce* meanders through the courts at the most leisurely pace, ruining the litigants and enriching the lawyers.

And, on this continent, Lincoln wrote in 1850:

> There is a vague but popular belief that lawyers are necessarily dishonest. I say *vague*, because when we consider to what extent *confidence*, and *honors* are reposed in, and conferred upon lawyers by the people, it appears improbable that their *impression* of dishonesty is very distinct and vivid. Yet the impression is common – almost universal. Let no young

> man, choosing the law for a calling, for a moment yield to this popular belief. Resolve to be honest at all events; and if, in your own judgment, you can not be an honest lawyer, resolve to be honest without being a lawyer. Choose some other occupation, rather than one in the choosing of which you do, in advance, consent to be a knave.[4]

Today, it is fashionable, if not commonplace, to criticize the modern practice of law as having forfeited its idealistic soul in exchange for the economic rewards of business imperatives. Only a scholarly history of the legal profession could validate the view that modern lawyers are obsessed with money, if not dishonest, in a way that their forebears were not.

It is true that law firms have had to focus more on the purely business side of their operations: they have had to become much more efficient, as clients are insisting that they reduce their costs and offer better "value for service." While this phenomenon – the demand for better services at lower cost – is not limited to law firms, it does pose a challenge for lawyers in general, and advocates in particular, to ensure that they can discharge their duties to their clients and provide competent representation to anyone entitled to it.

That is the world you will be soon entering, and I trust that we will leave it sufficiently imbued with the ideal of "justice for all" that motivates the best advocates. It will then be up to you to take up the challenge confronting every generation of lawyers to reconcile the conflicting demands of justice and economic efficiency.

The increasing demands of the profession

One of the effects of what I call the "businefication of law" is that all lawyers – young and not so young – feel that the demands of the profession are increasing at an alarming pace and encroaching upon their personal lives to an unprecedented and unacceptable extent. But it seems to me unlikely that the life of the modern advocate should be much more challenging now than that of the callow English barrister 100 years ago. With no guaranteed income, all that barrister could do was wait for some brief to land on his desk and a chance to make a reputation that, over time, would provide some financial security.

There was no starting salary of $100k, as some firms are reported to pay first-year lawyers. More than a century ago, even the eventually

4 Sheppard, *supra* note 1 at 490.

famous barrister Marshall Hall flirted with bankruptcy for the first few years of his outstanding career before he could be confident that he could earn a living.

And while I envy my elders, many of whom apparently took the summers off when no court was sitting to occupy them, I cannot imagine that they were not harassed by worries proportionate to their time, as we are by those commensurate to our own.

Beyond the perennial worries about money and reputation, your main challenge as an advocate will be what it has always been: to discharge the obligation to defend the interest of your client to the best of your ability. That will require, as it always has, incredibly hard work and thorough preparation; it will demand mental agility as you are being challenged by judges and opponents in court. And, once more, it will require that you summon the courage to confront the haunting second-guessing that follows every advocate worth his or her salt, as he or she reflects on the argument that could have been made, the question that should not have been asked and the case that should have been won.

Every great advocate is equally obsessed with the pursuit of perfection, knowing all the while that – at best – it is occasionally approached, but never achieved. Still, the futility of the chase is no reason to abandon it, for the advocate's commitment is not only a matter of personal choice: it is the command of his or her chosen calling to represent the client as well as can humanely be done. *And there can be no valid excuse for ever falling short in the attempt, even when doing so in the result.*

IS THE ADVOCATE STILL RELEVANT? THE ADVOCATE'S ROLE IN THE SEARCH FOR JUSTICE

Anyone who has attended a legal conference in the past few years is unlikely to have escaped without prominent judges and experienced lawyers decrying the legal system as hopelessly broken. They denounce the staggering cost of taking any case to court and complain that trials – the few that actually take place – are too long and too expensive.

In the era of the "vanishing trial," the role of the traditional advocate is questioned as fewer disputes are settled by judges in open courts; and those that are, are increasingly being compressed by various devices: greater reliance on written advocacy, "minitrials," strict time limits, in the name of efficiency and "proportionality."

At the appellate level, one routinely hears judges say, if not complain, that oral advocacy rarely affects the result of the case and so justify the imposition of strict time limits on oral arguments.

Indeed, a parallel semi-private system of justice – known as alternative dispute resolution ("ADR") – has grown alongside the public justice system. Many claim ADR to be more cost-efficient and reliable than the antiquated public system of open courts. More and more firms composed of retired judges and senior members of the bar have thrived in this ADR world as mediators and arbitrators. This phenomenon was barely conceivable when I was called to the bar in 1984.

It would of course be foolish and futile for me to predict what the future holds for aspiring advocates. But I do want to seize this occasion to remind those who have all but given up on attempting to address the genuine problems besetting our court system that it is indeed worth salvaging, notwithstanding the genuine merits of ADR.

It is imperative that it should be repaired, rather than thrown out, if only in the name of the old maxim that justice must not only be done but must also be *seen* to be done. An advocate, after all, is nothing more but no less than the client's voice. Yet one must wonder: how often is that voice really being heard, when access to the courts is effectively denied to all but the wealthiest, and those few "*téméraires*" souls, undeterred by cost, time and uncertainty.

For all the vicissitudes associated with our legal process; for all the inefficiencies we need to address; for all the access to justice issues that cry out for some solution, advocates do matter still. For they contribute to the public search for *real, practical* justice, if not always in obtaining the result the client hoped for, at least in allowing that client to see and hear his or her cause being assessed by an impartial judge presiding in an open courtroom, in full public view.

Every work of philosophy dedicated to defining what justice demands – from Plato's *Republic* to John Rawls's *A Theory of Justice* – every constitution that has ever been adopted – including our own *Canadian Charter of Rights and Freedoms* – can only give us the most theoretical and broad outline of what that elusive concept – justice – really demands.

The interstices of daily life, where reality adopts unforeseen shapes and surprising complexity, is where actual, practical justice must be found. And the advocate is retained to help the client, the court and ultimately society itself, in finding the best way to make *concrete* the ideals of justice.

For no society has yet been devised whose laws are so clear, precise and farsighted that they can easily and clearly resolve each and every dispute that can arise between citizens. And yet resolved they must be, to the satisfaction of all, including especially the disappointed litigant who must feel that he or she can accept the result *because* it was reached fairly and openly. It is there – in this country's public courts and tribunals – that the advocate toils: mining the jurisprudence, searching for the relevant facts and probing his or her mind for new ideas and fundamental principles to guide the decision maker to where the just legal solution lies.

For the courtroom is but a stage where vignettes of real life – in all its infinite variety – are presented. The place where the best advocate is called upon to understand human nature beyond his or her own experience of it. It is the ultimate reality show. If you do your job properly, putting forth all that can be said for the client's cause, both as to law and fact, you will be doing your part in bringing about some measure of justice.

To illustrate why it is proper and necessary that the search for justice be conducted in open courts, and that there be committed advocates to assist those in need of seeing the ideals of justice made real for *them*, let me tell you of a case with which I had the privilege of being involved.

Réjean Hinse was a Quebec man who, while in his early 20s, was arrested just before Christmas 1962 in a small town not far from Mont-Tremblant, Quebec, for allegedly participating with other accomplices in a violent break-and-enter robbery. With no lawyer to assist him, he was thrown in jail following a ridiculously flawed line-up, where the police chief put a hat on his head and had him stand beside known policemen and other accused in prison garb, all of them hatless. Even by the standards of the day, this could not be considered a proper or reliable identification parade. Later, the victim of an incompetent lawyer, a confused judge who explicitly said he could not tell to which accused the evidence applied, and an overzealous prosecutor, Mr. Hinse was condemned to 15 years in jail. He was released after seven years, but was put through the tortures of the damned, convinced that his life had been ruined, though he knew himself to be totally innocent. Mr. Hinse began a lengthy campaign to write to every official charged with the administration of justice to seek their assistance in correcting the obvious wrong that had robbed him of his most precious years.

But he confronted 40 years of institutional indifference that defies understanding. Letters written to the Quebec Minister of Justice were returned with the advice that only the federal Minister of Justice had the power under the law to correct such errors the police, the prosecution and the judiciary may have committed. Upon following that advice and writing to the federal authorities, he was told that only the provincial government could help. On and on it went, with lost files and total indifference for the plight of a man who on occasion was flirting dangerously with insanity.

Finally, in the mid-1990s, after the federal Minister of Justice had refused yet again any assistance, Mr. Hinse took his own case to the Quebec Court of Appeal. That court did find that his conviction was unsafe but refused to declare him not guilty. It decided not to order a new trial, however, as the passage of time made that practically impossible.

Not satisfied with this ruling – Mr. Hinse wanted a public declaration that he was not guilty – he then sought leave to the Supreme Court of Canada, which initially denied it. Writing directly to then Chief Justice Lamer, he got that decision reversed – a virtually unheard-of event in the annals of the Supreme Court of Canada.

In 1997, Réjean Hinse was at last acquitted by the Supreme Court of a crime he had not committed. He immediately launched a civil lawsuit for damages against both the federal and Quebec governments, for their negligent investigation and failure to assist a wrongfully accused man. But he soon found himself with no lawyer; left to his own devices, Mr. Hinse's lawsuit inevitably stalled.

Then, a few years ago, I was asked by the Associate Chief Justice of Quebec whether I would represent Mr. Hinse *pro bono*. The case had lingered, as the government defendants essentially did everything they could to frustrate its progress. I was fortunate to be assisted by a number of younger lawyers in my firm – a few just out of law school – who dedicated hundreds of hours of their time *pro bono* to the vindication of Mr. Hinse. They undoubtedly deserve much, if not most, of the credit for the result we eventually achieved.

The trial took several weeks in 2011. Again, the federal and provincial governments gave no quarter, denying any wrongdoing. The federal government even called an expert psychiatrist to say that Mr. Hinse actually benefited from his long stay in jail, as it had given "structure" to his life.

And notwithstanding the Supreme Court of Canada's acquittal, we were forced to prove Mr. Hinse's innocence, even though it could not be seriously challenged, as the evidence of the hopeless line-up, the flawed investigation and the confessions obtained from those really involved in the crime all demonstrated conclusively that Mr. Hinse was not there when it was committed.

After the evidence was all in but before final argument, the province settled for $4.5 million. But the Feds persisted. Ultimately, the Quebec Superior Court found the federal government liable and awarded Mr. Hinse some $8 million, including punitive damages and costs. This judgment was appealed, and the Court of Appeal has yet to render its decision. But whatever the court's decision, it is manifest that a huge injustice – one that you don't expect governments to ignore – has been identified and partially corrected.

Now, I thought that I knew what *justice* was, but let me tell you:

- to be sitting at the counsel table when Mr. Hinse was testifying, describing the humiliation of being shoved in a rigged police line-up, his voice still full of rage;
- to hear him recount the depression he endured, and describe how he would physically hit his head on the cement prison walls hoping that this would help dispel the chronic headaches he was prone to;
- to hear him ruefully recount his having lived in his "mental prison," as he called it, for nearly 50 years;
- to see Mr. Hinse's daughter in tears in the courtroom as she saw and heard her father *finally* getting his day in court; well, if I ever knew what justice *meant*, I certainly had neither understood nor felt it like that before. It was being moulded, was taking shape before our very eyes, in a public courtroom, for all to see – including, most important of all, Mr. Hinse himself.

When I made my oral submissions on behalf of Mr. Hinse, I could hardly control my own emotions. I had to pause on occasion, overcome by the wrongs he had suffered, yet joyful that the promise of justice had – albeit belatedly – been fulfilled for a man now nearing the end of his human existence, robbed of a normal life just as he was becoming a young adult.

This unjustly accused man of meagre formal education; this haunted man beset by debilitating mental challenges; this lonely man – Mr. Réjean Hinse – could not possibly assure the pursuit of his own rights without the assistance of advocates – advocates doing no more than what their calling required them to do. Countless lawyers could have played that role at least as well as we did. As it happened, serendipity gave us the chance and privilege to assist Mr. Hinse, to *be* the voice speaking on *his* behalf in the halls of justice.

CONCLUSION

None of us involved in Mr. Hinse's case will ever achieve fame, let alone glory, because of it.

For it is the curse of even the greatest advocates and judges to be all but forgotten by the generations following them. Indeed, it is disconcerting that my idols – Mr. Robinette, Ian Scott and Chief Justice Brian Dickson – are barely known by younger lawyers. Perhaps it is because an advocate's performance, even when it is recorded, has a very short shelf life – except perhaps in the advocate's own mind.

Therein lies an important lesson for the aspiring advocate: one should not choose advocacy as a calling if one is looking for a career that will lead to a permanent place in the history books. That fate is reserved for the likes of Cicero and Abraham Lincoln, who were not only accomplished advocates but also great statesmen. If perchance you should be tempted by the practice of law for the glory that the great advocates achieve, you may want to recall Shakespeare's words:

> The painful warrior famoused for fight,
> After a thousand victories once foil'd,
> Is from the book of honour razed quite,
> And all the rest forgot for which he toiled.[5]

So forget about the glory, even of the ersatz type the media tantalizingly reserves for those involved in high-profile cases. What should matter to you is that your performance will live in the hearts and minds of those whom – like Mr. Hinse – you have been privileged to help. *That* legacy should be incentive enough to motivate you to acquire and hone the skills this exceptional advocacy program affords you.

When you leave this law school, you will have, if you choose to become advocates, to adhere to a credo that every advocate is duty-bound to embrace, namely, to represent any person who requires your assistance – whether the cause be big or small, popular or controversial, remunerative or *pro bono* – to the very best of your ability.

---

5 William Shakespeare, *Sonnet XXV*.

And whether you stand up to address the Supreme Court of Canada, sit down in any other courtroom in this country after a successful cross-examination, or spar with a Court of Appeal judge in a valiant attempt to persuade her of the merits of your position, you will be able to tell yourself – I promise – "It does not get better than this." For you will have played a small, yet critical role in one of humanity's great endeavours: the pursuit of justice, however imperfect the attempt or uncertain the result.

For that reason, you will take on the next case, the case after that, and all the ones that follow, until the day you decide – as you might – that it is time to change direction to become a judge, teach at law school, or answer the tantalizing, sweet call of retirement. But until that day – if it should ever come – you will answer your calling with the same urgency, the same passion, the same obsession that causes you so much pain and brings you so much satisfaction – sure in the knowledge that you are doing your part in bringing about some measure of justice, however fleeting, in this unfair world.

Nothing more can be asked of you, even though it is likely that you will ask it of yourself.

That is the curse of the advocate and the advocate's calling.

Part Four

TRIALS AND SETTLEMENTS

TO TRY OR not to try, that is the question. "Whether 'tis nobler in the mind to suffer the slings and arrows" of an enraged or uninterested judge or "to take arms against a sea of troubles and by opposing," settle? (With apologies, of course, to the Bard.) How is a client to know? In Texas, some lawyers and law professors propose that trial counsel must disclose to prospective clients as part of their professional duties, the extent of their experience, particularly in front of juries. All this in an age of the "vanishing" trial, let alone lawyer rating services on the Internet. Interestingly, it is often harder to settle a matter than simply to try the case. A client can be critical of the result either way, but at least with a trial, someone else made the decision. In this chapter, a retired and witty judge and a noted media counsel offer their distinct views.

The unsettling truth about settling: PART ONE

THE HONOURABLE JOSEPH W. QUINN*

OVERTURE

HOW DO YOU become a talented trial lawyer? You become a good golfer by playing golf regularly. You become a proficient pianist by playing the piano frequently. You become a skilled skier by skiing often. You become ...

If you tell me that you know where I am going with this, I will cease using these annoying alliterative references. *Experientia docet* [experience teaches].[1]

SO, YOU SETTLE ALL YOUR CASES

Do you settle all your cases? Why? Is it because you have had a fortuitous run of excellent pre-trial and settlement conferences? Really? Is it because opposing counsel consistently have been reasonable and obliging? Lucky you. Is it because you have a fear of, or at least an anxiety toward, trials? Oops. Have I touched a nerve?

---

* This article was prepared for Conduct of the Family Law Trial, a program jointly sponsored by The Advocates' Society and the Law Society of Upper Canada in Toronto on October 28, 2016.

1 Tacitus, Histories, Book 5, chapter 6.

If you settle all your cases prior to trial, some of your clients are not enjoying the outcome they deserve. Settling every case is not a virtue. A bank loans manager who boasted a zero percent default rate would be fired for not taking sufficient risks. Litigation is all about risks: They must be assessed, reassessed, managed and, occasionally, taken.

If you have not had a trial in, say, five years, do you advise a new client, "I will be happy to take your case, but I must tell you that my parking privileges at the courthouse have been revoked for lack of use"? How fast and how far would you run if the surgeon you consulted announced that he or she had not seen the inside of an operating room in five years?

Furthermore, if you settle all of your cases, you are damaging your reputation. When I would ask my trial coordinator, "What do I have for Monday, and is preparatory reading required?" she would often reply, "It is a three-day trial, but Mr./Ms. X is on for the plaintiff and he/she always settles, so do not bother with any preparation." Do you want this to be your professional epitaph? Surely you do not aspire to be a litigation-lightweight.

You cannot call yourself a trial lawyer unless you do some trials. I recall an occasion in my law practice when I would not settle a particular family case. The other lawyer was miffed and said, "Why won't you settle? I settle all of my cases." I replied, "Good for you. Perhaps you should be a social worker."[2]

ARE YOU GUN SHY?

For a senior lawyer with an established reputation for trying cases, a prolonged absence from the courtroom does not equate with reluctance or inability to do a trial. However, young lawyers without a track record of trials can quickly become gun shy. If you do not draw your gun on a regular basis in your early years as counsel, when you do, you will be shooting blanks.[3]

Should your trial experiences be ones for which you are ill equipped, the effect on you will be traumatizing and, perhaps, permanent. You will be both scarred and scared. Therefore, you *must* get trial experience. But how? I will get back to you on that in a moment.

---

2 Do I hear chants of, "Unkind, unkind, unkind"?

3 If I had an editor, this sentence would have been redlined for deletion.

THE BROCCOLI IMPERATIVE

Trials are like broccoli. Regular consumption is necessary to develop a tolerance.[4]

MIRROR, MIRROR ON THE WALL

I once acted for the owner of an auto body repair shop that was destroyed by fire. His insurance company refused to pay, suspecting arson because the premises were heavily mortgaged and he was having financial difficulties. The action ambled through the usual stages and, on the Friday before the Monday on which our jury trial was to begin, I received a telephone call from counsel for the insurer with an offer. Had the offer been proffered a year earlier it might have been marginally acceptable; but not three days before trial. I was angry – but I also was embarrassed. What was there about me that led the other lawyer to think I would cave at this late date? Had I developed a reputation for being a settler of cases?

I reviewed with my client the risks associated with the situation, and I added one factoid: If we went to trial, and were unsuccessful, I would not charge a fee.[5] He instructed me to reject the offer. I was pleased. No, I was thrilled. Insurance counsel was stunned. Counsel even telephoned the lawyer who represented the first mortgagee, urging the lawyer to apply some pressure. (The settlement offer would have paid out the first mortgage.)

We were successful at trial for the full amount of the claim and, in addition, the jury awarded $50,000 in punitive damages. I mentioned earlier that litigation involves assessing, reassessing and managing risks. Sometimes you, as counsel, must be prepared to take risks. Had I convinced my client to settle for the amount offered (and, I suppose, I could have subtly coerced him into doing so), I would not have been able to look in a mirror.[6]

4 Again, if I had an editor ...

5 Remember, I was angry.

6 As I get older, I find it difficult to look in a mirror at any time. However, that is a different issue.

GUT CHECK

For a litigator, the gut is your most important organ. It will tell you whether you are selling out your client by way of an unreasonable settlement. In trial work, given the choice between guts and brains, I choose the former. Guts and hard work trump brains.[7]

A TRIAL IS A TRIAL IS A TRIAL

Whether you are in Small Claims Court, the Ontario Court of Justice or the Superior Court of Justice, all non-jury trials are pretty much the same: They have issues, and they have evidence in the form of witnesses and documents. Issues are defined and argued. Witnesses are examined. Documents are proved and tendered to the court. In other words, a trial is a trial is a trial; the stakes are the only distinguishing feature.

All trials offer valuable experience.[8]

GET TRIAL EXPERIENCE BY SOLVING THE TRIAL EQUATION

A trial can be reduced to an equation:

Trial = time + solicitor-and-client costs + party-and-party costs

You can eliminate the solicitor-and-client costs of a trial by waiving your fees.

The spectre of party-and-party costs in a trial can almost be eliminated where the opposing litigant is self-represented. That leaves "*time.*" You have an abundance of time. You are young. You do not need sleep. The more that you can neutralize the risks associated with the right side of this equation, the more likely you will be able to reduce the left side to a takeable risk.

How do you get trial experience? In my opinion, there are two main options:[9]

---

7 Imagine, in 2016, using "trump" and "brains" in the same sentence.

8 Even contested motions provide some transferable lessons.

9 Apart from stealing something or breaching a few contracts and then representing yourself in the ensuing litigation.

1. Family trials frequently involve self-represented litigants. (In fact, it was the epidemic of self-represented litigants that drove me to an early retirement.) I think they offer the best path for anyone seeking courtroom experience. Self-represented opposing parties present a low costs downside. Also, family cases typically have modest disbursements.
2. Take trials in Small Claims Court. They are relatively low risk as far as costs are concerned (particularly where the other side is self-represented and you waive your fees) and are a valuable forum for the novice litigator.

The other options are ones that are commonly touted and I mention them for completeness, but without enthusiasm:

1. If you are part of a firm with a litigation department, presumably you will be given the opportunity to act as junior co-counsel.
2. Do *pro bono* work for a legal clinic or organization in your community. Frankly, however, I think that if you are going to do *pro bono* work, it – in the first instance – should be for your own clients, where you are able to pick the specific beneficiary of your generosity as well as the subject matter of the litigation to be undertaken.
3. Motions are not a waste of time for inexperienced counsel. I am overstating the point slightly, but contested motions are trials without the witnesses. A morning spent sitting in motions court will expose you to many types of on-your-feet advocacy.

Taking trials without charging fees will have immediate financial drawbacks, but the long-term benefits to your career are incalculable.

FINALE

Without the ability to competently and comfortably conduct a trial when needed, you are destined to become a salt lick in the field of law; and a mere condiment for the big dogs.[10] At that point, your only recourse will be to seek an appointment to the bench. It worked for me.

10 Once more, the editor thing.

The unsettling truth about settling: PART TWO

THE HONOURABLE JOSEPH W. QUINN*

ONCE UPON A time, in a Kingdom far away, I was a lawyer. I recall that 99 percent of my professional headaches were caused by fewer than 5 percent of my files. A friend of mine referred to those problem files as "movers." He would stack them on a corner of his desk and, every week or so, move them to a different corner. Even today, when I am asked what it takes to be a trial lawyer, I reply, "A big desk with as many corners as possible."

Is there anything more satisfying than settling a problem file without a trial and being paid a nice fee for doing so? What about taking some of those files to trial and getting a successful result? Realistically, if you are light on courtroom experience, a trial is unlikely to happen.

Are you content being a trial lawyer who does not do trials? Really? If, on a golf course, you hit every green in regulation figures but then pick up your ball and walk to the next tee because you do not know how to putt, are you still a golfer? Just asking.

---

* Portions of this article formed the basis of an oral presentation by the Honourable Joseph W. Quinn, Superior Court of Justice (retired), at the annual general meeting of the Canadian Defence Lawyers Association in Toronto on June 8, 2017. The article is a sequel to "The unsettling truth about settling" (*Advocates' Journal*, Winter 2016).

WITHERING HEIGHTS

Advocacy skills are withering because trials (in particular, civil trials) are an endangered species headed for the Canadian Museum of History. Even worse, those skills are not being developed in the first instance. There is nothing to wither.

How many lawyers can expect to match the trial experience of, say, Francis L. Wellman (1854–1942), a New York attorney who, it is estimated, examined or cross-examined 15,000 witnesses during his courtroom career? If one were to arbitrarily assume an average of 10 witnesses per trial, it would mean Wellman participated in 1,500 trials. Raise your hand if you are on track to reach that number.

THE UROLOGICAL CONNECTION

One lawyer I knew was well on his way to Wellman numbers.

Peter Kormos was called to the Ontario bar in 1980. He quickly developed a large criminal practice in the Niagara area. Peter was an avowed anarchist. In keeping with that trait, he took all his cases to trial. Every one. His goal was to create chaos in the courts by tying up the Crown's office with cascading trials. Peter did not sleep much and, for him, cigarettes were a food group. Thus, he was able to juggle trials in circumstances where others would require an intravenous drip.

His try-them-all approach likely would not work in a civil practice, where there are incessant interlocutory proceedings and often crushing disbursements. But it is quite possible in a criminal practice,[1] which in general is not as labour intensive and lends itself to a freewheeling, shoot-from-the-lip approach where the task is not so much to prove *your* case but to find a crack in the *opposing* case.

Fortunately, for the Crown, in 1988 Peter was elected to the provincial parliament as a member of the Ontario New Democratic Party. From 1988 until his retirement from politics in 2011 (a period during which he never lost an election), Peter brought that same talent for courtroom chaos to the halls of government. He died in 2013 at the age of 60, proving that anarchy is destructive on more than one level.

1 And in a family practice.

It takes a certain personality to try all one's cases. Who does such a thing? We are given a hint by former Premier Bob Rae. With mixed feelings about doing so, Mr. Rae appointed Peter as Ontario minister of consumer and commercial relations when the NDP came to power in 1990. In his book, *From Protest to Power: Personal Reflections on a Life in Politics*, Rae wrote: "It was better to have [Peter] inside the tent pissing out than outside the tent pissing in. The problem was that he ended up inside the tent pissing in."[2]

So, now we know the magical combination needed to produce a try-them-all counsel: an anarchist with a urological disorder.[3]

Although you probably need not worry about whether you try too many cases, there is room for concern about whether you settle too many cases. I am particularly interested in why you settle and the influence of pre-trial conferences in the settlement process.

THE EDUCATION IMPERATIVE

Counsel must always be aware of the need to educate their judge. This is particularly important on a pre-trial conference. At trial, you might have several weeks during which you will be able to educate your judge on the legal principles relevant to your case. However, on a pre-trial, neither you nor the judge has the luxury of time. A judge could have six or more civil pre-trials in one day; and you are restricted to what you can fold into a pre-trial brief.

Educating your judge over the course of a multi-week trial is one thing, but having to do so within the confines of a pre-trial conference is almost impossible unless your case is blessed with one or two very narrow issues (and, then, only if those issues fall within an area of the law for which the pre-trial judge has some expertise).

I was a generalist judge sitting in a generalist court, which meant that, as each year passed, I knew less and less about more and more until I reached the point where I knew very little about an awful lot.

---

2 Bob Rae, *From Protest to Power: Personal Reflections on a Life in Politics* (Toronto: Penguin, 1996), 134.

3 Lyndon Johnson is quoted in *The New York Times* (October 31, 1971), when speaking about keeping J Edgar Hoover (1895–1972) as FBI chief: "It's probably better to have him inside the tent pissing out, than outside the tent pissing in."

When you have a case privately mediated, you properly pick a mediator with the appropriate knowledge of the law for your case. Would you ask a family lawyer or a corporate lawyer to mediate a motor vehicle claim? What about a judge with the same pedigree? Welcome to your pre-trial. Enjoy.[4]

In 2000, I received a letter in circumstances that cannot be conveniently summarized here. It was from the Honourable Mr. Justice Alvin Rosenberg. He died in 2013 at the age of 87. He was appointed to the Trial Division of the High Court in 1983. As you know, that was a circuiting court and, at one point, he was sent out from Toronto to preside at a murder trial in Napanee. Three prisoners, serving sentences in Millhaven, were accused of killing a third inmate with a baseball bat. Justice Rosenberg gave this background in his letter:

> When the preparations were made for the hearing it became obvious that there were real dangers involved in that the alleged murders were the result of an Anglophone–Francophone confrontation in Millhaven. There was concern that the Francophones would attempt to [avenge] the murder of their leader by having outside friends assassinate the accused. There was also concern that friends of the accused would attempt to help them escape while they were being transferred to the courthouse in Napanee. The result was that the prisoners were brought to the courthouse in a snow plough which it was felt could break through any barrier that was erected to try to stop the safe transport of the prisoners to the courthouse. There were helicopters hovering overhead and guard dogs used to assist in escorting the prisoners.
>
> Almost every complication that can arise in such a criminal case arose in this trial, from the selection of the very first juror until the verdict and sentencing.

With that background, let me add three facts to the story: (1) Justice Rosenberg had been appointed to the bench only several weeks before the trial; (2) he had not previously been part of, or witnessed, a criminal trial; and (3) he had never even been present at the selection of a criminal jury.

---

4 This does not mean I am opposed to lawyers from a general practice being appointed to the bench. After all, I was such a lawyer. My concern is with continuing as a generalist once on the bench.

To complete the picture that I am attempting to paint, the letter from Justice Rosenberg continued:

> I had been advised when I was appointed that all of the members of the High Court and the Court of Appeal were ready to assist whenever a problem arose. I took advantage of this situation and was in touch with John Brooke of the Court of Appeal almost hourly for advice [Justice Brooke sat on the Court of Appeal from 1969 until 1999]. My calls were frequent, even to his home when he was not in court. I once received a message from John while I was on the bench advising me that he was going out to the supermarket for an hour or so and that if I had a problem that arose while he was out, to stall for a while as he would be back shortly.

And you probably thought that the only reason for frequent short adjournments in a trial was a weak judicial bladder. Well, now you have a second working hypothesis: Your judge is seeking advice. On a regular basis judges preside over trials and pre-trials covering areas of the law in which they are less knowledgeable than counsel.

Surely the minimum requirement for an efficient and dependable legal system is to have judges who know at least as much law as the lawyers who appear before them. Those unfamiliar with our courts would be shocked to learn how often this minimum requirement is not met. In the Superior Court of Justice, this requirement, in my opinion, is consistently satisfied only in four instances: (1) the Family Court branch; (2) class proceedings where certain judges have been designated to handle such cases; (3) matters on the Commercial List in Toronto (established in 1991 for the hearing of actions, applications and motions involving issues of commercial law); and (4) some criminal cases heard by judges with a particular expertise in criminal law who seem to sit only on criminal trials. The rest of us are engaged in on-the-job training.

The fact that Justice Rosenberg survived his experience and went on to enjoy a long and distinguished judicial career does not flatter the system. He succeeded despite the system, not because of it.

PRE-TRIAL CONFERENCES AND DETRIMENTAL RELIANCE

In civil actions, some lawyers seem to think they have fulfilled their duty to a client with completion of the pre-trial conference. It is not so.

A crutch or a tool?

Are your pre-trials an excuse for settling or a reason for settling? In other words, do you use pre-trials as a crutch or as a tool?

Civil pre-trials are valuable if they are treated as a tool to uncover weaknesses in your case of which you were unaware. They become a crutch where you blindly rely on the settlement recommendations of the pre-trial judge so as to avoid a trial. I hold to the heretical view that lawyers should not be unduly influenced by a pre-trial. Very good lawyers know their case far, far better than does the pre-trial judge. Such lawyers do not materially benefit from a pre-trial. Typically, lawyers have lived with a file for two or more years before it reaches the pre-trial stage. If your case is scheduled for a 10-day trial, can you meaningfully address the key issues and evidence within the confines of a pre-trial brief? And how can the pre-trial judge, in one hour or so, fairly and reasonably address the resolution of those issues (even assuming the judge has expertise in the relevant area of the law)?

Thanks, Your Honour, but no thanks

I never saw my judicial role in a pre-trial conference to be one of actively seeking a settlement between the parties.[5] Frankly, I was thoroughly disinterested in whether the case was settled.[6] I gave to counsel my views on the issues in dispute and how I thought those issues would be decided at trial. Counsel could figure out for themselves what weight to give to my views and what compromises they were prepared to make. They did not require a judge to determine a midpoint between two positions. Thanks, Your Honour, but no thanks. Anybody with a calculator or a pencil and a scrap of paper could fulfill that function.

All right, show me yours if you wish – but I might not show you mine

When I was in practice, I knew a tough and experienced Welland counsel[7] who once complained to me that he disliked pre-trials because often the judge would identify the weaknesses in his opponent's case and either suggest cures or at least alert the opponent to the need for a

5 I was not appointed to the Superior House of Mediation.

6 I was not employed on a piecework basis.

7 Earle A Blackadder, Q.C.

cure.[8] I see nothing wrong with that mindset. As I have mentioned, for very good lawyers, pre-trial conferences are of debatable utility. They are merely thumb-twiddling, time-wasting money burners. In a pre-trial conference with a skilled lawyer on one side and a mediocre counterpart, a pre-trial judge effectively becomes co-counsel for the latter.

Why would you reveal your full case on a pre-trial? According to Article 17 under the *Geneva Conventions of 1949*, a prisoner of war is required to provide only his name, rank, serial number and date of birth. There are some pre-trials where you should adhere to Article 17. "Tactics" is not a four-letter word. Litigation is war with rules.[9]

Beware the ambiguity of inscrutable silence

As a lawyer, I assumed judges possessed more knowledge of the law than I did.[10] Why? It was because they sat in inscrutable silence throughout the case and appeared all-knowing. How wrong could I be? Very wrong, it turns out. When I became a judge and sat in silence, it was because I was not comfortably familiar with the area of the law in issue. Why would I ask a question and expose my ignorance? On those occasions when I interrupted and sprayed counsel with questions, it was because I *thought* I knew something. (The exceptions were criminal trials, where I always sat mute. If a fire were to have broken out at the front of the courtroom, I would have remained silent for fear that to do otherwise might upset the carefully crafted strategy of one of the parties.)

How does your judge perform on a muddy track?

Thoroughbred handicappers have the *Daily Racing Form* as their resource for researching the past performances of racehorses under varying conditions. Lawyers have *Quicklaw* and *CanLII* for doing the same in respect of the judges before whom they appear.

How do you gauge the past performance and expertise of your judge? Research. For example, if you checked up on me you would find, I think,

---

8 His complaint came after a mutual pre-trial wherein the judge had suggested a cure for a flaw in my case in circumstances where I had not even noticed the flaw, let alone crafted the cure (and Mr. Blackadder had been aware of both).

9 Please. Enough with the raised eyebrows.

10 Okay, okay, there were one or two notorious exceptions.

that I last presided over a motor vehicle trial in 2003.[11] (This was not by design. It was simply the way the docket unfolded. I had many motor vehicle pre-trial conferences since then, but no trials.) Imagine the learning ladder that I would have to climb if you and I were starting a motor vehicle trial tomorrow. And, if the trial included accident benefits issues, one ladder would not be enough.

In addition to the usual pressures preparing for trial, why should you have the extra burden of my education to worry about? That will always be a problem with generalist judges; and the problem is compounded by the limitations presented by a pre-trial conference.

Tabula rasa: *A poor business model*

You are well aware (but too polite to mention) that lawyers who never saw, say, a family file or a personal injury file in their law practices are appointed to the bench and preside over such matters. Imagine if this same business model were found in the health care system; we might have the following conversation between a hospital nurse and a doctor recently appointed as head of cardiology:

NURSE: Congratulations on your appointment.

DOCTOR: Thank you. Those years of bake sales and fundraising for the hospital paid off for me.

NURSE: The patient in Room 312 is complaining of arrhythmia, palpitations, light-headedness and chest pain. What is your diagnosis?

DOCTOR: You're asking me? Before I was appointed head of cardiology last Tuesday, I was a urologist. But, gosh, it sounds serious. My neighbour had the same symptoms. He was a nice man. I miss him.

NURSE: Do you have any idea about a diagnosis?

DOCTOR: It sounds like the heart.

NURSE: That's it? Can you be more precise?

---

11 *Mercier v Royal & Sunalliance Insurance Co of Canada*, 2003 CanLII 21638 (ON SC); aff'd (2004), 72 OR (3d) 94 (CA), in which I commented that anyone able to understand the world of statutory accident benefits should be entitled to claim bilingual status.

DOCTOR: I'll have to telephone someone. Do you have the number for Dr. Michael DeBakey?[12]

NURSE: What if something happens to the patient in the meantime?

DOCTOR: Not to worry. There is a panel of three doctors to whom the patient may appeal, posthumously if necessary.

NURSE: But aren't two of those doctors also former urologists?

DOCTOR: Good point. And the third used to be a dermatologist.

I once accompanied my wife on a visit to a medical specialist. When the nurse who did the pre-appointment prep-work learned that I was a judge and, as part of my duties, actually presided over medical malpractice cases, she was horrified. "What medical training do you have?" she asked, still horrified. Good question. I explained to her the *tabula rasa* ("blank slate") approach to judging. She was not impressed and remained horrified to the point of distraction. Can you blame her? The only other occupation where people routinely obtain serious employment for which they have no previous experience, learning as they go, is politics.[13]

Well intentioned, but not well informed

If it is your plan to hide behind the recommendations of a pre-trial judge, always be mindful of the need to educate the judge by outlining the legal principles and case law at play in your action so that you receive informed recommendations. As but one example, claims for loss of competitive advantage are common in personal injury actions. In your pre-trial conference briefs, I would like to see you set out the basic governing principles found in the leading cases. No counsel *ever* did this in any personal injury pre-trial conference over which I presided. Surely, from the 858 cases that came up in my last *CanLII* search under "loss of competitive advantage" (at the trial and appellate levels in Ontario), some are useful. If your judge finds all this education to be pedantic and demeaning and says, "You must think that I am an idiot," your reply should be, "No, Your Honour, but we were told that Justice Quinn would be hearing this pre-trial conference."

Judges are not any smarter than you are and although, in an efficient legal system, the judge would always know the law at least as well as

12 Dr. Michael DeBakey (1908–2008) was a Lebanese-American cardiac surgeon, scientist and medical pioneer.

13 And how is that working out?

counsel, the fact is that, in many cases, I knew less about the law than you knew. I was more well-intentioned than well-informed. In what other field of endeavour do the latter take guidance from the former?

When you step into a courtroom or conference room, educate the judge and you will have a best friend forever. Should you not want to bother doing so, but still require a judicial opinion, bring darts, dice and a Ouija board.

It is a silly system that appoints people to do work for which they have no experience. It is stressful for the judge,[14] it unnecessarily complicates the life of counsel and it can be a disservice to the litigants. Therefore, whether you have a favourable or unfavourable pre-trial conference, it could be immaterial. If your pre-trial judge is inexperienced in the relevant area of practice, you might as well have a urologist conduct the conference; and, if you settle your case on that basis, shame on you.[15]

Forceful, but still not well informed

The fact that your pre-trial judge may express his or her views forcefully is irrelevant. I know of one judge who adopted the motto, "Sometimes right, sometimes wrong, but never in doubt."

The epitome of futility

Perhaps there is some room for argument over what I have said so far. However, this point is inarguable: Certain issues do not lend themselves to a pre-trial, with the result that the conference is as productive as Question Period in the House of Commons. I will give two examples.

First, liability in a motor vehicle case or in a slip-and-fall case is an issue that the janitor at your courthouse is as equipped as a judge to resolve. Second, credibility issues are a poor fit with a pre-trial. Apart from the difficulty of conveying sufficient information to the pre-trial judge, why would you telegraph at a pre-trial how you intend to discredit a party at trial, thereby giving that party months to prepare and rehearse?

If your pre-trial presents those issues, adjourn the conference and go bowling.

---

14 If you want to witness pure fear, look into the eyes of a judge on the morning of his or her first jury trial (civil or criminal).

15 I have just noticed that urology has assumed a curious prominence in this article. I will look into that.

PLAYERS AND PRETENDERS

You cannot always validly excuse your avoidance of a trial by saying that the case was settled in accordance with the recommendations of the pre-trial judge. It is only where those recommendations reflect the true merits of the case, and where the judge has sufficient expertise, that the excuse is valid.

Some counsel are players and some are pretenders. You cannot be a player if you settle all your cases. A bank loans manager who boasts a zero percent default rate would be fired for not taking sufficient risks. Litigation is all about risks. They must be assessed, reassessed, managed and, sometimes, taken. You cannot become a competent counsel while camped in your office.

Do not fear losing a case. If you win a high percentage of your trials, I suspect you are selling many clients short because you obviously are not litigating the tough cases. Most high-profile counsel in the United States and Canada lose more often than they win. Losing is a part of advocacy – a *big* part. Your willingness, if not eagerness, to go to trial is the most effective weapon in your advocacy arsenal.

Lawyers avoid going to trial for various reasons. It is important that you honestly identify the basis for your avoidance of the courtroom, because there are both good and bad reasons for doing so. A good reason would be one that takes into account the risks associated with a trial. A bad reason would be fear.[16] The only basis for fear is inexperience, and there is a foolproof cure for inexperience. Another bad reason is laziness. Unfortunately, there is no known cure for laziness.

WHY TRY (CASES, THAT IS)?

Try some cases. Be a player.

I assume you do not want to be in the position of having to obtain a Google map to find your way to the courthouse. Apart from that, why should you try cases? I offer several reasons. Although they are obvious, it might be helpful to hear them mentioned out loud.

16 Are you uncomfortable hearing that word? Pity.

A professional trifecta

By trying cases with reasonable frequency, you achieve a professional trifecta. You (1) enhance your reputation; (2) protect the interests of your client; and (3) preserve your mental health.

How can you call yourself a trial lawyer if you do not do trials? What does that do to your professional reputation? And how can that be in the best interests of your client? A settlement that does not reflect the risks reasonably associated with taking a case to trial probably is an unreasonable settlement.

Fear snowballs. The longer the gap between your trials, the greater the apprehension and even the fear that results.[17]

I was called to the bar in 1972. Although I had tried several cases in Small Claims Court as an articling student, jury trials were a mystery. I dreaded having my first jury trial. Nothing in my legal education and training had prepared me for a jury trial. And the written precedents of the day (both civil and criminal) were utter garbage compared with the excellent material now available.

I did everything possible to avoid getting stuck with a jury trial. It was a foolish decision, for my anxiety rose to an irrational crescendo. I was drowning in fear.[18] I have no memory of my first jury trial, much like the lone survivor of a plane crash from whose conscious thought the body blocks out all the gory details. Given a second chance, if I were called to the bar on Monday I would arrange a jury trial for Tuesday.

Because advocacy can be learned, it makes sense that watching other counsel argue a motion or try a case will be beneficial. In fact, watching bad lawyers[19] is as enlightening as observing good ones. I rarely see young lawyers linger in motions court after their matter has been heard, and it is equally uncommon to spot such a lawyer serving as a spectator in a trial involving experienced counsel. These are missed opportunities to add to your courtroom toolbox. In 1972, I should at least have sat in on a few jury trials. I have no idea why that did not occur to me at the time.

Taste-test your judgment and analysis

Another reason for taking trials is to periodically test your assessment of what constitutes a reasonable settlement. In doing so, you are honing

17 To this point, I have used the word "fear" six times.

18 Seven times.

19 In this article, I am using "lawyer" and "counsel" interchangeably.

your judgment and analysis for future settlements. If a chef never taste-tests the food, how does he or she know the dishes are palatable and the correct recipe is being used? A trial is the best way to taste-test your work.

Try steering the bus for a change

Occasionally, a case will present a novel legal issue. What personal price are you prepared to pay to advance the case law and become part of the jurisprudence in your field? Do you not feel even a small duty to your profession? Sorry to hear that.

Are you merely along for the ride? Why not try steering the bus from time to time?[20]

Good news – you are not as important as you think

Inexperienced or otherwise poorly prepared counsel create disorganization and sometimes chaos, but it is difficult to lose a case where the facts are on your side. Injustice is likely to result only where an important witness is not called or a relevant document is not tendered in evidence.

Justice John Sopinka once estimated the importance of counsel to the outcome of a case as follows: at trial, up to 50 percent; on appeal to the Court of Appeal, about 25 percent; and, in the Supreme Court of Canada, 10–20 percent.[21] Thus, you probably are not as important to the case as you think.

A strong case likely will offset your inexperience. Facts should defeat fear.[22]

THE YOUNG OFFENDER GRACE PERIOD

Putting yourself in a position to get early trial experience means you will be doing so at a relatively young age. Judges, even curmudgeons, generally are kind and sympathetic to young, inexperienced counsel.

In the 1970s, the world of fashion suffered a nervous breakdown and I was a willing victim. One morning, I was in motions court in Hamilton. I had been a lawyer for about 12 minutes. I was wearing a green blazer, an orange shirt and a tie that might have glowed in the dark. Mercifully, I have no memory of the colour of my trousers and I can only assume

20 The overuse of metaphors is a criminal offence. My sentencing hearing is tomorrow.

21 See *The Advocates' Society Journal*, March 1990 at 3.

22 Eight times.

I was wearing shoes. I must have looked like a clown school freshman. The presiding judge did not criticize my physical appearance, but he did chastise Nick Borkovich,[23] a well-known Hamilton lawyer (10 years my senior) who was in court that morning, for wearing a somewhat sporty outfit, and sarcastically asked him when he was due at the yacht club. Much later, Nick was appointed to the bench and, when I subsequently joined him, he never missed an opportunity to complain that it was me the motions judge should have criticized. It was not until I went to the bench and discovered an urge to be protective of young, inexperienced counsel that I realized the motions judge humanely wished to send a message to me about proper courtroom attire without scarring me for life. His Honour had correctly concluded that Nick was better able to shoulder the criticism and it was better to annoy Nick than to scar me.[24]

Young lawyers should have trials early and often, when judicial empathy abounds.

THE YOU-SHOULD-KNOW-BETTER PHENOMENON

Running a trial is not like riding a bicycle (except for the falling-down-and-getting-banged-up part). You can forget.

Senior counsel do not enjoy the same level of tolerance from the bench as that available to junior counsel. It actually is sad to see a senior lawyer conduct a trial in circumstances where his[25] advocacy skills have atrophied. It produces a curious phenomenon: a lawyer who makes mistakes and commits protocol *faux pas* but does so with the panache of someone who does not know what he does not know.

SOME FINAL WORDS

Imagine we are on opposite sides of a case. Do you actually think you will get a reasonable settlement offer from me if I know you are an inexperienced or anxious litigator? The truth is that, in fulfillment of the duty to my client (and in furtherance of my predatory nature), I will try to take

23 (1935–2017).

24 Today, if you were to walk into my clothes closet you would think you had suffered detached retinas because my wardrobe consists of all blacks and greys. Too late.

25 I have not used the pronoun "her" because I have never encountered an inexperienced senior female counsel.

advantage of your inexperience or anxiety. I will take your lunch money every chance I get (but with a kind word, a smile and civility throughout).

Most counsel do not have enough trial experience. You can attend pre-trial conferences on an hourly basis until you die, but that will not advance your skills as a trial lawyer.

Trial lawyers try cases. Trial lawyers who settle all their cases are social workers.

Declare war on fear.[26] Try your brains out.

Get courtroom experience, even if you must take cases to trial for little or no fees (pick those cases carefully; but *pick* them). Do not view all your files from a financial perspective.[27] Treat some as educational opportunities that will advance your reputation as counsel and may lead to profitable future files.

I must tell you that the quality of advocacy is falling. Although there still are top-notch counsel to be found, they are becoming fewer and the number of mediocre counsel is swelling. Counsel today are as intelligent as their predecessors, but they lack the training and experience to be effective in court.

I was presiding in motions court in St. Catharines a few years ago when a lawyer approached the counsel table as his case was called. He addressed the court by saying, "Hi." How can that happen? How can it possibly happen?[28] Looking back I like to think that, maybe, I was mistaken and he was not a lawyer. Perhaps he was a urologist.

---

26 Nine times.

27 I am aware that litigation is expensive for clients. "I was never ruined but twice: once when I lost a lawsuit and once when I won one": Voltaire, pseudonym of François-Marie Arouet (1694–1778).

28 I suppose it could have been worse. He might have greeted me with, "Hi, dude."

Summer 2016

In support of open courts

IRIS FISCHER

IN FEBRUARY OF this year, many were captivated by Jian Ghomeshi's sexual assault trial. That case, and the social media posts and reporting that preceded the charges, started a national conversation about sexual assault and the criminal justice system. It also raised important questions about court openness and privacy interests, and where the balance should lie.

In the Ghomeshi trial, a coalition of the media applied to get access to the trial exhibits, as the media does in other trials where there is a significant public interest – the James Forcillo trial and Tim Bosma murder trial, to name two recent examples. But unlike Forcillo and Bosma, in Ghomeshi the media was the subject of strong criticism, even virulent online attack, for its application to unseal a photo exhibit – the "bikini photo" of the first complainant.

I acted for the media coalition in the Ghomeshi case. Here's why the media applied to get access to all the exhibits in that case, which was granted subject to the right of any interested party to object to the release of a particular exhibit. And here's why the media sought access to the bikini photo, which it didn't get.

I will start with some first principles.

We have decades of case law that makes it clear: Our courts are presumptively open, and exhibits are presumptively accessible. This is the case even when what is being adjudicated upon is highly personal, as it often is, given that our courts deal with everything from difficult family law cases to sexual assaults. The two categories of exceptions to openness are mandatory publication bans or sealing orders, found in the *Criminal Code* and elsewhere, and discretionary judicial restrictions on openness that satisfy the high threshold test set out by the Supreme Court of Canada in the landmark cases of *Dagenais v. Canadian Broadcasting Corporation* and *R. v. Mentuck*. The *Dagenais/Mentuck* test says that restrictions on openness are justified only if they are necessary to prevent a serious risk of harm to a recognized interest, and if preventing harm to that interest outweighs the harm to the public's interest in open courts.

The importance of openness in a free and democratic society has to do with our ability to hold public institutions to account. Transparency helps ensure that everyone does their job and the system functions as it should. The integrity of our justice system is based on public scrutiny of all the players – judges, lawyers, accused persons, witnesses, and institutional players such as the police.

The Supreme Court of Canada has been clear on the role of the media in the maintenance of democratic society: The media functions as the public's eyes and ears. As the court said in *Edmonton Journal v. Alberta (Attorney General)*, most of us can't take time off work or away from children or other obligations to attend court every day. Instead, we rely on the press to tell us about court proceedings. Members of the public are listeners or readers who have a right to receive the information gathered by the press, and only then can they assess an institution.

It is nothing new to recognize that open courts are fundamentally important to democracy and the maintenance of public confidence in the administration of justice. Openness is not a creation of the *Charter* era. In the seminal cases of *Scott v. Scott* and *McPherson v. McPherson*, the House of Lords and Privy Council in the early 20th century confirmed that even the very private stuff of matrimonial disputes is to be dealt with in open court, and not behind closed doors.

This does not mean that there are never occasions when openness legitimately needs to be curtailed. Of course there are. Openness does not foreclose a respect for privacy. Our legislatures have balanced these two interests by enacting limited carve-outs to openness, and our courts do the same thing in applying the *Dagenais/Mentuck* test. For instance, in some cases our laws protect the identity of patients where their personal health information is put in evidence in a public hearing. The *Youth Criminal*

Justice Act protects the identity of young people dealt with under that legislation. And, of course, sexual assault complainants have their identity protected by a mandatory publication ban in the *Criminal Code*. Sometimes discretionary publication bans or sealing orders are appropriate.

The media understands and respects the needs for certain exceptions to openness. But to maintain our justice system, these need to be carefully considered exceptions to presumptive openness and they need to be narrowly tailored to their purpose, and no broader. And there is often a concerning tendency to expand them.

As an example, in a 2015 case in Brampton, *R v. Hosannah*, the identities of two parents found guilty of manslaughter in the death of their toddler were initially protected by a publication ban. The rationale was that this was necessary to protect the pair's living children. The uncomfortable result was that these individuals, found criminally responsible in open court for the death of their child, were able to keep their identities secret from the general public. The *Toronto Star* applied to narrow the ban to the names of the living children only, on the basis that such a ban protected the children's privacy interests while not overly encroaching on the open court principle. The court agreed, holding that denying the public access to the names of convicted adult offenders was too great a restriction on openness, could lead to speculation and distrust of innocent third parties and could have a corrosive effect on the administration of justice.

Returning to the Ghomeshi trial, on the importance of court openness it offers a good example of the media's role in giving the rest of us a window into what is happening in the courts. Like many others, I closely followed reporters' tweets from the trial, intrigued and compelled by Marie Henein's expert cross-examinations and the unfolding of strategy on both sides. As a litigator, I asked myself many questions as I followed along. Would I have elicited more in direct examination of the complainants? What about the role of the police in digging out information in pre-charge interviews of complainants? And the much debated question: If I were Crown counsel, would I have called an expert witness to testify to the emotional and mental responses of sexual assault victims and the reasons some go back to their alleged assaulter? And would such expert evidence even have been admitted by the court?

Regardless of the answers to these questions, the point is, I was thinking about the issues. I was highly engaged, and I was able to be so engaged because of the media presence in the courtroom and the committed, almost verbatim, live-tweeting of questions and answers during witness examinations. I was able to be so engaged because I watched the police interviews of the complainants – trial exhibits obtained and made available to the public because of the media coalition application – and developed my own views about the sufficiency of the questions asked and the level of preparedness of the witnesses. And when Justice Horkins released his judgment, I – along with many others – was in a position to understand it and to agree or disagree to an unusual extent.

More than this, the detailed reporting of the trial made possible a broad and impassioned debate – not limited to lawyers – about how our criminal justice system functions in sexual assault cases and whether it ought to function differently. This is public scrutiny of the justice system that is made possible by open courts, and it is how it should be.

On the balance between court openness and privacy interests, the Ghomeshi trial provided another useful point of discussion. The "bikini photo" exhibit was entered by the defence during the cross-examination of the first complainant, who was confronted with two emails she sent to Mr. Ghomeshi a year after the alleged assault. To the second one she had attached a photograph of herself in a string bikini on a Toronto beach. When pressed by Ms. Henein, she told the court that this was intended to be "bait" to try to get Mr. Ghomeshi to contact her so she could seek an explanation from him. Many found this to be a highly incredible explanation. The photo was not shown on a screen to those in the courtroom, as other exhibits were, and this was the only exhibit during the trial that was not made available to the media and was sealed by the court pending a decision by the media on whether to apply to unseal it. The media did bring an application, which was opposed by the Crown and the complainant, and ultimately denied by the court.

It is important to recognize the difference between access – getting a copy of an exhibit – and publication of an exhibit by the media. In applying for access, the media was not committing to publish the photo exhibit. Each newspaper or broadcaster in the broad coalition that sought access would have made its own editorial decision on this point, probably after vigorous newsroom debate.

We will never know what decisions would have been made. But the media fought for access to this photo because it was an important piece of evidence in this trial of great public interest. It was part of the record the court considered and ruled upon in deciding Mr. Ghomeshi's guilt or innocence. It was tendered to assail the credibility of the first complainant, and what we didn't see may have been important, too.

The court ultimately held that the complainant's privacy interests and the societal interest in complainants coming forward justified keeping the photo sealed. The court also held that the media and the public did not need to see the photo to understand the issues. For this, we have to take the court's word.

To be clear, there was never any question of identifying the complainant even if the photo had been published – her face would have been blurred, and any other identifying marks obscured. Though the complainant's lawyers argued she could still be identified online even if the photo was blurred, there was no evidence to support this argument and it did not appear to be part of the basis of the court's ruling. So in this contest between openness and privacy, it wasn't ever all or nothing. Instead, the media position was that the complainant's privacy would remain protected by the publication ban on her identity, and that a further constraint on openness was not warranted. The court rejected that position, but did so thoughtfully and with a reasoned discussion of the relevant law.

Whether ultimately successful in a particular case or not, the media's vigilant push for openness and transparency should be important to all of us. Without the media's exercise of its watchdog function, there might not be anyone watching to make sure publication bans are not ordered summarily; or anonymity orders granted without consideration of the Supreme Court's carefully calibrated test; or exhibits peremptorily sealed without consideration of their public interest. There might not be anyone else willing to fight discretionary court applications and incur the costs of doing so.

Even when the media loses the fight for openness, an important function is served. The courts, the parties and the public are reminded of the importance of this principle and of the willingness of the fourth estate to monitor courts and fight for transparency.

Without that vigilance, the risk exists that, next time, we simply won't know what we don't know.

PERSONAL REFLECTION | SUMMER 2011

The advocate as loser

JONATHAN LISUS

EVERY TIME WE advocates try a case, there must be a loser. Our system is designed to create a loser and to ensure that the loss is permanent. After all, most appeals are unsuccessful and deference to the decision at first instance is the rule. This is unique to our adversarial system of justice. It isn't so in business (where second chances are encouraged), other professions or other forms of lawyering. No doubt solicitors can make costly mistakes, but the context in which they operate isn't premised on causing an opponent to lose. And if their clients do "lose," it's likely due to an insured error, not because their lawyer was bested in a duel.

This brute reality makes it tough to be a trial lawyer, which itself is odd, because the certainty of loss is baked right into the process. It's what we sign up for. One would think that we would understand and internalize this. Yet, of all the sacrifices we make and the tests we endure – the long hours, the difficult clients, the obstructive opponents and grumpy judges – nothing tests us more than a loss.

Losing really rocks us. It knocks some of us right off our game and into a career of motions, discoveries and mediations. And losing can be bad for business. If we are trying cases, the spectre of losing – its consequences for our client and future clients – hangs over much of what we do. We either master it or it, us. Paul Brown, head coach of the Cleveland franchise that took his name, counselled his players: "When you win, say nothing. When you lose, say less." The second part of Coach Brown's advice seems to be the approach taken by most lawyers. Lawyers, particularly trial lawyers, like to talk about what they do, but there isn't a lot of talk about their losses. The fact is, our losses teach much more than our wins, and not just about the craft of trying cases. So it's important to talk about them.

The medical profession learned this lesson early. Mortality and morbidity rounds – in which bad outcomes and the price that patients pay for them are presented to staff doctors, nurses and students – are a central part of life in a teaching hospital and a core element of medical professionalism. Sometimes these outcomes are the product of mistakes. Sometimes they are the inevitable result of the process, and to that extent doctoring is a lot like lawyering.

In reality, the sports analogy, although good for inspirational metaphors, is incomplete. Athletics are mostly a contest, and not much more (although the fan base of the English Premier League and some very good sociologists would strongly disagree). On the other hand, a case is often so much more than a contest. It's the path through which a wrong is righted, a freedom is returned, or the ability to carry on with the natural course of life is restored. This is why we so often identify with our clients and their causes, and why losing is so hard.

I looked for some insight from our medical colleagues because of the dramatic nature of the losses they deal with and the formalized discussion process they have. In fact, I quickly realized that the focus of M&M rounds, as they're euphemistically called, is a pure causation analysis.

There is precious little written on the impact of the loss of a patient on the treating physician. I did find two terrific articles, one in the *British Medical Journal* ("*BMJ*") titled "Doctors' Emotional Reactions to Recent Death of a Patient"[1] and another in the *Journal of the American Medical Association* ("*JAMA*"), "The Inner Life of Physicians and Care of the Seriously Ill."[2] The *BMJ* article is data-based and poignant in a stiff-upper-lip sort of way. It crunches statistics and discusses the different reactions of

1 Ellen M Redinbaugh et al, "Doctors' Emotional Reactions to Recent Death of a Patient: Cross-Sectional Study of Hospital Doctors" (2003) BMJ 327: 185 doi: 10.1136/bmj.327.7408.185, online: <www.bmj.com/content/327/7408/185.full>.

2 DE Meier, AL Back & RS Morrison, "The Inner Life of Physicians and Care of the Seriously Ill" (2001) JAMA Dec 19; 286(23):3007–3014, online: <http://jama.ama-assn.org/content/286/23/3007.full>.

interns and "house staff" to the loss of patients. These reactions include disrupted sleep for long after the event and "intrusive thoughts" about the patient. The *JAMA* article examines more closely the impact on clinicians beyond the starch of the white coat – their inner life.

The *JAMA* article notes that "[s]eriously ill persons are emotionally vulnerable during the typically protracted course of an illness. Physicians respond to such patients' needs and emotions with emotions of their own, which may reflect a need to rescue the patient, a sense of failure and frustration when the patient's illness progresses ... These emotions can affect both the quality of medical care and the physician's own sense of well-being, since unexamined emotions may also lead to physician distress, disengagement, burnout, and poor judgment." Do you see the parallels?

The *BMJ* article cautions that "although it is normal to have feelings arising from the care of patients, physicians should take an active role in identifying and controlling those emotions." This is easier said than done, but the point is that much in this description of the physician–patient relationship is reflected in the advocate–client relationship.

The *BMJ* article also says that "caring for dying patients is part of every doctor's clinical experience both during training and in subsequent practice. However, the literature on doctors' experiences in caring for the dying is sparse and mostly anecdotal. Many of these stories reflect the sadness, guilt and stress caused by caring for dying patients. Such stress has been linked to professional burnout and may put doctors at risk of psychiatric disorders." Although the issue of psychiatric disorders at the bar is a topic for another article, there is little doubt that we often have the same. It would thus appear that like doctors, we keep our losses bottled up, except perhaps to explain the central role played by the client, judge or jury (and sometimes all three) in the unhappy outcome. I don't know of any firm that has a monthly breakfast meeting to discuss its biggest recent losses. And, as far as I know, The Advocates' Society has not yet sold out a symposium on the topic.

I spoke with Bryce Taylor, the former surgeon in chief at the University Health Network, about what he learned about losing from 38 years on the surgical floor. He told me that the losses got harder to deal with over the years, not easier, perhaps because medicine and science are supposed to advance. He recalled being the trauma surgeon on call in 1980, when two patients were rushed on to his service at the Toronto General

Hospital. One was Constable Michael Sweet, and the other was Craig Munro. These men were the protagonists memorialized in the infamous robbery turned hostage-taking that culminated in the Supreme Court's constructive homicide ruling *R. v. Munro*. The trauma team lost Constable Sweet but saved Craig Munro from dying from his multiple gunshot wounds. He said that the events of that day, and the dreadfully unfair outcome, which he considered a loss, still live vividly with him.

So, what can we learn from losing? I thought the best way to get an answer would be to ask people who knew a lot about the issue. "Show me a good loser and I'll show you a loser," this *Journal*'s editor answered when I asked him what he learned from losing. I tried again, but Paul Pape told me he really didn't know anything about losing. Happily, that call wasn't wasted because I heard a lot about his upcoming appeal and the inside story of the last two.

In fact, the process of asking was itself instructive. Many experienced trial lawyers were surprised by the request and declined the invitation to talk publicly and candidly about their losses. Forced into primary research, I discovered a few great pieces on the topic, although, far fewer than have been written on how to win. My favourite is a 2002 article by Glenn Bradford, "Losing," and I've leaned heavily on it.[3] Bradford identifies what he considers the two aspects of losing that every trial lawyer must reckon with: the fear of losing and the reality of losing.

These are two very different things. At some level, all of us fear losing. Some permit that fear to stunt their approach, whereas others use it to motivate them. The same is true of the reality of losing. Losses are the anvil on which the advocate is forged. Without taxing the sports analogy, let me quote Vince Lombardi: "It's not whether you get knocked down, it's whether you get back up."

One of the most enthusiastic responses to my request for help came from Roger Oatley, an advocate who has tried a few high-risk cases. Roger described a formative loss: one of his early jury trials. His client was a lovely, intelligent high school student from a close-knit, working-class family. She had been in woodworking class, operating a table saw, when she asked her teacher for help in adjusting the blade. The teacher didn't have her stand clear from the machine and bumped her

3 Glenn Bradford, "Losing" (2002) 58:4 Journal of the Missouri Bar (July–August), online: <www.mobar.org/7a326e79-70f6-4087-bf14-a8ee890d6655.aspx>.

elbow, knocking her hand into the still-spinning saw. She lost three fingers, and her hand was horribly disfigured. The disfigurement caused her to suffer a profound emotional disturbance, and by the time of trial she had dropped out of school, was abusing substances and was living on the street. The trial went well, but during closing argument defence counsel postulated a theory of causation that had no foundation in the evidence. The jury returned a plaintiff's verdict, but it was very modest and with a large finding of contributory negligence.

The client and her family were devastated. The Court of Appeal refused to interfere. Oatley "just couldn't believe the case had worked out so badly for such a deserving plaintiff. I found my own sense of failure almost unbearable." He told me that the loss taught him that he had "no idea how to properly present a jury trial and that [he] had to do something about it." I suspect that this is an overstatement, but it is a highly revealing overstatement. As difficult as the loss was, it was galvanizing, not debilitating. Oatley started reading everything he could on jury persuasion and decision making. He went to every course he could on the subject. The loss affirmed, not undermined, his belief in the jury process. He started to win a lot more, and went on to write a book to share what he had learned. He describes that case as changing his entire career.

New York plaintiff's personal injury lawyer Thomas Moore has said, "If I lose a case, it's a disaster, the losses live with me, it's like a grieving process." But his grief has not stood in the way of delivering over 100 verdicts in excess of $1 million and settlements exceeding $1 billion. These two statistics are closely connected. Ian Binnie recalled from his counsel days the "aftershocks of losing," which would sometimes reverberate for months. He also remarked on the often overlooked impact that appellate reversal, the judicial form of loss, has on trial and appellate judges. After all, in the case of a trial and appeal, it is really the position of your client that is not ultimately accepted, isn't it? But when a carefully considered judgment is overturned for error of law, or even worse, palpable and overriding error, there can be no doubt about the reason for reversal.

Perhaps the hardest part of losing is its unpredictability. Henry Miller, a renowned New York trial lawyer, observed from the perspective of 40-odd years of trial work that "[w]e must accept that in our careers we are going to lose a certain number of cases. We just do not know which ones they will be."

This brings us to the first lesson of losing: humility. Humility, not to be confused with meekness, is tightly bound up with courage and honesty, which are essential elements of strong advocacy. Whatever else it includes, humility is the ability to understand that every case can be lost and that, like our losses, our wins often occur in spite of ourselves.

Anyone who has tried more than a handful of cases understands that the line between a win and a loss is often very thin and is frequently drawn not by counsel but by other incalculable factors, some seen and understood, and others invisible and silent: documents not found or even asked for, memories lost, theories not explored, silent persuaders in the mind and life experience of the trier of fact.

John Robinette, arguably Canada's greatest advocate, lost a lot of cases. In approximately 148 appearances in the Supreme Court, he lost 68. Now, 80 wins is a lot, but so is 68 losses. That's because Robinette was a lawyer of last resort, and most of those cases were lost before they ever reached his hands. Abraham Lincoln, one of America's greatest advocates, had a similar record: of 87 judge–alone cases for which there are records, Lincoln won 40 and lost 47; of 82 jury trials, verdicts in favour of his clients were achieved in "only" 43. The consensus of the British bar is said to be: "Of every hundred cases, ninety win themselves, three are won by advocacy, and seven are lost by advocacy."

Edward Bennett Williams, the Washington trial lawyer who counted Frank Sinatra, Hugh Hefner, Michael Milken, Jimmy Hoffa, Senator Joseph McCarthy, Reverend Sun Myung Moon and *The Washington Post* among his clients, said:

> If you turn over any given football team to the best coach in America, he may win two more games than the most incompetent coach would win with the same material. Likewise, if you take a hundred criminal cases and assume that fifty of them should be won on the merits and that fifty should be lost, and then turn them over to the most able and experienced advocate in America, he will probably win sixty and lose forty. Turn the same cases over to the most incompetent trial man and he will win forty and lose sixty. The concept of a great trial lawyer who always wins has no foundation in reality. It is a television or Hollywood fiction.[4]

4 Evan Thomas, *The Man to See* (New York: Simon & Schuster, 1992) at 157.

This leads to losing's second lesson: the ability to distinguish a win from a loss. Whether you're on for the plaintiff or for the defence, you must recognize that many cases are actually about damage control. Some outcomes, while technically a loss, are far better than the deal on the table before trial and are a substantial improvement in the pre-trial position of your client.

Conversely, some "wins" have very little value when the initial event and transaction costs are taken in to account. The ability to distinguish a loss from a win and to explain the distinction to the client at the appropriate stage of the case is a key lesson to learn. On this topic John Rosen, who has more than 300 murder trials to his credit, surprised me by saying that the losses he minds least are those in which he did everything right. The rulings all went his way, the jury was engaged and responsive, and the credibility of the prosecution witnesses was left in tatters. But the jury still convicted.

In those cases, Rosen felt that he had discharged his role as an advocate and had upheld his oath to his client and the court. But even the best counsel can't entirely rewrite history or change the laws of physics. In such cases, a loss is measured not so much by the ultimate outcome but by the process – something the advocate can control and is accountable for. Cases such as *R. v. Brown* (the "Just Desserts" trial), *R. v. Felderhof* and *Marchand v. Public General Hospital Society of Chatham* are good examples of cases in which judgment was rendered in favour of one side or the other but advocacy was the loser.

The third lesson of losing is that it completes us as advocates. We must be prepared to lose. It must not frighten us. After all, we did not create the problem our client is saddled with. Embracing the prospect of loss is an essential element of strong advocacy. Without doing so, we can never develop that most essential character of the advocate – courage. And courage can be developed.

Courage can be developed by learning from bitter experience that the world does not end with a loss. I have always admired those counsel who shake off the Big Loss and gallop right into the next contest, secure in the knowledge of their limited ability to influence the ultimate outcome. Pericles said that "those who can truly be accounted brave are those who know the meaning of what is sweet in life and what is terrible and then go out undeterred to meet what is to come." In the life of an advocate, winning is surely sweet and losing terrible, but the true advocate goes out undeterred to meet what is to come. And if you are so deterred by what is terrible, you will never know the sweetness.

If you have the courage and the tenacity to get up from a loss, there is – sure as day – a win around the corner. My father, who has had more than his share of losses and wins in life, is fond of saying, "*Môre is nog n'dag*" (tomorrow is another day). Until we have lost a good number of cases, including those we thought we had won or should have won, we cannot really claim to be complete advocates. As Glenn Bradford points out, we must embrace our losses, use the hard times to build "psychic muscles" and take pride in our "scar tissue."

Coming to terms with the prospect of loss not only leads to good preparation but creates the confidence to take the case to its natural end point, whether that point be judgment or a fair settlement. The fact is that we cannot be the best advocates for our clients unless we fully understand and accept the possibility of losing, and it is important that our opponents know that we are not afraid to lose again. This awareness often leads to better settlements and is one good reason not to be shy about gaining scar tissue.

This leads to the fourth lesson. Courage leads to confidence, and confidence to civility. And civility in losing is critical. We must know how to lose, or, at the very least, appear to our colleagues and the court as knowing how to lose.

Fortunately, this lesson isn't a long one and often means doing not very much more than Coach Brown's "saying less." But something should be said to our opponent, even if it's by e-mail if we can't quite bear to make "the call." And don't forget the court: sometimes we can see a loss coming in court, and it's rarely a good idea to get into a fight with the judge about it. This doesn't mean we don't stand our ground – in fact, it's imperative that we do – but the line between tenacity and impudence must be kept in sight. Courage and scar tissue leads to the fifth and final lesson of losing: perseverance. This recalls Winston Churchill's 1941 speech to the graduating class of Harrow: "Never give in. Never give in. Never, never, never, never – in nothing, great or small, large or petty – never give in, except to convictions of honour and good sense."

When I asked Earl Cherniak to reflect on some of his most memorable losses and what they taught him, he instantly recalled the case of a young woman left with badly disfigured legs as a result of a car accident. The case was tried by a judge and jury. Following a completely inadequate charge, to which Cherniak took great exception, the jury came in with a middling award for general damages. Cherniak appealed. He was careful to have the appellant in court, wearing a skirt that would reveal the sad consequences of the accident. As it happened, each time the appellant stood up, the seating obscured her legs. She presented to the panel as a healthy, attractive and able young woman. The court "reluctantly" dismissed her appeal.

On appeal to the Supreme Court of Canada, where the appellant was nowhere to be seen, the court noted: "[T]his young woman will bear now for the rest of her life two badly scarred legs, and those scars will not appreciably improve, and that in addition to the surface being scarred the function of the legs is visibly altered so that she walks with a most awkward and ungainly gait ... even in today's atmosphere of independence, young ladies still put some value upon marital prospects, and the marital prospect of a young woman with badly scarred legs and awkward gait is most materially affected."[5] The Supreme Court close to doubled the damage award. This case, a "loss" at trial and appeal, taught the most important lesson of losing – tenacity and perseverance, or, as Cherniak succinctly puts it, "He who wins last wins."

One of the aspects of the perseverance lesson I find the most challenging is driving on in the face of important interlocutory losses and, often, the attendant costs. Why isn't the judge seeing the case the same way? Am I missing an important signal from the court? Will the client have the appetite to see this through? How will this play out later? Bob Harrison and Richard Swan, who tried *Waxman v. Waxman,* describe the "tens of interlocutory losses" their client had sustained, the early exhaustion of the retainer and the rocky start before a chilly and skeptical trial judge. Early in her reasons, the judge remarked that at the outset of trial she preferred the defendant's version of events – a version she ultimately concluded was a "fabrication."

And in *Lac Minerals Ltd. v. International Corona Resources Ltd.,* Alan Lenczner and Ron Slaght persevered after the claim was struck multiple times, until Justice Mac Craig graciously allowed the long-shot pleading of "breach of confidence" to stand. The rest, of course, is history.

To the extent that Roger Oatley, Earl Cherniak and John Rosen can offer a single lesson from their losses, it is this: if you try your cases, you

5 *Honan v Gerhold,* [1975] 2 SCR 866 at 879.

will have losses. And you will have wins. They are closely intertwined. Do not let the losses deter you from trying cases. If you try more cases you will have more wins, but you will also have more losses. Winning and losing are flip sides of the same coin, the one we toss high into the air every time we walk into court and begin a trial.

We can influence the height to which we flip the coin, the force with which we flip it, how carefully we position our hand beneath its downward arch and how closely we watch it rise, then fall. But there is much we cannot control, and this is set by a myriad of factors and forces. If we do not try our cases because we fear the losses, we will quickly not have any wins and the bar will quickly identify us as being afraid to lose. And fear is the advocate's greatest foe.

Part Five

APPELLATE ADVOCACY

MY LATE PARTNER and the former Attorney General Ian Scott hated trials. They were unpredictable. A witness might well say anything despite exhaustive preparation. Ian preferred judicial reviews and appeals, where the record is available and the evidence is immutable. Meanwhile, I keep seeking an answer to the question, "What persuades?" To answer the question, we have reflections by two esteemed jurists and two formidable advocates. To get there, as Justice Coulter Osborne famously put it, you must show that your client occupies the "moral high ground."

March 2005

Losing tip no. 16:

1066 AND ALL THAT

THE HONOURABLE MARVIN CATZMAN

WHEN WE WERE in high school, our history teacher made us read *1066 And All That.*[1] Although a small book, it was majestically subtitled "A Memorable History of England, comprising all the parts you can remember, including 103 Good Things, 5 Bad Kings and 2 Genuine Dates."

One of the "2 Genuine Dates" was 1066.[2] That was the year William the Conqueror, Duke of Normandy, invaded and conquered England.[3] At the Battle of Hastings, a Norman arrow mortally wounded the Anglo-Saxon King Harold, and the English language proceeded off in a whole new direction.[4] For one of the principal consequences of the Norman

1 Walter C. Sellar and Robert J. Yeatman, *1066 And All That* (London: Methuen, 1931).

2 The other was 55 B.C., when Julius Caesar landed at the Isle of Thanet with ten thousand of his closest friends. The Romans hung around, off and on, until the A.D. 400s, speaking a lot of Latin so that the locals wouldn't understand what they were saying. But the locals outsmarted them and learned a little Latin without letting on: see note 6.

3 Hence the name "William the Conqueror." Some people called King Harold "Harold the Conqueree" for a while, but the name never stuck.

4 This is what our high school English teacher called a "cat-and-dog" sentence, the first half of which appears to have nothing to do with the second half. But then again, we always liked history more than we liked English: see note 12.

invasion was the imposition on the invadees[5] of a vocabulary that was very different from the one they had previously used. The aristocracy employed a form of the Norman French language; the commoners, their traditional Anglo-Saxon language. The result was the creation of legal phrases that combined the two languages (often, with a little Latin thrown in for good measure[6]) so that they could be understood by everyone who plied his[7] lawyerly trade. They said the same thing, but in different languages. Sometimes they spoke in duplicate, saying such things as:

- "aid and comfort"
- "last will and testament"
- "cease and desist"
- "null and void"
- "goods and chattels"
- "covenant and agree"
- "force and effect"
- "free and clear"
- "save and except"

Sometimes, if duplicates weren't enough, they spoke in triplicate, saying things like:

- "right, title and interest"
- "rest, residue and remainder"
- "ordered, adjudged and decreed"

And sometimes, when they were really, really desperate, they spoke in quadruplicate, like this:

- "give, grant, devise and bequeath"

---

5 It is not generally known, but judges are required to attend mandatory courses in composing goofy names for people on the receiving end of things. That is why they keep using words like "abductees," "detainees," and "representees." My particular favourite is "escapees," which means exactly the opposite of what it is intended to convey. "Escapees" is used to describe prisoners who have gone AWOL from the place in which they are incarcerated. Strictly speaking, they should be called "escapers"; it is the warden and the prison guards who are the "escapees." But I digress.

6 See note 2. Haven't you been paying attention?

7 This possessive pronoun is not politically, but is historically, correct. Women weren't lawyers then.

Think about it for a minute. Remember Paul Revere and his celebrated midnight ride to Concord in 1775, warning about the coming of the British? And the famous signal of the lanterns hanging in the belfry arch of the North Church Tower?[8] How fast do you think the colonial army would have been able to react if Paul had had to figure out the hanging of the lanterns using the code "One, single or individual if by land, terra firma or real estate; two, duple or distichous if by sea, the bounding main or the briny deep"? Had that been the signal, the Americans would to this day be trying to figure out what on earth[9] Revere was talking about.[10]

You may well wonder[11] how all this erudition ties in with losing appeals. The answer is this. Just like the post-1066 invadees of England, good losing counsel generously sprinkle in duplicate, triplicate, and even occasionally quadruplicate, meaningless words and phrases that are designed to confuse the daylights out of every court in which they appear.[12] In their factums,[13] they make sure to present the same point at least three different times in three ever-so-slightly different ways, thereby leaving the unmistakable impression that they consider the court to be too dumb to have understood it the first, second, or (occasionally) third time. Similarly, they cite not one but two, three, or four cases in support of every proposition they advance, no matter how pedestrian. The factums read something like this: "A driver may enter an intersection when

8 The well-read among you will know that I can't take any personal credit for this impressive historical allusion. The real credit belongs to a guy named Longfellow who, in 1860, captured Paul Revere's famous ride in poetry: "Listen, my children, and you shall hear," etc. See "Paul Revere's Ride," in *Complete Poetical Works of Henry Wadsworth Longfellow* (New York: Amereon, 2000).

9 Or, to be precise, "where on earth, soil or alluvium?" See how complicated this is?

10 In which case, of course, they wouldn't be called "Americans," either.

11 Or, if you lost interest several paragraphs ago, you well may not.

12 This sentence originally ended "they appear in." Then I remembered our high school English teacher, who taught us 117 unbreakable rules of grammar, including the one about never ending a sentence with a preposition. Is it any wonder we liked our history teacher more?

13 Or, if you are a Latin purist, "facta." But this assumes that a factum has been filed. Many losing counsel prefer to employ the Lost Factum Gambit. They file no factum (lest, by accident, they disclose that their appeal has some merit) and then, when a member of panel says that she couldn't find their factum in the court papers, they affect an awestruck look and tell the court with a straight face that they did file one and the court office must have lost it.

the light is green:[14] see *Lockstock v. Barrel*, [1968] S.C.R. 742 (S.C.C.); considered in *Hammer v. Tongs* (1973), 43 O.P.C.R. (2d) 529 (Ont. Police Court); approved, *in obiter*, in *Murder v. Mayhem* (1984), 27 Admin. L.R. (2d) 390 (Manitoba Domestic Violence and Stalking Prevention, Protection and Compensation Commission)."

While we are on the subject of factums, there is a Practice Direction out there that says that a factum should not be longer than thirty pages. Losing counsel, who know that they can say everything they have to say in ten pages, never ever file a ten-page factum. Instead, good losing counsel fill twenty pages, saying the same thing over and over again. And exceptional losing counsel fill the whole thirty, saying the same thing over and over and over again.

Ditto the oral argument. Suppose that an appeal can be fully argued in fifteen minutes, but the appellant has been allotted forty-five minutes for oral submissions. Only an amateur would make his[15] argument in fifteen minutes and sit down. Practised losing counsel will stretch it to thirty. And really accomplished losing counsel will stretch it to the full forty-five. And why not? The only jeopardy is incurring the undying enmity of the panel of judges who have to suffer through this torture. But that's the object of the exercise, isn't it? To so infuriate the judges that pure fury will blind them to any possible merit the appeal may have?

In preparing for an appeal, losing counsel should take every available opportunity to sharpen their talent for longiloquence.[16] The art of unintelligible prolixity is not perfected overnight; it requires a great deal of practice. Among the readily available subjects on whom you may wish to consider honing your burgeoning ability to confuse are the members of your own family. I know several truly dedicated losing counsel who

---

14 This proposition is not, strictly speaking, pedestrian; it is more like vehicular.

15 I agonized over this pronoun. In these articles, I have used "she" and "her" for good lawyers, judges and clients, and "he" and "his" for the other variety. Strictly speaking, this should read "her." But the label "amateur" conveys a certain opprobrium, and for that reason I decided to use "his" instead.

16 Those of you who doubt that "longiloquence" is really a word (or, for that matter, those of you who have too much time on your hands and are simply looking for ways to fill your waking hours) can find it in *The Shorter Oxford English Dictionary*, 3rd ed. (Oxford: Oxford University Press, 1973), just between "longilateral" and "longimetry."

nightly confound their unsuspecting children by singing to them, at bedtime, the famous nursery rhyme:

> A triumvirate of murine rodents totally devoid of ophthalmic acuity was observed in a state of rapid locomotion in pursuit of an agriculturist's uxorial adjunct. Said adjunct then performed a triple caudectomy utilizing an acutely honed bladed instrument generally employed for subdivision of edible tissue.[17]

Try it. It always worked when my kids were small. I cannot remember even one occasion when they didn't fall asleep in the middle of it.

So the moral, for all wannabe losing counsel out there, is this: never, ever say only once what you can say twice or even thrice. Remember: if it worked for Xerox, it can work for you, too.

17 Or, as non-losing counsel refer to it, "Three Blind Mice."

September 2009

Some appellate advocacy advice

THE HONOURABLE MARSHALL ROTHSTEIN[1]

BEING INTRODUCED BY Jack [Major] is a great honour; it is no exaggeration to say that he is an icon of the Canadian legal community and of this College.

His introduction brings to mind the story of the Pope. He had an engagement, he came down to the car that was waiting for him and he decided that he wanted to drive, so he told the chauffeur to get in the back, and he started driving. Unfortunately, he was going too fast and he was stopped. The officer came to the car window. When he saw the Pope, he decided he had better call headquarters.

He said, "We have an incident here." The desk sergeant said, "What is the problem?" The officer said, "Well, I have stopped someone really important for speeding." Desk sergeant said, "Who is he?" Officer replied, "I am not sure, but the Pope is his chauffeur." Today, I feel like the guy sitting in the back seat, with the Pope as my chauffeur.

As Jack told you, I never made it as a real member of the College, but I am happy to get in any way I can. Consider me a late bloomer.

1 Canadian Supreme Court Justice Marshall Rothstein was inducted as an Honorary Fellow of the American College of Trial Lawyers at its annual meeting in Toronto. The presentation was made by his predecessor, retired Justice Jack Major, Q.C., S.C.C., FACTL. The edited text of Justice Rothstein's acceptance remarks follows.

ADVICE CONCERNING CANADIAN APPELLATE PRACTICE

I want to talk, just for a moment, and say to you that lawyers are very mobile these days. I know that Canadian lawyers have appeared in U.S. courts, and American lawyers may soon appear in Canadian courts. Canadian lawyers will be familiar with what I propose to say, but the College I know is concerned about continuing legal education, so I thought it would be instructive for me to help our American visitors with the practice and procedure they will encounter if they come to the Canadian Supreme Court. I am going to cover ten points.

One, getting leave to appeal: Generally, advocacy before our Supreme Court starts with the application for leave to appeal. Some lawyers complain that it is hard to get leave in our court, but there is no secret to getting leave. Our *Charter of Rights* came into force in 1982. We like to write judgments about the *Charter*. It doesn't matter whether the case is about the *Charter* or not. You just have to sprinkle the *Charter* through the application at least half a dozen times. If it is bolded and put in large font, we won't miss the point. Colour is good. If we see the *Charter* enough times, and it is highlighted, we will grant leave.

Two, the brief: We call the brief a factum. In our court, you don't have to worry about the factum. You can patch up any errors or omissions in oral argument. If you don't put an argument in the factum, and you argue it orally, you will gain the advantage of surprise. Don't worry about the page limit in the rules for the factum. Those limits are not meant to be taken seriously. Factums should be as long as possible. It gives weight to the argument. If the other side has raised a good argument, don't get sucked into providing a response. Focus only on your winnable arguments, and if necessary, go off on tangents. That way, you will divert the judges from the difficult and contentious point. Judges get bored with reading dry legal writing. So you should make the factum as rhetorical as possible. References to Greek mythology, Shakespeare or John Grisham are a welcome change.

Three, approach to the oral hearing: As a senior, well-known lawyer, certainly someone who is a member of the College, you can usually rely on your reputation. The judges will hang on your every word. The judges will be so star-struck by your mere presence before them that they will be won over even before you stand up. Whatever you say, you will have them eating out of the palm of your hand. But if, in the remote case, things go badly, becoming meek and timid will turn the tide. After all, we are the Supreme Court of Canada. Make sure you keep saying, "It is respectfully submitted," and calling the judges "Your Lordship" or "Your Ladyship." "Your Holiness" only works with some judges. If you really want to make points, you should call the Chief Justice "Your Majesty."

Four, time: Your time for oral submissions is limited: for a party, one hour; for an intervenor, only 15 minutes. So, how do you cover everything you have to say in the limited time you have? The answer is, talk fast. The judges are always impressed by someone who can talk fast, even if they can't understand the argument.

Five, presenting the arguments: If you have a weak case, in our court, you should do four things. One, argue the facts in excruciating detail, especially when they are agreed, and your opponent won't contradict them. Two, read from the record. Make sure you do so in a monotone voice. Three, indicate a real sense of grievance and frustration with the Court of Appeal. It will show victimhood. That is always useful. Four, show a genuine desire to get even with your opponent. The judges will identify with your desire for vengeance. In describing your opponent's argument, use terms like "absurd" and "preposterous."

Six, dealing with the material: Some counsel prepare a condensed book for the day of the hearing that they will refer to in oral argument. You shouldn't bother with this, especially if you are going to be referring to several different volumes of the record during argument. Judges are always impressed by counsel's ability to flip from book to book, and all the commotion helps to keep them awake. They even keep a tally of which counsel referred to the most books. It helps to decide the case. When you refer to the record, or to books of authorities, don't waste time taking the judges to the material you are referring to. Just paraphrase. Your paraphrases will be better than the excerpt from the record of the case itself.

Some lawyers spend a good portion of their time dictating the tab and page numbers from the record to the judges. That is good. The judges like to write down lists of numbers. If they do follow up on the references, they will enjoy seeing if they can link the tab and pages you dictated with the material in the record, and then figure out why you wanted them to look at it in the first place.

Seven, dealing with an authority that is against you: There are two ways to deal with a previous Supreme Court of Canada decision that is adverse to your position. One, tell the court they got it wrong, and that they should overrule the prior decision. Two, better still, tell the judges what they really meant in their prior decision. That will be especially effective if the judge who wrote the decision is still on the bench.

Eight, dealing with questions: My pesky colleagues have a tendency to use up the time allotted to counsel with their pointless questions. I also ask questions, but they are always good. Some useful answers in our court, if a question happens to strike a weak spot in your case, are: one, "I wasn't counsel at the trial or at the Court of Appeal"; two, "Another lawyer prepared the factum, and she isn't here"; three, "I will get to it later"; four, "My colleague will address the point"; five, "You are missing the point"; six, "The question is irrelevant"; seven, "You are trying to trap me, and I won't answer."

Nine, dealing with theoretical questions: Sometimes a judge will ask a hypothetical question about the application of the principles of law that go beyond the facts of the case. You shouldn't answer. It is a trap. You are there to win the case for your client. You should just tell the judges there are no broad implications, and that they will only confuse themselves if they think there are.

And ten, persistence: As you argue, you must be persistent. You can't give in. If the court says it disagrees with your point, just carry on. If the court says it isn't interested in your point, don't be discouraged. Just make it again. Judges will eventually get it. And never sit down. When you are finished, if your time hasn't run out, just start all over again. Don't worry about the red light. Continue until the Chief Justice pleads for mercy, and begs you to sit down.

Well, if you believe any of what I have said, you really do need continuing legal education. But let me assure you, we have seen it all, or at least almost all.

INDEPENDENCE OF BENCH AND BAR

Seriously, I want to say what a truly great honour it is for me to be inducted as an honorary member of the College. We often talk about the independence of the judiciary, and about the independence of the bar. In North America, we take these things for granted. We shouldn't. When we look around the world, we see many examples where the bar and the bench are not independent. Independence is a fragile thing. As lawyers, you have to be free to take on all kinds of cases, to engage in courageous advocacy ... Even for the most unpopular clients and causes, in litigation lawyers are often acting against the government in one form or another, or for the government, or for large and powerful clients, where there can sometimes be pressure to break the rules or to act in ways that are not consistent with professional standards. In that context, nothing is more important than the integrity and independence of counsel.

The college, with its objective of elevating the standards of trial practice, the administration of justice and the ethics of the profession, is a key participant in contributing to an independent bar and bench. As judges, we are reliant on the integrity and independence of counsel, and in turn, on the important work and influence of the College, and I will be proud to be an honorary member.

CANADIAN CONFIRMATION PROCESS

Now, I was appointed, as Jack told you, in 2006, and as he said, to get my job I had to appear before that parliamentary committee to answer members of Parliament. And it was the first time, and as he told you, it was fairly benign. It is nowhere near as rigorous an exercise as the process before the [United States] Senate confirmation committee. The difference in Canada is that the parliamentary committee can advise, but it does not have the power of consent. Under our Constitution, the Prime Minister has the authority to appoint a judge to the Supreme Court with or without the approval of the parliamentary committee. But whether the new process is good or bad is, as Jack indicated, controversial. Judges and lawyers generally don't like it because, as he said, they are concerned that it is going to degenerate into nasty, intrusive questioning of a nominee and overly politicize the appointment process. But the press and the public like it. They want to see the individual who will fill the position.

JUDGES AS ORDINARY PEOPLE

What they see is that ultimately, we are ordinary people, at least most of us. I am sure I am. Last week, I opened a can of tuna fish, and threw the empty can in the garbage. Next morning, my wife sent me an e-mail in the office: "Rules: One, wrap all fish products before putting in garbage; Two, close blinds in living room. Sun bleaches couches; Three, put toilet seat DOWN." We are ordinary people.

One thing that comes from that parliamentary hearing process is that it creates a lot of publicity for the nominee. A couple of months after I was appointed, I called Air Canada to order a ticket on a personal matter. After the agent completed the process, she said, "Rothstein. So you are the guy they appointed to the Supreme Court?" I said, "Yes." She said, "I have a problem. I have to come to work very early, and I leave my house at 5 a.m. when it is dark. And some mornings on my way to the bus, I run into a raccoon. I don't like that raccoon; it scares me." And she said, "Can I kill the raccoon?"

I paused for a moment, thinking there were probably laws against killing wild animals in the city, and then wondering about self-defence and whether that would be an exception, and I end up saying, "Well, I don't know." She said, "You don't know? You are a judge of the Supreme Court! Can I or can't I?" Well, I retreated to the judge's safe harbour, and explained to her that as a judge I couldn't give legal advice. My answer did nothing to enhance her confidence in the administration of justice.

I thank you for the honour that has been bestowed upon me today ... and for your attention. Thank you very much.

How to lose an appeal in the Court of Appeal: THE NEXT GENERATION

THE HONOURABLE DAVID M. BROWN

ALMOST A GENERATION has passed since Justice Marvin Catzman published his groundbreaking article, "The Wrong Stuff: How to Lose Appeals in the Court of Appeal."[1] In it he offered, in seven succinct tips, surefire ways to lose an appeal. His advice still rings clear and true: (1) Always file an incomprehensible factum. (2) Never begin at the beginning. (3) Never start with your strongest point. (4) Never say the magic words. (5) Always make a speech for the jury. (6) Never answer a question directly or, better still, at all. And (7) Never keep your promises.

Several years' experience on the Court of Appeal has demonstrated to me the enduring legacy and power of Catzman's seven tips for losing an appeal. However, I have slowly realized there are other ways to successfully drive down the road to appeal failure. This article offers some additional losing tips that counsel can use at each stage of an appeal.

TIP #1: APPEAL TO THE WRONG COURT

The fastest way to lose an appeal is to file your client's appeal in the wrong court.

1 Justice Marvin Catzman, "The Wrong Stuff: How to Lose Appeals in the Court of Appeal," in 19:1 *The Advocates' Society Journal* (Summer 2000).

The novice litigator might be forgiven for thinking that choosing the right appellate court is a straightforward matter: If the civil order of a Superior Court judge is final, the loser trots off to the Court of Appeal; if it is interlocutory, off one goes to the Divisional Court. On its face, a distinction of great simplicity.

But "final" means "final" only to the uninitiated.[2] Those better versed in the labyrinth of appellate jurisdictional jurisprudence know they must consult Hendrickson and Ball, *Final or Interlocutory? Theory, Practice and Frustration*, the definitive three-volume work on the topic.[3]

And why the insistence of judges that litigants must pass this threshold existential test of final or interlocutory before presenting the merits of their appeal to an appellate court? The answer lies in the tactile nature of the remedy granted by an appellate court when an appellant, instead of choosing Door Number One for appeal, wrongly chooses Door Number Two. When that occurs, the appeal is quashed. And "quash" is such a viscerally satisfying word for a judge to write. Few words in the judicial lexicon exude onomatopoeia like "quash." One can both hear and feel the terminal nature of the remedy, writing "quashed." And when one's colleagues ask how the day has gone, what more satisfying answer can one give than to say, "We started our day by quashing an appeal." So, go ahead. Make our day.

TIP #2: FORGET REVIEW AND CORRECTION – TREAT APPEALS AS SECOND KICKS AT THE CAN

Embrace the old saying: "If at first you don't succeed, try, try again." The judge below did not accept the credibility of your client's witnesses? No problem. The beauty of an appeal court is the judges don't see your witnesses. Problem solved.

---

2 Watch the Monty Python "Argument Clinic" sketch on YouTube, substituting the word "final" for "argument," and "interlocutory" for "contradiction."

3 Hendrickson championed the School of Simplicity: A final order finally disposes of the rights of the parties. *Hendrickson v. Kallio*, [1932] O.R. 675 (C.A.) 680. By contrast, Ball championed the Issue-by-Issue School, which enjoys multiple trips up to the Court of Appeal during the life of a lawsuit. For Ball, final orders include those that finally dispose of an issue raised by the defence, even if they do not finally dispose of the rights of the parties. *Ball v. Donais* (1993), 13 O.R. (3d) 322 (C.A.) 324.

Ignore the whole notion of appellate standard of review. *Housen v. Nikolaisen*?[4] So passé. Palpable and overriding error? An incomprehensible phrase; best to let it go.

Keep your game plan simple: Argue that every minor mistake or misstatement by the judge below calls out for appellate intervention or else *the world will come to an end*. Argue the non-material and irrelevant in painstaking detail. For justice lies in the irrelevant minutiae of a case, not in the big picture.

TIP #3: USE JAMES JOYCE AS YOUR MODEL FOR WRITING YOUR FACTUM

James Joyce developed the stream of consciousness writing style into a High Art Form, so you should follow his style of writing when putting your factum together, because there is nothing judges enjoy more, when reading a factum, than participating in an author–reader relationship that incorporates the elements of the High Art Form, even though it may make it difficult for the reader to follow the thread of your argument, but the beauty of the High Art Form, at least in the postmodern world, is that the reader really doesn't matter as much as the writer, and the satisfaction in writing a factum lies not in crafting an argument persuading a judge to your client's point of view on an issue, but in showing the judge you can use the High Art Form and, as such, should be regarded as a cutting-edge, postmodern advocate, even though you don't end up communicating a single idea to the judge, but only put the judge to sleep – no doubt a well-earned sleep – by ensuring that each page of your factum manifests, exquisitely, the High Art Form, and avoids the tainted, bourgeois, but strangely understandable, style associated with the now thoroughly discredited It-Was-Bluebell-Time-in-Kent School of Clear Legal Prose.[5]

TIP #4: TURN YOUR FACTUM INTO A FUN GAME OF *WHERE'S WALDO?*

Reject the requirement in the rules that your factum contain a concise overview statement, describing the nature of the case and of the issues, as

4 [2002] 2 S.C.R. 235 at paras 8, 10, 23, 36.

5 From the judgment of the master of the style, Alfred Lord Denning, in *Hinz v. Berry*, [1970] 2 Q.B. 40 at 42.

well as a statement of each issue raised, immediately followed by a concise argument. Adopt, instead, the *Where's Waldo?* approach to factum-writing.

A losing factum, like a *Where's Waldo?* book, buries the object of the quest in gloriously distracting detail. Where an appeal involves a single issue – a legal error made by the judge below – write so that, like Waldo, the error-at-issue merely pokes its head out of the grocer's store window, lost in the riot of the hundreds of people shown milling about the town's marketplace.

Judges read factums carefully in advance of oral hearings. They enjoy the time it takes to find the "Waldo" issue. Where a factum is an especially fine example of *Where's Waldo?*–writing, judges delight in showing their colleagues the factum, so all can enjoy the fun in trying to find the "Waldo" issue and comparing their guesses.

TIP #5: OVERSTATE YOUR CASE

In your written and oral arguments, choose hyperbole and exaggeration over accuracy and balance. Spin the findings of fact below into alternative facts. Ensure the responding party can never accept your statement of facts as accurate. And assert that a case stands for a binding proposition of law which will defy discovery upon an actual reading of the case.

Sweep the (inevitable) weaknesses in your client's case under the rug. Pretend they are not there. Or bury them in an obscure footnote in your factum. Follow the adage, "out of sight; out of mind." But do not take offence when the panel does not call on the other side to respond to your submissions. Remember: The object is to lose your appeal, not to win.

TIP #6: FORGET THE PITCH – DAZZLE THEM WITH YOUR WIND-UP

The conventional wisdom for factum-writing is: Forget the Wind-up and Make the Pitch.[6] Wrong, wrong, wrong.[7]

6 Justice John Laskin, "Forget the Wind-up and Make the Pitch: Some Suggestions for Writing More Persuasive Factums," in 18:2 *The Advocates' Society Journal* (Summer 1999). Available online on the Court of Appeal website: <www.ontariocourts.ca/coa/en/ps/speeches/forget.htm>.

7 Of course, it is right, right, right. But only if you want to win an appeal. This article strives to teach you how to lose your appeal. So ignore the right advice.

Losing an appeal is all about dazzling the panel with your wind-up and ensuring you never make the pitch that really counts – identifying where the judge below made the Really Big Reversible Mistake. Emulate Eddie Feigner, the king of "The King & His Court," whose wind-ups dazzled crowds for decades.[8]

Make sure your factum leaves the panel guessing: So, just what is the real issue in this case? Rely on the High Art Form of stream of consciousness factum-writing to work its obfuscating magic.

TIP #7: TALK *TO* THE COURT, NOT *WITH* THE COURT

Court of Appeal judges have time built into their schedules to prepare for the oral hearing. They use it. They come prepared to a hearing with specific questions about specific issues. They want to focus on those questions and issues. They want to talk with counsel about them.

Rebuff the panel. Stick to your script. Talk *to* the court, not *with* the court. Remind the panel that your client was allocated a certain amount of time for oral argument and you want to use it as you see fit. Stick to your guns on this point. Don't relent. Your client is entitled to no less.

CONCLUSION

Let me finish by repeating Justice Catzman's final piece of advocacy wisdom: "I hope that you will find these tips helpful in significantly lowering your batting average in the Court of Appeal. If they do, console yourself by remembering that winning isn't everything."

8 On reflection, perhaps not the best example. I saw *The King & His Court* (three other players; The King always used a four-man team) at work in Iron River, Michigan, one summer at the local rodeo. The King's dazzling wind-up always led to a devastating pitch. In a 1960s celebrity charity softball game, The King struck out, in order, Willie Mays, Willie McCovey, Brooks Robinson, Roberto Clemente, Maury Wills and Harmon Killebrew. To enjoy The King, watch the YouTube clip labelled "Eddie Feigner Newsreel."

Beside the Supreme Court bench:
A LAW CLERK'S REFLECTIONS ON ADVOCACY

DAVID SANDOMIERSKI

BEFORE I STARTED my clerkship at the Supreme Court of Canada, I expected to discover a magic key to advocacy, a foolproof technique that would translate universally into effective persuasion.

Instead, I was disabused of the moot-court attitude that any one style of argument is best. The fist-slammer, the professorial lecturer, the line reader, the slow talker, the fast talker, the outraged crusader, the orchestra conductor – all of these, at various moments, commanded the judges' attention and consideration. When it came to style, I was reminded of that hard-won law school lesson: be your own person. One must play to one's own strengths, respect one's own particular way of thinking and speaking and do so boldly.

The triumph over inhibition is only a starting point, but it draws attention to my key discovery about advocacy – the superficial is unimportant. From the clerk's perch, I learned time and again that it is the big picture that matters. It is the familiar, but tough, demands of law that translate into success in the courtroom.

These are some of the lessons I learned.

PREPARATION

I learned that there is no substitute for excellent preparation. This seems so trite as to waste ink, but it deserves emphasis. The best-prepared advocates were not only familiar with the authorities and their own argument but were also on top of their side's weaknesses and the opposing side's strengths.

It was painfully obvious when the person speaking before the court was not the person who wrote the factum. This appears to be an inevitable part of advocacy today, but I was often left wanting to hear more from the junior who spoke 10 minutes than from the senior advocate who spoke 50. As a clerk (and a judge may feel the same way), I arrived ready to get at the heart of the case. When a lawyer recounted the written arguments or skirted questions to "stay on track," time and momentum evaporated. The more familiar one is with the case, the more one realizes the depth behind each question and the more one can truly answer it. There really is no greater authority than preparation.

EMPHASIS

Justice Binnie is famous for writing that the argument for any case should fit on the back of an envelope. This requires tough intellectual work but, having seen many good lawyers lose their way in minutiae, I believe distillation is the key to persuasion. Details may be the currency of legal practice, but their importance lies in serving *principles*. The best advocates I saw reminded the court how each point reinforced an overarching principle. Through all the precedents, statutes, regulations and contracts cited, the best lawyers gave the judge a reason why it all mattered, why one *wanted* to believe in their side.

The tricky thing about advocacy, especially at the Supreme Court, is that the court is often called upon to balance competing interests. One common pitfall I observed was the tendency to short-sell the other side. It never fooled anybody. The best advocates have cultivated the art of effective concessions. Justice Fish once interrupted a lawyer mid-sentence to remind him of Abe Lincoln's words: "In law it is good policy never to plead what you need not, lest you oblige yourself to prove what you cannot."

FRAMING

Perhaps the most important piece of "big picture" advice I heard while clerking is "Frame the case." There is so little one can control: the facts, the precedents, the other side's representation. But the lawyer who can successfully persuade the judge that the case before him or her is not really about X, but about Y, and that this characterization tilts the outcome of the case, is the Dumbledore of advocates. I rarely saw this technique used successfully, but when it worked, it was a sight to behold. It reflected a mastery of the case, the law and the courtroom. Any advocate who has the opportunity to develop or observe this skill should seize it.

A FEW LITTLE POINTS

I learned a number of more specific lessons from watching so many cases. Although I don't think any of these lessons would make or break a case, they are still worth highlighting, if only to give an impression of some common conduct I observed:

- Getting through all one's arguments is rarely more important than answering the judge's questions. The best lawyers I saw treated oral arguments as an opportunity to *complement* the written submissions, not reiterate them.
- Formalities such as "May it please the court" add very little, as does the unsolicited reviewing of facts. I once observed nine judges suppress their questions for half an hour while enduring a bullish recounting of uncontroversial facts. A wasted opportunity!
- Being familiar with both the English and the French versions of applicable legislation adds to the impression of one's mastery over the case. Twice I saw a judge ask a question about a material difference between the two versions. The difference between the lawyer who was prepared and the one who wasn't was more than evident.
- Finally, the timeless lesson of civility toward members of the profession really matters in court. Any time the word "disingenuous" was used, the collective cringe was palpable.

These observations, which can be made in any given court on any given day, are mere bagatelles compared with the tough stuff.

While there may be no silver bullets of successful advocacy, my year at the Supreme Court suggested to me the beginnings of a mantra: *Be prepared, distill your argument and frame the case.* With these essentials, any advocate, of any personality stripe or style, can work magic.

Part Six

STANDARD OF REVIEW

I REFUSE TO BE cynical and I'm sure it's just me, but I find the concept of standard of review beyond perplexing. Indeed, there must be a "better way," as the Toronto Transit Commission describes its service. It always seems like *ex post facto* reasoning to me. Correctness? Reasonableness? Discretion? It depends. Deference to be afforded a statutory tribunal and/or a trial judge? Sure, except when it isn't. To me, it's illusory. In this chapter we have two looks at the problem: one from a fine and vastly experienced former trial and now appellate judge and the other from an amusing and insightful civil practitioner trying to deconstruct the most recent utterance on this subject from the Supreme Court of Canada.

Tipping the balance in the Court of Appeal

THE HONOURABLE KATHRYN N. FELDMAN*

MY FRIEND STEPHEN Grant wanted to know, what speaks to the judges of the Court of Appeal, what moves them? Two very important components are written and oral advocacy and the art of persuasion, which was the topic of my colleague John Laskin's extraordinary address to this conference last year. My topic is the standard of appellate review and the limits on what the Court of Appeal can do. Is there a way to identify when you have a winning appeal or at least a potential winner? And when should you advise your clients, who lost at trial, that the Court of Appeal is not going to be able to help, even if the result appears unjust to them?

The scope for interference by the Court of Appeal has been circumscribed by the Supreme Court of Canada over the last thirty years and was even more strictly limited two years ago in *Housen v. Nikolaisen*.[1] How many times have you been in the Court of Appeal when the president of the court says (hopefully to your opponent): "You know, counsel, that we cannot retry the case."

---

* EDITOR'S NOTE: This article is the edited text of an address delivered to The Advocates' Society Fall Convention in Scottsdale, Arizona, on November 21, 2004. The author wishes to thank her law clerk, Colin Grey, for his assistance in preparing this article.

1 [2002] 2 S.C.R. 235.

You all know the test for the review of findings of fact – there must be a "palpable and overriding error."[2] I can tell you that in many cases, the court also struggles with whether an error meets that test. In *Housen*, the majority of the Supreme Court of Canada emphasized that "palpable" means "plainly seen."[3] One problem is that I may not plainly see what you plainly see, and vice versa. Palpable can be in the eye of the beholder. Similarly, in the 1996 case of *Schwartz v. Canada*, the Supreme Court said that "overriding" means "determinative ... with respect to that factual issue."[4] But who determines what is determinative?

I want to talk today about the development of the standard of review on appeal, the latest word from our court, and to emphasize how important it is that in order to win an appeal, you have to be able to demonstrate a reviewable error. Finally, I want to weave in something that Raj Anand adverted to yesterday when he was talking about judicial review of administrative tribunals: where does ensuring a just result fit in?

FROM *THE KATHY K* TO *HOUSEN V. NIKOLAISEN*

Before the decision of the Supreme Court of Canada in *Stein v. The Kathy K* in 1976, Bora Laskin stated in a dissent in *Hood v. Hood* that the call to deference was "a mere homily, from which each judge can proceed in his assessment of the appeal as he sees fit."[5]

However, since then and over the last thirty years, the Supreme Court has made it clear that appellate courts should be extremely reluctant to interfere with the decision of a trial court unless a palpable and overriding error of fact or a pure error of law has been made. Here, I want to briefly discuss the two leading cases in this area. The first was *The Kathy K* case. More recently, in *Housen v. Nikolaisen* in 2002, the court extended the reach of deference and strengthened the logical foundation for it.

In his judgment in *The Kathy K*, Ritchie J. made what was for twenty-six years the definitive statement on the standard of review when he said that findings of fact made at trial "are not to be reversed unless it can be established that the learned trial judge made some palpable and overriding error which affected his assessment of the facts."

2 *Stein v. The Kathy K*, [1976] 2 S.C.R. 802.

3 *Supra* note 1 at para. 6.

4 [1996] 1 S.C.R. 254 at para. 35.

5 *Hood v. Hood* (1971), 19 D.L.R. (3d) 669 (S.C.C.) (per Laskin J., dissenting).

He cited several authorities in support of this standard. One important thing to note about those authorities is that they all advocated deference for the reason that the trial judge had the advantage of seeing and hearing the witnesses while the appellate judges did not. Lord Sumner is quoted as saying the appellate judges were "in a permanent position of disadvantage as against the trial judge."

Because this was the rationale cited for deference to the trial judge, in the following years there remained doubt about what to do in cases where the trial judge did not have this comparative advantage. In fact, one could say that, following the *Kathy K*, there were two clear categories at either end, with many unclear categories in between. On the one hand there were questions of law, in which case the standard of review was correctness. On the other hand there were determinations of fact based on the credibility of witnesses or the assessment of evidence, where the trial judge had an important advantage and where the standard was palpable and overriding error. There was an ongoing debate about what to do with anything in between the two extremes.

This is a gloss, but I don't think it's an inaccurate one. One did not know what to do, for example, with findings of fact based on documentary evidence, with inferences of fact, or with issues of mixed fact and law. Although the judicial consensus was that appellate courts should also defer on these issues, they did not know by how much. As my colleague, John Laskin, said in the *Equity Waste Management* decision in 1997: "It is not easy to articulate a standard less deferential than 'manifest error' but falling short of 'correctness.'"[6]

What resolved this issue was that it came to be recognized that there were other reasons to show deference to the trial judge's decision. *Housen* picked up on these, and in the process it strengthened the case for deference. In *Housen*, the majority of the Supreme Court restated the underlying rationales for deference as three basic principles. A higher standard of deference is required because (1) it limits the number, length, and cost of appeals; (2) it promotes the autonomy and integrity of trial proceedings; and (3) it recognizes the expertise of the trial judge and his or her advantageous position.

6 *Equity Waste Management of Canada v. Halton Hills (Town)* (1997), 35 O.R. (3d) 321 at 336 (C.A.).

Based on these rationales, the majority held that the following standards of review would apply: (1) the standard of review for findings of fact and for factual inferences is "palpable and overriding error"; (2) the standard of review for legal error is correctness; and (3) the standard of review for questions of mixed fact and law is also highly deferential, unless the judge has made some extricable error of law that would be subject to a correctness standard.

What *Housen* did was fill in the grey areas between findings of fact and pure questions of law. And it filled in those grey areas, in essence, by extending the reach of the palpable and overriding standard.

EIGHT "RULES" FROM *WAXMAN V. WAXMAN*

The latest word on how strictly the court is going to apply and enforce the rules on standard of review came from our court last April in *Waxman v. Waxman*.[7]

I'm sure you all know about the case, an unfortunate and bitter feud between two brothers over the family business; but you all may not have read the 752-paragraph judgment of the Court of Appeal. In that judgment – which was written by Justices Doherty, Laskin, and Goudge – the court both explains and elaborates on *Housen*, and I have identified eight rules or tips, discussed in *Waxman*, that help the court, but perhaps more importantly help counsel, consider whether it can be shown that the trial judge made the type of error that will allow the Court of Appeal to interfere.

First, most cases involve evidence that is open to more than one interpretation. An appeal court will defer to the trial court on factual conclusions even though it views the evidence differently and would make different findings. This includes findings based not only on credibility, but on the weighing of competing evidence, the drawing of inferences, and, very importantly, the interpretation of documents.[8]

Second, the court defined a palpable factual error as one that is obvious or clear, such as a finding made in the complete absence of evidence, findings made in conflict with evidence that the judge accepted as true, findings based on a misapprehension of the evidence, and findings

7 [2004] O.J. No. 1765 (C.A.).
8 *Ibid.* at paras. 300–305.

drawn from primary facts that are the result of speculation rather than inference.[9]

Third, an error may be palpable but not overriding. This is key to any decision about the strength of your case on appeal. To be overriding, it must go to the root of a finding of fact so that the challenged finding is unsafe because of the palpable error.[10] In *Waxman*, for example, the trial judge made a finding that by the late 1970s, Chester Waxman was trying to take control of the business and push Morris Waxman out. That conclusion was based, in part, on the terms of a proposed trust for an estate freeze drawn on Chester's instructions, which the trial judge found would give Chester voting control. The Court of Appeal agreed with Chester that the trial judge had misapprehended the effect of the trust document. However, the effect of the trust document did not go to the root of the trial judge's conclusion that Chester was trying to take control. There were many other facts that led to that conclusion. In the end, although the Court of Appeal found a palpable error, it was not an overriding error, and therefore it had no effect on the outcome of the appeal.[11]

Fourth, following the *Housen* case, appellate courts will not review findings of fact or inferences drawn from facts by asking whether, on the record, the findings are reasonable, but with this caveat: if the findings of the trial judge are not reasonable, then the judge probably at least made a palpable error. Otherwise, there is no explanation for the unreasonable conclusion. With that caveat, this rule allows an appellate court some room to ensure that unfair or unjust results can be overturned.[12]

Fifth, when examining reasons for judgment looking for palpable and overriding errors, the fact that the judge did not refer to a piece of evidence does not mean that she did not consider it. Judges are not obliged to refer to every piece of evidence in their reasons. The appellants must point to something in the record or the reasons that demonstrates that the trial judge ignored a piece of evidence. Only then can one decide if ignoring that piece of evidence resulted in a palpable and overriding error.[13]

9 *Ibid.* at para. 296.
10 *Ibid.* at para. 297.
11 *Ibid.* at paras. 298–299.
12 *Ibid.* at para. 306.
13 *Ibid.* at paras. 307–308, 343–345.

Sixth, although it would be an error for a trial judge to make directly inconsistent findings of fact, a trier of fact is entitled to believe some, all, or none of any witness's testimony.[14] That is part of the standard instructions that trial judges give to juries. Therefore a trial judge may base a finding on one thing a witness said, although the rest of that witness's evidence is rejected. Of course, judges also tell juries that if they find that the witness has deliberately lied about one thing, they should consider carefully whether that witness can be believed about anything else. You will want to see if the trial judge has given a full explanation for believing any of what a deliberately lying witness said.

Seventh, it will be a palpable and overriding error if a trial judge fails to make a finding of fact that is essential to the ultimate determination of the issues in dispute. However, what is essential will not always be clear.[15]

Eighth, credibility findings are the most difficult to overturn on appeal, but they are not immune to appellate review if they are based on a misapprehension of the evidence or on an irrelevant consideration.[16] I was surprised to learn how many times credibility findings in fact are set aside. In a talk given last month at the Criminal Lawyers' Association conference in Toronto, Professor David M. Tanovich said that his research has uncovered as many as seventy-five recent criminal cases in Ontario where the Court of Appeal has allowed appeals based on errors in the trial judge's credibility assessments.[17]

THREE EXAMPLES FROM RECENT CASES

I want to give you some examples from recent cases of how judges struggle with the question of when to interfere.

14 *Ibid.* at paras. 346–347.

15 *Ibid.* at paras. 348–349.

16 *Ibid.* at para. 364.

17 See David M. Tanovich, "Assessing Defence Evidence: How and Why Judges So Often Get It Wrong in Credibility Cases," Paper presented to the Criminal Lawyers' Association 2004 Fall Conference, October 2004 (unpublished) at 11: "Although I have not undertaken any empirical study, the sheer number of relatively recent appellate cases referred to in this paper where convictions were overturned is, I think, compelling evidence of the systemic nature of the problem." He gave the figure of seventy-five cases in his oral presentation.

Before I do, it is important to remember what happens when an appellate court finds an error. In criminal cases, unless there is an unreasonable verdict, inevitably a new trial is ordered. But in civil cases, after saying that the Court of Appeal does not retry the case, if you are able to convince the Court of Appeal that the trial judge has made a palpable and overriding error, a new trial is virtually never ordered. Instead, the court rejects the erroneous finding of the trial judge and comes to its own conclusion about the proper outcome. That is your opportunity to convince the court of the merit of your position.

Medical malpractice cases often involve complex issues of fact, and because the evidence is technical, they involve difficult inferences to be drawn from facts. *Hassen v. Anvari* is an example of such a medical malpractice case from last year.[18]

Briefly, the evidence was that while performing a hernia operation laparoscopically, the surgeon mistakenly cut the patient's aorta, the major artery leading from the heart. The doctor's position was that although what he did caused the damage, it was an unfortunate mistake and did not amount to negligence. He was a leading expert in this type of operation; he had performed two similar operations that same day; there was nothing wrong with the trocar or cutting instrument that he used, and he did the operation in the same way he always did. Furthermore, while no expert witness said that the defendant was negligent, an expert went so far as to say that the doctor had to have used enough pressure to push the abdominal wall down and to bring the trocar in the proximity of the aorta. The trial judge inferred from the evidence that the surgeon's feel and touch failed him when he inserted the trocar too far, too hard, or too fast, and that he was negligent. The trial judge rejected as speculative the surgeon's innocent explanations for what occurred.

I was on the panel on each of the two medical malpractice cases discussed and authored the decisions.

At the appeal, skilled counsel on behalf of the doctor argued that the trial judge made two errors of law and one palpable and overriding error in his factual findings. He argued that there was no basis for drawing an inference of negligence when there were two non-negligent explanations for the mishap, that the findings of negligence did not amount to

18 [2003] O.J. No. 3543 (C.A.).

negligence but only to misadventure, and that the trial judge failed to consider certain evidence in coming to his findings of fact.

The Court of Appeal considered each of these arguments in detail and closely reviewed the findings of fact and the inferences drawn by the trial judge to see if they were inferences that were available to be made. Counsel made a compelling argument that this was a case where something unexplained went wrong but where the doctor was not at fault. But the issue is not whether the Court of Appeal finds an argument attractive or even compelling, but whether there is a basis to interfere with the conclusion reached by the trial judge. Ultimately, the court was satisfied that having rejected the two non-negligent explanations, the trial judge was entitled to reach the conclusion that the only explanation for the doctor's error was negligence. The trial judge asked the right question of law: whether the doctor fell below the standard of care. The inferences he drew from the facts were entitled to deference.

A recent case, *Kennedy v. Jackiewicz*,[19] presented a similar situation, but in that case, the trial judge came to the opposite conclusion – that is, he declined to infer that the defendant Dr. Jackiewicz had been negligent.

Dr. Jackiewicz had burned Mrs. Kennedy's bowel while performing laparoscopic surgery to remove her ovaries, using an electrosurgical device known as a bipolar laparoscopic cautery. The trial judge found that when performing the operation, the doctor had made an error that caused the burn. An expert in the use of electrosurgical devices who was not a medical doctor had testified that burns of the kind suffered by Mrs. Kennedy "are always the result of an error in technique." The issue then became whether the error was the result of negligence by the doctor. A medical expert in the same field as the defendant testified that, assuming the defendant applied the cautery in either one of two places during the operation, he did so negligently by applying it at too high a power or for too long.

The problem was that Dr. Jackiewicz testified that he applied the cautery in a third location, about which Mrs. Kennedy's expert did not testify. The trial judge concluded that because of this gap in the evidence, he could not infer that Dr. Jackiewicz had been negligent when he applied the cautery at this third location.

19 [2004] O.J. No. 4816 (C.A.). This decision was released on November 26, 2004, after this address was delivered.

In the Court of Appeal, counsel for Mrs. Kennedy argued that the trial judge had before him sufficient evidence to draw the inference that the doctor had been negligent in his application of the cautery at the third location, because to cause the burn, the cautery must have been applied at too high a power or for too long. However, because this was a question of the proper inference to draw from proven facts based on the evidence, the court concluded that this was a case for deference, stating: "Although it was open to the trial judge to infer from the expert evidence that the respondent applied the cautery either with too much power or for too long, and that this would have been the case in respect of any location within the surgical field that was near the colon, it was also open to him not to draw that inference."[20]

In another recent case, *Wang v. Metropolitan Life Insurance Co.*,[21] the question was the proper interpretation of two terms in an insurance policy – "accident" and "illness." Because the issue was the interpretation of an insurance policy and the application of the terms of the policy, correctly interpreted, to the facts of the case, the question before the court was one of mixed fact and law.

The insured was a woman who died during childbirth from a rare complication of pregnancy called amniotic fluid embolism. The woman's husband claimed the accidental death benefit on the basis that her death was an accident that was not caused by illness, because pregnancy is not an illness. The motions judge agreed with the husband.

On the appeal, the court split, with both judges giving persuasive reasons for their conclusions. Justice Charron for the majority held that the motions judge erred in her interpretation of what constitutes an accident and in failing to consider the amniotic fluid embolism as an illness. The majority determined its own interpretation of "accident," concluding that death from natural causes could not be an accident, and drew its own conclusions that, although pregnancy is not an illness, amniotic fluid embolism is, and it was what caused the wife's death.

Justice Laskin in dissent disagreed on both counts. He found that the motions judge asked the right legal question to determine whether the death was an accident – "Did the wife expect to die from her pregnancy?" – and that her answer – "No" – was entitled to deference. Relying

20 *Ibid.* at para. 3.

21 [2004] O.J. No. 3525 (C.A.).

on *Housen* and *Waxman*, he concluded that there was no basis to interfere with the conclusion of mixed fact and law reached by the motions judge. He went on to say that, even without deference, his view was that the motions judge was correct in her interpretation of the term "accident" and that the death in this case, being unexpected, was accidental.

On the second issue, he said that the term "illness" in an insurance policy must be given its ordinary, popular meaning, and amniotic fluid embolism, being like an allergic reaction, would not in ordinary parlance be considered an illness. He also considered policy reasons for interpreting this policy to accord coverage. The insurer had not excluded death by natural causes from the definition of accident. Where there is ambiguity in an insurance policy, it is to be interpreted in favour of the insured.

Obviously in this case two judges, including the motions judge, saw it one way and two saw it the other way. It turned out to be a losing case in the Court of Appeal, but it could have been a winner. There are compelling arguments both ways. It is also interesting that the judges took opposite views of the justice of the case.

So how do you win in the Court of Appeal? After *Housen* and *Waxman*, I would say that the rules that limit appellate interference are going to be strictly enforced. Your main stage is before the trial judge. But with this caveat: the Court of Appeal will always be concerned with the justice of the case. And one other thing I find is that at the outset, it may be hard to know whether or not an error is palpable and overriding. But in retrospect, the outcome can seem inevitable. I don't think that is an accident. It is excellent advocates that convince the court of the inevitability of their position.

Advocacy in the Court of Appeal:
ONE LAWYER'S PERSPECTIVE

PAUL J. PAPE

IN PREPARING TO appear in the Court of Appeal and, for that matter, in any court, my goal is winning, pure and simple. I try to craft an argument that will convince the panel to find in favour of my client. How the court finds in my client's favour is of limited interest to me; only results count.

How, then, does one craft a convincing argument? I have always been guided by Professor Charles Nesson's approach to this problem. Professor Nesson is the William F. Weld Professor of Law at Harvard University Law School and the founder of the Berkman Institute for Internet and Society. He teaches evidence and tort litigation. Nesson has said that the way to win an argument in court is by telling a short story which will convince your mother[1] of the righteousness of your position. If you cannot persuade your mother, you certainly will not persuade the court.

Nesson's focus is first on the auditor. If you imagine your mother as your adjudicator, it becomes easy to prepare an argument in the way I suggest. Selecting her implicitly recognizes what he and I believe: judges are swayed, influenced and governed by the same considerations as ordinary people. Judges come to their task with a sense of humanity and justice. Just like your mother. Taking the oath does not change this. Judges

1 I have maintained Nesson's choice of parent, notwithstanding that some might see it as biased. I refer to "your mother" here because, to my mind, she is reasonable, humane and has common sense. Your father does not have these qualities.

recognize that they have one job, namely, to do justice between the parties. Your mother, in making a decision, would try to do the same. In addition, your mother (generally speaking) is practical and sensible. She tries to solve family problems with a dollop of common sense. Judges try to do the same. This means that your argument should appeal to the panel's common sense and sense of justice. In my view and Nesson's, this is what wins. Next, Nesson requires that it be a story told to your mother. It is not a submission, presentation or argument. It is a story. If you want to convince your mother of something, you need to capture her attention and keep her interest. Almost everything we learn comes through the medium of the story. The information we receive from the media is often delivered in the form of a story. Everyone is accustomed to receiving information through stories. This includes judges, and an appeal is not any different. Why should the form of your presentation differ from what the panel is accustomed to hearing? It is also worth remembering that we are in the age of the "sound bite." Shorter is always better.

Finally, Nesson chooses the righteousness of your position as the end point of your story. Coulter Osbourne, when he was the Associate Chief Justice for Ontario, described this as the struggle for "the moral high ground." Either way, in telling your client's story, your aim is to convince the panel that justice is on your side.

THE STORY: WHAT WILL ENGAGE YOUR MOTHER'S ATTENTION?

Consider that the panel before whom you appear is sitting for a fortnight, followed by a fortnight off to prepare for the next sitting. While it is sitting it will hear, on average, two appeals per day, or 20 appeals for ten hearing days. Thus each judge must read at least 40 factums and 20 sets of reasons. Some of these factums will not be models of clarity, and that includes the underlying reasons that are the subject of the appeal. What type of factum will speak more to the panel? What type of factum will the panel more easily absorb? What type of factum will it want to finish reading? What type of factum will it remember?

To ask these questions is to answer them. Look at your last three factums. Would your mother – or anyone, for that matter – be interested in anything you have written, let alone be persuaded by reading it? I know that my mother would have paid attention only as long as I was telling her an engaging and interesting tale. Judges are no different. How can they be persuaded when you cannot hold their attention?

Most importantly, the story must be interesting. I have yet to argue an appeal where I was unable to tell an interesting story. Appeals, in the end, are all about people. And people are inherently interesting. You have certainly told a dinner party or group of friends about your latest case. Therefore, you do know how to make the tale interesting. Move on from there. The style of writing is entirely yours. You are, in the best sense of the word, an artist. Words are an advocate's stock-in-trade. Use your imagination and your own experience to create a finished product that you will be proud to show to anyone because you know they will read it and enjoy it, much the way you would recommend a great novel to a friend.

I cannot overemphasize the advantage you hold in preparing your factum; you know the record and the panel does not. You control the story they will read, particularly where you are the appellant. Many judges read the factum before the reasons for decision to find out what you are putting into issue. When you present your oral argument, you will know the facts and record better than they do. Do not squander this advantage.

Structurally, the story must be ordered. A beginning, middle and end should lead the listener to your point(s). The story must be written in simple, concrete terms. Leave abstractions for others. The writing must be specific and detailed. Generalities are an anathema. Details are the colours on your palette. They should be used for both interest and persuasion. A plaintiff who is a single mother of three preschool children and who works night and day immediately becomes more sympathetic than a corporate shareholder or insurance policy owner. While these facts (details) are irrelevant to the determination of the *lis* before the court, they are highly relevant to your story. The story must be brief. Here, as in most things, less is more. I recognize that this runs counter to the received wisdom of making the factum as long as the Court of Appeal office will allow through the use of smaller typeface, minimal spacing and extensive footnotes. But if your mother has a choice between long and short when she is burdened with at least 20 appeals, what would she choose? Remember that oral submissions are restricted in length and that the court is content to rely on limited argument. You suffer nothing when you are brief. In my view, you gain a distinct advantage. Here, more is less.

The story should be told in the overview (where you will articulate the one or two issues underpinning the appeal) and facts sections of the factum. The sections for issues and argument (as mandated by the Rules) are, for me, of minimal significance. I complete my story and, therefore, my argument by the end of the facts. The latter two sections are for emphasis and summation. I write short paragraphs, trying to limit each to one or two facts. I try to use short sentences. I shun, in no particular order, conjunctions, the intricate, the convoluted, the complex, the dense, the verbose and the legalistic.

I use adjectives carefully. First, I try never to use superlatives and emotive terms. By this I mean words like "outrageous," "impossible," "irrational" and so on – they add nothing and generally detract from the story. For example, if there is no evidence to support a finding of fact, simply say so. To add that there is not a scintilla or a shred of evidence is counterproductive. It will most certainly put off the judge. Moreover, adjectives like "egregious" or "scandalous" are also off-putting. In adding value-laden language such as this, you are attempting to usurp the role of the judge. Rarely, if ever, do you see words like this in a judge's reasons. Instead, let the panel reach its own conclusion. If the facts do not drive the panel there, your overblown language won't do it. While important to the story, the colour and heat are to be found in the facts themselves. Leave the characterization of these facts to the panel. Hyperbole undermines your credibility as an advocate.

THE LAW

Appeals, like trials, are determined on the facts of the case, not the law. The role of the law in appeals is greatly exaggerated. There are legal principles that underpin the result, but they are subsumed in what I consider to be the common sense of the argument. Not only will your mother have no interest in the law, but judges as well share that lack of interest when reaching a decision. Legalities, procedural niceties and, for that matter, the law itself are distractions. Many of my factums cite no law. I find it gets in the way and uses up space better spent in advancing the tale. In any event, the court knows the law far better than you do or ever will. This applies equally to "the standard of review." If the panel wants to help you, it will find the law to do so. If, however, you must recite the applicable legal principle, be brief. The best advocacy lies in a story convincingly told.

THE FACTS

I generally accept the trial judge's factual findings. Rarely do I attack a finding. It's a fool's errand to do so. I try to tell the story with the facts that the judge has found. There are exceptions, of course, but these factual errors must be both clearly wrong and pivotal to the argument. When in doubt, accept the finding. In drafting the factum, I try to use the judge's findings wherever possible. It simplifies and shortens the text. Generally there is no need to go into the underlying evidence when the finding itself is not in issue. I also try to use the facts adduced at trial by the opposition.

Nothing strengthens an argument (particularly an oral one) more than saying that this was "my friend's" evidence. The facts I include are only those that are necessary for telling the story. Editing is critical. There is no point in including facts that do not advance the tale. Remember, your audience is your mother. Superfluous facts are distracting and dilute the argument. You have often heard that the Court of Appeal is not there to retry the case. At one level, this is true; at another, it is not. Certainly the appeal court is not there to weigh the evidence, draw inferences or make findings of credibility. That is what I understand when I hear that it is not there to retry the case.

However, appeal judges always check the reasonableness of the result and the reasoning process by which the trial judge arrived at it. Accordingly, I will always argue that the result is reasonable (or not) on the basis of the facts as found. It is only in this sense that I attempt to have the case retried. Ultimately this finds its way into the story I am telling.

I use direct quotations wherever possible. The witness always has far more credibility than I do, and summarizing a witness's words is a poor substitute. Short quotes worked into the body of the paragraph are effective. Where the evidence is a critical part of the story, I use chunks of the transcript. Where the transcript is convoluted or close to unintelligible, a summary is in order. Facts can also be dealt with in the negative. You can write that there was no evidence on a particular point. You can write that the witness was not challenged by cross-examination on a point or that your opponent led no evidence to the contrary. On an effective cross-examination, you can say counsel made no attempt to rehabilitate the witness in re-examination.

In the context of a just result and credible advocacy, I cannot overemphasize the critical importance of accurately reciting the facts and the evidence. Nothing is more damaging to your case than misstating the evidence. It undermines your credibility as an advocate and the justness of your position. Your mother would not be happy if she thought you were trying to fool her. If you are trying to mislead the court, how just can your case be? I read every line of evidence that affects the fact or point about which I am writing to ensure the accuracy of my writing.

ISSUES

There are three categories of issues on appeal. The first issue is the same on every appeal. Whether you appear for the appellant or for the respondent, you will argue the justice of the result. This, of course, is the point of the story you are telling. If you appear for the appellant, the result you are seeking is just. If you are appearing for the respondent, the result you have obtained is just.

The second category is more familiar to appeal lawyers. It contains the issues you will articulate in the issues section of your factum. In the second category there are generally no more than two issues. These issues are governed by the "no harm – no foul" rule for judging. This means that if the error does not directly affect the result, no foul will be called by the judicial referee because no harm has been caused by the error. In other words, if you cannot connect the error to the result, as in cause and effect, don't bother raising it in this section. A good example of the application of this rule can be found in *Marchand v. Public General Hospital Society of Chatham*,[2] where the conduct of trial counsel for the defendants deprived the plaintiff of her fair day in court. However, on a reading of the trial evidence, the appeal panel determined that the result would not have been otherwise even if counsel had behaved properly. There was no point in giving the plaintiff a second trial if, with properly behaved counsel, she would still be unsuccessful. The appeal was dismissed: no harm, no foul.

There are always mistakes made at trial. A trial is not an exercise in perfection. Errors such as the improper use of discovery transcripts, interference with counsel by the judge, improperly striking the jury notice, applying the wrong law/legal test, misapprehending the evidence or delivering

2 (2000),51 O.R. (3d) 97 (C.A.).

incomprehensible reasons are ever present. The errors become meaningful on appeal only where they directly connect to an erroneous result.

Generally, there are few errors like this. Choose your issues carefully: again, less is more. Adding weak issues to this list will only dilute the powerful issues. Where no such causative issues exist on appeal, all is not lost. Remember that the prime issue is whether the result was just. Where the panel determines that the result is wrong, as in unjust, it may well substitute its discretion for that of the trial judge and do justice between the parties. For this reason, the first issue always takes precedence.

The third category contains what I call the unlisted issues. These are articulated more informally as you tell your story. Here you can raise the errors the judge has made that fall short of the "no harm – no foul" rule. They can easily be worked into the written argument and your oral presentation. I do this to undermine, in the eyes of the panel, the judge's reliability as a sound trial judge. This, of course, also goes to the *justness* of the result. Many other issues can be woven into the text. What did the judge not deal with that he or she ought to have dealt with? How did the opposite party handle the trial – for example, what arguments were not made or made, what evidence was not led? All of this will show that your opponent's position was constantly shifting. By dealing with these points at this level, the panel is not likely to attack you for raising them because you are not asking the court to act on them.

This approach is part of my "goldfish theory" of argument. When you feed a goldfish, you sprinkle morsels of food across the top of the bowl. They rest there upon the surface of the water. Although you can never predict where the fish will rise to the surface and nibble, you can be certain that it will not eat all the food. Only some bits will appeal to it. Arguing an appeal is the same: in my argument, I try to sprinkle the facts and issues that may appeal to the panel's sense of justice. I do not know what they will nibble at, but I do know that they (and my mother) will be interested in the "food."

RIGHTEOUSNESS

In every appeal in which I have been involved, there has been only one issue, and that issue is always the same: was the result just? My aim is to convince my mother that my position is just, reasonable, fair and righteous. The word does not matter; the sentiment does. It is an easy argument to make. Remember you are in a court of justice. That should remain your focus. Appeal judges see the issues the same way. They are not there to write law, correct law, castigate judges, discipline lawyers or the like. These activities are mere byproducts of their doing justice.

THE COMPENDIUM / THE ORAL ARGUMENT

The rules specify what the compendium must contain. In addition, I ask myself what the court will want to read. For example, in a jury trial I always include the entire charge. I try to include enough excerpts of the evidence to place in context the item referred to in the factum. Do not underestimate the importance of the compendium; in argument you will refer to it much more than to your brief of authorities. This highlights the importance of the facts of the case – the story – as opposed to the law. More importantly, I recognize that the court will not read the transcript before the hearing. Indeed, you now need to file only one copy of the transcript. The judges, when preparing, will read parts of the compendium in conjunction with your factum. So here I include more rather than less.

When you arrive in court to make your oral argument, much time will have passed since you wrote your factum and thought about the case. Furthermore, your time will be limited. You will neither be able to tell the story that is in your factum nor want to do this. What you want to do is engage in a dialogue with the court and answer the panel's questions. You should not fear these questions; you should welcome them. They should be seen as the sprinter's starting blocks. This requires you to anticipate the questions. What will the panel want to know about? I craft my oral argument to answer these questions.

When crafting my oral argument, since I am considering the matter anew, I know that I will have different and perhaps fresh insights into the case. Matters will occur to me for the first time. New ways of expressing issues will also appear. With this in mind I prepare a second compendium, one that will support my oral argument. I prepare it the day before I argue. It is something I hand up to the panel. It is the basis of my oral submissions. It is substantially smaller than the compendium mandated by the rules. It is organized to follow my oral submissions. By this I mean that I hope to start at the beginning and move numerically through the tabs. The idea is that I want my argument to be seamless. I do not want the panel fishing for their place in the volume or searching on their desk for other volumes. That is a waste of time and distracting.

CONCLUSION

Will your mother accept your argument? If she won't, try another. Generally, it is easy to find the moral high ground. The argument should be obvious; capturing it is another matter. Start with a story about the people involved. Tell it as if your mother were across the kitchen table. Add all the details you believe will interest her and keep her attention. Forget about the law. Use the judge's facts and your friend's facts. Use excerpts from the transcripts.

Tell it in the most compelling way you can. Ask your spouse what she or he thinks of it. Ask your mother. When your mother listens and ultimately agrees with you, you are on the road to winning – which is all that matters.

Standard of review:
ONGOING CHAOS OR A PATH TO ORDER?

GREG TEMELINI

I'LL ADMIT SOMETHING to you as long as you agree not to pass it along. I am a bit of a nerd when it comes to law. When it comes to standard of review, I am a full-on nerd.

So that's why I found the Supreme Court's decision in *Wilson v. Atomic Energy of Canada Ltd.*[1] so fascinating. It's a decision that came out in mid-July – absolutely the best time to release intriguing decisions on standard of review. There is nothing better than sitting on a beach in 40 degree weather with a cold recreational beverage of your choosing and contemplating the state of Canadian administrative law.

The headlines generated by the *Atomic Energy* decision were about the interpretation of the *Canada Labour Code* ("*Code*"). Specifically, the big issue was whether non-unionized employees in federally regulated industries can legally be dismissed without cause so long as reasonable pay in lieu of notice is provided – an important and interesting issue to be sure.

The part of the case that did not prompt sound bites on the national news concerned the real divisions in the Supreme Court about the standard of review of administrative tribunal decisions.

The case spawned four sets of reasons. It's always enjoyable when the Supreme Court offers us four sets of reasons. It's like playing a game

1 *Wilson v Atomic Energy of Canada Ltd*, 2016 SCC 29.

of Where's Waldo to find out who won and what part of which decision creates binding law.

In *Atomic Energy*, the Supreme Court reviewed a decision of the Federal Court of Appeal which had overturned a decision of an adjudicator under the *Code*. The adjudicator interpreted the "unjust dismissal" provisions of the *Code* to mean that a non-unionized federally regulated employee cannot be dismissed without cause merely by providing reasonable pay in lieu of notice. The dismissed employee is entitled to other remedial options akin to those that a unionized employee enjoys, including the possibility of reinstatement. I will leave it to others to parse this significant ruling and the long history that led to the adjudicator's interpretation.

Instead, I will take you briefly through the four sets of reasons, focusing primarily on standard of review issues.

#1 – "LET'S HAVE A FRANK CHAT ABOUT STANDARD OF REVIEW" BY ABELLA J.

Part of Abella J.'s reasons, the part necessary to decide the issue, attracted the majority of the court. Abella J. held that the standard of review of the adjudicator's decision was reasonableness and upheld the adjudicator's decision as reasonable.

For my purpose, Abella J.'s reasons are interesting and important for the *obiter dicta*. Abella J. took the opportunity in this case to critically consider the *Dunsmuir* framework and ask whether it could be simplified. She made absolutely clear that she was only beginning a conversation and that her "proposal [was] not intended in any way to be comprehensive, definitive, or binding" (para. 19).

Stopping there, I find Abella J.'s approach, to start a conversation, reflects a refreshing openness about the evolution of law. The approach recognizes that law does not simply flow, fully formed, from the minds of geniuses. It is not pre-ordained or blatantly obvious. Abella J. is inviting all the bright minds out there to consider an issue that has bedevilled the courts for a long time.

There are some who might view this as a sign of weakness – perhaps even as an admission that law is not principled and is simply driven by the whims of individual judges. As you might have guessed, I disagree. I don't think injecting some honesty and reality into the process can ever be a bad thing. It makes the legal system more transparent and legitimate.

Abella J. recognized that the *Dunsmuir* decision, which did away with patent unreasonableness, "has not proven to be the runway to simplicity the court had hoped it would be. In fact, the terminological battles over which of the three standards of review should apply have been replaced by those over the application of the remaining two [correctness and reasonableness]" (para. 25). Abella J. acknowledged the criticism about "inconsistency and confusion in how the standards have been applied" (para. 27).

This echoes, albeit to a lesser degree, the assessment of Stratas J.A. of the Federal Court of Appeal, who wrote a provocative article imploring the Supreme Court to offer some guidance on the administrative law standard of review. In one of his most quote-worthy lines, Stratas J.A. summed up the state of administrative law: "Our administrative law is a never-ending construction site where one crew builds structures and then a later crew tears them down to build anew, seemingly without an overall plan."[2] Interestingly, Stratas J.A. authored the decision of the Federal Court of Appeal in *Atomic Energy* with which the majority of the Supreme Court disagreed.

In many ways, the conversation Abella J. invited is more important than the prescription offered. The invitation represents a recognition that we don't have it right, that the arguments focus on the wrong things and that, if you have an idea, Abella J. is looking to hear it.

Having come this far, I would be remiss if I didn't at least tell you Abella J.'s solution. She proposed a single standard of review: reasonableness. The analysis would focus on "whether the outcome falls within a range of defensible outcomes" (para. 33). In rare instances, there might be only one defensible outcome whereas in most others, there can be more than one defensible outcome.

#2 - "THANK YOU ABELLA J., BUT WE ARE NOT QUITE READY YET" BY McLACHLIN C.J. AND KARAKATSANIS, WAGNER AND GASCON JJ.

The chief justice, joined by three members of the court, sided with Abella J. on the main issues. That's the boring part. What did they think of Abella J.'s conversation and her proposal? "We appreciate Justice Abella's

2 Stratas, David, "The Canadian Law of Judicial Review: A Plea for Doctrinal Coherence and Consistency" (February 17, 2016). Online: Social Science Research Network, ssrn.com/abstract=2733751 or dx.doi.org/10.2139/ssrn.2733751 at 1.

efforts to stimulate a discussion on how to clarify or simplify our standard of review jurisprudence to better promote certainty and predictability" (para. 70). However, they were not prepared to endorse any proposal to revise the *Dunsmuir* framework "at this time" (para. 70).

These reasons do not say "never." They simply say, "not now." To quote Jim Carrey's character in the movie *Dumb and Dumber*, "So you're telling me there's a chance."

#3 - "WE'RE ALL GOOD, THANKS" BY CROMWELL J.

Cromwell J. joined with Abella J. on the disposition of the appeal, but stated clearly that "our standard of review jurisprudence does not need yet another overhaul and ... as a result, I respectfully disagree with the approach that Justice Abella develops in *obiter*" (para. 72). I don't think Cromwell J.'s position needs any further elucidation. Cromwell J. has since retired from the Supreme Court.

#4 – "NO THANKS, AND YOU'VE GOT IT ALL WRONG" BY CÔTÉ AND BROWN JJ. (AND JOINED IN BY MOLDAVER J.)

It is safe to say that this set of reasons (the dissent) is totally at odds with those of Abella J. on virtually all issues. There was even disagreement over the standard of review which the dissenting justices determined to be correctness.

The primary justification for the correctness standard was the fact of conflicting interpretations of the "unjust dismissal" provisions of the *Code* over the years. The dissenters determined that they were required to resolve the disagreement: "We believe, therefore, that where there is lingering disagreement on a matter of statutory interpretation between administrative decision-makers, and where it is clear that the legislature could only have intended the statute to bear one meaning, correctness review is appropriate" (para. 89). And the dissent determined that the adjudicator was incorrect.

On the issue of a rethink of the *Dunsmuir* framework, the dissenting justices were not receptive:

> "We note Abella J.'s proposed revisions to the standard of review, expressly made in *obiter dicta*. While we appreciate the constructive spirit in which

they are proposed, and while we harbour concerns about their merits, we prefer to confine any statement regarding what is already the subject of a peripatetic body of jurisprudence to a judicial pronouncement" (para. 78).

WHERE DOES *ATOMIC ENERGY* LEAVE US?

We are no further ahead on a simplified and understandable standard of review framework than before *Atomic Energy*. If you are keeping score, using the *Dunsmuir* framework, six justices found that reasonableness was the appropriate standard and that the adjudicator's decision was reasonable; and three justices held that correctness was the standard and the adjudicator's decision was incorrect. One justice wants to start a conversation on standard of review, four are not ready quite yet to have that conversation and the remaining four (one of whom has retired) are not interested in a conversation.

The benefit, as I see it, lies in the chaos that *Atomic Energy* reveals. The *Dunsmuir* framework is not being applied in a consistent manner, and *Atomic Energy* underscores that reality. We can hope, as the saying goes, out of the chaos will come order.

PERSONAL REFLECTION | SPRING 2009

The heroic advocate

THE HONOURABLE ELEANORE A. CRONK

I'VE CHOSEN TO discuss the topic of the heroic advocate, for three reasons. First, because in these times there is a great need for heroic advocates. Second, because an examination of the lives of heroic lawyers may remind us why we went to law school in the first place. Margaret Ross, a past president of The Advocates' Society, said in a recent speech, "For most of us, it was to serve the public ... through the pursuit of justice."[1] The demands of contemporary legal practice may result in this being easily forgotten. Third, because the occasion for this discussion is the Society's annual evening of celebration. It marks the notional completion of another busy court year, when advocates gather in fellowship, to toast the joys and difficulties of life at the bar. On this special occasion, it is fitting to speak in praise of advocates, to honour that which is best in the barrister.

I approach this topic with some trepidation. I well recall Theodore Roosevelt's disparaging comment about Oliver Wendell Holmes, Jr., when Holmes, who was Roosevelt's first appointment to the United States Supreme Court, dissented from a majority Supreme Court decision that enforced Roosevelt's antitrust legislation of 1890. Roosevelt reportedly

1 Margaret A. Ross, "Challenges to the Standards of Professionalism in the Legal Profession," a speech presented to the Chief Justice of Ontario's Advisory Committee on Professionalism: 10th Colloquium on the Legal Profession, Ottawa, March 28, 2008, online at <www.lsuc.on.ca/media/tenth_colloquium_ross.pdf>.

said, "A lawyer with more backbone could have been carved out of a banana." How wrong he was!

I am reminded also of a dark jest, attributed to Henry Adams, that a succession of senior lawyers with whom he was familiar "disproved the theory of evolution." Heroism, it appears, is often in the eyes of the beholder. What makes someone a hero? Heroism involves excelling beyond the norm – accomplishing something extraordinary. A heroic person is one admired for courage, outstanding achievements, nobility or similar qualities. A noted American law professor has said, "Whether through exceptional bravery, wisdom, imagination, fortitude ... creativity, perseverance, compassion or intelligence ... extraordinary contribution to humanity – for [these qualities] we consider ... people to be heroes."[2]

In speaking of the heroic advocate, I do not mean the lawyer as gladiator who wages war on the public stage or, indeed, even in the courtroom with worthy and sometimes unworthy adversaries. Unlike Willie Nelson, my heroes have never been cowboys. I speak instead of advocates – like so many in this room – who dedicate their lives to the rule of law, who speak truth even when the larger community seems determined not to allow truth to disturb the existing order, who approach their roles with compassion and sensitivity and who go quietly about the business of helping people in trouble. These are the truly heroic in our profession.

It is difficult for a lawyer to be heroic. We all know that "there are good clients and bad clients, winning causes and losing causes. Sometimes, weak cases are won and good cases are lost."[3] As one commentator observed, "Lawyers are constantly tempted to do wrong and challenged to do good ... there are many divergent interests pulling at the lawyer's sleeve."[4] Yet, despite these challenges, there are many heroic lawyers among us.

I suggest that four qualities are essential in the heroic lawyer:

1. Commitment to the rule of law, and the courage to defend it when the need arises.
2. Integrity – a sense of the dictates of one's own conscience.
3. Compassion.
4. Honesty.

2 Cynthia L. Fountaine, "In the Shadow of Atticus Finch: Constructing a Heroic Lawyer" (2003) 13 Widener L.J. 123.

3 *Ibid.*

4 *Ibid.*

My remarks will focus on one exceptional advocate who lived a long time ago. You might ask: what do the experiences of an advocate from a bygone age have to do with us? My answer is simple: everything. Only by understanding the past heroism of advocates can we help secure heroism at the bar in the future.

Let me turn now to history, to my choice of the finest exemplar of the heroic advocate: Sir Thomas More. More lived in mid-sixteenth-century England, in the early years of the reign of his friend, Henry VIII. Contrary to both Spanish and English law, Henry married his brother's widow, the Spanish princess, Catherine of Aragon. To do so, he was required to obtain a papal dispensation because the marriage violated the law that forbade marriage with a brother's widow. But, after almost 20 years of marriage, Catherine had yet to give birth to a son upon whom to settle the succession. This led to the great conflict between More and Henry.

The succession problem was serious. Moreover, Henry liked women (lots of them, at least initially), and he had fallen in love with Anne Boleyn. He decided to marry her and sought to have his marriage to Catherine annulled by the pope. Spain resisted, and the pope refused – there would be no annulment and no divorce.

What followed changed England forever.

An accommodating cleric, Thomas Cranmer, the bishop of Canterbury, agreed to the divorce and Henry married Anne. The ensuing conflict between More and Henry was immortalized by Robert Bolt in his famous play *A Man for All Seasons*, which premiered in London at the Globe Theatre on July 1, 1960, with Paul Scofield in the role of Sir Thomas More, the ultimate man of conscience.

This is Bolt's introductory description of More:

> He is in his late forties, Pale, middle-sized, not robust. But the life of the mind in him is so abundant and debonair that it illuminates the body. His movements are open and swift but never wild, having a natural moderation. The face is intellectual and quickly delighted, the norm to which it returns serious and compassionate. Only in moments of high crisis does it become ascetic, though then freezingly.

Opposition to Henry's marriage to Anne was treason and could well spell More's death. Henry wants More to sanction the divorce and the marriage because More is highly respected. He is also the lord chancellor of England. But More cannot do so – he knows that the divorce from Catherine is unlawful. As a result, so too is the king's marriage to Anne.

More tries to avoid conflict with the king and to save himself and his family by invoking the rule of law. If he does not declare his opposition to the marriage – if he makes no utterance against the king – he cannot be condemned as a traitor, for no one will have proof of his opposition, only suspicion about it. The law requires more. So More reposes his trust in the rule and the letter of the law and seeks, by all legitimate means, not to cross the king. The law becomes his shield and his safety net.

More's unshakeable faith in the rule of law is the first hallmark of the heroic advocate. It is evident early in the play, when More is summoned to meet with Cardinal Wolsey. More is pressed to commit to helping secure a divorce for the king from Queen Catherine. Wolsey threatens that if the king dies without an heir, the country, which has just emerged from the Wars of the Roses, will again plunge into civil war. More's reply defines one of the central features of his own character:

> I believe, when statesmen forsake their own private conscience for the sake of their public duties – they lead their country by a short route to chaos.

Faith in the rule of law reflects the very essence of More. This is revealed in one of the most famous exchanges in Bolt's play. Richard Rich, a sycophantic academic who hopes to exploit a friendship with More to gain riches and fame, comes to More and begs for a job. More declines because he knows Rich is untrustworthy and shallow. When Rich leaves, More's family pleads with him to arrest Rich because, they say, he is dangerous and a "bad man." When More replies "There is no law against that," his son-in-law Roper, a freshly minted barrister, asserts, "There is! God's law." More retorts, "Then, God can arrest him." And he tells Roper, "The law, Roper, the law. I know what's legal not what's right. I'll stick to what's legal."

Roper alleges that More is setting "Man's law above God's," but More rejects this, saying:

> No, far below; but let me draw your attention to a fact – I'm *not* God. The currents and eddies of right and wrong, which you find such plain-sailing, I can't navigate, I'm no voyager. But in the thickets of the law, oh, there I'm a forester. I doubt if there's a man alive who could follow me there, thank God.

By this time, Richard Rich has departed and More's wife warns, "While you talk, he's gone!"

MORE: And go he should if he was the devil himself until he broke the law.

ROPER: So now you'd give the Devil benefit of law.

MORE: Yes. What would you do? Cut a great road through the law to get after the Devil?

ROPER: I'd cut down every law in England to do that.

MORE: Oh? And when the last law was down – and the Devil turned round on you – where would you hide, Roper, the laws all being flat? This country's planted thick with laws from coast to coast – Man's laws, not God's – and if you cut them down ... d'you really think you could stand upright in the winds that would blow then? Yes, I'd give the Devil benefit of law, for my own safety's sake ... [W]hoever hunts for me, Roper, God or Devil, will find me hiding in the thickets of the law. And I'll hide my daughter with me. Not hoist her up the mainmast of your seagoing principles. They put about too nimbly.

More's profound faith in the rule of law and in the actual words of the established law are what makes him such a compelling model for advocates. He shelters himself in the letter of the law, trusting that it and his own abilities will ensure justice and save him in the end.

The second marker of More's heroism is his integrity and his sense of identity and conscience.

In due course, Parliament succumbs to Henry's pressure and passes the *Act of Supremacy*, which declares the king to be the supreme head of the Church of England "so far as the law of God allows." It paves the way to the divorce from Catherine and the marriage to Anne.

More invokes this important caveat in the Act: "so far as the law of God allows." He resigns as Henry's lord chancellor, an office in which, in good conscience, he can no longer serve, declaring: "How far the law of God does allow it remains a matter of opinion, since the Act doesn't state it." He knows that if he once utters his opinion on the divorce and the proposed marriage to anyone, he will, under the law, be vulnerable to the charge of treason. He keeps his own opinion on the matter resolutely to himself.

In the end, if More had been willing to publicly approve Henry's marriage to Anne, his life would have been spared. But his approval was sought under oath, in a form that required him to swear that he believed what he didn't believe. An *Act of Succession* and accompanying oath are passed by Parliament. More demands to know the exact wording of the law, particularly the oath. The inexperienced barrister, Roper, suggests that it wasn't necessary to know the wording because "We know what it will mean." More, however, rebukes him with the cry of a "lawyer's lawyer":

> It will mean what the words say. An oath is *made* of words. It may be possible to take it. Or avoid it.

In fact, the *Act of Succession* states that the king's marriage to Catherine was unlawful, she being previously his brother's wife, and the pope had no authority to sanction it.

For More, an oath was sacred and perjury invited damnation. In essence, an oath was a contract with God. The taking of an oath is concerned with who a person is – by swearing an oath, a person guarantees his word with his integrity. More explains to his beloved daughter Meg:

> When a man takes an oath, Meg, he's holding his own self in his own hands, like water [cups hands], and if he opens his fingers, then – he needn't hope to find himself again.

More is eventually imprisoned in the Tower of London for his steadfast refusal to take the oath. Although he has yet to be charged with anything, he is endlessly interrogated by Norfolk, Cranmer and the relentless Thomas Cromwell. When he tells his interrogators that he will not take the oath and will not tell them why he will not, Norfolk suggests that More's reasons "must be treasonable." But More corrects him, saying: "Not 'must be'; may be ... The law requires more than an assumption; the law requires a fact."

We see again More's firm belief in the dictates of the law, and in justice, when Cromwell – bully that he is – crudely threatens that the state has harsher punishments than mere imprisonment:

> MORE: You threaten like a dockside bully.
> CROMWELL: How should I threaten?
> MORE: Like a Minister of State, with justice.
> CROMWELL: Oh, justice is what you're threatened with.
> MORE: Then I'm not threatened.

Eventually, More is summoned to the Hall of Westminster to answer to the charge of high treason.

The law fully protects More until it is subverted by a perjurer – a man for whom an oath in court means nothing. The trial is rigged – Richard Rich sells his soul and his meagre supply of honour in order to become attorney general of Wales. He perjures himself, falsely claiming that More declared to him that Parliament had "not the competence" to make Henry head of the church. More is sentenced to hang and is executed the following day. In this tragic end, we see the third and fourth qualities of the truly heroic advocate.

The third quality is compassion – or, if you will, humanity. When he is condemned by Rich's treacherous lies, More sorrowfully remarks, "In good faith, Rich, I am sorrier for your perjury than my peril." Then More tries, not for the first time, to get through to Rich, to teach him that there are some principles that transcend in importance personal gain or promise of advancement. Indeed, there are some bedrock principles worth dying for. He famously says to Rich: "For Wales? Why, Richard, it profits a man nothing to give his soul for the whole world – But for Wales ... !"

More's moving exchange with his close friend Norfolk, before the treason charge is laid, is shaped by the depths of More's compassion. Norfolk will not forsake their friendship – thus exposing his own person and family to great danger. When More's pleading with him fails, More picks a quarrel – a stinging one that wounds Norfolk to the core, compelling him to reject More in anger. In this way, More, much the smarter of the two, saves his best friend's life and loses his one remaining ally in Henry's court.

Finally, More's profound compassion illuminates the scaffold as he mounts to meet his death. After consoling his daughter Meg, More says to the hangman himself: "Friend, be not afraid of your office. You send me to God."

The final quality displayed by More that I believe defines the heroic advocate is simple but essential: honesty. More is in peril precisely because he is honest. Unlike Richard Rich, he cannot be bought by promise of favour or wealth. And because he is known as an honest and principled man, his failure to approve the marriage taints its legitimacy in the eyes of the public.

At More's trial, when death is certain but at last he is free to speak, he confronts and shames his accusers with the naked truth. He bluntly tells them that his blood has been sought not "for the Supremacy" but, rather, because he "would not bend to the marriage."

As Hannah Senesh once said:

> There are stars whose radiance is visible on earth though they have long been extinct. There are people whose brilliance continues to light the world though they are no longer among the living. These lights are particularly bright when the night is dark.[5]

Thomas More is one of those lights.

Why is it that the life of Thomas More so ignites the imagination and illuminates the human spirit? Why is he, quintessentially, the heroic advocate?

I suggest it is because society has a strong need for advocates who represent a defined set of values – who are certain of what they believe, and why, and who are prepared to defend those values in the face of adversity – however great the consequences: in other words, for heroic advocates. More is almost everything that advocates "wish to be and hope to become."[6]

A Man for All Seasons is set in the 1530s. Imprisonment without trial and examination under torture – on the rack – were common practice then. So was lengthy detention in the infamous Tower of London, without trial or charge. Almost five centuries have passed. Yet, we are witness again in our world to imprisonment without trial, in a place called Guantanamo Bay, interrogation by torture and rendition (the name of Arar comes to mind).

We live in an uncertain and insecure time, where we are "vulnerable to terrorists, vulnerable to the fear of terrorists" and vulnerable to those who would ignore or compromise the law in the name of defending against terrorists. In the post-9/11 world, no one would seriously debate the need to preserve our nation's security. But it is essential that members of our profession, above all others, remember that if we "trade freedom for security [we will likely] have neither."[7]

---

5 *Hannah Senesh, Her Life and Diary* (Woodstock, VT: Jewish Lights, 2004), epigraph, p. 1.

6 Michael Asimow, "When Lawyers Were Heroes" (1996) 30 U.S.F. L. Rev. 1131 at 1138.

7 Walter Herbert Rice, "I Am Proud to Be a Lawyer, and You Should Be, Too" (1999) 34:4 International Society of Barristers Quarterly at 431.

In his book *The Future of Freedom*, Fareed Zakaria has suggested that we also live in a world where democracy is flourishing but where constitutional liberalism – which seeks to protect the individual from arbitrary authority and coercion – is not.[8] At heart, this is an attack on the rule of law as we know it. We live, as well, in a time when many in the world suffer still from great inequities, poverty and hopelessness. The need to foster human dignity and maintain respect for others is pronounced. The world is awash with the innocent and the powerless.

In times such as these, there is great need for courageous advocates, advocates who are prepared to defend the rule of law and the right to equal justice, advocates who have the mettle to stand firm. The lessons to be learned from Thomas More resonate still. Heroic advocates believe unequivocally in the importance of the rule of law. But to defend the rule of law effectively and heroically, more is required than mere knowledge of the law: compassion, integrity and honesty are critical allies in the defence of the law and in the conduct of a heroic life.

Thomas More possessed all these qualities. He stands as a shining example of that which is heroic in the advocate and that which is finest in ourselves.

I do not wish to be taken as suggesting that we can all be heroes. As the pundit said, "Someone has to sit on the curb and clap as they go by." But I do say this. There have always been quietly heroic lawyers, and many are practising today. Heroic men and women toil in our courts everywhere, working competently for ordinary clients. Clients come to advocates burdened by troubles they find too great to support, and they depart "leaving their weight upon stronger shoulders."[9]

We see many advocates serving pro bono in public interest cases or volunteering in clinics. We find many others doing underpaid jobs as prosecutors, acting for legally aided clients or as advocates for the physically or mentally challenged and the poor. Others simply approach each day and each case with the resolve to do the best that they are able to do, with what they have, for those that they can assist.

We also see the monumental contributions of many lawyers on the international stage. This is a different but equally indispensable form

8 Fareed Zakaria, *The Future of Freedom: Illiberal Democracy at Home and Abroad* (New York & London: W.W. Norton, 2003).

9 "The Law," a speech presented at the Suffolk Bar Association Dinner, February 5, 1885; in Oliver Wendell Holmes, Jr., *Speeches* (Boston: Little, Brown & Co., 1913), 16–18.

of heroic advocacy. The names of Louise Arbour, Mary Robinson, Peter Cory, Albie Sachs and Bella Abzug come to mind. They are tenacious and fearless defenders of human rights and the champions of the rule of law on a global scale. They are heroic advocates.

Holmes believed that the law is made by the bar even more than by the bench.[10] Every case you conduct as trial and appellate lawyers becomes a part of our pattern of civil and criminal justice. What you say, when you say it and how you say it matters. Yours is a vital role and a profound responsibility.

It was Chief Justice Brian Dickson who warned that "lawyers who fail to recognize the moral quality of their work misunderstand the nature of their calling and ignore their larger responsibilities to society."[11] He also said,

> Without the dignity, independence and integrity of the Bar, impartial justice and maintenance of the rule of law are impossible ... However unpopular the task may be in the heat and passion of the moment, it falls upon the ... Bar to vindicate the rights of even the reprehensible, and to ensure that society deals fairly and justly with its weakest members.[12]

When advocates of courage, advocates who promote the rule of law, advocates who hold fast to their integrity, advocates who speak the truth – in short, heroic advocates – appear in circumstances where there is confusion, fear, tyranny, suffering or frustration, the dynamics of justice inevitably change. As Holmes reminded us: "To [achieve greatly], lawyers must be heroes as well as idealists." For it is only then "that you can know that *you have done what it lay in you to do* – can say that you have lived, and be ready for the end."[13]

Thank you for allowing me the privilege of speaking, once again, in the company of heroes.[14]

---

10 *Ibid.*

11 Brian Dickson, "Counsel's Duty to the Court and to His Client," Continuing Legal Education Society, Halifax, November 17, 1984.

12 Brian Dickson, "Remarks to the Criminal Lawyers' Association Conference," Toronto, November 4, 1989.

13 "The Profession of the Law," conclusion of a lecture delivered to undergraduates of Harvard University, February 17, 1886; in Oliver Wendell Holmes, Jr., *Speeches* (Boston: Little, Brown & Co., 1913), 22–25.

14 This article is an edited version of remarks presented at The Advocates' Society End of Term Dinner in Toronto on June 11, 2008.

Part Seven

ETHICS AND PROFESSIONALISM

OF THE MANY changes wrought in our profession over these years, perhaps the most profound relate not to the nature of advocacy but to our roles and responsibilities as advocates. The standards of ethics and professionalism loom large in our day-to-day practices, more so as self-represented litigants, especially in the family law sphere, find their way into courtrooms. Ethics and professionalism are hallmarks of the privilege of practising law as advocates in a fiercely adversarial profession, the modern equivalent of gladiatorial combat. For the last decade at least, one case has occupied as much academic and jurisprudential air time as any (*Groia v. The Law Society of Upper Canada*) and the saga is only now nearing an end, but not yet resolved as of this writing. Two judges – one now retired, one now deceased – and a former Law Society treasurer offer their thoughts on these critically important aspects of our work.

September 2008

The ethics of advocacy

GAVIN MACKENZIE

I DON'T SPEND A lot of time wringing my hands about the ethical standards of the lawyers of Ontario, which are very high. I have been practising for 30 years, and I can think of few cases in which my clients or I have been exposed to unethical conduct by lawyers on the other side of a case. Despite the egregious exceptions that we see occasionally at the Law Society, I do think there is a civility at the bar of Ontario in which we can take great pride. Those of us who practise as advocates confront ethical choices continually, however, at every phase of the litigation process: in deciding what clients to act for, and what cases to act on; in advising clients about whether matters are actionable; in deciding how to plead a claim or defence; in compiling documents for production and drafting affidavits of documents; in conducting examinations for discovery; in interviewing witnesses; in preparing motion materials and arguing motions; in leading evidence at trial; in cross-examining witnesses; and in arguing on our clients' behalf at trial and on appeal.

In each of those activities, the choices we make will depend on how we conceive of the role of a lawyer in an adversary system. The fundamental tension is between what our American colleagues refer to as their duty of "zealous representation" of their clients (our own rules of conduct say we have a duty to represent clients "resolutely") while at the same time fulfilling our duties as officers of the court, which include a duty to be candid with the court.

In the United States the duty to the client is generally seen as the lawyer's primary duty, while in Britain the duty to the court is preeminent. In our rules, the two duties are given equal prominence – which may make ethical choices in advocacy more difficult in our jurisdiction. I want to discuss how the different ways we conceive of our duties in an adversary system affect the ethical choices we make as advocates, and then refer briefly to two particular illustrations: the conduct of discoveries and the preparation of witnesses.

In a famous address in 1906, Roscoe Pound identified the pervasiveness of the "sporting theory of justice" as one of the causes of public dissatisfaction with the administration of justice. "The idea that procedure must of necessity be wholly contentious," he asserted, "disfigures our judicial administration at every turn."

Other untoward consequences that have been ascribed to the sporting theory of justice range from a disinclination among lawyers to resolve disputes to the selection of judges based on inappropriate criteria. Professor Roger Fisher of Harvard Law School (whom The Advocates' Society, the Ontario Bar Association and the Law Society of Upper Canada, among other organizations, recently honoured in Toronto) has imputed the aversion of many lawyers to discharging their ethical responsibility to settle disputes to their love of the contest:

> They find pleasure in representing a client with the full zeal that the legal canons of ethics call for. For some lawyers, negotiating the settlement of a case being prepared for trial has about as much appeal as negotiating the settlement of a football game or a prize fight would have for the athletes.

A former American judge, Marvin E. Frankel, analogized the practice of selecting judges from among trial lawyers to selecting umpires from among former baseball players: "Reflective people have suggested from time to time that qualities of detachment and calm neutrality are not necessarily cultivated by long years of partisan combat." The untoward effects of the adversary system's preoccupation with gamesmanship and contentiousness include forensic excesses, discovery abuse and an often significant discrepancy between lawyers' and non-lawyers' notions of ethical conduct.

Adversarial tactics tend to escalate despite the best of intentions in a competitive system. Lawyers adopt adversarial tactics – for example, unfounded objections that are calculated to break up the flow of damaging testimony – because to refrain from doing so would put their clients at a competitive disadvantage relative to the clients of lawyers who show no such restraint. Game theorists have a label for this phenomenon: the prisoner's dilemma.

But we have seen a few illustrations of cases in which this tendency to reduce lawyers' conduct to the lowest common denominator has worked to the disadvantage of both parties. The *Felderhof* case[1] is one example with which everyone is familiar. *Walsh*[2] is another. *Walsh* arose out of a lawyer's conduct of an examination for discovery. Discovery may be the most common forum for forensic excesses bred by lawyers' notions of the adversary system as a "win at all costs" professional sport.

THE HARD QUESTION IS WHERE TO DRAW THE LINE BETWEEN PROPER AND IMPROPER INFLUENCES ON WITNESSES' TESTIMONY

In *Walsh*, the court imposed costs personally on counsel for the plaintiffs, who had conducted what the court described as a "sprawling" examination of the defendant, and who appeared not to have been well prepared. He laughed and snickered throughout the examination, asked frivolous questions and intimidated and demeaned the witness. He answered his cell phone and left the room while the defendant's counsel was speaking. (This has happened to some of us while speaking, but not usually on a discovery.) The court wrote that the lawyer's "generally self-indulgent approach was more troubling than most of his outrageous questions."

One interesting feature of the case was that the court reduced the costs that would otherwise have been payable by the plaintiff's counsel on the ground that some of the time wasted on the discovery was attributable to the defendant's counsel. The court referred to the prisoner's dilemma (without giving it that label) and intervened to provide a financial disincentive to competitive forensic excesses.

The court wrote that the defendant's counsel's conduct could not be excused on the basis that he was merely responding to the plaintiff's counsel's improprieties: "That cannot be allowed as an excuse," the court

1 *R. v. Felderhof*, 2002 CanLII 41888 (Ont. S.C.J.), aff'd (2003), 68 O.R. (3d) 481 (C.A.).
2 *Walsh v. 1124660 Ontario Ltd.*, [2002] O.J. No. 4069 (Ont. S.C.J.).

held, "or we will have established a recipe for a downward spiral into increasing incivility." The court added that by surrendering, unprofessionally, to the temptation to respond sarcastically to provocative questions, the defendant's counsel had compromised his right to complain of comparable improprieties on the part of the plaintiff 's counsel. So responding in kind, or taking the bait, may not be such a good idea.

Preparing witnesses is an area in which lawyers encounter some of their most troubling ethical problems. Their honour is likely to be tested regularly. Under our rules of conduct, you cannot "influence the course of justice" by "suppressing what ought to be disclosed" and you must "take care not to subvert or suppress any evidence."[3] That does not mean, of course, that you have to take a purely passive role, or be a mere scribe, in interviewing witnesses.

We have all heard the suggestion that you may advise a witness how to testify but not what to say. That oversimplifies the problem, but at least it recognizes that lawyers may take an active role in preparing witnesses to testify, as long as it remains the witnesses' evidence.

We may of course advise witnesses on how to address the judge and the lawyers, and what procedure will be followed in eliciting their evidence. We may also draw their attention to relevant issues, probe in an effort to refresh their memories by referring to known facts or other evidence, even if the effect of doing so is to prompt answers that the witness may not have volunteered if it were not for our probing. We may prepare witnesses to stand up to a hostile cross-examination.

At the other end of the spectrum, we must not suborn perjury, persuade witnesses to avoid summonses or obstruct access to witnesses by other parties. You'll recall from *Meek v. Fleming*[4] that we must not permit witnesses to be presented in a misleading way. That was the case in which the defendant's counsel stood by silently while both the plaintiff's counsel and the trial judge referred to his client the defendant, a police officer, as "Chief Inspector," though the defendant had been reduced in rank because he had deceived the court in another case. Lord Justice Pearce said that in his judgment, "the duty to the court was here unwarrantably subordinated to the duty to the client."

3 Law Society of Upper Canada, *Rules of Professional Conduct,* Rule 4.01(2)(e).

4 [1961] Q.B. 366.

I think the same would be said of the lawyer in the movie (and play) *Anatomy of a Murder*, who said to the client who had just given him an inculpatory account of a murder: "If the facts are as you stated them you have no legal defence and will probably be electrocuted. On the other hand, if you acted in a blind rage, there is a possibility of saving your life. Think it over and we will talk about it tomorrow."

So those are the easy questions. The hard question is where to draw the line between proper and improper influences on witnesses' testimony. Is it proper, for example, to elicit answers from witnesses in interviews by means of leading questions? Witnesses' memories of an event may, without dishonesty, be influenced by both the form and the content of lawyers' questions. Psychologists who have studied memory have concluded that the process of "remembering" events involves more reconstruction that recollection. Much of what is said to be perceived is in fact inferred. Recollection is influenced by many factors, including, prominently, the witness's prior experiences and the witness's interest. Even honest witnesses suppress and invent facts, without realizing that they are doing so.

One of the strongest influences on memory, however, is the way in which the question is asked. In one American study, witnesses' estimates of the speed of a car they observed in a collision varied depending on the verb used by the questioner in describing the impact. When the car "contacted" another car, its speed averaged 31.8 miles per hour. When it "hit" it, its speed was 34 mph. When it "bumped" the other car, its speed increased to 38.1 mph. When it "collided" with the other car, it was travelling at 39.3 mph. And when it "smashed" into the other car, it did so at 40.8 mph. So the verb used by the questioner may make the difference between whether the driver was careful or negligent. Besides that, in the same study, twice as many witnesses reported seeing non-existent broken glass on the ground when the questioner used the verb "smashed" rather than "hit."

There is no prohibition against asking leading questions when interviewing witnesses, and there is a fine line between what you can properly do to influence a witness's evidence and what may influence it improperly.

I will say only this, by way of conclusion: we should be skeptical of justifications of questionable conduct that appeal to the ethics of the adversary system. Particularly in civil cases, we should conceive of the adversary system as a proven mechanism whereby trained advocates present their clients' cases in their best light, in accordance with rules by which they are bound, before a passive and neutral adjudicator whom they are there to assist. I remember Ian Scott saying to me once – and I'm sure the expression goes back long before his time – that the reason we have lawyers is that clients don't fight fair. The best advice is still the old maxim that if you have to ask whether you are crossing the line, you are probably standing too close to it.

Professionalism: AN OLD IDEA BUT A NEW IDEAL

THE HONOURABLE JOAN L. LAX

IN OCTOBER 1999, Justice Rosie Abella delivered what has become an iconic speech to a retreat of Law Society benchers. Her title was "Professionalism Revisited." Her speech was about values, and her thesis was "that there are three basic values that merge in a good lawyer: a commitment to competence, which is about skills; a commitment to ethics, which is about decency; and a commitment to professionalism, which transfuses the public interest into the two other values."[1] This triumvirate of values – competence, ethics and service to the public – has long been regarded as the foundation of the claim that law is not merely a trade but a higher calling – a profession – comprising elements of scholarship, integrity, honour, service, pride and independence.

Historically, the early professions of law, medicine and theology were built around philosophical or ethical codes featuring some kind of service to others and "a calling to some higher satisfaction than a commercial gain,"[2] and professionals "declared that choice openly in front of the

1 The Honourable Rosalie Silberman Abella, Justice, Court of Appeal for Ontario (as she then was), "Professionalism Revisited" (Opening Address, Bencher's Retreat, October 14, 1999), (Toronto: Law Society of Upper Canada, 1999) at 1 [Justice Abella].

2 E.W. Roddenbery, "Achieving Professionalism" (May–June 1953) 44:1 *Journal of Criminal Law, Criminology, and Police Science* at 109; cited in Jordan Furlong, "Professionalism Revived: Diagnosing the Failure of Professionalism among Lawyers and

community."[3] Although lawyers served the interest of their clients, the lawyers' other duties – to the court, to the opposing party, to truth and to society – were viewed as equally if not more important.[4] The transition from a public-centred model of service to a client-centred one is usually attributed to Sir Henry Brougham's 1820 speech, in defence of Queen Caroline against treason[5] charges brought by her husband, King George IV, when he said that an advocate in discharge of his duties "knows but one person in all the world and that person is his client."[6] Some have suggested that this philosophy of lawyering emerged much later,[7] but all commentators agree that the dominant and current model of lawyering is that of the zealous advocate. In the 2003 *R. v. Felderhof* decision, Rosenberg J.A., speaking for the Court of Appeal, described zealous advocacy as "a cornerstone of our adversary system,"[8] which it has been.

However, the centrality of client autonomy and a lawyer's unqualified loyalty to the client's interests is a narrative of the legal profession that some say has run its course. Today's lawyers, argues legal academic David Tanovich, are looking for ways to practise law as a means of securing justice rather than maximizing clients' goals.[9] Today's lawyers, argues legal academic Trevor Farrow, want narratives of the profession that make good on aspirational promises of equality, access to justice and protecting the public interest.[10] So does the public. Historically, professionalism was the pursuit and service of others' best interests.

Finding a Cure" Chief Justice of Ontario's Advisory Committee on Professionalism, 10th Colloquium, March 2008 at 2, online: <www.lsuc.on.ca> [Furlong].

3 Furlong, *supra* note 2 at 2

4 *Ibid.* at 3.

5 Some sources characterize the charges as treason (see, e.g., Fred Zacharias & Bruce A. Green, "Anything Rather Than a Deliberate and Well-Considered Opinion – Henry Lord Brougham, Written by Himself" (2006) 19 Geo. J. Legal Ethics 1221 at 1221, n. 2); others characterize the charges as adultery (see, e.g., Monroe H. Freedman, "Henry Lord Brougham and Zeal" (2006) 34 Hofstra L. Rev. 1319 at 1320 [Freedman]).

6 2 *Trial of Queen Caroline* 3 (1821); cited *inter alia* in Freedman, *supra* note 5 at 1322.

7 See, e.g., Michel Proulx & David Layton, *Ethics and Canadian Criminal Law* (Toronto: Irwin Law, 2001) at 3–5; cited in David M. Tanovich, "Law's Ambition and the Reconstruction of Role Morality in Canada" (2005) 28 Dalhousie L.J. 267 at 272 [Tanovich].

8 *R. v. Felderhof* (2003), 68 O.R. (3d) 481 at para. 84.

9 See Tanovich, *supra* note 7.

10 See Trevor Farrow, "Sustainable Professionalism" (2008) 46 O.H.L.J. 51.

Helping people, alleviating misery, fighting injustice and any conversation about professionalism must recall these ideals.

Ethical practice and conduct has long been recognized as a key element of professionalism, and the terms "legal ethics" and "professionalism" are often used interchangeably. Lawyers are expected to observe codes of professional conduct established by their governing bodies. As a self-governing profession, the legal community establishes its own standards of professionalism and ethics. Harry Arthurs has been a persistent and powerful critic of the efficacy of the professional codes and of the failure of the Law Society to effectively discipline its members. In an article colourfully titled "The Dead Parrot: Does Professional Self-Regulation Exhibit Vital Signs?" he asserts that many if not most of the chapters of the Canadian Bar Association Code and their provincial counterparts are not in fact used to discipline lawyers. He wrote:

> I personally would be pleased to hear that someone had been suspended for not representing clients resolutely, not adhering to high standards in the discharge of public office or not trying to improve the administration of justice. I would be delighted to know that someone who was discourteous to members of the profession or derelict in his or her duty to make legal services available to the public had attracted professional censure. But, alas, such professional norms are violated with impunity.[11]

Professor Michael Code (recently appointed to the Superior Court of Justice) takes up this argument in a compelling article on counsel's duty of civility in which he argues that there is an enforceable right to be protected against the uncivil behaviour of opposing counsel because it undermines fair trials.[12] He calls on counsel, the courts and the Law Society to rededicate themselves to the ideals of civility, both for pragmatic reasons of trial efficiency and for normative reasons relating to public respect for the administration of justice. Similar themes show up in the report prepared by former Chief Justice Patrick LeSage and Professor Code on complex criminal case procedures. According to press reports,

---

11 H.W. Arthurs, "The Dead Parrot: Does Professional Self-Regulation Exhibit Vital Signs?" (1995) 33 Alta. L. Rev. 800 at 802; cited in Michael Code, "Counsel's Duty of Civility: An Essential Component of Fair Trials and an Effective Justice System" (2007) 11 Can. Crim. L. Rev. 97 at 136, n. 121 [Code].

12 See Code, *supra* note 11.

the report includes recommendations that unprofessional lawyers be cut off legal aid funding and subjected to professional discipline.[13]

More than a decade separates the Arthurs "Dead Parrot" article and the Code "Civility" article. Until recently, the legal community had shown little interest in critically examining the conduct of lawyers or the role of the legal profession. In an essay published eight years ago, legal scholar Adam Dodek described the barren landscape of Canadian legal ethics as "a subject in search of scholarship,"[14] echoing the oft-heard lament of Harry Arthurs that the legal profession led an unexamined life. For decades, Arthurs was the only legal academic teaching and writing about the legal profession, painstakingly "tilling the scholarly soil" alone.[15] Why this indifference?

Professor Allan Hutchinson argues that unlike the United States – which in the 1970s had the defining cultural moment of Watergate, where all but three of those implicated in the scandal were lawyers – we did not experience the same pressure to consider the legitimacy of our professional norms.[16] South of the border, the participation of lawyers in a series of scandals, from the collapse of the savings and loan industry in the 1980s to the collapse of Enron in 2001 to the O.J. Simpson trial, kept the debate alive when it had hardly begun here.

When the Supreme Court of Canada released its decision in *Macdonald Estate v. Martin*[17] in 1990, the legal profession sat up and took notice because it brought the "abstract ethical discussions of conflicts of interest down to the reality of the practice of law in the 1990s."[18] It hit lawyers in their bank accounts. But conflicts of interest are only the tip of the ethical iceberg. The Ken Murray trial, 10 years later, raised an ethical storm and has been described as "something of a mini-Enron

13 Kirk Makin, "Ontario review takes aim at disruptive lawyers" *The Globe and Mail* (29 October 2008), online: The Globe and Mail <www.theglobeandmail.com>.

14 See Adam M. Dodek, "Canadian Legal Ethics: A Subject in Search of Scholarship" (2000) 50 U. Toronto L. J. 115 [Dodek, "Subject in Search of Scholarship"].

15 Adam M. Dodek, "Canadian Legal Ethics: Ready for the Twenty-first Century at Last" (2008) 46 Osgoode Hall L.J. 1 at 23 [Dodek, "Twenty-first Century"].

16 Allan C. Hutchinson, *Legal Ethics and Professional Responsibility*, 2nd ed. (Toronto: Irwin Law, 2006) at 5–6; cited in Dodek, "Twenty-first Century," *supra* note 15 at 9.

17 [1990] 3 S.C.R. 1235.

18 Dodek, "Subject in Search of Scholarship," *supra* note 14 at 119.

for the legal profession."[19] It was followed by other mini-scandals that have removed our complacency: the grades scandal at the University of Toronto, a cheating scandal at the bar admission course, the resignations of the president of the Law Society of British Columbia after a conviction for impaired driving and of the treasurer of the Law Society of Upper Canada following a sexual relationship with a client, and the Conrad Black trial. Each attracted huge media attention, public scrutiny and self-examination. The publication last year of Philip Slayton's book on lawyers, which was sensationalized as a *Maclean's* magazine cover story, led to outrage and protest from the bar but only one published letter to the editor from a member of the Canadian public, who pointed to the outcome of the O.J. Simpson trial as proof that "indeed, lawyers are rats."[20]

In the aftermath of that article, the Ontario Bar Association compared *Maclean's* to Nazis, suggesting that lawyers are all that stands between civilization and tyranny.[21] The Canadian Bar Association called on the magazine to apologize, but no apology was forthcoming.[22] In a powerful editorial, *Maclean's* editors reminded us that the whole point of being a self-governing community is that we are collectively responsible for the welfare of the profession and that every Canadian lawyer is implicated in its failures. They suggested that we tone down the rhetoric and look at ourselves in the mirror.[23] To our credit, this is what we have been doing.

The creation of Pro Bono Law Ontario, the Ontario Justice Education Network and the Chief Justice of Ontario's Advisory Committee on Professionalism was initiated in recent years under the leadership of former Chief Justice Roy McMurtry and with the encouragement and dedication of Justices Stephen Goudge and Robert Armstrong, who have played a very significant role in putting professionalism in the spotlight. Last month, the advisory committee held its 11th Colloquium on the Legal Profession at the University of Windsor Law School examining how well today's legal profession is doing in its role of service to the public, particularly vulnerable and marginalized communities. The colloquia series began in 2003 and has engaged participants from the profession,

19 Kent Roach, "Ethics and Criminal Justice" (2003) 47 Crim. L.Q. 121 at 121; cited in Tanovich, *supra* note 7 at 270.

20 For further discussion see Dodek, "Twenty-first Century," *supra* note 15.

21 "Not Just a Lone Voice in the Wilderness," Editorial, *Maclean's* (13 August 2007).

22 *Ibid.*

23 *Ibid.*

the judiciary, the Law Society and the academy in ideas, arguments and issues that have become an integral part of the research agenda for a growing cadre of Canadian legal scholars who are thinking and writing critically about the legal profession, legal ethics and professionalism.

Be prepared to hear more from legal scholars Code, Hutchinson, Farrow, Dodek, Tanovich, Sossin, Woolley and others. Be prepared to be challenged by their ideas and the ideas of their students as initiatives have taken root at Canadian law schools in the form of mandatory and elective courses on legal ethics and professionalism.

Some law schools, such as Osgoode Hall, seek to join the theoretical discussion with mandatory public interest law-related work reinforcing the ideal of public service. Although professionalism has long been ignored as a subject worthy of academic discussion, this generation of law students is learning about professionalism as part of its legal education and will bring this into the profession. This year saw the establishment of the Centre for the Legal Profession at the University of Toronto under the direction of Professor Lorne Sossin.[24] The centre's goal is to broaden and deepen an understanding of professionalism, ethics and public service and the relationship between them. This year also saw the establishment of The Advocates' Society Institute for Civility and Professionalism. And, fittingly, Adam Dodek has published another article in which he surveys the 2008 landscape of Canadian legal ethics scholarship and declares that it is "ready for the twenty-first century at last."[25]

That we are having a conversation about professionalism can be disquieting to those who believe they learned their professional ideals and values by osmosis from the generation that preceded them. Many of us had no formal education in legal ethics or professionalism, yet we emerged from law school and the bar admission course with an understanding that the world we were entering had a professional culture, a vague term of shared values, traditions, ambitions, symbols and expectations. At one time, to obtain and maintain membership in that culture required a considerable adaptation to the norms and expected behaviours of the culture, which could be difficult if you were not of that culture – a culture that was overwhelmingly male, white and privileged, often evoking the image of

24 Centre for the Legal Profession, <http://www.law.utoronto.ca>.

25 Dodek, "Twenty-first Century," *supra* note 15.

the English gentleman.[26] The English bar was in fact an important reference point for the cultural norms that took root in the Canadian legal profession, particularly among advocates, but the legal profession has not resembled an English gentleman for some time. In a profession that is increasingly diverse, we cannot assume a shared understanding of the lawyer's role.

History can be a lesson for us here, and while we are holding up the mirror let's remind ourselves that we must always be vigilant about intolerance. As legal historian Constance Backhouse has documented, the legal profession sometimes perverted professionalism, turning it into a club and using it to erect barriers to admission and to discriminate on the basis of gender, race, class and religion. Difference was noticed and resisted each time there were new entrants, whether they were Jews, women or visible minorities. It is known, for example, that Bora Laskin was forced to take an unpaid articling position and, after graduation from Harvard Law School, wrote headnotes for a law publisher when he was unable to obtain a paid position with a law firm.[27]

It is disheartening to read Ellen Anderson's biography of Madam Justice Bertha Wilson, in which she describes the exclusion and hostility that Justice Wilson faced when she became the first woman appointed to the Court of Appeal for Ontario in 1976 and to the Supreme Court of Canada in 1982.[28] Madam Justice Claire L'Heureux-Dubé, the second woman appointed to the Supreme Court of Canada, had been on the court for 12 years when the release of her decision in *Ewanchuk*, a sexual assault case, prompted an unprecedented public attack on her.[29] She was vilified in national newspapers by members of the bar and publicly accused of disgracing the Supreme Court of Canada. Mr. Justice McClung, whose decision she had overturned, published a letter in the *National Post* accusing her of feminist bias and, astonishingly, suggesting that she was responsible for the growing number of male suicides in Quebec. A very senior

26 Constance Backhouse, "Gender and Race in the Construction of 'Legal Professionalism': Historical Perspectives" Chief Justice of Ontario's Advisory Committee on Professionalism, 1st Colloquium, October 2003 at 3, online: <http://www.lsuc.on.ca> [Backhouse].

27 *Ibid.* at 6.

28 Ellen Anderson, *Judging Bertha Wilson: Law as Large as Life* (Toronto: University of Toronto Press, 2001).

29 *R. v. Ewanchuk*, [1999] 1 S.C.R. 330.

member of the criminal defence bar wrote a letter to the editor of the same newspaper accusing her of intemperance, lack of balance and terrible lack of judgment. He forecast that the feminist influence posed a potential danger to the independence of the judiciary. Although Justice McClung was disciplined modestly by the Canadian Judicial Council, the Law Society took no action against those members of the bar who publicly denounced Justice L'Heureux-Dubé, leaving some to wonder what exactly the regulator had in mind when it drafted its rules on unprofessional behaviour and conduct unbecoming a barrister.[30]

There are of course narratives of the profession of which we can be extremely proud and which illustrate the profession's capacity to learn, to change and to grow. This past fall, I heard Justice Robert Armstrong deliver a memorable eulogy for former Chief Justice Charles Dubin.[31] He spoke of his deep admiration and affection for Justice Dubin, for whom he articled in 1964 and to whom he remained close until his death. In the sanctuary of a large Jewish synagogue filled with lawyers and judges, women and men, Armstrong J.A. quoted from the Torah and eulogized his Jewish mentor, who became a beloved Chief Justice of Ontario. Justice Dubin will be remembered not only as a part of a tradition of legendary lawyers that included John Robinette, Arthur Maloney and Arthur Martin, among others, but as someone whose life was a metaphor for the building blocks of professionalism – scholarship, integrity, honour, leadership, independence, pride, spirit, collegiality, service and balanced commercialism.[32] It is these cherished values that we want to pass on, but we must find new ways to share the legacy left to us by these iconic figures.

There is no doubt that senior lawyers must continue to serve as role models for the next generation, but as we all know, the opportunity to learn how to be a good and honourable lawyer by watching good and honourable lawyers in action is extremely limited, depriving many new entrants of a significant channel of professional education to learn the triumvirate of values about which Justice Abella spoke. As Justice Armstrong's account attests, mentorship was an important tool used by the

30 For further discussion of this issue, see Backhouse, *supra* note 26.

31 The Honourable Robert P. Armstrong, "Eulogy for the Honourable Charles Leonard Dubin, Q.C." (Spring 2009) 27:4 Advocates' Journal 3.

32 Chief Justice of Ontario Advisory Committee on Professionalism, Working Group on the Definition of Professionalism, "Elements of Professionalism," October 2001 (revised December 2001 and June 2002) at 1, online: <www.lsuc.on.ca>.

bar to foster civility, professionalism and ethics in its junior ranks. The Advocates' Society has been a leader on these two important fronts – civility and mentorship – and is once again showing leadership by putting professionalism on its agenda. It joins an energetic discussion that seeks answers to challenging ethical and professional issues that not only confront individuals within the legal system but also raise larger questions that go to the very heart of the legitimacy of the legal profession and the legal system.

Few are unfamiliar with Shakespeare's most well-known and lasting popular legacy to the law, which appears to stand out as a stinging comment on the legal profession. Lawyers have long said that when one of the rebels in *Henry VI* says, "The first thing we do, let's kill all the lawyers,"[33] Shakespeare was not disparaging lawyers but praising their role in society. If we want the public to accept this interpretation, if we want the public to accept that lawyers are all that stand between civilization and tyranny, we must begin to take seriously the 1994 Role Statement of the Law Society that the legal profession exists in the public interest to advance the cause of justice and the rule of law.[34] If we are a profession dedicated to advancing the cause of justice, then, as former Chief Justice Roy McMurtry has said, the profession should want to participate in making justice accessible.[35] As Chief Justice Beverley McLachlin has said, "the most advanced justice system in the world is a failure if it does not provide justice to the people it is meant to serve."[36] The result is injustice. We must be open to discussing new models of lawyering that may challenge what we perceive to be our core values but may better address our aspirations – equality, access to justice, protection of the public interest. We must be ready to demonstrate by our actions that the pursuit and service of others' best interests is at the core of what we do.

33 William Shakespeare, *Henry VI, Part II*, Act IV, Scene ii, lines 83–84.

34 Law Society of Upper Canada, "Strategic Plan 2000–2003" at 3, online: Law Society of Upper Canada <www.lsuc.on.ca>.

35 The Honourable R. Roy McMurtry, Chief Justice of Ontario, "The Legal Profession and Public Service" Chief Justice of Ontario's Advisory Committee on Professionalism, 3rd Colloquium, October 2004 at 15, online: <www.lsuc.on.ca>.

36 The Right Honourable Beverley McLachlin, Chief Justice of Canada, "The Challenges We Face" (Remarks to the Empire Club of Canada, 8 March 2007), online: <http://cfcj-fcjc.org>.

September 2009

Looking back and looking forward on learning in professionalism

THE HONOURABLE STEPHEN T. GOUDGE

I SUSPECT WE ALL remember the day when we first told our family and friends that we were going to law school. Undoubtedly, some of us were met by the most recent lawyer joke – something about lawyers and rats, or lawyers and sharks or lawyers and light bulbs. But underneath, there was almost always a quiet admiration and pride that we had decided to become a part of something both important and valued – the legal profession.

We did not consider it to be a cult, although undoubtedly it had its ceremonies and rituals and thought of itself as an "in group." Nor did it really seem to be a culture, although it clearly had its distinctive customs and outlooks, and it would give us the label by which we would be identified from then on: lawyers. Rather, it was a profession – although we had only the vaguest understanding of what that meant.

Little did we know then that most of us would inevitably spend time exploring this question, either explicitly or implicitly, either consciously or subconsciously, attempting to answer in one way or another what it means for a lawyer to say that he or she is a member of a profession. The ongoing quest for how best to live one's professional life as a lawyer necessarily lasts a lifetime. It is inevitably a journey of lifelong learning.

Lawyers love – indeed, are addicted to – definitions, and professionalism is a slippery term. Many alternatives can be conceived. Let me describe just several.

For lawyers, the most venerable conception of professionalism focuses on the paradigm of the zealous advocate. The sole professional obligation of the lawyer is described as the duty to advance the client's objectives "zealously within the bounds of the law." The discharge of this duty is not only a necessary but also a sufficient condition of professionalism, because it is assumed that if this happens, justice will be done. In the famous words of Lord Brougham:

> An advocate in the discharge of his duty knows but one person in all the world, and that person is his client. The lawyer's first and only duty is to save that client by all means and expedients, and at all hazards and costs to other persons, among them to himself.

A somewhat broader, but related, conception reflects the notion articulated so well by Benjamin Cardozo that being a lawyer is a privilege overlain with responsibilities. Legal ethics viewed this way are mostly about rules that prohibit a lawyer from engaging in specified conduct. As Anthony Kronman put it:

> One assumes that one becomes an ethical lawyer by mastering the complex body of rules that govern a lawyer's relations with clients, adversaries, officials and other third parties and that these rules define, perhaps exhaust, the subject of professional responsibility.

Although broader than the first conception, this remains at heart a negative approach to professionalism in a world where I think lawyers seek more. In a paper done in 2002, the Chief Justice of Ontario's Advisory Committee on Professionalism described a considerably richer vision. It uses language that is much more positive than the proscriptions of a rules-based notion. It begins this way:

> Professionalism as a personal characteristic is revealed in an attitude and approach to an occupation that is commonly characterized by intelligence, integrity, maturity and thoughtfulness. The expectation among lawyers, whose occupation is defined as a profession, and in the public who receive legal services, is that professionalism will inform a lawyer's work and conduct.

The advisory committee's conception goes on to describe what it calls the building blocks of professionalism:

> Defining the elements of professionalism involves identification and discussion of its various components. They are: scholarship, integrity, honour, leadership, independence, pride, spirit, collegiality, service, and balanced commercialism.

The committee then goes on to unpack each of these notions. For example, scholarship refers to the capacity to provide competent legal services, independent advice and sound judgment, acquired through formal education, experience, mentors, the example of peers and continuing legal education. Integrity is described as not just the observing of ethical standards established by the Law Society, but also a shared collective responsibility for ensuring, so far as practicable, that the profession as a whole discharges its roles appropriately and in the public interest, which is its part of the social contract under which society has delegated to it the power of self-regulation. Balanced commercialism is described as being dedicated to serving the public, with income and status being worthy but not primary goals. This was famously described by Roscoe Pound in 1953:

> The term [professionalism] refers to a group pursuing a learned art as a common calling in the spirit of public service – no less a public service because it may incidentally be a means of livelihood. Pursuit of the learned art in the spirit of a public service is the primary purpose.

The last conception I want to refer to is that described as sustainable professionalism by Professor Trevor Farrow in a thoughtful article in the *Osgoode Hall Law Journal*. He builds on the positive approach by adding to it qualities such as pursuing equality and access to justice, and protecting the public interest – qualities that introduce seeking substantive justice as a piece of the puzzle. He argues that this makes space for lawyers' principles, interests and life preferences, and seeks to balance them with other important interests including, but not dominated by, those of clients. He closes his article with this challenge:

> We need a sustainable model of professionalism to facilitate change. As Socrates commented in *The Republic*, the question of how we should live our lives – or in this case how we should view ourselves as professionals – is no light matter. This is because as Martin Meyer argues, in all likelihood "this society ... and the world of our children will largely depend on how we view ourselves as professionals."

This brief tour of various approaches to the concept of professionalism demonstrates the richness of the discussions that are possible in addressing what it means for a lawyer to say: "I am a member of a profession."

What is clear, I think, is that settling on a "right" answer is not a precondition to advancing the cause. Whether one focuses primarily on the mandatory or regulatory aspects of professionalism or on its aspirational aspects, there is a shared recognition that being a lawyer means something more than having a job, something valuable. It entails duties to others and ways of acting in living one's professional life.

But then one might ask: why is professionalism important? Why does all this matter? Let me answer in three ways. First, it is essential if the public is to have confidence in the justice system. As the advisory committee's paper says, the public expects that professionalism will inform a lawyer's work and conduct. Lawyers perform services that are essential for the proper functioning of a civil society. They make the system of justice function, and they occupy significant positions of leadership in the community. In return, they are accorded a certain stature and prestige because of the expectation that they will bring to their tasks the values and attitudes that are expected to be exemplified by the lawyer as professional. If this expectation is disappointed, faith in the justice system is eroded – at great cost not just to the system, but also to the rule of law that depends on it. It is not to be forgotten that, as Oliver Wendell Holmes said,

> Law is nothing unless behind it stands a warm, living public opinion.

The second reason I offer is rather more mechanical. If the justice system is to effectively resolve disputes, it is essential that lawyers bring to their work a healthy sense of professionalism. Many of the regulatory aspects of professionalism play a role here. Rules designed to ensure confidentiality between lawyer and client, or to prevent conflicts of interest, are but two examples. However, aspirational aspects of professionalism are important as well. Seeking to ensure access to justice is just one obvious example.

Third, I think professionalism matters if we are to ensure that we will be able to provide the satisfying career opportunities for the young people of tomorrow that will be so necessary if the legal profession is to continue to successfully renew itself. Every year, when I have the privilege of spending a week with the first-year students at this law school and when I do so at law schools elsewhere in Ontario, I am forcibly struck not just by their intelligence but also by their sense of idealism. For most, there is a deep-seated desire to make a contribution to the justice system and to help make their world a better place. If we are not to leave them disappointed and seeking alternative careers, it is vital that we nurture professionalism in all its dimensions, but perhaps most of all in its aspirational dimensions.

If professionalism matters in these ways, and undoubtedly in others, it is very tempting to immediately embark on an inquiry into the current state of its health. How bad is it, and how much worse can it get? Indeed, in the past, much of the work on professionalism has been in response to a sense – sometimes studied, more often anecdotal – that there has been an unfortunate decline in professionalism throughout the practice of law. I will resist that temptation for two reasons. First, it would be all too easy to talk oneself into a pessimistic funk by doing so; and second, it was ever thus. As Professor Deborah Rhode has said:

> Lawyers belong to a profession permanently in decline. Or so it appears in the chronic laments by critics within and outside the bar.

So I will attempt my sketch of where we have come from in learning in professionalism in a way that is simply descriptive but does not seek to determine whether the curve of history is rising or in free fall.

Historically, for lawyers in Ontario, learning about professionalism was mostly about being a gentleman, something that was considered rather more about breeding than about education. While from its beginning in 1797 the Law Society of Upper Canada promulgated rules for compliance with professional standards, throughout the 19th century the legal profession was governed, in Christopher Moore's phrase, as much by codes of gentility as by books of rules.

By the early 20th century, professionalism had built on the shared social culture from which lawyers came, to centre on definitions of inappropriate professional behaviour as defined by the Law Society. In the 1920s, organizations like the newly formed Canadian Bar Association began crusading for higher professional standards than the narrow "thou shalt not" of the regulator. This resulted in the Canadian Bar Association's canons of ethics which purported to describe a lawyer's obligations as a minister of justice, an officer of the court, his client's advocate and a member of an ancient, honourable and learned profession. However, the focus still remained very much on a rules-based notion of professionalism.

By the middle of the last century, little had changed save the level of detail of the proscribed conduct. For example, although it might surprise today's Law Foundation of Ontario, accounting rules prohibited pocketing the interest on trust accounts. Advertising was prohibited. Even the way in which lawyers should list their names in the phone book was prescribed, in the name of the dignity of the profession. The rules of the regulator – concerning what conduct could not be engaged in if one wished to call oneself a lawyer – had become a major vehicle for learning in professionalism.

The more aspirational dimensions of professionalism – how a lawyer should aspire to behave in pursuit of true professionalism – were left to other less explicit means of communication. The coherence of the bar, its shared professional values, and the mentoring provided by older lawyers were of vital importance in this exercise. In an article written in 1968, the eminent Arthur Martin described this way of learning professionalism:

> A magnificent tradition exists among the senior members of the bar of willingness to make their judgment and experience available to their colleagues and especially to the younger members of the bar without regard to compensation.

This went beyond ethical challenges that might arise in a particular case. For example, Justice Martin described the expectation that existed before legal aid that defence lawyers would devote a substantial part of their time to the defence of the indigent. In ways like this, aspirational dimensions of professionalism were passed from generation to generation.

Through much of the last century, one way in which learning in professionalism did not take place was through the formal teaching of it. Even someone as youthful as Justice Rosie Abella could describe her own legal education experience this way:

> When I graduated from law school no one taught ethics or professionalism. In the Bar Admission Course the then Chief Justice of the province gave a one hour lecture on how lawyers should behave. He told the over 500 students never to wear brown suits and white socks – a largely irrelevant observation for the ten women in the room who nonetheless shared the Chief Justice's view of brown suits.

However, by the 1990s, significant winds of change had started to blow. In its 1994 role statement, the Law Society explicitly took on professionalism as its brand, declaring that the legal profession exists in the public interest to advance the cause of justice and the rule of law. By the turn of the millennium, it had completely revised and modernized its rules of professional conduct to simplify the mandatory aspects of professionalism and to expand its attention to the aspirational aspects of what it means for lawyers to be professionals.

At the same time, leading organizations of lawyers were putting their shoulders to the wheel. For example, The Advocates' Society produced and disseminated valuable materials to assist lawyers in improving the civility with which they conduct their activities.

In addition, the realization was rapidly growing of the need to advance the learning of professionalism by formally teaching it. The Bar Admission Course had come to include sessions on professionalism. In the legal academy, Professor Brent Cotter published his seminal report, addressing two questions: the status of the teaching and learning of professional responsibility in Canadian legal education today; and how to change the lack of resources, co-ordination and pedagogical excitement that seem to impair the efforts of legal education providers who want to contribute more to an ethically aware profession.

In 2000, the Honourable Roy McMurtry, then the Chief Justice of Ontario, and Justice Robert Armstrong, then the treasurer of the Law Society, established the Chief Justice's Advisory Committee on Professionalism. Responding to a widely perceived need to more effectively promote professionalism, it had the moral authority derived from its makeup, senior leaders of the three pillars of the justice system: the bench, the bar and the legal academy. It sought to advance the teaching of professionalism both in law schools and across the profession and to encourage the creation of original materials on the many aspects of professionalism through a series of colloquia.

Thus, the last 15 years have seen many positive changes in what is being done about the learning of professionalism. That brings us to the present and to what we can envisage as we look forward, something that requires a hard-eyed assessment of the challenges that face the cause of advancing professionalism today. I think the most important challenge is the rise of the practice of law as a business. Although there has always been tension between the commercial dimension of law and its professional dimension, the last 25 years have seen changes that are of a wholly different order of magnitude. We have seen the rise of national mega-firms, with their magnetic allure for the best and brightest of the younger members of our profession. These firms tend to spread their business ways well beyond the upper reaches of the profession that they are seen to inhabit. The measure of success becomes profitability. Income expectations become the primary driver of legal activity. Billable hours come to reflect the lawyer's ability to serve the needs of the client and the justice system. Business techniques are imported that previously would have been regarded as anathema – notions of corporate governance, firm branding, and marketing techniques are now simply a part of everyday life in law in the urban setting. While this paradigm is far from universal, it sets a powerful example that others seek to emulate. The challenge this presents is clear. Will lawyers increasingly see anything but the narrowest aspects of professionalism – such as the most minimal compliance with the rules of professional conduct required to escape the discipline process – as a luxury they can no longer afford in the frantic scramble to do law as business? A second challenge is the growing diversity of the profession.

Here I am referring not to the wonderful growth in the ethnic and cultural diversity of the younger profession as it comes to more closely reflect the faces of the communities it serves, something that thankfully has been the final nail in the coffin of breeding as a source of professional values. Rather, I mean the growth of specialization that has also occurred over the last several decades. This is the inevitable result of the growing complexity of law. A consequence has been that lawyers no longer all share an identical professional culture, at least when compared with the era of a simpler and more homogeneous bar. This comes at a cost to what was once an easy medium for the transmission of what remain common professional values for all lawyers.

A third challenge comes from the dramatic growth in the size of the legal profession. While the profession has its modern heroes, they seem fewer in number than once was the case. Indeed, in a relative sense that is true. As a consequence, we perhaps cannot look, as we might have in the past, to role models and mentors to play quite as central a role in spreading professional values.

But there are considerations of a more hopeful sort. One has to do with the expectations of the younger profession – both expectations of lifestyle and expectations of fulfillment derived from the practice of law. My perception is that for many young people, the business of law will not be allowed to become the exclusive master it might have once been. Moreover, the desire to use the practice of law to make a difference, to improve the world, may resonate rather more broadly than it once did. If this is so, and is not simply the wishful misperception of aging eyes, it is an important reality for those engaged in meeting the challenge of improving the professional responsibility of lawyers.

At Ontario's law schools, it is clear that the teaching of professional responsibility is really starting to flourish. There is now at least one course on the subject offered at virtually every law school, and in many instances these courses must be taken by all students. Last fall, a group of the leading academics in the field published the first text on lawyers' ethics and professional regulation. In January, I had the privilege of attending the third annual symposium on legal ethics teaching and scholarship. Academic leaders like Dean Cotter and the cadre of young turks who were there are all deeply committed to teaching, research and writing about professionalism. It gives one great hope that in the future, law students are assured of a good grounding. Moreover, the new Centre for the Legal Profession at this law school is not only responsible for today. It demonstrates how the legal academy can and will apply its learning and teaching skills to the benefit not just of law students but also of those already in practice.

The Law Society too has undertaken initiatives that carry promise for learning in professionalism in the years ahead. To qualify for call to the bar, law students will be required to undertake a 30-hour educational program during the articling year. A large portion of the program will be devoted to professional responsibility.

Of significant interest is the fact that it will be delivered electronically, a pedagogical technique that is likely to be much more successful than traditional methods have been. In addition, the Law Society has resolved to enter the world of mandatory continuing education for those in the early years of practice, and again professionalism will be part of that curriculum. The use of 21st-century teaching techniques and a mandatory approach will undoubtedly both be important for the future success of learning in professionalism.

The bar can also claim its share of the growing momentum in advancing professionalism. The best example is the establishment last fall by

The Advocates' Society of its institute for civility and professionalism to promote the principles of professional responsibility.

Even the judiciary has become engaged in the enterprise. Judges experience the impact of professional-responsibility shortcomings every day in their courtrooms, sometimes with devastating consequences. The Code/Lesage Report graphically describes how this can and does happen. In our own continuing education programs, judges are beginning more frequently to examine the norms of professionalism to be applied in their courtrooms and how to better ensure that this happens. For example, my colleague, Marc Rosenberg, in his program on managing criminal trials effectively, addresses the significant issues of professionalism that judges must often cope with in that context.

Thus, while the challenges are significant, I think the present does carry great promise for the future, as we in the justice system collectively seek to enhance the role of professional responsibility in how lawyers live their lives in the profession. This challenge extends throughout a lawyer's career. Almost by definition it is a lifelong problem that requires lifelong learning in response. An assessment of the current context simply cements this reality. The days when it was enough to be born a gentleman in order to know what is required are centuries behind us. Nor can law schools be asked to do it all. Learning professional responsibility is not like learning to ride a bicycle. It is a perpetual endeavour, as issues and their contexts change. Nor can we expect a monolithic professional culture or a plentiful supply of heroes and role models to bail us out.

The reality is that lifelong learning is essential if we are to build professional responsibility so that the legal profession can serve the justice system and the public interest as it must. Successful lifelong learning requires that each of the major participants – the legal academy, the Law Society as regulator, the bar and the judiciary – plays its part. We are all in this together. For me, the good news is that with a little good luck and a little good management, this is within our grasp. Let me sketch out how my utopia might look. For the legal academy, I think it means continuing to deepen its involvement in the field. It means enhanced teaching, both with stand-alone courses and within existing courses so that law students will get an even stronger grounding in the issues of professionalism. It means enhanced scholarship, that I hope over time can become even more empirically based, a situation that will finally erase any lingering doubts about the academic legitimacy of this subject.

And it means making this learning accessible not just to law students but to the whole profession. The academy should not be diverted or alarmed if regulators require stand-alone courses. This is meant neither to implicitly limit ways of teaching professional responsibility nor to signal an offloading of the responsibilities of the other major participants in the justice system. It is, I think, meant only to advance the objective we all share.

The enhanced engagement of the legal academy will undoubtedly require resources. We must all recognize this and assist in addressing it. In my utopia, the profession would set up a Canadian counterpart to the ABA Institute of Professional Responsibility in Chicago to provide invaluable support for teaching and research in the subject. As part of this kind of partnership, the legal academy would continue to broaden its engagement with the profession, bringing with it its teaching skills and its scholarship.

The bar will have to play a significantly enhanced role if the cause is to succeed. The Advocates' Society has set a wonderful example with its centre. It is easy to imagine other legal organizations – the Criminal Lawyers' Association, the Ontario Bar Association and the County and District Law Presidents' Association to name a few – following suit.

Law firms, too, must play their part. They must be persuaded that, if nothing else, it is in their self-interest to ensure that their lawyers act professionally, for example, when the mandatory dimensions of professionalism, such as avoiding conflicts, are engaged. This will, I hope, involve not just participating in or encouraging CLE but also enhancing mentoring, encouraging pro bono programs and participating in substantive improvements of the justice system itself. In these ways, and undoubtedly others, the bar can discharge its obligation to practise law in ways that promote professionalism.

As regulator, the Law Society has a critical role. It must continue its commitment to lifelong learning in professionalism in order to protect its brand. I think this will mean continuing to enhance its emphasis on professionalism at the gatekeeper stage of professional life. It also will mean continuing to evolve mandatory continuing legal education beyond the early years of a lawyer's career in ways that embed professionalism in the process for lawyers at all stages of their careers.

In doing this, the Law Society will have to work with the bar, the legal academy and adult educators to determine what techniques work best in the modern world. This is one of the biggest challenges we face today: how can this learning be effectively brought to bear on those who need it most? The judiciary, too, must play its part. This will require a broader awareness of this obligation among judges. It will also mean enhanced efforts to educate themselves about issues of professionalism, the proper norms of professional responsibility that can be expected in the courtroom, and how best to ensure that they are observed. Judicial participation in continuing education – both in and outside their courtrooms – will be important to success.

Let me conclude by saying that all this may sound impossibly idealistic and perhaps slightly naïve. However, the stakes are vital, and every step along the way gets us closer to the goal; but there is much more to be done. In due course, we will need to gather again to assess our progress and recommit to the lifelong learning of professionalism that is essential if the legal profession is to play its proper role in society. If anything is clear, however, it is that this challenge matters, and that acting separately we probably cannot meet it. But together, to borrow a phrase, "Yes we can."

How I do it

JASMINE AKBARALI

YEARS AGO, NEWLY returned from a maternity leave, I was talking to a colleague about a book we had both read that was popular among new parents. A hilarious *Bridget Jones's Diary*–style story of a professional woman trying to juggle kids and career, it was called *I Don't Know How She Does It.* Another woman joined our conversation and asked the name of the book we were discussing. In what must have been a Freudian moment, burdened by the pressures of just having returned to work, I said, "It's called *I Don't Know Why She Does It.*"

Of course, I do know why I do it, and I knew back then too. But it isn't always easy. In addition to my appellate practice, I have four children, ages five to thirteen. My husband has a demanding tax practice. We are both involved in our communities. It's a full life, in a good way – and sometimes in a bad way, too.

Like the protagonist of the book, I am often asked how I do it. I usually say "inertia" – an object in motion (that's me) stays in motion (I do).

Then Stephen Grant, the editor of the *Journal,* asked me how I do it. And now I'm writing this article. He's very persuasive.

Over my nearly 20 years at the bar, I've adopted a set of rules that help to keep me sane. It's not perfect. Most of the time, I feel there's something I'm not doing as well as I could be doing it. But I'm still here. And that counts.

What follows are some of my rules to stay sane while practising law. They are not about work–life balance (a phrase I dislike, because meaningful work is part of a meaningful life). They are guidelines that help me stay happy by directing my energies toward the things that satisfy me and away from negativity.

RULE #1 – PUT THE WOMAN DOWN

Who hasn't nearly lost their temper when dealing with someone unreasonable on the other side of a file? The interactions between counsel can sometimes be so enraging that we carry them with us. Lawyers, and especially younger lawyers, need to learn to let go of that anger. No one should be mentally drafting the response to a nasty email at 3 a.m.

I share a fable with the students and juniors at my firm. It comes from *Zen Shorts*, a beautiful children's book by Jon J Muth. Two Buddhist monks come across a young woman with two attendants. The woman is stuck on one side of a large puddle. She can't wade across; it will ruin her silken robes. Her attendants are carrying her packages, so they can't help her cross the puddle. She is very unhappy.

The older Buddhist monk wades through the puddle, picks up the woman and carries her to the other side. She doesn't thank him but pushes him away and leaves. The monks walk on. The younger monk is brooding. Several hours later he speaks up. "The woman was selfish," he says. "She did not even say thank you!"

The older monk replies, "I set the woman down hours ago. Why are *you* still carrying her?"[1]

It isn't always easy, but this is one of my golden rules: To be a happy litigator, you have to put the woman down.

RULE #2 – DELEGATE

Delegate. Delegate. Delegate. As much as you can. As often as you can. In as many ways as you can.

As an example, I tell younger lawyers to learn how to use their dictating machines. Dictating is a form of delegation that is falling out of favour. People tell me they can type, so why would they dictate? *Because*

1 Jon J Muth, "A Heavy Load" in *Zen Shorts* (New York: Scholastic Press, 2005).

dictating is faster – that's why. The fundamental premise should not be, *I delegate what I cannot do.* It should be, *I delegate what I don't have to do myself.*

At home, I am a master of delegation. I have an amazing nanny who looks after my children when I'm at work. While the kids are at school, she picks up groceries and dry cleaning, buys birthday presents, takes my car in for servicing, clears out the toy chest and so on. I couldn't live without her. Other people (including my kids) help in different ways. I don't garden or clean, and I rarely cook. I pay a woman to prep meals for me. She makes my lunches for the week – all I have to do is pack them. And before you tell me that's too expensive, call me and let's compare what you spend at the food court for a week with what I pay her (a decent wage) and the cost of my groceries. I'll bet I'm ahead – and I'm eating better food, too.

I use delegation to free up as much time as possible. Delegation lets me spend my evenings helping with homework, reading to my daughter, driving my son to soccer or catching up on work, rather than folding laundry and making lunches. Yes, I'm less involved in the daily running of my house and things aren't always done exactly the way I'd do them. I think it's a good trade-off.

RULE #3 – YOU CAN'T BE TOO CAREFUL WHO YOU HAVE KIDS WITH

Years ago, I heard a story about a friend of a friend's family. The woman was dating a rotten guy. My friend's family watched in dismay and said, "You can't be too careful who you date."

Then their friend decided to marry the rotten guy. The family was dismayed again, and all agreed that you can't be too careful who you marry.

The newlyweds had a child, and unfortunately if predictably, the guy turned out to be rotten.[2] The marriage was breaking up, and he caused no end of troubles. Of course, the wife was now stuck with him in some capacity because they had had a child together. My friend's family

2 There is probably another side to this story, but it's irrelevant for the purpose of my rules.

concluded, with absolute certainty, that you can't be too careful who you have kids with.

Need to work late? Is something going on at home? Is something happening in your life that is leaving you feeling overwhelmed, furious, sad or confused? If you have a partner at home, the relationship had best be a solid one. Otherwise, all your challenges just got worse, not better. You really can't be too careful.

RULE #4 – BE SELFISH

I did not invent this rule, but I practise it. There is always someone who needs something from you, whether a client, a partner (work or life), a child, a parent or a charity or community organization you are involved with. You could spend every waking minute delivering for other people. But that would be a miserable existence.

It is imperative to carve out time to feed yourself first. First the basics: Get some exercise; don't eat at the food court – ever – because it will destroy your soul and your arteries; and sleep more.

Also, breathe. Deep belly breaths calm us. Experts recommend them as a tool to improve oral advocacy,[3] so take a few before you rise for your next submissions in court and you'll see why. (Yes, you're right. I do practice yoga as well as law. But that doesn't make me wrong.)

Beyond that, your self-care depends on you. Paint. Start a charitable foundation. Join a book club. Meditate. Play in an adult soccer league. Meet your high-school buddies for a regular game of Scrabble. Whatever floats your boat. Just do something.

A corollary to self-care is caring for your relationships. Make time to see your family. Make sure you have a decent sitter if you have kids who need one, and go out for dinner with your partner. Investing in your relationships yields returns. Ignoring them has consequences, too.

And note that successfully practising Rule #2 makes Rule #4 easier to follow.

---

3 See e.g. Brian K Johnson and Marsha Hunter, *The Articulate Advocate: New Techniques of Persuasion for Trial Lawyers* (Phoenix, AZ: Crown King Books, 2009); Janice Mucalov: *Better Public Speaking for Lawyers* (Canadian Bar Association, online at <www.cba.org/Publications-Resources/CBA-Practice-Link/Young-Lawyers/2014/Better-Public-Speaking-for-Lawyers>).

RULE #5 – GET OUTSIDE

Research shows that spending time in nature improves mental well-being.[4] I try to get out for a hike as often as I can. I think Halton has the best trails in the Greater Toronto Area, but I'll take a city park or garden if I have only a little time. There is something about being among the trees that I find rejuvenating. It helps clear my head and creates space for me. It's a great antidote to an oppressive to-do-list, and it makes me more productive overall.

And although it's not what I mean by getting outside, enjoying a beer on a patio on a beautiful summer day will do in a pinch.

RULE #6 – FOCUS BUSINESS DEVELOPMENT ON PEOPLE YOU LIKE AND WORK YOU WANT

This rule is a controversial one. The consequence is that you don't focus your efforts on lucrative work that is less enjoyable.[5] For that reason, it's not for everybody.

But when I work for people I like, doing work I enjoy, I'm happier. It's not rocket science.

RULE #7 – BE FLEXIBLE

Sometimes I work a predictable day – in the office during business hours, home in the evening, maybe some work after the kids are in bed.

Sometimes my day looks nothing like that. I may be at a school presentation in the morning and then take a kid or a parent to a doctor's appointment. It may be 3 p.m. before I start working, and I may work until late in the night.

I usually have work with me at the dance studio or at soccer practice. I'm stuck waiting, so I may as well make it productive time.

Sometimes I work crazy hours for a few weeks in a row, and I start to feel guilty that my children have forgotten who I am.

---

4 "The physiological effects of *Shinrin-yoku* (taking in the forest atmosphere or forest bathing): evidence from field experiments in 24 forests across Japan" by Bun Jim Park et al. (<www.ncbi.nlm.nih.gov/pmc/articles/PMC2793346>).

5 Credit goes to Jane Southren, who taught me this rule.

Sometimes I have a lull and I can take a day off unexpectedly, or leave early and take my kids to a weeknight movie or get an extra workout in.

The flexibility that comes with a law practice is, I think, a blessing. It allows me to meet other obligations while still meeting my obligations to my clients. To embrace the beauty of it, one has to be prepared to be working at 11 p.m. on a Saturday night without resentment, to work the crazy hours when they come and to take advantage of the lulls when they present themselves.

RULE #8 – ASK FOR WHAT YOU NEED

I haven't always followed this rule, but I'm a convert.

Our lives are busy and often stressful. It isn't always easy to juggle the demands we have. Sometimes we need help. When we do, we need to ask for it. It comes easily when we ask.

Whether it's getting ergonomic furniture in your office, arranging a leave of absence to deal with a critical personal issue, organizing a ride for your kid, borrowing a costume or finding a shoulder to cry on – from the big to the small, we benefit from the help of a strong community around us.

High-functioning people often feel like they should not need help. But we all need help, and help is there. We just have to ask. (And remember to accept it with thanks when it's offered.)

RULE #9 – TRUST YOURSELF. FORGIVE YOURSELF

This rule applies really well to parenting. Never mind the experts, your mother-in-law, the annoying parent on the playground, or that stranger in the elevator. Trust yourself to get it right. You will. You know your kid best.

Except when you get it wrong – and you will. So forgive yourself.

Once I liberated myself from the worry that every decision I made would put my kids into therapy, I became a happier parent. But the rule also applies to other aspects of our lives.

Of course, the rule assumes you have a reasonable basis to trust yourself. I don't suggest that you should trust yourself to give securities advice to a client if you practise family law – and then simply forgive yourself when you screw it up. I'm not advocating cheerful irresponsibility.

But sometimes we make judgment calls. We have to trust ourselves to make the right call when we believe we have the appropriate experience and knowledge to make it. Sometimes we later wish we'd made a different call. We need to forgive ourselves for not being perfect; we can't be. Maybe there's a lesson to be learned from the experience. If so, learn it. Then move on.

RULE #10 – BE GRATEFUL

Over the Christmas holidays, my 10-year-old son and his friend went out to his friend's backyard where they kicked a soccer ball around for an hour – probably my son's favourite activity on the planet. It was a cold day, and when the boys came inside they couldn't feel their faces.

My son's friend's mother told me that as the boys drank their hot chocolate, she heard my son say to hers, "Aren't we lucky? We get to play, and then we have a warm place to come to and hot chocolate to drink."

I loved how present he was in the moment, and how grateful he was – for the big things and for the little things.

It's easy to get bogged down in the day-to-day. I get annoyed when my shower leaks. But we are a privileged lot. We may have personal challenges, but we are still among the luckiest people on this planet. Remembering to practise gratitude makes me happier.

These rules, or my adherence to them, are a work in progress. In truth, sometimes I aspire to them more than I practise them. But overall, the closer I follow them, the happier I am.

So, Stephen, there's your answer. These rules, plus constant motion – are how I do it.

Diversity and the future of advocacy

IMAN ABOKOR AND M. GREG ABOGADO

AS WE COMMEMORATE The Advocates' Society's 50th anniversary, it is important to address the issue of diversity in the legal profession. Diversity will inform the future of advocacy as the face of the advocate continues to reflect Canada's changing demographics. Diversity, in all its manifestations, has received much attention in recent years. There have been some notable efforts in the legal community to promote diversity, including diversity committees at law firms, diversity working groups at professional associations and an increased consciousness of diversity in judicial appointments. What is less clear, however, is the connection between diversity and the working lives of everyday lawyers. When we arrive at work in the morning, we do not think about how we can make the legal profession more diverse; rather, our focus is on how we can best serve our clients. Certainly when diversity in the legal profession is mentioned, we nod in approval. No one denies that diversity as a concept is a good thing. But the belief that diversity is key to law firms' success is a leap that we as a profession have not yet made. What will change in the next 20 or so years? In this article we argue that Canadian corporations will give much more weight to law firm diversity because they will realize that law firms that are more diverse will deliver better legal services. Simply put, diversity will be good for business. We focus on racialized communities (visible minorities and Aboriginals) and highlight how their presence in your firm may determine whether you get the client or lose out to the more diverse firm down the street. We conclude by highlighting some barriers that lawyers from racialized communities face.

DIVERSITY MEANS BUSINESS

In recent years, Canadian corporate clients have been increasingly looking for diverse legal representation. An Association of Corporate Counsel online *Quick Poll* found that one in two Canadian in-house counsel consider a firm's diversity in determining whether to retain that law firm.[1] Also, the organization Legal Leaders for Diversity and Inclusion ("Legal Leaders"), launched in 2011 and made up of in-house counsel from over 60 major corporations, encourages its members to advise law firms that they expect to see diversity and inclusiveness in their legal teams.[2] Another group, A Call to Action Canada, boasting a less robust nine members, is similar to Legal Leaders in being made up of in-house counsel with a commitment to diversity. It goes further than Legal Leaders of Diversity in requiring its members to limit or sever their relationships with firms "whose performance consistently evidences a lack of meaningful interest in being diverse."[3] Corporations in the United States have been even more proactive in their commitment to diversity. Since 1992, diversity is one of the six criteria that the U.S. DuPont Company has used to choose the law firms it would award the bulk of its legal work.[4] In 2006, Wal-Mart announced that it had fired two of its outside law firms for failing to meet diversity goals.[5] Since 2008,

---

1 Julius Melnitzer, "50% of Canadian general counsel look to diversity in choosing law firms", *The Financial Post* (5 June 2012), online: *The Financial Post,* <http://business.financialpost. com/2012/06/05/50-of-canadian-general-counsel-look-to-diversity-in-choosing-law-firms>.

2 "Mission Statement," online: Legal Leaders for Diversity and Inclusion, <http://legalleaders-fordiversity.com/about-us>.

3 "A Call to Action Canada's Mission Statement is:", online: A Call to Action Canada, <www.acalltoactioncanada.com/mission-statement>.

4 Karen Donovan, "Pushed by clients, law firms step up diversity efforts", *The New York Times* (21 July 2006), online: *The New York Times* <www.nytimes.com/2006/07/21/business/21legal.html?pagewant-ed=all&_r=0>.

5 *Ibid.*

Microsoft has offered a 2 percent bonus to firms that achieve one of the following: increase by 2 percent the number of hours that women and visible-minority attorneys at the firm work on Microsoft matters; increase the number of women and visible-minority attorneys at the firm by 0.5 percent, compared with the previous year; or become more diverse than the Microsoft legal department itself, 54 percent of which is composed of women, visible minorities and lawyers who are lesbian, gay, bisexual or transgender.[6] Microsoft also reduces firms' rates by 1 percent if they do not meet at least one of these standards.[7] This trend of giving greater priority to diversity in the procurement of legal services will rise in Canada in the coming years. It is evidenced by the values we share with our American counterparts and our economic interdependence. Furthermore, as new markets emerge in various parts of the globe, corporations will require lawyers who can understand and manage cultural differences. Corporations' increasing demands for diversity in their legal teams will require law firms to hire more visible-minority and Aboriginal lawyers if they want to maintain a competitive advantage.

DIVERSITY MEANS BETTER SERVICES

In the next few decades, Canadian corporations will increasingly give more weight to a law firm's demographics as they begin to realize that law firms that are more diverse deliver better legal services. As Rose Mary Wentling, an associate professor at the University of Illinois, notes: "While the need for incorporating diversity may appear to grow out of notions of social and economic fairness and morality, the real need is to maintain and increase profits in national and global competition."[8] The increased emphasis on diversity will stem from corporations' increased recognition that organizations with a strong commitment to diversity

6 Catherine Ho, "Microsoft's chief legal officer talks about the company's diversity benchmarks", *The Washington Post* (24 March 2013), online: *The Washington Post* <http://articles.washingtonpost.com/2013-03-24/ business/37989954_1_law-firms-diversity-scholarships-microsoft>.

7 *Ibid.*

8 "Diversity Initiatives in the Workplace: Work in Progress at the University of Illinois" (Summer 1997) 8:2 CenterWork, online: National Center for Research in Vocational Education, University of California, Berkeley, <http://ncrve.berkeley.edu/CW82/Diversity.html>.

are outperforming their peers. The proof is in the statistics. A 2005 study by the *Harvard Business Review* found that the top 50 U.S. companies that emphasized diversity as part of their corporate strategy had a higher median difference in their net profit margins than their counterparts and had higher median returns on equity.[9] Likewise, a 2007 study of Fortune 1000 firms and some of the United States' largest private companies found diversity among corporate leaders to be "significantly related to revenues, net income, and book-to-market equity."[10] There is also a host of evidence that diversity increases the performance of organizations. For example, in a study of 28 teams by Henley Business School, heterogeneous teams solved complex tasks better than homogeneous teams. The diverse teams exhibited a higher level of creativity and a broader thought process.[11] This is understandable, as people with differing experiences bring new ideas and problem-solving techniques to the task at hand. In addition, people from diverse backgrounds can have an in-depth understanding of cultural nuances to assist firms in serving clients from around the world. As Raj Anand, lawyer and chair of the Law Society's working group The Challenges Faced by Racialized Licensees states, "It only stands to reason that bringing in people who will be able to speak the language, understand the customs, be more involved in their community will benefit the bottom line quite apart from making the workplace a more welcoming and productive environment in which to work."[12] The cultural fluency that lawyers from racialized communities bring enriches law firms both by attracting clients and by improving the general work environment. Furthermore, having advocates from diverse backgrounds can assist law firms in the courtroom. Justice Michael J. Moldaver observes, "It is vital in any decision-making process that you have a range of ideas to work from. The greater the depth and the breadth of your knowledge, the better chance you have of coming to

9 Stanley F Slater, Robert Weigand & Thomas J Zwirlein, "The Business Case for Commitment to Diversity" *Harvard Business Review* Case Study (15 May 2008).

10 Quinetta M. Robertson & Hyeon Jeong Park, "Examining the Link Between Diversity and Firm Performance: The Effects of Diversity Reputation and Leader Racial Diversity" (2007) 32 Group & Organization Management 548 at 560.

11 MJ Higgs, A Plewina & G Piloch, "The Influence of Team Composition on Team Performance and Dependence on Task Complexity", Henley Working Paper Series, HWP 0314 (Reading: Henley Business School, University of Reading, 2003).

12 Interview of Raj Anand by Iman Abokor (18 September 2013).

a solution that is just, equitable and reasonable. It is important to have ideas from all ends of the spectrum, put them in the hopper, consider them, weigh them and arrive at a solution that is broad-based and inclusive of all members of society."[13]

THE CHALLENGE FOR LAW FIRMS

Many law firms are paying increasing attention to the importance of diversity to their bottom line. Mahmud Jamal, a partner at Osler, Hoskin & Harcourt LLP, states: "It is common now for requests for proposals to contain questions regarding our diversity and inclusion policies. It is no longer enough for law firms to tout their expertise or discuss their rates without also addressing the makeup of their legal workforce."[14] However, many law firms are working in the dark in this area because, unlike their counterparts in the United States, Canadian law firms do not collect, keep and release demographic data.[15] In order to create a more diverse legal profession in Ontario, law firms need to collect and release information on the backgrounds of their lawyers and the experiences of racialized lawyers within their firms. Sabrina Lyon and Lorne Sossin have drafted a paper[16] in which they conclude that generating quantitative and qualitative data would advance a culture of inclusion and accountability in the Canadian legal community.[17] Diversity statistics would demonstrate which firms have been successful in increasing diversity within their organizations and which firms are lagging behind. In an environment in which the diversity of a law firm is increasingly important to the firm's reputation, statistics on the diverse makeup and culture of law firms can be an important motivating factor for law firms to improve in this area. As a Diversity Institute Report put it, "What gets

13 Interview of Justice Michael J. Moldaver by Iman Abokor (16 September 2013).

14 Interview of Mahmud Jamal by Iman Abokor (16 September 2013).

15 Although a few Canadian firms collect demographic data, no firm makes this data public.

16 "Data & Diversity in the Canadian Justice Community" (2013) [unpublished], draft online: Canadian Association of Black Lawyers, <www.cabl.ca/PDF/Data&Diversity_in_the_Legal_Community. pdf>.

17 *Ibid* at 2.

measured gets done."[18] The other issue law firms encounter is removing the barriers that lawyers from racialized communities face in advancing to leadership positions in their firms. A 2011 study that tracked the rates of diversity among leaders in the Greater Toronto Area, where 14.4 percent of lawyers then were visible minorities, found that only 6.8 percent of legal leaders were visible minorities.[19] Michael Ornstein, in a 2010 report to the Law Society of Upper Canada, found that compared to white lawyers, Aboriginal and visible-minority lawyers were more likely to be law firm associates and employees.[20] He also found that the median earnings for racialized lawyers was $77,400, compared with $115,000 for white lawyers.[21] He concluded that there was strong evidence that Aboriginal and visible-minority lawyers made less money than white lawyers who were the same age and that this difference in earnings was much larger than the gender difference.[22] The barriers that racialized communities face limit the contributions they can make to a law firm. To eliminate these barriers, the legal profession must confront their systemic nature and work toward meaningful solutions.

CONCLUSION

It is often believed that the commitment to diversity comes at a cost. Diversity is a benefit to law firms, increasing their business prospects and the quality of their services. In the next few years, Canadian corporations will assess a firm's diversity much more closely. They will pay increasing attention to statistics demonstrating that businesses with

18 "Improving Representation in the Judiciary: A Diversity Strategy" (27 June 2012), online: Diversity Institute, <www.ryerson.ca/content/dam/diversity/resources/Powerpoint%20-%20 Improving%20Representation%20 in%20the%20Judiciary %20-%20 June%2027.pdf> at 20.

19 DiverseCity: The Greater Toronto Leadership Project, "Diversity Counts 3: A Snapshot of Diverse Leadership in the GTA 2011", online: Diversity Institute, <http://diversecitytoronto.ca/wp-content/uploads/CountsReport3-full.pdf> at iii.

20 Michael Ornstein, *Racialization and Gender of Lawyers in Ontario: A Report for the Law Society of Upper Canada*, online: The Law Society of Upper Canada, <www.lsuc.on.ca/media/convapril10_ornstein.pdf> at 35.

21 *Ibid.* at 26.

22 *Ibid.* at 35.

diverse teams outperform their peers. This trend linking greater diversity with increased business has already begun with the establishment of organizations like Legal Leaders for Diversity and Inclusion and A Call to Action Canada. We should not, however, ignore the barriers faced by lawyers from racialized communities. They encounter limited opportunities to advance to leadership positions and receive lower salaries than white lawyers their age. As we celebrate The Advocates' Society's 50th anniversary, we should renew our commitment to eliminate these barriers.

Part Eight

MEDIA RELATIONS

IN THIS INCREDIBLE age of the profusion of online communication – LinkedIn, Twitter, Facebook, etc. – that there's still a print medium is somewhat surprising. Print was vibrant when I asked several noted legal writers to share with counsel the best ways to deal with journalists. Our contributors (one now retired but writing freelance, one now deceased) offer different takes on how counsel can get their message into the public domain or at least explain the nuances of the case at hand. These are subtle considerations and handled here with aplomb, confidence and dexterity.

The care and feeding of reporters: A LAWYER'S GUIDE

TRACEY TYLER

JOURNALISTS AND LAWYERS seem ever-fascinated by each other's work. Perhaps it is the case, to borrow from Harry Kopyto, that we are stuck together like Krazy Glue.

I once had a call from a lawyer with a case he wanted to publicize and a plan for making that happen. He decided to provide documents in advance to my colleague Kirk Makin so that he could break the story exclusively in *The Globe and Mail*. According to the plan, I was to come along the following day and write a "softer" story about his client.

More recently, in another memorable encounter, I found myself at a legal conference seated beside a veteran criminal lawyer who was quite curious about how much I made. I didn't tell him, but his interest in the subject wasn't abating. He said he was shocked to discover most print reporters in Canada earn less than $100,000. With pity in his eyes, he told me how tragic it was that I would never know the thrill of going to the Kitchen Table grocery store and filling a cart with $100 worth of impulse buys, as he had the previous weekend. In retrospect, what was most astonishing about these conversations was that I was having them with lawyers – members of a profession to whom words matter, but who, at those moments, seemed to have little appreciation of the effect of what they were saying.

It happens. Lawyers are human. Sometimes, in dealings between journalists and lawyers, it's the non-verbal issues that trip you up. It can happen even when a lawyer has the *savoir faire* of a Stephen Grant, as I was reminded when we met to discuss this story. As we sipped our tea, a waiter arrived with the cheque. The question: Who pays? (Stephen didn't think it was an issue, but it can be a nagging little question for a reporter.) Whether you are being contacted by a member of the media or it's you picking up the phone and calling a journalist, as a lawyer you are probably on unfamiliar terrain. But it's not as complicated as you might imagine. After all, every day, in newsrooms across the country, reporters are talking to lawyers. Stories get written. Nobody is found in contempt of court. A lot of people are doing something right.

But there are times when we can still be nervous around each other. Rather than anticipating what concerns or questions might go through your mind when a reporter calls, I decided to go to the source. I asked a half-dozen civil and criminal law litigators, and their responses follow. I'll try to address their concerns from a reporter's perspective.

WHEN A REPORTER CALLS

Are they going to ask me case-specific questions that are going to send my judge into a tizzy? Usually these are questions that require me to speculate about the effect of evidence or the result.

This is the number one concern of lawyers. But there is every chance that I am not calling about one of your cases at all. Quite likely, I am writing about a legal issue and would like you to weigh in with your perspective. The subject could be the legal aid tariff. New family law rules. A recent crime bill. Even if I am writing a story about your case, I can't imagine asking you to assess your chances of victory or to pronounce on the strength of your opponent's evidence. Like lawyers, journalists face restraints, and we have to be very careful about treading into that territory. The *sub judice* rule still exists.

I am probably interested in obtaining an electronic version of your factum. If your trial or appeal is only weeks away, there is a very good chance that the material you have filed with the court has been transferred to the judge (or judges) and is no longer available for me to read. I want to see that material, possibly because I would like to write a story in advance. But also because I would like to better understand the case when I am sitting in court listening to your argument.

Some lawyers are too afraid to provide even a factum, because they are worried that the judge will find out and won't like it. I can only say that attitudes are changing, as the three members of the Ontario Court of Appeal's media committee noted in a jointly authored piece for a recent issue of *The Justice Reporter*, an online newsletter devoted to open court issues. "Many in the legal system have traditionally been apprehensive about the media and media coverage," wrote Justices Russell Juriansz, James MacPherson and Eleanore Cronk:

> In the mid 1970s, the culture of civil litigators towards the media was fearful. It was considered inappropriate to discuss matters with the media for cases going in the court. Attitudes towards the media have evolved over the years and this apprehension towards the media has changed. Now there is a greater realization that the media act as the eyes and ears of the public, who cannot attend court proceedings ... The media provides the primary means of public discussion of the work of the courts in administering justice. In this way the media performs an important public service by informing the public about what public institutions are doing. The media also plays an increasingly important role in ensuring access to justice.
>
> ... By ensuring that the media can do its work, we ensure that accurate information concerning justice issues will be provided to the public, which in turn promotes a well-informed public. Viewed in this way, facilitating the work of journalists is not an accommodation or favour, but serves the public interest and gives effect to the *Charter's* guarantee of the freedom of the press and other media of communication.[1]

Is it in my client's interest for me to speak, or does my client even want me to speak?

As a reporter, that's something I can't address. Some lawyers feel that when you are taking on public-interest cases, part of the calculation is to consider whether it is in a client's interest to go public for the purpose of provoking broader debate. The Law Society of Upper Canada's *Rules of Professional Conduct*, of course, anticipate that there are times when the

1 "Promoting a Well-Informed Public: Facilitating Work of Journalists Is Not a Favour, Judges Say," *The Justice Reporter*, vol 1 (Spring 2009) at 1–2, online: <www.justicereporter.ca>.

lawyer's role will encompass talking to journalists. Rule 6.06(1) says: "Provided that there is no infringement of the lawyer's obligations to the client, the profession, the courts, or the administration of justice, a lawyer may communicate information to the media and may make public appearances and statements."

My job as a defence lawyer is not to publicize my client's case. I know that my client will have to return to his or her community after the case, and I do not want the glare of publicity on my client.

This is understandable, but it wrongly assumes that the lawyer is in control of whether or not there will be a story. And it could be that your client was the subject of publicity even before you were retained – from the moment the police or the Ontario Securities Commission or the College of Physicians and Surgeons issued a news release about their charges.

Some lawyers take the view that if the case is going to be covered anyway, they might as well get their oar in. Almost nobody these days says, "No comment." At the very least, you could say that you prefer to withhold your remarks and make your submissions in court. It is hard to imagine a judge holding that against you. And it is better than having a journalist report that you did not return calls. The reason reporters say this in a story is to let readers know that we did attempt to contact you and give you an opportunity to speak on your client's behalf.

The commentary accompanying Rule 6.06 says that there will be circumstances in which a lawyer is under a specific duty to contact the media to properly serve a client. It also notes that lawyers often are involved as advocates for special-interest groups attempting to bring about changes in legislation or government policy, or even heightened public awareness about certain issues, and describes this as an important role for lawyers to play. Some lawyers believe that the best way to protect their clients and minimize the glare of publicity is to speak with journalists and, in some cases, allow their clients to be photographed in comfortable surroundings, rather than have reporters chase them down a street or camp in front of their house.

Can I speak on background?

I've never said no. Why would I? Quite likely, I'm going to learn something. Also, I find that when lawyers ask to speak on background, it's usually not because they have anything particularly sensitive to discuss. It's a way of buying some time so that they don't feel pressured at the outset of our conversation, worried that if they say something dumb it's going to end up in the paper. It's a way of gaining control, really. And that's just fine with me. Sometimes I might ask lawyers afterward if they would mind me including in my story one or two of the points they mentioned in our background discussion. Most of the time, they have no problem with that.

I worry that I'll sound stupid or that I'll go too far, if the story involves something I am passionate about. On the other hand, if I am too bland, what use is that?

There's no question, a story needs quotes. They're sometimes called the lifeblood of a story. They break up large blocks of black type, make reading easier on the eyes and inject humanity into a news story. But remember, you're probably not going to be quoted more than once or twice in a story because space is at a premium. Colourful or pithy will win out over an uninspiring remark filled with legal jargon. Lawyers with high-profile cases often give a lot of thought not only to what they say in court but to what they say to reporters outside of court later. Being prepared in this way can help you as well as help a reporter. But always remember, that line you worked so hard to craft may never get used.

If I say something that I think is unfair or stupid or defamatory, can I take it back?

It's difficult to do when TV cameras are rolling, but easier with print reporters. If you are particularly worried about a quote, it's usually not a problem to highlight and delete. (Although if it's a real zinger, I might be disappointed.) We can usually find some other, less worrisome way of making the point you would like to get across.

Some lawyers like to go away and think about a question, then call me back with their response.

Will the reporter call me back after he or she has written the story and read my quotes back to me?

This is a somewhat unusual request, but most reporters I know do it from time to time. I have as well. We want to be accurate, and if reading back a quote puts someone we've interviewed at ease, that's all for the better. It would be difficult to do it with every story, though, simply because of the time involved.

I worry about defamation.
So do we. Worry might not be entirely the right word, but it is something we strive to avoid. One lawyer I know thinks it can be helpful in some cases to couch what you are saying to a reporter as your opinion, rather than fact. For example, "In our view ..." or "As we see it ..." or "From our perspective ..."

If it's a reporter I don't know, I want to know if "off the record" and "background" mean the same to me as to her.
This is important to establish. There are many definitions. Are you seeking assurances from a reporter that what you are about to say will never appear in a story? Or do you mean the journalist can use it, as long as you are not identified as the source? (This is sometimes known as "not for attribution.") Reporters would rather not quote unnamed sources; identifying where information comes from enhances a story's credibility. But sometimes there's no way around it. Beat reporters talk to lawyers all the time on a background basis. My contacts know that if I want to quote them in a story, I'll tell them and establish that we are speaking for that purpose. Otherwise, we're just talking.

Can I read and approve the story before it is published?
I'm sorry, but I can't let you do that. That would really amount to giving newsmakers editorial control over the news. If we did that, we would not be independent.

Can I trust this reporter?
If you've dealt with the reporter before, that's easy. But what if you've never met? You might check with colleagues. You can also look at the news organization that employs the reporter. Is it credible? You might ask the reporter if you could speak off the record first, to get a better measure of who he or she is. You might even want to meet first for coffee.

Reporters are often seen as cynical, but just about all the journalists I know take their job seriously, work hard to get things right, don't burn sources and are mortified if they've made a mistake. As with lawyers, their reputation is important.

WHEN YOU ARE CALLING A REPORTER

Let's turn the tables. You have clients with a case that warrants attention. Maybe they've been jailed in another country for reasons that are suspect, or they believe that social assistance rules are discriminating against them. Perhaps they've brought a complaint against police or have launched a class-action lawsuit against the manufacturer of a defective product. How do you get a reporter interested? As a lawyer, you're already off to a good start, because you know how to tell a story. But it might help if we review a few truths about newsrooms and how they work.

Let's begin with editors. Which of the following images most resembles 21st-century editors in their natural habitat?

If you guessed E, you might be onto something, especially when it comes to editors after their 5 p.m. news meeting. You'll still find shades of Jason Robards as Ben Bradlee in today's newsrooms, but not too much of Cary Grant in *His Girl Friday*. Some would argue the romance, such as it was, has vanished. In fact, the drink box our furry friend is clutching is fitting because, instead of finding editors perched on a stool at their neighbourhood watering hole at 7 p.m., you're more likely to find them behind their desks, planning the next day's – or next weekend's – paper. Some days, entire news sections of the paper are on the presses by 1 p.m. the day before. All of which is to say that story decisions are made earlier than ever, and pages are often laid out well in advance. So the sooner we know about your case, your news conference or your hearing, the better it is for you and for us.

You might consider providing material to reporters on an embargoed basis, so that they can read through court materials or reports ahead of time, on the understanding that no story will be published until a given date. The Ontario Law Reform Commission used to do this. The Association in Defence of the Wrongly Convicted, among other organizations, does it on occasion. Recently, the Court of Appeal for Ontario has offered "lock-ups" for reporters prior to the release of major decisions. The court provides a room where journalists can spend part of a morning reading through the judgment (or judgments, as in the case of a lock-up for some terrorism decisions released last December 17) and writing a story that will be ready for publication or broadcast later in the day, at the moment the rulings are officially released and posted on the court's website.

But while the news business has undergone changes, one universal truth remains: every reporter wants a scoop. Nobody wants to play second fiddle. That's also true of news organizations as a whole. If it's a good story and we know it is ours exclusively, it has a better chance of ending up on the front page. You should also know, however, that if one newspaper breaks a story, others are not always so keen to follow. Sometimes, preferring to chase their own stories, they pretend it never happened.

ALSO WORTH NOTING

- Decisions on whether a story will be placed in the paper and how prominently it will be displayed are often made on the basis of skedlines – short, two- or three-sentence descriptions of what the story is about. Editors read these and meet through the day to decide what ends up where. It's part of a reporter's job to distill a story to its essence and capture the attention of these decision makers. Anything you can do to help the reporter grasp your point is welcome. Think of your opening statement to a judge or jury. How would you pitch your case?
- If you're sending out a press release, make sure the contact number you have included is accurate and that your spokesperson is available. If possible, include an after-hours number and an e-mail address.
- Try to return calls promptly. With the arrival of the Internet, our deadline is always now.

NOURISHING YOUR NEWSHOUND

Although this piece is entitled "The Care and Feeding of Reporters," you needn't take that literally; I'm pretty sure I can't be bought for a cup of coffee. But at my paper and many other news organizations, reporters are not permitted to accept anything that could be considered a gift.

A couple of years ago, a young lawyer who was pleased about a story sent me a Chapters gift card as an expression of thanks. I mailed it back to him. I appreciated the sentiment, and it was nice to hear that he liked the story; we don't get much feedback at times. But the card was something I couldn't accept. As for lunches, I don't like to make too big an issue out of the bill. I prefer to pay, and many dining companions have been happy to let me do it. Others suggest splitting the cheque, which is a good compromise.

Some insist on paying, because they were the ones who invited me. Or because they are a bit old-fashioned, but charmingly so. In most cases, that's okay, on one condition. We must have lunch again, and I'll pay next time.

Summer 2011

When a journalist comes calling

KIRK MAKIN

MY LEAST PLEASANT encounter with a lawyer occurred in the early 1980s, back in the days when exotic *Charter of Rights* challenges were all the rage. After one such challenge had crashed and burned on appeal, I quoted the unsuccessful litigant moaning about the more than $100,000 she had blown on legal fees in her failed cause.

Later that day, the high-profile Toronto litigator who had represented her called to accuse me, in so many words, of printing a figure so outlandish that I had to have known it was false.

I was incredulous. "Are you actually suggesting I'm lying?" "If the shoe fits, wear it," he snarled.

Early in their careers, journalists become used to dealing with aggrieved parties and hurt feelings. However, it's one thing to dispute and object, quite another to malign and level accusations of dishonesty. Five thousand articles later, I have yet to call or quote that lawyer again – a record I intend to maintain.

Happily, the incident was an aberration rather than a harbinger of horrors to come. In the intervening years, I have interviewed, lunched and chatted with thousands of lawyers without ever encountering another as insufferable or mean-spirited. The truth is, most lawyers – in common with most journalists – are dedicated, opinionated individuals who tend to maintain a cheerfully jaundiced outlook on the world.

Why, then, is the relationship between our professions sometimes fraught with tension? I begin my inquiry with three possible causes: distrust, fear and frustration.

If one journalistic shortcoming drives lawyers to distraction, it is surely the fact that many reporters sent to cover legal stories have little or no understanding of the law. Yet, their managers still expect them to produce an accurate, informative story on short notice. The resulting reports are liable to be naive, incorrect or lacking in context.

Not surprisingly, lawyers bruised by encounters of this sort become wary, particularly of journalists they have not encountered before. They relate their negative experience to colleagues; and they, too, suddenly become unavailable when a journalist comes calling.

Lawyers have an inherent need to mould, fashion and control their cases. No wonder, then, that they break out in perspiration when obliged to cede control of their words, their arguments and, perhaps, their public image, to a slovenly stranger wielding a notebook and a tape recorder. Indeed, I am aware of only one other group as nervous about entrusting its fortunes to the press – journalists themselves. After all, we know how the sausages are made.

My prescription for smooth relations between our professions begins with respect. Until proven otherwise, a journalist ought to be seen as a well-meaning character who wants to get it right. We journalists do not come in a single size or stereotype, any more than lawyers do.

True, some of us are reckless and sloppy. Others are intense and obsessive about accuracy. Still others are rude, aggressive boors who consider framing a question politely as a sign of weakness. Some would prefer decapitation to using the word "I," whereas others believe that readers crave their opinions on everything from the testimony of a rape victim to a lawyer's taste in neckties.

In short, we are an unruly, ungovernable lot. Still, I marvel when I encounter a lawyer who proudly tells me that he "never speaks to the press" – as if this is a mark of heavenly virtue that I'm bound to appreciate and admire.

Writing off an entire profession on the basis of the acts of a minority is as thoughtless as any other bromide or myopic stereotype. Rather than rejecting all journalists based on the failings of a few, I suggest engaging in some basic research when a reporter calls for an interview.

Can she suggest someone you know who will vouch for her integrity? Has a colleague dealt with her? Would a quick perusal of her online articles provide a quick clue to her professionalism?

Lawyers have to also face the incontrovertible fact that, once in a while, they have little choice about press coverage. Inevitably, some cases and events are going to be covered. The only real question is whether the lawyer will try to influence the course of that coverage, or simply sit back and take what comes.

There is no denying that co-operation can carry risks. There are times when a journalist is out to "get" your client, usually in cases where the press has long since adopted a certain approach or slant to a case that does not accord with your own. (And let's face it: some people deserve to be "got.")

You must also live with the reality that journalists do sometimes wheedle, implore and employ the most facile tactics to keep a recalcitrant subject on the phone. We can bait our hooks with painfully obvious incentives and come-ons. It is our job to do so – just as it's our job to troll for quotes that elucidate a thought or an argument trenchantly, succinctly and perhaps even provocatively.

For all that, however, co-operating can swing a story toward a client's direction, even if only a smidgen. If you take the time to educate a journalist about your view of the law and your client's position, you can swing the direction of a story. Even the less reputable among us find it difficult to be unfair to an interviewee who is personable and helpful.

Moreover, many journalists will reduce the risk to you by agreeing to an advance, informal, off-the-record discussion of terms and provisos. (And just to dispense speedily with this vital topic, "off the record" means the material discussed will not be used in a story; "unattributed" means that the information may be used, but not in a way that identifies you.)

Just make sure that you think twice before putting your words on the record, unless you are comfortable with them, because interviewees who ask to revise what they have said place a journalist in a very difficult position.

For those lawyers who choose to live with us and who perhaps even thrive on the relationship, what follows is my list of ingredients for a fruitful relationship.

The best contacts know that 98 per cent of what they say will not be quoted, but recognize that the interview process is necessary to provide a general context and elicit key quotes.

The best legal contacts don't take it personally when a story idea they supply slides off my overburdened desk, is felled by managerial disinterest or simply doesn't pan out.

Savvy and considerate lawyers know that the clock is invariably a journalist's worst enemy. Even in the pre-Internet days, we were invariably in a hurry; now, our pants are on fire 24/7. Thus, our most cherished contacts willingly supply us with factums, rulings or transcripts that are publicly available, saving us vital hours without risking their reputation or their client's welfare. The contacts we cherish embrace the idea of answering questions by e-mail, since it provides immense advantages in time and accuracy.

Legal journalists know that wise counsel are quite sensibly wary of annoying judges; they think twice before arguing their case in front of a microphone. There are, however, an infinite number of ways to make a statement that falls well short of being indiscreet or provocative.

My best legal contacts know that editors sometimes eliminate quotes and paragraphs without our knowledge. They recognize that we journalists are usually more frustrated about it than you are when your voice goes missing from a story.

Good contacts do not ingratiate themselves with a rival journalist by disclosing the nature of a story someone else is working on.

A good contact understands that we are sometimes forced to spread our net wide on a breaking story and call several sources, even though we can only interview the first two who call back. We don't mean to exploit you or treat you as a disposable commodity.

Valued contacts soon come to understand that we have no interest in betraying their trust; thus, it is unnecessary to pepper a casual conversation with: "This is off the record, right?"

If you want a sense of the questions we intend to ask, many of us will provide you with a rough preview. However, no, you cannot see a draft of a story that has not yet been published.

Ultimately, the simple fact is that you may just have to trust that we will do our best professional job. Bear in mind, though, that a journalist who acquires a reputation for being slipshod, disrespectful or ignorant will not remain long on a particular beat. Most journalists recognize that editors and publishers have a wide circle of contacts and keep their ears to the ground. An aggrieved person who makes a convincing case that a journalist has misbehaved can damage the journalist's standing with his superiors.

In the end, as wild and unregulated as we are, there are built-in incentives for journalists to be fair and to get it right.

Talk to reporters:
IT'S YOUR PROFESSIONAL DUTY

CRISTIN SCHMITZ

AS A JOURNALIST from a "legacy" medium (meaning that my stories are still printed on dead trees), I was flattered to be invited to write about dealing with the media. Certainly, lawyers are taking an increasingly sophisticated approach to those dealings.

For example, hardly a day goes by that I do not receive a press release from a large firm, or a university law faculty, offering its lawyers as commentators on the important legal developments of the day. Lawyers are raising their professional profiles and attracting new clients by sharing their expertise (and trumpeting their victories) through social media, blogging and even slick current-affairs-style podcasts on their own websites.

Yet the gold standard for publicity probably still remains a mention in a story by a professional journalist from a reputable media outlet.

So what are today's deadline-harried reporters looking for from lawyers? Above all, we need instant access to your expertise. Start by providing us with your cellphone and Blackberry coordinates. Many journalists, whatever their medium, are filing first to the web – almost immediately after important court judgments or legal developments. If you are a lawyer who can instantly provide reliable information and/or trenchant quotes, you will quickly find yourself on a reporter's speed dial.

Of course, not every reporter deserves your trust and respect. Get to know who you are dealing with. If a reporter has a solid reputation, cultivate a relationship with that person, and do so early in your legal career. I can personally vouch for the fact that many prominent lawyers and judges built their reputations not only by honing their legal skills, but by being media-savvy and media-friendly.

A relationship of mutual trust and respect with selected journalists will always be useful to you and your clients. I recall, for example, a woman whose wealthy husband was taking what her lawyer saw as an extremely unreasonable position in their matrimonial litigation. Her lawyer tipped off a reporter, on a not-for-attribution basis, about a newsworthy development in the case that turned into front-page national headlines. I'm told the publicity wound up moderating her ex's position. Of course, that was a matter of indifference to the reporter, but it was undoubtedly what her canny lawyer had in mind.

In my experience, lawyers and judges who have made the needs of their clients or of the public the touchstone for their contacts with the media rarely set their feet wrong in their media dealings. On the other hand, I have seen otherwise competent lawyers and judges – some at their profession's pinnacle – trip themselves up when they let their egos do the talking.

Here I am not referring only to self-promoters and other publicity hounds. Some of the biggest egoists I have come across are lawyers who refuse to speak with the media – ever – even when their silence ill-serves their clients and/or the public's interest in getting a clear, accurate picture of arcane legal issues and court proceedings. I recall speaking with an experienced counsel whose client was fighting to overturn a lower-court ruling. The lawyer told me he had no comment whatsoever, citing his unwavering policy not to speak to the media about his clients' cases. Imagine my surprise weeks later when his upset client called to demand why she hadn't been contacted.

Did her lawyer seek her instructions before he refused comment, I wonder? But, speaking generally, I query whether lawyers who maintain blanket "no comment" policies – and there are still some – can properly serve their clients in the 21st century. Isn't this inflexible approach motivated more by a lawyer's preoccupation with his or her own public image, rather than the clients' interests?

But how does a lawyer build a good relationship with a reporter?

We welcome tips on interesting cases or legal developments. Be as fair, open, clear and accurate as you can. Expect the same from the reporter. If errors creep into a story, contact the reporter immediately – even if you are not seeking a correction – to avoid repetition. Most errors should be corrected, and as soon as possible, because with electronic databases such errors are otherwise likely to be repeated endlessly.

You are entitled to expect that your remarks will not be taken out of context or otherwise distorted. When necessary, complain to the reporter, news outlet and/or press council or ombudsman for redress. All reputable news organizations take such complaints seriously.

At the same time, lawyers should treat members of the media fairly. This means not passing on information gleaned from one reporter to a reporter from a competing news outlet. A lawyer who blows a reporter's scoop has blown the relationship.

Also, please don't demand to see a story before it is printed and/or broadcast – that privilege is reserved for editors. If you fear that errors could creep into a complex or sensitive story, volunteer to address any follow-up questions the journalist might have as she or he prepares the story, or even, out of an abundance of caution, e-mail to the journalist those points you wish to make crystal clear.

Finally, it would be a mistake to think that the number one reason lawyers should talk to the media is to attract clients, or to promote themselves or their law firms – although these are often by-products.

We reporters seek out the views of lawyers because, as members of a self-governing and learned profession, lawyers are both uniquely placed and uniquely qualified to understand and interpret for the rest of us the many complex and profound dimensions of the rule of law in our society. This aspect of your professional duties – similar to being an officer of court – exists separately from your duties to your clients or firms.

I have spoken with thousands of lawyers, both famous and obscure. To the profession's great credit, nearly all were willing to take on this role of demystifying the law and the legal system for the public good – even when they knew their names would never appear in print.

What litigators and broadcast journalists have in common

SCOTT ARNOLD

WHETHER YOU'RE STANDING in front of a judge, 12 jurors or the business end of a TV camera, you're working to communicate in the most effective way possible. Regardless of whether your viewers are in the same room or in another country, the best way to make your points involves doing a lot of the same things, including speaking in a conversational way, simplifying and bottom-lining things as much as you reasonably can, recognizing and addressing what the crux of the issue actually is, and putting yourself in the shoes of those who are listening to you.

Before becoming a lawyer who spends most of my days on my feet in court, I spent nearly a decade as a TV news reporter covering everything from crime to politics to groundhog activity on February 2. In both lines of work, I've also had a front row seat to watch others on the job and have seen the full quality-range of advocacy and oral communication – from the masterful to the gruesome.

In my experience, the most effective litigators and most effective broadcast journalists have a number of qualities in common. Here are a few of them.

THEY SPEAK THE WAY PEOPLE ACTUALLY SPEAK

"Officer Chan, did you have occasion to make observations with respect to the accused's attire while conducting the initial stages of your surveillance on the

evening in question?" Resorting to this kind of flabby, formalized wording is one of the more common challenges among the trial advocacy students I've taught. (Speaking too quickly is also up there.) It often takes effort and experience to work up – or down – to more accessible and aerodynamic language like, *"What was he wearing when you first saw him?"* Relaxing and uncluttering the wording need not be at the expense of linguistic precision.

The tendency to use non-conversational or flowery language may in part come from the desire we all have to sound professional, authoritative and intelligent. In reality, needlessly complex syntax and esoteric words make the language less clear, make the communicator less effective, and can sound awkward or pretentious or both.

Just as wooden, over-formality can be the default style of uncomfortable litigators, a TV reporter delivering news of some squabble at City Hall or of the first minor snowfall of the year with breathless, end-of-the-world gravity can be an indication that that journalist would benefit from more experience and confidence. The grandmaster of the clear, straightforward, unaffected and compelling delivery was the late ABC *World News Tonight* anchor Peter Jennings, whose manner was supremely self-assured and whose language was confidently restrained. He seemed to speak into the camera and address his millions of viewers the same way he would have politely ordered a coffee. Whether on camera or in court, that ability to be one's natural self is often difficult to master but is a feature that is universal among the best and most watchable modern communicators.

THEY SWIFTLY RECOGNIZE WHAT THE REAL ISSUE IS

We've all seen some version of it: an exhaustively researched and well-articulated legal argument that is excellent in nearly every way except that it just misses the point. The ability to avoid that sidetrack, to promptly appreciate and then focus on the essence of a matter, and to disentangle important information from less relevant or irrelevant information are abilities that productive lawyers and journalists share.

For the litigator, promptly seeing the point, getting to that point and staying on point have the obvious pre-courtroom benefit of a more focused and efficient preparation. Among the incourt benefits is building credibility with a trier of fact who will no doubt appreciate the lawyer conceding non-issues and avoiding doomed, time-wasting arguments while shortening motions examinations, submissions and trials.

For a broadcast journalist up against rock-hard daily deadlines and slots in news shows timed to the second, it's also essential to know what story you're telling (which can be a moving target), to recognize and present competing arguments, and to efficiently triage a flood of information. Judgment calls about what information to seek, what to prioritize and leave out, where to cut off sound bites, what images to voice over and what to describe in an on-camera stand-up or in a live conclusion can be made properly only if the reporter has no uncertainty about the central purpose of the story.

THEY SIMPLIFY, SIMPLIFY, SIMPLIFY (BUT DON'T OVERSIMPLIFY)

Einstein said, "Everything should be made as simple as possible, but not simpler." If an explanation of quantum mechanics or special relativity can be at least somewhat simplified, surely any legal concept, expert evidence or fact pattern can also be. For lawyers who are good communicators, that includes boiling things down as much as is reasonable, making timelines and sequences of events as easy to follow and remember as possible, using headings or road signs, making apt analogies, numbering points, avoiding distractions, and painting crisp pictures of events, concepts and issues.

For logically complex matters or those with a massive amount of information, the old Henry Ford adage about nothing being particularly hard if you divide it into small jobs is instructive. The effective advocate breaks things down into manageable, understandable pieces and then explains how those pieces fit together to form the big picture.

Of course, simplifying is relative and a journalist is far more constrained by time. A two- or two-and-a-half-minute news story often requires radical simplification and will never be sufficient for a deep analysis. However, with proper focus, efficient explanation, appropriate use of graphics and, when necessary, show-and-tell on-camera standups, stories can and should convey the essence of a matter, event or development. That commitment to reasonable simplicity while being ruthlessly economical with time maximizes the value of the story. Like effective lawyers, good reporters get to the point and don't complicate the point when they get there.

THEY THINK FROM THE PERSPECTIVE OF THEIR VIEWERS

By the time you're writing your opening to a jury, you know the case backward and forward but – as effective advocates know – every word in that situation must be written and then spoken for people who are hearing things for the very first time. That means not only making it flow logically and intuitively, but also considering little things to make a narrative easier to follow. For example, instead of rattling off a bunch of dates, contextualize a timeline by saying "a month later ..." or "the year before ..." Or, in giving the jurors an overview of the evidence you expect they'll hear, if the proper names of some witnesses are not yet important, it may be more helpful to first refer to them simply by the roles they play. Whatever the stage of the proceedings and whether it's jurors or judges, always being considerate of the perspective of the listener helps to have information come out in a reasonably paced, understandable and retainable way.

Like jurors, TV viewers can't ask for the speaker to repeat something, to slow down or to explain the information in a different way. So it's important that reporters make thoughtful estimates about the knowledge of the average viewer in order that the content, the wording and the pace neither lose them nor bore them. That includes reasonable judgments made about when to give wide-angle views of a story and when – both metaphorically and literally – to go in for a more detailed close-up.

A worthwhile exercise for new journalists is writing a number of stories on the same general topic but for different audiences. A story written for a local audience (when, for example, explaining the location of an event might involve referring to a major intersection by name) should be written differently from one written for a national audience (when a location may be best described as being in "the west end of Toronto") or an international audience (when the location may be simply in "Toronto, which is Canada's largest city").

The most effective television reporters also understand the importance of describing for viewers the images they are seeing. Because what we see generally takes precedence over what we hear, not "writing to the pictures" is a recipe for your words being missed by viewers who are seeing and hearing things that don't match. Thinking about how the viewer is likely to process images and words that they may see and hear only once helps to convey information most successfully.

The litigator/journalist skills-in-common go beyond these interrelated abilities and include being an alert, agile and responsive listener whether asking questions or answering them, understanding and dealing with rival versions of the truth, and staying composed under sometimes intense pressure. All are capabilities of the most effective at their craft, whether the audience is wearing a sash, sitting in the jury box or watching on a screen.

Why good judgment comes first

JOHN ADAIR

I RECENTLY INTERVIEWED YOUNG lawyers for a position with our firm. I asked all the applicants what quality they believe is the most important for a successful litigator. It is, admittedly, a bit of an unfair question, both because there probably is no "most" important quality and because it is so difficult for anyone who has not spent any considerable amount of time doing this job to answer that question. However, posing the question caused me to revisit my own thoughts on the subject.

I have long heard my father say that judgment is the single-most important quality for a good litigator. I now believe that I can adopt that answer based on my own thinking and experience. There are of course many other options, and no doubt a compelling case can be made for a number of them. This is not a question that admits of a "right" answer. But in this space I want to defend my answer by (1) explaining how I got to it, and what "judgment" means; (2) explaining why, to me, judgment is so important in the context of today's litigation landscape; and (3), considering what, to me, is the critical question that follows from my answer: whether we can "learn" better judgment. My effort starts with a podcast about California resident Larry Williams.

WHAT I MEAN BY JUDGMENT

I am probably well behind the times, but I started listening to podcasts about 12 months ago, and I'm hooked. The variety and quality of podcasts has surprised me. One podcast I enjoy is *Planet Money*, produced by National Public Radio. (*Planet Money* is, in my view, a misnomer, because it does not generally deal with finances.) Episode #685 tells the story of Larry Williams, who found himself asking whether he really did have a legal obligation to pay income taxes in the United States, or whether perhaps there was a legal argument that would overcome this obligation. Larry's was an ambitious task given that income taxes are considered such an ironclad obligation that they are listed together with death as one of only two certainties in life.

The story goes like this. Larry and some friends were camping in the mountains of New Mexico in the mid-1980s. One night around the campfire, one of them asked: "Do you really have to pay your income taxes?" These are sophisticated businessmen, and it was a serious question (or at least a question posed in a serious manner). Some members of the group claimed there were people who had found legal ways not to pay income tax. Larry, who seems to have been earning a fairly substantial income, felt that the government was collecting far too much in taxes, and he took up the question with interest.

One of the men sitting around the campfire was a lawyer, Jim Knowles. Jim had never studied the issue, but he had an understandable gut reaction: He told his group they were talking nonsense – everyone has to pay taxes. Larry's response was to ask Jim to look into it. Jim brushed Larry off ("Sure, I'll look into it"). Larry didn't hear back for a while, until he received a call one day from Jim. Jim explained that he was reasonably confident he had found a lacuna in the income tax code and that Larry, and anyone else, didn't actually have a legal obligation to pay income tax.

Jim's conclusion after researching the issue carefully was that tax can be levied only on income paid *by* the federal government and, in any event, is applicable only to citizens of the United States. Larry, by renouncing his citizenship, could avoid the obligation.

Larry was thrilled with this advice. From the interview of Larry, it's clear he genuinely believed the advice because Jim "is a lawyer" – he has the credibility of having gone to law school, and practised as an attorney for more than 30 years.

Larry decided to rely on Jim's arguments and stop paying taxes. He didn't hide this decision from the government. Instead, he wrote to the state and federal governments and declared himself a "sovereign citizen." He also set up a trust, routing all his income through it so that it was not "his" income (a curious move given that his premise was that *he* was not obliged to pay income tax at all).

The IRS did not get around to Larry for three or four years. When it did, however, the consequences were severe and the IRS pursued him vigorously. Without getting into all the details, Larry ended up a fugitive living in Australia and was ultimately brought back to California by two US Marshals, an experience Larry clearly did not enjoy. The upshot of the legal proceedings was that Larry did not go to jail, but he did have to pay all the back taxes, plus substantial interest and penalties.

What Larry (or, rather, Jim) can teach us

Larry's story is not really, for my purposes, Larry's. It is Jim's. From the interview clips in the podcast, Jim sounds like an intelligent guy. He also had what I consider to be the only rational gut reaction to the campfire question: There is no way on earth that any court would accept a legal argument that a person in the United States does not have to pay income tax (leaving aside foreign citizens who may have the benefit of various tax treaties).

What is so interesting to me is that Jim fell into a trap that can too often catch us as litigators: He was asked to develop an argument to support a position and, somewhere during that process, he lost sight of whether the position had any hope of succeeding. (It plainly did not.) Jim used his skills as a lawyer to undertake careful research, and then he creatively came up with arguments that were consistent with the text of the legal authorities. But he abandoned his good judgment in the form of his initial reaction.

Jim's story to me highlights why judgment is the most important quality we possess as litigators. To explain, let me start by stating what I understand "judgment" to be in the context of a litigation practice.

WHAT IS "JUDGMENT"?

I understand judgment to be the act of considering the facts, determining what position your client should take to achieve the most successful outcome possible and then identifying the argument most likely to persuade the court to achieve that outcome. In litigation, judgment is manifest in almost everything we do. But in my view, it's most apparent when we undertake the specific task of trying to determine what a court is likely to do with the dispute (whether that means a larger dispute between the parties at a trial; or a more narrow interlocutory dispute such as over whether certain documents must be produced).

Judgment understood in this way is different from *advocacy*. The former is, at a general level, about deciding what position to take and what will persuade a court to accept that position, while the latter consists of the skills necessary to make that argument effectively. Excellence in advocacy therefore requires mastery of the essential skills with which we are all familiar: cross-examination, persuasive writing, knowledge of the rules of evidence, etc. However, as explained below, excellent advocacy cannot overcome poor judgment.

Why judgment comes first

So why do I say that judgment is the most important quality a good litigator can possess? What elevates judgment above hard work, intelligence, determination and advocacy skills? For me, judgment is paramount simply because those other attributes do not do the client much good in the absence of the ability to exercise sound judgment in formulating the client's position. Paul Pape, for whom I had the pleasure of working for a few years, is fond of saying: "We're lawyers, not magicians." What that "Pape-ism" means to me is that we can be excellent advocates, but excellence will not turn a loser into a winner. Although I suspect this point is obvious to any intelligent lawyer who thinks it through, the problem is that it is far too easy for us to jump right into advocating for the client's position. I suspect that this tendency happens for a variety of reasons, including that we are prone to believe we are being paid to advocate, and because we put so much of ourselves into the advocacy that we become "married" to our clients' positions and fail to see the warts on those positions.

The current litigation landscape is such that our clients are, probably unconsciously, placing a premium on judgment. Judges are doing so, too, though much more consciously. For clients, the premium on judgment is seen in the rejection of the hourly rate billing model. Clients now routinely demand alternative-fee arrangements (AFAs) that are predicated on value billing. Clients increasingly don't care how long it takes us to draft a factum, and they don't want to pay for our time. What they will pay for, I believe, is good judgment because good judgment means they are getting quality insight into the likely outcome of litigation and are getting someone who can achieve that outcome efficiently (for example, by making the one or two arguments that have a real chance of success, rather than the nine arguments that come to mind). That, to me, is the "value" at the heart of any notion of "value billing."

Judges also demand judgment from counsel. They see too many motions, too many briefs and too many pages of written submissions. Counsel who have the judgment to cut through that and advance the one or two arguments which really need to be made will benefit greatly. Counsel who do not have it will see their clients suffer.

CAN WE "LEARN" GOOD JUDGMENT?

Regardless of whether you agree that good judgment is the most important skill a litigator can possess, there is no doubting that it is a significant and important attribute. Recognizing that, one can reasonably wonder whether we can improve our judgment, or whether it is simply an innate skill dished out in heaping amounts at birth to the likes of Earl Cherniak and Alan Lenczner. Is it akin to the ability to recognize the difference between a 96 mph fastball and an 82 mph change-up right out of the pitcher's hand, genetically bestowed upon great hitters such as Ted Williams?

I do believe that good judgment involves an innate grasp of human nature and notions of fairness, and to that extent cannot therefore be "learned." However, I also believe that we can learn to *improve* our judgment as litigators, probably significantly so. Perhaps this is nothing more than putting ourselves in the best position to succeed in exercising our judgment. The concluding section of this article is dedicated to a discussion of three ways in which we might approach that exercise.

What really happened here?

The first essential task seems to me to be obtaining from your client and other available sources the best understanding of "what really happened here." This lesson is another thing I learned from Paul Pape, though I don't believe he used that particular phrase to describe what he was doing. Paul is the best lawyer I have seen at interviewing the client to understand the facts. What makes Paul so good is that he never takes the client's words at face value; instead, he constantly cross-examines the client. Paul has a remarkable ability to grasp quickly what was really motivating the players in the client's story, including, most importantly, the client. All these skills help him determine the key question in any case – "What really happened here?"– and develop a theory of the case that is consistent with the answer to that question.

Although most of us will never be as good as Paul at interviewing the client or witnesses, it is fundamentally important when conducting the initial interview with our clients that we listen critically to their stories, cross-examine them as much as necessary without any regard to their "feelings" or reaction, and determine not what the client wants us to believe happened but what a judge is likely to conclude happened. That will put us in a position to be best able to exercise the innate part of good judgment.

Be objective

We must also ask ourselves what a judge is likely to think about the parties and the circumstances and use the answer as the basis for our advice to our clients. Our clients are generally not paying us to advocate their position regardless of the merits (though there are, of course, rare cases of principle in which our clients are doing precisely that). Rather, they want genuine insight into what will happen if the dispute goes to court, whether that be the overall dispute or an interlocutory skirmish. It is simply too expensive these days to have a full-day motion about documentary production and refusals, or the adequacy of pleadings, to be wasting such resources on arguments that, while made effectively, never had a chance. I suspect that well over half of such motions should never have been brought.

To exercise good judgment, we must be more than cheerleaders, and even more than advocates. We must be objective and honest with our clients. It is helpful in that regard to run the situation or issue by our colleagues. Give them the *Coles Notes* version of the situation and ask them for their gut reaction. This approach is particularly important because, despite our best efforts (or perhaps because of them), we are too quickly sucked into our client's position and how we can shine that up and pursue it as effectively as possible.

Learn from your mistakes

I hate this particular way of developing better judgment. I hate it because it makes me think about the mistakes of judgment I have made that cost my clients. We have all lost cases, but there are a few losses where you look back and realize you had it all wrong from the start. Not that you were unprepared for court, or misunderstood the applicable law. It's that you simply should have known from the start that your client would not succeed in court. This is usually because of the equities. Each outcome, whether by settlement or hearing, provides an opportunity for critical analysis of what advice we gave the client at the outset, what the outcome was, and why and where (if at all) our judgment could have been better.

CONCLUSION

I do believe that good judgment is to a certain degree innate. However, there is a reason why experience is so valuable in any profession – including, especially, litigation. Lawyers who have seen thousands of cases unfold are in a better position to predict the outcome of the next case. We can expedite that process to some extent by working hard to develop better judgment and, thereby, serve our clients more effectively.

Part Nine

HUMOUR

LAW HAS ITS amusing side. As storytellers, lawyers can regale others with tales of defeat, woe, frustration and any vexing quality one can imagine. A good rule about humour, exemplified in the *Rumpole of the Bailey* series from the 70s, is that in any courtroom, it's best to let the judge make the quips; but, often, lawyers can't help themselves. With the proliferation of professional awards and honours, however, lawyers can take themselves seriously ... or not. Our witty observer describes the folly of a self-aggrandizing awards night banquet, much to the amusement of most of us.

And the winner is …

MARIE HENEIN

I WAS RECENTLY INVITED by friends to attend an august awards ceremony. Assured that it was a pre-eminent, black tie, legal awards event, I was sort of honoured to be included – even though I had to pay to attend. What a night it was.

I should have known something was up when many of my friends – litigation luminaries all, who did not need any award to acknowledge their talents – asked why I was there. Not in an "I'm surprised to see you" way, but in a "Don't you have something better to do?" way. I didn't take the hint to make a run for it, though, probably because there was an open bar and I was standing right beside it.

I spent much of the evening asking people, including the organizers, how someone wins one of these awards. People smiled knowingly and said they would explain it to me later. The selection criteria remained as mysterious as the Holy Grail. I decided to try to convince the organizers that I should win the Bankruptcy Lawyer of the Year award, and I got awfully close.

In school, the rationale for handing out awards was simple: they went to the people with the highest marks. But we've long left Kansas, Dorothy, and Oz has different rules. It's just that the Wiz won't tell. Less Oscars, more People's Choice. The yearly Las Vegas Porn Star Awards have more identifiable, merit-based selection criteria. We've entered the realm of prom king and queen. Clearly, the prettiest boy and girl in the room win. But even this is not necessarily an indicator of how winners are nominated or selected.

Indeed, this is true of many of the awards ceremonies in the legal profession. While some are awarded by a publicly identified and qualified selection committee that has published standards, you may have noticed that the legal profession has a plethora of privately sponsored awards ceremonies. The private sponsor invents them, directs them and gains revenue from them. This is brilliant marketing to a captive audience: who could resist shelling out $7,500 per table when they are going to be named Best Lawyer in Ontario?

Apparently, some awards are chosen by a selection committee that spends months travelling the country and "consulting" with clients to select their nominees. Notwithstanding this apparently in-depth research, let me tell you that there were many stunning upsets that night. Don't even get me started on this year's Yukon Insolvency Lawyer of the Year award. Completely out of left field. I'm still processing that one. Back to that evening. Each time an award was announced, music that sounded like royal coronation music (including trumpets) played.

No kidding. The award winner would get up on stage, pose uncomfortably with the organizers of the event and sit down. They really should have given each winner a tiara as well.

There were many awards. I lost count after my first bottle of wine. As we all sat there stunned – in awe, really, of what was happening – it occurred to me that we could simply get up and leave. But nobody did. Smart, bright, aggressive litigators were glued to their chairs. Enduring the nightmare. In tuxes. Sheepishly. Sort of like Stockholm Syndrome.

You knew you should run, but you just couldn't. I thought of rushing the stage, Kanye West style, just to spice things up, but my law partners restrained me. I tried to convince someone to let me accept the award on their behalf, Marlon Brando style, so I could conscientiously object, but there were no takers. It was time to leave. And I did. Loudly. I would not go gentle into that good night. No way.

Law firms proudly display the awards they have bought, I mean won, for themselves. Recently, our firm was thrilled to receive an e-mail informing us that we were going to be included in the list of Best International Mergers and Acquisitions Firms, for a small price. Clearly our innate talent for this type of work was shining through. We accepted, and we look forward to doing our first merger and acquisition case soon.

I'm hoping that one day I will win an Admiralty Law award – after all, I was on a boat once. What's next? Surely someone, somewhere, is organizing a dinner to give out the award for Best Lawyer in the Universe or Best Intergalactic Lawyer Specializing in Interspecies Mergers. I want one of those. The opportunities for impressive-sounding accolades are endless. But with this article I have ensured that I will never win such an award. Unless, of course, my firm buys a whole lot of tables.

Why lawyers like baseball

PETER HRASTOVEC, LSM

I WAS NEVER ONE of those kids who could say that I had big-league baseball dreams. First, that would be a little too clichéd. Second, though I could throw a knuckle ball at the age of 12, my curve ball would rise higher than floodwaters after a spring thaw, and it lacked as much in control as any raging river. But a dearth of talent didn't stop me from playing the game I loved in my own "field of dreams," in a park near my home for hours on end every summer, long before W.P. Kinsella made that term a baseball staple in his celebrated book, *Shoeless Joe.*

Though law school was supposed to be a stepping stone to a budding career in journalism, somewhere along the way I balked and sidestepped my way into the practice of law.

After 30 years of law practice, the anniversary coinciding with the start of baseball season, I have concluded that as interesting, rewarding and challenging as law practice may have been, it was only one of several ways to measure my life. Along with my family, my community and my law practice, baseball has ranked pretty high on my list of "likes and loves." It has cast a constant shadow, long and lingering like those balls we'd throw on a hot, late summer afternoon at the ballpark.

As a litigator, I have found baseball to be a great conversation starter, a pleasing segue for dialogue with opposing counsel before commencing an intense discovery or a sensitive mediation. "Say, did you see the game last night?" or "Did you read what so-and-so said in the paper about our manager?" Baseball gossip would often take the edge off of a difficult situation or breed a little familiarity between litigation rivals, reminding us of the less pedantic side of our adversarial nature.

Here in the deep south – Windsor, Ontario – most of us cheer for the cross-border Detroit Tigers, a team that dates back to 1894. The Tigers are said to be the oldest continuing one-name and one-city baseball franchise in the American League of Major League Baseball. And, by an unusual twist of geographic irony, we find ourselves "south" of the American border. Yes, that's right ... south of the border, a border that we cross with abject compliance and appropriate paperwork – passports – all the while wearing intense smiles of excitement. And once we clear U.S. Homeland Security with the officer waving us through with an "enjoy the game" salute, we are only minutes away from the architectural splendour that is Comerica Park, a Major League Baseball stadium that is a joy to behold.

While it was under construction several years ago as a necessary replacement to the fabled but time-worn Tiger Stadium (Briggs Stadium, it used to be called), I remember making my way to the GTA for a discovery, travelling down a lonely and quintessentially boring stretch of Highway 401. In the westbound lane, heading toward Windsor (and presumably Detroit), were two rather large flatbed trucks, each bearing what looked like a large baseball bat, big enough to be swung by the likes of Paul Bunyan. I knew then and there that they were destined for Comerica.

And there you can find them, sentinels at the gate of this brilliant ball park, creating an archway of enchantment. At this moment, I couldn't tell you what my discovery entailed, who the client was or even the name of the file. But I do remember those majestic bats! Though I attend only a handful of games every year (the full 81 home games would probably end my legal career and my marriage – and not in that order), I have to say that I have probably encountered a member of the local bar, a client or someone from my hometown at every game that I have seen since my call to the bar in 1984. And, I can tell you most assuredly, I have seen a few judges in the stands as well. Whether it is an afternoon game where I can slip over in my suit and tie looking like an extra in a remake of *Pride of the Yankees* or a night/weekend game where my casual attire will include something sporting the old English "D," I know that I will invariably run into someone from my side of the border. And if I have an encounter with a colleague with whom I have a file, we can grab a beer or a hot dog (or both) and perhaps discuss the case between innings while on the concourse that overlooks the field. In my view, the concourse is akin to "no man's land" and is as good a place as any to discuss or settle a case. Then, when play resumes, we will not miss one vital pitch or a crucial swing at the plate with the plethora of television monitors hanging from the concourse ceilings. Sometimes, a case is settled or the facts narrowed all between the cheers and jeers that become the soundtrack to our lawyers' dance.

I have always found that baseball is a wonderful icebreaker with out-of-town counsel as well. "Who's your team?" "Who's your favourite player?" "Can you believe what they're paying that guy?" Counsel from the GTA have always found it an interesting anomaly that those of us in Windsor-Essex support the Detroit Tigers over the Blue Jays of downtown Toronto. That's more a function of history and, as we all know, old habits die hard. But the rivalry between the Blue Jays and the Tigers, despite having to play in different divisions, is evident especially when the two teams square off all too infrequently.

If you have the capacity (and if tickets are available), it is fun to do a home-and-home series with lawyers from Toronto, the invitations (and the creative trash talk) going back and forth like an exchange of documents. In the old days, it was a joy as well to get up to Montreal and see the renowned Expos play. Regrettably, business did not take me to Montreal! More regrettably, the Expos are a footnote to baseball history and, in my mind, a tragic loss to their fans.

When spring training arrives every February, I often think of the late Justice Randall Echlin, who – in addition to his brilliance both as a competent lawyer and then, in later years, as a revered judge – would, given the right moment, wax eloquent about his beloved Blue Jays. I got to know him through law, both through litigation and through his incredible seminars. His appreciation for the game was legendary. Though law introduced us, I feel that I got to know him better because of baseball. Though we talked about it, I regret never having had the opportunity to enjoy a game with him.

In an informal poll of some colleagues and friends who are as passionate as I am about the game (perhaps more so), I learned that insights about baseball are as various as the blades of grass in the infield. Borden Ladner Gervais partner Matt Certosimo is a brazen and shameless supporter of the New York Mets, despite practising law in Toronto just minutes from the Rogers Centre. He says, "I love baseball because, while it is a game, like life, it inspires hope. Each spring, every team has a chance. Each day, either team could prevail. Each pitch presents so many possibilities. All the while, we the fans have the privilege of being the tenth player on the field." Baseball, it would appear, breeds optimism, even for a Mets fan!

Windsor poet laureate and journalist Marty Gervais finds that baseball is like religion. He says that "baseball is meditative – it slows me down, provides a comfortable pace that lends itself to reflection, and thinking and feeling, and finally makes me see the purity in everyday life." Baseball clearly has a holistic appeal.

A seasoned litigator and a past president of The Advocates' Society, Bert Raphael quips that he likes baseball because "unlike when I am in court, I can close my eyes and doze off between innings and also have the odd beer." Such honesty, such zeal!

Patrick Ballantyne, general counsel for the Registered Insurance Brokers of Ontario and a gifted musician/songwriter, originally hails from Windsor. He says he will "still listen to as many Tiger games as I can on the radio. Even though Tiger Stadium is long gone, the smell of the grass and the franks are still there – in my car, in my home, in my office, in my mind." He sums it up quite nicely: "It breaks down the years and places me back into a much simpler time." Baseball is, after all, timeless!

Baseball has had a long history and connection with litigation. In the early part of the 20th century, it was the subject of antitrust rallying by a competing league and a celebrated case that found the United States Supreme Court exempting all of baseball from anti-trust legislation.[1] It is a virtual monopoly in its prohibition of competition, and it is protected from attack, if not from criticism for fashioning its own rules on ownership or exclusive membership in its select club, as a result of this 1922 controversial decision. Of interest to lawyers (and theoretical logicians) is baseball's ironic exclusivity and status above and beyond the law – directly as a result of the law!

Courts in the United States revisited the anti-trust case 50 years later, when, in 1972, the St. Louis Cardinals' Curt Flood attempted to oppose

1 Alex Belth, "Ending Baseball's Antitrust Exemption: What Would It Mean?" Baseball Prospectus (26 November 2001), online: <www.baseballprospectus.com/article.php?articleid=1286>.

his trade from the team. Though he failed in his lawsuit against baseball commissioner Bowie Kuhn, Flood was in effect a pioneer when Major League Baseball and the Major League Baseball Players Association finally came to terms on a structure for free agency. However, baseball's antitrust exemption remained in full force as free agency was created on consent, outside of the courts and the legislature, and in spite of the exemption (or because of it!). The Supreme Court has made it abundantly clear that it would not overturn the exemption, leaving that to the U.S. Congress.[2] So, Curt Flood's defiant stance led to the multi-million-dollar player contracts that have now become the topic of water cooler discussions by lawyers and non-lawyers alike.

It doesn't end with civil litigation, protracted contract negotiations or free agency. Criminal lawyers, administrative tribunals and government counsel all got into the act when baseball began to investigate itself in recent years in the wake of the wide and rampant use of performance-enhancing drugs. United States grand juries, congressional committees and comprehensive investigations all centred on marquee players, turning the game of baseball into a front-page frenzy of veritable wrongdoing, with iconic role models tumbling like fallen angels as a result of long suspensions from the game we have all come to love. And after they "pay the price" with their suspension, the teams and the fans – baseball itself – often welcome the wrongdoers back to the fold as if nothing had happened!

Baseball umpires normally call strikes. In 1999, their job action and mass resignations conducted in lieu of illegal strike action led to the demise of one union and the creation of another.[3] Speaking of strikes, the seemingly most sacrilegious of events in baseball history occurred with the 1994 work stoppage that led to the cancellation of the entire baseball season. Instead of precision pitching, long-ball dingers rocking out of the stadium and textbook double-play defences, the sporting news covered the details of collective bargaining with players suited up like their lawyers, walking in and out of hotel rooms and into waiting limousines. This, we all asked, is baseball?

The negatives are, however, few and far between. Baseball for lawyers – for everyone – has "marked time ... is a living part of history ... and

2 *Ibid.*

3 Murray Chass, "Baseball: Umpires threaten to quit on Sept. 2" *The New York Times* (15 July 1999); "New umpire union ratified" *Today's News-Herald* (25 February 2000).

it continually reminds us of what once was."[4] Baseball is a lot of things to a lot of people. Above all, it is about statistics, meticulously kept, filed and analyzed. Law has its version of stats: its precedents. Baseball and law both continue to evolve, to become better than they have been, with deference to the past and hope for their future. Baseball is as simple as it is technical, as relaxing as it is complicated. It is a sweet respite from the day-to-day.

But it is not a free-for-all. Baseball has laws like the infield fly rule and the ban on pine tar. It is not played in the rain, and its desired end is in gloomy October and November. Yet, for the better part of the better days in our year, it is there for the taking.

Lawyers like baseball because, like baseball players, lawyers have to amass many skills. Where a ball player has to hit, throw, catch, run and adapt to numerous situations on the field, lawyers have to speak, write, listen, multi-task and balance the interests of team members. Lawyer Joe Masiuk says, "Being a baseball player or a lawyer requires the mastery of various discrete and unrelated skill sets which, depending upon the position, will be used when appropriate. It's also true that, although some proficiency in every skill set is required for every player through a firm grasp of the fundamentals, every player need not be a specialist in every skill set."[5]

Baseball is a game of precision, a game of inches and degrees, a game of profound intellect and limited brawn, a game of skill, championed by fans who look for excellence – something that is fleeting yet coveted by the most ardent of aficionados. The pause between pitches, the interval of action restored when a batter steps in and out of the batter's box and the joy manifest in a great play enveloped by loud resounding cheers gives us a chance to escape from the nagging little things and annoyances that ferment into the minor crises of our existence. In baseball, there is a healing quality that erodes stress and soothes compulsion and, in some instances, allows for clear-headedness despite the agitation between headstrong umpires and obstinate managers arguing errant calls. It can be summed up by what the prolific baseball writer

4 W.P. Kinsella, *Shoeless Joe* (Boston: Houghton Mifflin, 1982) at 253.

5 Joe Masiuk, "Lawyers, Baseball Players and Social Media", *Lawyernomics* (31 May 2013), online: <http://lawyernomics.avvo.com/legal-marketing-2/lawyers-baseball-players-and-social-media.html#ixzz2zZxy-67Qn>.

Red Smith once said: "Ninety feet between home plate and first base may be the closest man has ever come to perfection."

Perhaps that's the attraction. Lawyers are like baseball players. We both play a game – a serious game. We win, we lose and we suit up to play again. We both have high regard for the rules, for the talent that we observe, for the excellence demanded from each of us and the way it keeps us humble but yearning to do our best and strive for more. Law, like baseball, is bigger than any of us, regardless of how good a knuckle ball you can throw.

FSC
www.fsc.org
MIX
Papier | Fördert
gute Waldnutzung
FSC® C083411

Kolibri 360 GmbH
Ferdinand-Jühlke-Straße 7
99095 Erfurt, Deutschland
produktsicherheit@kolibri360.de